Conflict Management
in the Middle East

Conflict Management in the Middle East

Edited by Steven L. Spiegel

Westview Press / Boulder • San Francisco

Pinter Publishers / London

Copyright © 1992 by Westview Press, Inc.

Published in 1992 in the United States of America by Westview Press, Inc., 5500 Central Avenue, Boulder, Colorado 80301-2847

Published in 1992 in Great Britain by Pinter Publishers Limited, 25 Floral Street, London WC2E 9DS

Library of Congress Cataloging-in Publication Data
Conflict management in the Middle East / edited by Steven
 L. Spiegel.
  p. cm.
 Includes index.
 ISBN 0-8133-8218-1
  1. Middle East—Politics and government—1979-   . 2. Conflict management—Middle East.   3. Persian Gulf War, 1991.   I. Spiegel, Steven L.
DS63.1.S87   1992
956.05—dc20   92-6018
                                                                                   CIP

A CIP catalogue record for this book is available from the British Library.
ISBN 1-85567-059-3

Printed and bound in the United States of America

The paper used in this publication meets the requirements
(∞) of the American National Standard for Permanence of Paper
for Printed Library Materials Z39.48-1984.

10   9   8   7   6   5   4   3   2   1

Contents

viii

Acknowledgments

This volume emerged from a workshop, which was co-sponsored by the Institute on Global Conflict and Cooperation of the University of California and the Center for International and Strategic Affairs at UCLA. Financial contributions were received from the United States Institute of Peace, International Studies and Overseas Programs (ISOP) at UCLA, the East-West Forum, Stanley Sheinbaum, L'Hermitage Hotels, Pan-American World Airways, the Center for Russian and East European Studies at UCLA, and the Institute on Global Conflict and Cooperation of the University of California. The participants of this project wish to thank these contributors for making this effort possible.

In addition they wish to credit the work of Susan Greer, Julia Ingraham, and Patty Patarek of the IGCC staff for their efforts in conjunction with Gerri Harrington of the UCLA Center for International and Strategic Affairs. Professor John Ruggie, director of IGCC, gave the project his unstinting support, as did Professor Michael Intriligator, the director of CISA at UCLA. The participants also wish to thank the following institutes in various countries for their cooperation: the Moscow State Institute for International Relations (MGIMO), the Jaffee Center for Strategic Affairs at Tel Aviv University, the Hebrew University Department of Political Science, and the Al-Ahram Strategic Studies Center in Cairo. The participants also wish to thank Ms. Joan Levinson for her concerted efforts to help coordinate the conference.

In terms of this manuscript, the editor wishes to thank Val Phillips and Kimberlee Ward for supervising the editing, collation and preparation of the manuscript. In addition, the work of David Pervin, Gitty Cannon, Adam Stohlberg, Michael Chan, Naomi Renek, Kathleen Najmzadeh, Nancy Lapp, Scott McIntosh, Craig Wu, Holly Urban, Samira Sadeghi, Renat Engel, Melissa Mograss, and Andrew Gomperts is recognized and appreciated.

x

This kind of intercontinental effort requires the cooperation of many from various countries, and we are indeed grateful that all of these participants made the publication of this volume possible.

S.L.S.
Los Angeles

Steven L. Spiegel and David J. Pervin

Introduction

The recent events in Europe and the Soviet Union have caused fundamental changes in the international system and challenged many of the assumptions upon which the analysis of international affairs has traditionally been based. For some forty years after the end of World War II the competition between the United States and the Soviet Union dominated world politics. The paradox of this competition is that while it was global, deliberate war between the two superpowers was inconceivable given the massive destructive potential of nuclear weapons.

Accidental war, on the other hand, remained a possibility, and a frightful one at that. Such a war was unlikely to occur in Europe, where the lines were clearly drawn and the interests obviously great. Where spheres of interests were not as clearly defined, mistakes were possible. The difficulty both superpowers had in controlling the actions of their respective client states, each of which had their own interests which at times conflicted with their patron's, increased the risk of such mistakes.

The Middle East, as the region with the murkiest delineation of superpower interests, the greatest independence of action by clients, and the most profound conflict among local states, created the most concern. It is not surprising that the Middle East was known as the Balkans of the late twentieth century. If accidental war, caused by miscalculation and escalation, was to occur, the Middle East was the most likely point of origin. Indeed, in 1973 the United States used a discreet but clear nuclear warning in order to deter a possible Soviet intervention. On a number of occasions American and Soviet naval forces jockeyed for position in the Mediterranean. Yet no shots were fired, and war did not occur.

The reasons that competition did not turn into conflict is the central focus of this volume. The chapters are unique in three ways. First, the authors are drawn from the United States, the Soviet Union and the Middle East. The unprecedented participation of scholars from the U.S.S.R. in itself reflects the radical changes in that country and the end of the Cold War. Second, theoretical, historical, and policy aspects of the interaction of the Middle Eastern states and the two superpowers are examined, with an emphasis on how the United States and the Soviet Union have attempted to manage their competition in the region. Third, these articles were written as the conflict between the United States and Iraq unfolded. Many therefore attempt to integrate the crisis and war into their analysis. The first chapter, by Steven L. Spiegel, provides an overview of the Gulf Crisis and War, focusing on its unique nature. Graham E. Fuller proceeds to present a regional perspective of the ongoing international changes.

The next section of this volume explores theoretical approaches to conflict management and crisis avoidance. Janet Gross Stein and Richard Ned Lebow argue that deterrence, the dominant security policy of the United States and Israel, may have contributed to each state's defense while also exacerbating the conflict with their respective rivals. They therefore suggest that a policy of "reassurance" might contribute to conflict resolution. With the end of the Cold War their suggestions take on added resonance.

Mark A. Heller and Abraham Ben-Zvi's chapter clearly delineates the conceptual distinctions among conflict resolution, management, and avoidance. As they note, the superpowers have not been successful in resolving the conflicts among their regional clients, in the main due to the profound interests at stake. They have been more successful, however, in managing regional conflicts, preventing the complete defeat of their regional clients. Regarding conflict avoidance, the record has been mixed. On the one hand, the superpowers have avoided a direct confrontation. On the other hand, both have been actively involved in support of their clients. The decline of the Soviet Union effectively means that conflict avoidance will be easier, as events in the Gulf War demonstrated, but whether it will facilitate conflict management, let alone resolution, remains unclear.

An interesting explanation as to why the superpowers have been more successful in avoiding direct conflict and in managing the regional crises than in conflict resolution is offered by Benjamin Miller. It is during crises, Miller argues, that the dictates of national interest come to the fore in the decisions made by political leaders. Since the horror of nuclear holocaust has an uncanny way of focusing the mind and forcing leaders to calculate conservatively, neither superpower was willing to directly challenge the other. In contrast, efforts at conflict resolution occur during non-crisis periods, when policy-makers must take into consideration the competing demands of domestic interest groups and are less willing to press their clients to make concessions. The dilemma is clear: During the Cold War the superpowers were neither willing to sacrifice their clients nor defend them to the hilt, but the extent of their support was in large measure dependent on the context.

Having explored several theoretical approaches to the interaction between the superpowers and their regional clients, we move to an examination of the historical record. Mostafa-Elwi Saif provides an overview of the superpowers' increasing involvement in the various Middle East wars. The Cold War competition, Saif argues, led both the United States and the Soviet Union to misunderstand regional dynamics. The competition between the two superpowers may have thus aggravated what was already a delicate local situation. Aharon Yariv notes that notwithstanding the competition of the Cold War and the intensity of the interests of each superpower in the region, neither superpower has directly challenged the other; they were thus successfully able to manage their conflict. By comparing crises that did not lead to war with those that did, Steven L. Spiegel demonstrates that both sides are right: by providing support for their regional clients the superpowers helped intensify and exacerbate local conflicts; on the other hand, by avoiding involvement the superpowers effectively limited the ambitions of regional actors.

Analysis of the superpowers' policies toward the region has traditionally focused on each country's pursuit of a vaguely defined "national interest" which responded to changes in the international environment. Students of American policy toward the region have long known that it is a mixture of both domestic politics and foreign policy goals. Because of the Soviet Union's closed nature, it has been more difficult for analysts to explore the influence of domestic politics on Moscow's policy-making. Richard D. Anderson Jr.'s examination of the competition among various factions of the Soviet Politburo and its effects on Soviet policy toward the region is thus a welcome contribution toward a better understanding of Soviet motivation and actions. As Fred Wehling points out, the goals of the Soviet Union have frequently been at cross purposes, with those regarding its relationship with the United States at times in conflict with regional interests. This conflict necessitated tradeoffs, and thus inconsistency in policy.

From examining the policies of the two superpowers, actors external to the region, we turn to two indigenous problems: the Palestinian issue, which is central to the dispute between Israel and the Arabs, and the Lebanon-Syria-Israel triangle, where the most recent war was fought and tensions remain high. Yehoshafat Harkabi cogently analyzes not only the political but also the emotional depths of the divisions between Israelis and Palestinians. The rawness of these emotions have led both sides to commit errors, to miss opportunities to ameliorate the conflict by taking concrete steps to reassure the other side of its limited objectives. Ziad Abu-Amr traces the history of American and Soviet policies toward the Palestinians. He describes how the evolution of their policies has reflected both the altered role of the PLO and changes in each superpowers' perception of its interests in the region. Shibley Telhami provides an analysis of Palestinian perceptions of the implications of the end of the Cold War. He also discusses the reasons for the PLO's support of Iraq in the Gulf War. Turning to the "triangle," Georgi Mirski argues that neither superpower has been able to control its respective client in this area of direct confrontation. He also reminds us that while the Soviet Union is no longer as powerful a factor as it used to be, in large part due to the demise of its ideological pretensions, it remains a great power with considerable interest in a region close to its borders.

Having examined the history of superpower conflict management in the Middle East, the authors next discuss policies that Washington and Moscow could pursue that may contribute to conflict resolution. As Andrei Shoumikhin argues, since both superpowers bear responsibility for aggravating regional problems and conflicts, they also have an obligation to be actively involved in facilitating peace. Much attention has been paid to the importance of the control of arms exports to the Middle East. Michael D. Intriligator and Dagobert L. Brito argue, however, that while arms control can lead to political agreements, political agreements that eliminate the sources of tension are the best form of arms control. As Dore Gold makes clear, from Israel's standpoint it is important that arms control measures be the outcome of direct negotiations between the regional parties. Any measures imposed from the outside, he argues, are doomed to failure.

Although the superpowers cannot impose a solution, the deep-seated nature of Arab and Israeli mutual fear and distrust of each other nonetheless make it unlikely that they can reach agreement in the absence of external involvement. Emile Sahliyeh argues that the ideological and territorial nature of the conflict makes Arab-Israeli agreement difficult, especially as long as the two causes are intertwined. He maintains that the superpowers can play a useful role by serving as channels of communication between the conflicting parties. An international conference, Alexei Vassiliev argues, is the best forum for any negotiations, and he notes that the Soviet Union has long favored this approach. Yet as Galia Golan and Gur Ofer point out, the most important contribution of the superpowers toward conflict resolution will be in offering incentives for peace. These incentives can be economic, as in aid or trade, or political, as in offering assurance that territorial concessions will not mean a dangerous compromise of security.

Conclusion

This volume, therefore, completes a cycle: It starts with an examination of theoretical perspectives on conflict management in the Middle East. It continues with an examination of the historical record, from which lessons can be learned. It concludes with a discussion of policies that may make the future one of conflict resolution instead of management. The circle thus moves forward towards a possibility of regional rapprochement.

Since the international system continues to be in a process of constant change, epitomized by the transformation of Soviet foreign policy, no single volume can hope to take account of all aspects of the tumultuous events that we currently confront. While the problems remain profound, the end of the Cold War has meant the opening of opportunities previously unimaginable. The concern of the authors from various countries has been to offer guidelines for improving future policies and actions of both the superpowers and regional states; the authors have been mindful of the shoals that have grounded even those with the best of intentions. In the gales of change, those with the best maps have the best chance of reaching their destination: peace.

PART ONE

The Changing International Setting

1   Superpower Conflict
Resolution in the Middle East:
Implications of the Persian Gulf Crisis

The Persian Gulf Crisis of 1990-91, which ended in the massive defeat of Iraq, represented neither the last of the Cold War nor the first indication of a new era. Unlike the Cold War's competition in which both superpowers jockeyed for political and military gains at the other's expense, in 1990-91 the United States and the Soviet Union were on the same side. Although the Soviet Union may have been more inclined to seek a diplomatic rather than military solution, it voted with the United States at the United Nations and coordinated its diplomacy with Washington. Even when the collaboration became frayed on the eve of the ground war, the Soviets did not maneuver to undermine the American position nor to increase tensions, as they frequently had done during the Cold War.

In previous Middle East crises from 1945 to 1990, war had occurred by the action of superpower clients, in some cases despite Soviet or American attempts to restrain them. The Soviets had at times meddled in ways that precipitated combat, with disastrous results, as in 1967. When the superpowers sent troops to the area on previous occasions, they did so in a limited manner for circumscribed goals: the United States intervention in Lebanon in 1958, the American role in the multi-national peace-keeping force in Lebanon in 1982, the U.S. reflagging of Kuwaiti oil tankers in 1987-88, the Soviet assistance to the Egyptians in the War of Attrition against Israel in 1970. In these cases the external power intervened to manage the conflict by preventing additional escalation and ensuring the survival of its regional client. The Persian Gulf

Crisis was the first time that a country from outside the region, supposedly engaged in restraining conflict, had actually engaged in full-scale war. If crisis management is defined as the prevention of war, then the management of this crisis was clearly a failure. The absence of Soviet-American competition may have actually led Saddam Hussein to seek to expand Iraq's power, and it facilitated the decision of the American-led coalition to go to war. In the absence of a major danger of escalation to superpower confrontation, there was little to prevent the coalition from attacking except for the fear of the use of unconventional weapons by Iraq. That fear militated in favor of employing a military option. Once Hussein invaded Kuwait, many in the coalition believed that hesitating to destroy Iraqi weaponry would only lead to a greater danger later.

Why did war occur in 1991? Central to any explanation are the miscalculations committed by both the United States and Iraq. While it has been argued that cultural differences played an important role in these miscalculations, this explanation is not convincing. The end of the Cold War, however, may have been a contributing factor in the failure of both sides to understand the "rules" of the "new world order." Let us examine these failures in greater detail.

American Miscalculations: A Failure of Deterrence?

In one sense the American failure to deter Saddam before August 2 was not so much an inability to prevent him from acting as it was a failure to try in the first place. With the major reflagging operation of Kuwaiti oil tankers in 1987 and 1988, the United States had in effect supported Iraq against Iran. Both the Reagan and Bush administrations had largely ignored Baghdad's use of chemical weapons against Iranian troops and Iraq's Kurdish civilians. The Bush administration reacted mildly to the increasingly harsh statements against the United States and Israel by the Iraqi government in 1989 and 1990. Indeed, until Saddam's invasion of Kuwait, the Bush administration had actively opposed efforts by many in Congress to impose sanctions against the Iraqi regime for its use of chemical weapons and its development and acquisition of long range missiles and weapons of mass destruction. The United States had thus given Iraq great latitude in its conduct of a controversial and aggressive foreign policy.

We will never know whether or not Saddam could have been deterred had the United States attempted to do so wholeheartedly. The Bush administration clearly miscalculated Saddam's intentions, in part due to inaccurate interpretations of intelligence reports in light of faulty assessments by Egyptian and Saudi leaders. These errors were compounded by the post-Iran-Contra Washington atmosphere, which led to the removal, resignation, or transfer of officials who had advocated closer relations with Iran as a balance to Iraq. Those who remained were reluctant to question the prevailing tilt toward Baghdad even if they had doubts about the wisdom of that policy.[1] Opposition to Iran, with a concomitant favoritism toward Iraq, was so well-entrenched that even had the Iran-Contra scandal not happened, it was highly unlikely that a change in policy regarding Baghdad would have occurred. The scandal made such a shift impossible.

If the Bush administration had not taken any steps to discourage Saddam, then technically the policy would not have been a failure of deterrence. Yet in a somewhat confused fashion a deterrence policy was pursued. The administration's effort to placate Iraq can be seen as an attempt to engage in positive inducement, in a roundabout route consistent with deterrence in the minimal definition of seeking to raise the potential costs of an action above any benefits. By offering benefits that could be removed, the administration was raising the costs of any negative policy pursued by Saddam.[2] If this logic is accepted, then the Congressional efforts to reduce or eliminate export credits and the readiness to impose negative sanctions *decreased* the potential costs to Iraq of an attack on Kuwait. Consistently applied tough sanctions, favored by many in Congress, might have conveyed to Saddam Hussein the dangers of aggressive action. Positive inducements, favored by many in the Administration, might have led him to give greater weight to maintaining good relations with the United States. In the end, the interplay between Congress and the administration undermined both approaches and left American policy toward Iraq confused and thus inadequate in the months prior to the invasion of Kuwait.

There is, however, evidence that the United States did indeed attempt to deter Iraq on the eve of the invasion. It can be found in the State Department's warnings of mid-July 1990, in response to a bellicose Iraqi statement concerning Kuwait and the United Arab Emirates (UAE). Baghdad was informed that the United States was "strongly committed to supporting the individual and collective self-defense of our friends in the Gulf with whom we have deep and longstanding ties."[3] These warnings were followed by the announcement on July 24 that there would be a joint military exercise with the UAE in response to the increase in Iraqi forces on the border with Kuwait.[4]

The next day U.S. Ambassador April Glaspie held a controversial and now famous meeting with Saddam Hussein. According to the Iraqi version of the meeting, Glaspie said that "we have no opinion on the Arab-Arab conflicts, like your border disagreement with Kuwait." Yet in a message which could be construed as a veiled warning, she also told Hussein that:

> we can . . . see that you have deployed massive troops in the south. Normally this would not be any of our business. But when this happens in the context of what you have said on your national day . . . then we see the Iraqi point of view that the measures taken by the UAE and Kuwait [are], in the final analysis, parallel to military aggression against Iraq, then it would be reasonable for me to be concerned.[5]

According to Glaspie's emendations to Congress in March, 1991, she had said *prior* to the first quote that "we would insist on settlements being made in a non-violent manner, not by threats, not by intimidation, and certainly not by aggression."[6] These words further strengthen the view that an implicit warning was made. In any case, according to both reports, Hussein assured her that there would be a peaceful resolution of Iraq's dispute with Kuwait. Instead of deterring the Iraqi leaders, American warnings only succeeded in convincing him to provide false promises.

Saddam's Miscalculations

It can be argued that the attack against Kuwait was neither irrational nor foolish. The United States, prior to August 2, 1990, seemed preoccupied with the end of the Cold War, uncertain as to its place in the world, and turning inward to confront its economic problems. In the months before Saddam's action any signals sent by the United States were at best ambiguous. Given Iraq's long-standing claims on Kuwait, in 1990 it would have been possible for a leader intent on conquest to convince himself that the United States would likely respond primarily with rhetorical objection but would not act in any forceful manner.

To the extent that the United States was indeed trying to deter Iraq, Saddam Hussein did not consider the signals very credible. His statements to Glaspie demonstrate a complex message, which included an assurance that American interests, in particular oil, would be taken into account no matter what developments ensued, a threat that Iraq could not be intimidated, and a disdain for U.S. capabilities:

> I assure you, had the Iranians overrun the region, the American troops would not have stopped them, except by the use of nuclear weapons. I do not belittle you. But I hold this view by looking at geography and [taking the] nature of American society into account. Yours is a society which cannot accept 10,000 dead in one battle.[7]

Indeed, he might have pointed out that in 1983 the United States could not accept even 241 dead in the attack on the Marine headquarters in Beirut.

Additionally, with American and world attention diverted from the Middle East by events in Europe and the Soviet Union, from Saddam's point of view it was logical to anticipate that the international reaction would be tolerable. Certainly no one would have been able to predict the immediate and strong American reaction to the invasion of August 2, much less the Soviet-American cooperation and the willingness of the Gulf Arab states to accept an American military presence. The only precedent for the kind of UN collective security operation that followed the invasion of Kuwait was Korea, which did not involve the U.S.S.R. and had occurred 40 years earlier.

We can thus accept that it was logical and even rational for Saddam Hussein to expect that an attack against Kuwait was worth the risk. Yet the tough stand taken after August 2 by the United States and its allies would have seemed to have pressed overwhelmingly in favor of an Iraqi compromise, especially after the allied preparations had proceeded as far as they had by January 1991. We may never know why Saddam Hussein refused to withdraw peacefully from Kuwait. Based on his statements, and the situation as it existed *prior* to January 15, it is possible to make a variety of educated estimates. The unspectacular demonstration of American military prowess in Vietnam, Grenada, and even Panama would not have contributed to predictions of the overwhelming superiority of U.S. arms that led to a quick victory. Many in the West expected an extended war with significant coalition, and in particular American, casualties. It is plausible that Saddam Hussein may have calculated similarly. He had made his contempt for America's ability to absorb casualties clear to Ambassador Glaspie on the eve of his invasion of Kuwait. The "Vietnam Syndrome" and America's reluctance to engage in substantial warfare in the Third World must certainly have been a factor in Baghdad's calculations, especially as it was perceived as an influence in the United States itself.

In the weeks prior to the coalition attack, the Congressional debate and anti-war sentiment, as expressed in demonstrations in the United States and Europe, could certainly have convinced an isolated leader that the United States was weak, divided and confused. As Hussein put it in his famous interview of January 29, 1991, with CNN's Peter Arnett, "all the people of Iraq are grateful to all the noble souls . . . amongst the United States people who are coming out into the street, demonstrating against this war."[8]

George Bush's own actions also conveyed a sense of uncertainty. The President had operated with exceptional skill in organizing the coalition and by January 15 had sent more than 500,000 troops to the area. However, after his shaky performance in the budget crisis in October and his uneven public reaction to the ebb and flow of events throughout the crisis, it was possible for an observer to conclude that in the end he would not go to war. Who could have anticipated that the United States would suddenly and effectively exert the full weight of its considerable military might?

It was even plausible for Saddam Hussein to believe that a limited military defeat could later be transformed into a political victory and a setback for the United States in the region. Saddam may have thought that the governments of the Arab states that supported the United States would be threatened by domestic instability in the face of their alliance with the "imperialists" and "paymasters" of Zionism. He may even have believed that an attack on Iraq would lead to their overthrow and replacement by radical regimes sympathetic to Iraq and antagonistic to the United States. Demonstrations in some Arab countries in favor of Saddam's cause could have reinforced this perception. If all else failed he planned to attack Israel in the hope that it would retaliate, transforming the conflict into an Arab-Israeli confrontation and thereby increasing domestic opposition in the Arab states aligned against him. On each point Saddam miscalculated, as none of the pro-American regimes were seriously threatened, much less overthrown, and in the wake of the coalition's successes Israel refrained from retaliating.

The Clash of Cultures:
A Failure to Communicate?

Why did the United States fail both to deter Iraq before August 2 and to convince Saddam to withdraw peacefully from Kuwait thereafter? A possible interpretation is that the difference in cultures did not permit accurate communication. This type of analysis suggests that the veiled warnings before the invasion and George Bush's efforts to convince Saddam Hussein to leave Kuwait were cursed by the President's inability to make points that would be effective in terms understandable to a leader imbued with "Arab culture." This position assumes that the differences in backgrounds between American and Iraqi officials made the transfer of a clear message impossible.

This argument, that "Arab culture" played an important role, while appealing to some, does not stand up to close scrutiny. The United States was effective at various times in the past in convincing Arab parties to take actions which they might not have otherwise pursued. In September 1970 Syria was persuaded to withdraw its forces from Jordan, in part by the impact of American diplomatic and military maneuvers. In Lebanon in 1958 the United States acted to prevent the accelerated spread of Nasserism throughout the area. The 1986 air raid against Libya did lead to a decline in Colonel Khadafi's backing of international terrorism. Most notably for the 1990-1991 Persian Gulf crisis, it is worth recalling the British intervention in Kuwait in 1961 to deter a threatened Iraqi attack. Given these examples, it is clear that "Arab culture" did not prevent other Arab leaders from understanding and respecting Western interests, especially when there was a clear determination to act vigorously to defend them.

Another argument that has been offered to explain Saddam's refusal to withdraw is that he was backed into a corner by President Bush's demand for the unconditional withdrawal of Iraqi forces from Kuwait, the transformation of the U.S. force to an offensive posture with its near doubling after November 8, 1990, and the December UN authorization of the use of force, accompanied by a January 15, 1991, deadline for Iraq's withdrawal from Kuwait. According to this view, if left with an opening Saddam might have withdrawn, but he could not possibly submit to the President's obstinacy without losing face--and ultimately power--in the eyes of his own people and the entire Arab world.

This argument for a kind of "Arab machismo" is belied by Saddam's own subsequent fate. Despite the humiliation of an overwhelming military rout and multiple rebellions in the wake of Iraq's decimating defeat, Saddam Hussein not only remained in power after the war but accepted a degrading cease-fire. He was not the first. An example of an Arab leader who had survived a humiliating defeat, albeit with his reputation tarnished, was Egypt's Gamal Abdel Nasser. This persistence in power is not explained by Arab culture, but by the authoritarian nature of both regimes. For these types of governments, military defeat does not necessarily lead to the overthrow of the old leadership, nor does political

11

compromise. Saddam was strong enough to take whatever action he chose, and could have justified a compromise if he had hen one or both sides are ready and willing to undertake them, and this was a cardinal case of such an example. At no point in the crisis was either side willing to see its goals compromised, while both were willing to threaten and subsequently to use force. Conflict management does not lend itself easily to a situation when compromise is not considered a viable option. Saddam represented a peculiar type of leader with a proclivity to violence, and George Bush, who was prepared to resort to force if necessary, could act with relative flexibility because of the end of the Cold War.

It is doubtful that the American intervention is a model of patterns that will evolve in the new era. In many ways, the Persian Gulf War was a unique event. First, with the demise of the Soviet Union's ability significantly to influence events, the United States had attained political and military hegemony, at least in the Middle East. The United States thus emerged as the only country that could exert a policing role if it chose to do so. Whether or not it will act as a *gendarme* in the future will largely depend on its economic conditions, the importance of the interests at stake, and the clarity of the threat.

Second, in 1990-91, the issue was exceptionally clear. Saddam Hussein had invaded Kuwait and destroyed an entire country, disregarding and challenging the foundation of international order: the right of all states to sovereign independence. The clarity of the issue appealed to so many nations that Iraq had precious little support around the world, with the exception of some radical Arab states, a portion of the Arab masses and some Third World countries. Despite some wavering on the part of China, the five permanent members of the United Nations Security Council were opposed to Baghdad's actions. Given the concerted response of the United Nations, such a challenge is not likely to be repeated soon.

The implications of the war for the future of the Middle East are not as clear. The new era may encourage attempts to address fundamental issues, which were not feasible in a Cold War distinguished by escalation to higher levels of conflict. We are likely to witness increased concentration on underlying problems such as the Palestinian or Kurdish questions, arms sales to the region, the proliferation of unconventional weapons, water issues, economic conditions, and haves versus have-nots. This focus may, at times, yield greater achievements of conflict resolution as a consequence of coordinated superpower efforts.

Yet it is also possible that the search for settlements and the end of the fear that conflicts will escalate may result in heightened local tensions. The new world order is likely to be punctuated by a series of seething, local conflicts--Arab-Israeli, Arab-Arab, or Arab-Iranian--with no possibility of escalation to global confrontation. In this sense, there is no guarantee that the increased stability at the superpower level will lead to increased stability in the regional arena. The early aftermath of the war--the failed Shiite and Kurdish rebellions against Saddam Hussein; his political survival; the confusion over the Kurdish refugees--may be a starker harbinger of future events than the clear military victory of the coalition forces. The end of the Cold War thus offers no reprieve. To deal with the multitude of diffuse problems that will face future policy-makers will take an even wiser and more careful diplomacy than was needed at the height of tension between the superpowers.

Notes

1. See Paul A. Gigot, "The Great American Screw-Up: The U.S. and Iraq, 1980-90," *The National Interest* (Winter, 1990-1), pp. 3-10.

2. For a general discussion of this point, see David Baldwin, "The Power of Positive Sanctions," *World Politics* 24 (October, 1971), pp. 19-38.

3. *The New York Times*, March 21, 1991.

4. *The New York Times*, July 25, 1990, p. 1.

5. The Iraqi version of the meeting can be found in *The New York Times*, September 23, 1990, p. 13.

6. *The New York Times*, March 21, 1991, p. A7.

7. *The New York Times*, September 23, 1990, p. 13.

8. Federal News Service, January 29, 1991.

2 Soviet-American Cooperation in the Middle East: The Changing Face of International Conflict

The New Era in International Relations: The Source of Change

The whole world has now come to recognize the stunning changes in the character of the international order. The Cold War, which in one sense dates back to 1917, stemmed from a communist ideological vision that liberal democracy and the free enterprise system were historically doomed, and that the revolutionary mission of the Soviet Union required that it advance this revolutionary process worldwide by any and all appropriate means.

This ideological stance of the Soviet Union was a direct challenge of unprecedented magnitude to the entire international order; the challenge, precisely because it was ideological as well as military in nature, was far more serious than the military challenge of Nazi Germany, lacked any meaningful intellectual component other than brute military force. In consequence, the Soviet challenge to the world engendered sharp reaction to it. The Soviet Union did indeed come to be encircled in a self-fulfilling prophecy. Two massive political-military blocs eventually emerged that in time touched nearly every corner of the globe.

If there is any doubt about the communist origins of the Cold War, one need only look at the breathtaking revolutionary change that has occurred in the world since 1986. These changes have come about almost exclusively because of change in the Soviet Union alone. The rest of the world has merely sat by and watched with rapt fascination. The two most influential figures of the twentieth century are ironically, therefore, both Russian. One is Vladimir Ilyich Lenin, the other is Mikhail Sergeyevich Gorbachev.

The Nature of International Change

The Cold War guaranteed that no nation could remain outside the armed camps of the long ideological struggle. In turn, the policies of virtually every nation had some impact on the East-West balance sheet. Indeed, in one sense, the international order was corrupted by the existence of this struggle, for it meant that almost no issue could be looked at in its own right; every new political development invariably raised the question in all major world capitals as to whose interests were being served by such events. American foreign policies came to be distorted to a similar measure as well, for it became nearly impossible to separate most events from Cold War calculations. The most America could aspire to were enlightened Cold War policies. American policies towards the Third World were the primary casualty of this state of affairs.

Today the East-West factor is now almost entirely absent from the international calculus. It is astonishing what a difference it makes. For the Cold War was not just about American vs. Soviet interests; it validated the idea of ideological struggle around the world, even in areas where the Cold War was not so directly involved. Today it is not too soon to say that the idea of ideological struggle of any kind is now losing acceptability in the international arena. Conflict, of course, will not go away, for it is part of the human condition. But it is hoped that the global ideological struggle has faded into history. In an increasing number of countries, the concept of peaceful reconciliation has gained new importance--even affecting struggles such as those in South Africa.

The end of ideology and ideological camps has already had an impact on the Middle East, starting at least by 1987. The Soviet Union gave notice to Syria and to the PLO that armed struggle did not represent a viable means for the solution of regional conflict. Of course, these regional conflicts were not of Soviet making, even though massive arms sales from the outside world had an inevitable impact on escalating conflict. Soviet diplomatic and military support to states like Nasser's Egypt, Iraq, Syria, South Yemen and Libya greatly increased their ability to destabilize the area at various times. Many moderate Arab states also believe that massive American military assistance to Israel has also helped to raise levels of tension. As a result of changing Soviet policies in the region, individual states can now act more independently, without consideration of whether such actions tend to fulfill American or Soviet interests. From the point of view of the outside world, the actions of regional states can now be treated much more on their own merits and not interpreted as a proxy action for the great powers.

The Impact of the Gulf Crisis

Prima facie evidence of this global shift is evident in the astonishingly different character of the Kuwaiti crisis compared with earlier international crises in the Middle East. It is truly the first major post-Cold War crisis. In its early unambiguous condemnation of Iraq's aggression, the Soviet Union left little doubt of its new commitment to the preservation of the international order rather than to fulfillment of ideological or historical commitments. (To be sure, the war also revealed other fissures in Soviet policy making that clearly demonstrate Soviet foreign policy is still in a state of flux and lacks a clear national consensus.)

Furthermore, it is amazing to see the difference that a basic change in Soviet foreign policy makes in handling an international crisis. No crisis is "easy," but this one was handled more easily and effectively than any other crisis in memory. The relative unanimity of world opinion on the issue was important not only to Soviet-American relations; general Soviet-American consensus on the nature of the problem made it easier, in part, for the Arab world to act with greater consensus on the unacceptable nature of the Iraqi invasion.

Few private agendas entered the calculus of action on Kuwait in this crisis: nearly all states were able to view the crisis as neither an ideological issue nor as an East-West issue, but as a direct matter of aggression and annexation. Saddam tried to invoke the vocabulary of much of the Cold War strategic world, but largely failed. In this sense, Middle Eastern politics are entering the first entirely new stage since the early 1950s.

The Arab-Israeli Crisis in the New Order, or
The Dog That Did Not Bark in the Night:
Israel's Role

Yet even with the end of the Cold War, the Kuwaiti crisis was not entirely free of outside factors. One outstanding regional issue still serves as a prism to distort perception and reaction to these regional events: the Palestinian-Israeli issue.

Yet there was still a striking feature even here: the almost complete irrelevance of Israel in the Gulf War. I do not mean this in any slighting sense towards Israel. On the contrary, this phenomenon is very good news for all states of the region--including Israel. It suggests that a crisis can take place in the Arab world in which Israel is neither the chief protagonist, nor the primary issue at stake. The irrelevance of Israel in this crisis hardly means that Israel is irrelevant in the region in general. Nor does it suggest that the Gulf War was irrelevant to Israel. But it does suggest that Israel may gradually begin to take a more "normal" role in the region.

The end of the Cold War clearly has a major impact on Israel as well as on the Arab states. If the radical Arab states no longer figure prominently in Russian calculations of their interests in the region, then Israel also will figure less in American calculations of its interests in the region. After all, one of the key features of the strategic alliance between the United States and Israel was Israel's potentially important role in the Cold War. In the event of Soviet-sponsored military activity in the Middle East, or even Soviet military involvement in the region, Israel's formidable military capabilities were considered to be of great importance.

It was generally acknowledged by Washington strategists, however, that Israel's great potential value in an East-West scenario was not matched by an equal role in regional or domestic Arab crises. The intervention of Israel into Arab politics simply carries too much baggage for it to be helpful to the United States in the majority of such situations. Israel cannot realistically intervene to stop an Islamic fundamentalist takeover in any Arab country. It cannot defend one Arab state against another under most circumstances. And, as we have seen in the Gulf War, Israel's most significant act thus far in intra-Arab conflict was to refrain from any military action, to stay out of the conflict. Israel cannot usefully intervene in support of Saudi Arabia without politically compromising the character of that regime. Nor could Israel even serve as an instrument for striking Iraq from afar; such an act would have automatically changed the character of the conflict and utterly polarized it, paralyzing even the role that U.S. forces played--which in itself already ran some risk of "delegitimization" of the states assisted.

The irrelevance of Israel in the Gulf War is the good news for Israel, for it suggests that there is some chance in the new international order that Israel may now be irrelevant as an "instrument" of American interests in the region. While such an Israeli role undoubtedly strengthened Israel militarily, and proved exhilarating to its spirit, the role of "instrument" did not in the long run serve Israel well. For what Israel now needs is to become a "normal" state, and not the perceived vanguard of someone else's interests. Of course Israel has its own national interests, and its future relations with America will more normally rest on cultural and political affinities and ties. Astonishingly, even Syria was prepared to admit Israel's right to defend itself in the course of the SCUD missile attacks upon Israeli cities. Such is the changing character of the Israeli role when it is no longer seen as pursuing a special pro-American, anti-Arab agenda.

The Palestinian Problem as Ideological Baggage

Yet, overtones of the Palestinian-Israeli problem were hardly absent in the Gulf War, for Iraqi President Saddam Hussein repeatedly appealed to it in an effort to legitimize his own aggressive grab for territory and power. In effect, the Palestinian-Israeli problem still manages to haunt nearly all aspects of the relations of the Arab states with the rest of the world. It is one of the last hold-outs of a series of long-festering international crises--after Eastern Europe, South Africa, Afghanistan, South East Asia, and other regions in conflict are moving toward peaceful resolution. It is therefore imperative that this last crisis move towards resolution if politics in the region are to be restored to a more normal state. "Normal" does not mean the absence of conflict; it means the ability of local conflicts to rise and fall without constant--indeed obsessive--reference to another, greater problem (the Palestinian) that overshadows the immediate local problem.

The imperative need to resolve the Palestinian question therefore emerged with greater urgency in the course of the Gulf War. Indeed, the cataclysm of the Gulf War may have brought the Arab-Israeli problem as a whole closer to a resolution than at any time in the past several decades. And in the absence of the immense, distracting, distorting nature of the Cold War, these problems seem more tractable. The most important thing is to take the problem out of the ideological arena and reduce it to a complex series of negotiations over the concrete needs of each side. The problem is soluble. But it must be shorn of its ideological character. That ideological character is no longer a question of Russian and American proxies in conflict in the region. The only remaining "ideology" is the deep psychological barrier on the part of Israelis and Palestinians regarding the willingness of each people to recognize the right to exist and the legitimate national aspirations of the other.

In all frankness, I see only two final "destinations" of the Arab-Israeli problem--two ultimate and inevitable stages of resolution that can scarcely be avoided if a lasting peace is ever to be achieved. First, there is no other solution to the Palestinian-Israeli problem than the creation of a Palestinian state in the West Bank and Gaza. The Palestinian movement towards self-conscious nationhood is far advanced, and international attitudes have now come to accept as reasonable that the Palestinians should be an independent people on their own land on the West Bank. Both sides must give up ideological dreams: the Palestinians will not be able to take over all of Palestine; Israel will not be able to become a "Greater Israel."

Once these ideological security blankets have been abandoned, the problem then becomes one of hard negotiations over complex details about the nature of the future intimate relationships between these two sovereign states.

The second inevitable "destination" is the full, complete normalization of relations between Israel and all of its neighbors, and with much of the rest of the Arab world as well--a "warm" peace, not a cold armistice. With an agreement between the Palestinians and Israel, a normalization of relations between Israel and the other Arab states must fall into place. This must be the basis upon which the world will insist that the Arabs and the Israelis reach an agreement. Each will have conceded what is most important to the other: fulfillment of Palestinian aspirations and Israel's search for acceptance in the region.

Other problems remain, but they are surely susceptible to solution for they are not zero-sum in nature. Resolution and compromise on the Golan Heights issue will be central to Syria's settlement with Israel. The only zero-sum problem in the region are the two old maximalist visions: the PLO vision of the recovery of all of Palestine--which the PLO is abandoning--and the Likud dream that it can annex the West Bank with or without the people. It is foolish to talk of solving the problems between the Arab states and Israel without first turning to the Palestinian question. Such talk verges on a willful desire to avoid any settlement that does not leave Israel in control of Palestinian territory. If the Likud Party cannot accept giving up the territories, then the external world must construct the framework of an agreement: a Palestinian state for a comprehensive Arab-Israeli settlement. Presented with such an offer it is extremely unlikely that the Israeli public will support Likud rejectionism of a comprehensive settlement. Indeed, an appeal to the Israeli public is now the only way to get around the impassable obstacles posed by the Likud leadership, which refuses to compromise.

Once the two-state solution is within sight--which in the eyes of the PLO leadership requires a "warm peace" between Israel and Palestine--a "warm peace" between Israel and Egypt then becomes possible. Jordan's problems with Israel would at that point be quite solvable, and will probably involve some confederational relationship with Israel and the Palestinian state. Syria remains the last potential hold-out.

While Syria has consistently been the most formidable barrier to an Arab-Israeli settlement for nearly twenty years, one senses that Syrian radicalism is waning. In the absence of major Soviet support, in the face of Syrian economic weakness and the aging of the genius of rejectionism, Hafez el-Assad, Syria seems less committed to a long-term policy of rejectionism. Syrian membership in the anti-Iraqi war coalition, and its membership in a post-Gulf War security arrangement in the Gulf for the benefit of the Gulf Cooperation Council, both suggest that it now may cast in its lot with the moderate states. It has neither the military nor financial support necessary to do otherwise.

Lebanon's problems, of course, remain a function of Syria and Palestine: with the settlement of the Palestinian issue in sight and the departure of the PLO from Lebanon, Syria will have less reason to maintain the permanent destabilization and fragmentation of Lebanon. Lebanon was Syria's key line of defense against Israeli and American threats to Syria's position; once peace is established with Israel, the strategic role of Lebanon in Syria's security is sharply diminished. But because Lebanon is dependent upon Syria, it comes last on the list of Arab neighbors that will settle with Israel.

To be sure, there will always be a Saddam Hussein who will seek to perpetuate the concept of Israel as an alien imperialist power in the region. But it will be more difficult to enlist major Arab states into this kind of a war in the future. The broad Arab state condemnation of Iraq's invasion of Kuwait will hopefully be a forerunner of a broad Arab state refusal to re-open the Palestinian question once a Palestinian state has been established. Israel will need to retain its military strength, but the supreme symbol of Arab humiliation, the Palestinian issue, will have lost most of its power.

Yet we must all watch for the emergence of the next center of Arab radicalism. There is no credible leader of the radical movement on the horizon. But the issues and grievances are still there to be exploited: the Palestinian problem until it is resolved, haves vs. have-nots, the inequitable distribution of wealth, the absence of democracy, the need for social reform, etc. What powerful Arab state will pick up these issues to propel itself forward as the new radical leader of the region? An Iraq rising out of the ashes and bent on revenge? Syria? A future radical Saudi Arabia after the monarchy? A new Egypt? Or Algeria? Only time will tell, and only a start towards the resolution of many of these other grievances will blunt a radical resurgence.

American-Soviet Differences
on the Middle East

As of today, there are no fundamental differences in how the United States and the Soviet Union view their own strategic interests in the Arab-Israeli problem. Both states recognize that stability and peace in the region are important to the interests of both. Both states recognize that the existence of weapons of mass destruction in the hands of the regional states is increasingly dangerous to the whole world. Both states believe in the security and right to exist of all states in the region, and in the inadmissibility of territorial conquest. Neither state any longer sees a specific regional state as a vehicle for its own interests in the region.

Yet inevitably there will be differences in the outlook of the United States and the U.S.S.R. in the future. We must remember that it is entirely proper for there to be such differences in Soviet and American interests in the Middle East. The United States has differences with other states in the world over a variety of issues, and such differences are normal. It is only when these concrete differences begin to take on a systematic and major character that the problem of serious divergence of interests emerges. In the current absence of ideological struggle between the U.S.S.R. and the United States, I cannot readily perceive such major differences.

But there will be minor differences. The Soviet Union, as an oil exporter, will probably prefer, on balance, to have higher oil prices. So do most other oil producers in the world. The Soviets will recognize, as does the Saudi regime, that some kind of balance on oil pricing policy is essential for the stability of the world economic order. Debates over equity of oil pricing will continue indefinitely into the future. The Soviet Union, as a major arms producer, will also have a long-term interest in arms sales to the region. So do the United States, France, Britain, Brazil, and a number of other countries with advanced arms industries. Here again, all of these states will have to develop some kind of code by which an arms race--even on a purely commercial basis--does not come to dominate the Middle East. That area has already squandered far too much of its wealth on arms--at the overall expense of its citizens.

Beyond that, the Soviet Union may seek particularly close working relations with certain states that might be able to invest in Soviet economic development in the future, especially Saudi Arabia. Other special Soviet interests that are likely to emerge should not conflict strategically with American interests. In short, I do not see any major reason why the United States and the U.S.S.R. should not be able to cooperate in helping to bring greater stability to the region.

The Gulf War, however, also demonstrated that Moscow's "new thinking" in foreign policy is far from universal inside the Soviet Union. Following Foreign Minister Shevardnadze's resignation in December 1990, multiple and dissenting voices were heard in the Soviet foreign policy arena. Conservative party members, supported strongly by much of the upper military echelon, condemned Moscow's policy of turning its back on its old ally Iraq in favor of supporting U.S. political interests in the Gulf. Many spoke bitterly of Soviet willingness to give free reign to American unilateral military action in the Middle East once again. New Party Chairman Polozkov called openly for a return to the old class-based foreign policy. The Soviets were clearly getting cold feet in the middle of the crisis as they pursued a drastically new set of policies. Moscow, of course, is still in the process of trying to figure out just what its national interests are now that the ideological basis of foreign policy is gone. The angry Soviet debate over the Gulf War and the sharp criticisms of U.S. military actions, including the long bombing campaign against Iraq and Washington's disinterest in negotiating with Saddam at any point, demonstrate that much more time is required before Moscow finds its own new voice in foreign policy. Moscow's efforts to come up with its own peace plan to end the war--prematurely in Washington's eyes--were not appreciated in Washington. Even though the plan was designed to strengthen

Gorbachev's own influence in foreign policy, and to further Soviet interests at the temporary expense of U.S. interests, Moscow at no time broke with Washington. A crucial testing period had passed.

However harsh much of the rhetoric against the United States was during the war, a return to the old ideological, zero-sum game is nearly impossible. Moscow will always have an interest in blunting the spectrum of American unilateral action now that the Soviets have largely retired from active competition. But a non-ideological analysis of genuine Soviet interests should not cause the U.S.S.R. to differ sharply or systematically with the United States on most issues in the future--unless the United States itself should increase the scope of its own unilateralism. That, too, is less likely given the considerable emphasis the Bush Administration placed on international legality and cooperation with the UN in the course of the Gulf War.

The New Multilateralism

Both the United States and the Soviet Union, for a variety of different reasons, are relatively weaker in the world today than a decade ago. The U.S.S.R. is far weaker due to its internal turmoil while the United States has emerged from the Gulf War with renewed clout--for a while. Both states possess considerable influence, of different kinds, that can help in bringing about a regional settlement in the Middle East. That influence is particularly important in bringing all parties around to a realistic sense of what is possible and not possible in this world.

At this point, however, the end of the Cold War also means that there is less reason for us to talk of "superpower" solutions to the region. The Soviet Union is not really a superpower any more, at least not to the extent that it once was; American power, while still considerable, is increasingly limited in its freedom to maneuver with the end of the Cold War. In speaking of "great powers" there is increasing reason to include Europe and Japan in the equation. In fact, it is imperative that we do so, for these two parties have greater interest in Middle East oil than either the United States or the Soviet Union. They will need to have a voice in any longer range discussion of energy supplies, the problems of price stability, and the issue of regional political stability.

In the past, both the Americans and Soviets sought to maintain some kind of "superpower" monopoly over strategic questions in the region in general. That monopoly is fading fast. Indeed, the Gulf War demonstrates that the new world trend is towards multilateralism in issues of regional security. Multilateralism will be increasingly important in solving questions relating to regional and international security, especially where weapons of mass destruction are involved. The U.S.S.R. has been moving towards this concept in the last several years, and Gorbachev has made it increasingly clear that he favors multilateral solutions as opposed to unilateral solutions--especially American unilateral operations.

If Gorbachev's restructuring of Soviet politics, economics, and relationships among the republics of the Soviet Union proves painful, it will also prove mildly painful for America to gradually wean itself from the idea of routine unilateral action. Multilateral action has the great benefit of moral authority; this is especially important in Third World issues where considerable sensitivity exists over "imposed solutions" by Western powers. The weakness of multilateralism, of course, is the slowness of getting the mechanisms to work. But, the Kuwaiti crisis again suggests that the post-Cold War world is making progress in this area. The United Nations' moment may finally have come.

There will indeed be major problems ahead of us in the Middle East, requiring more consultation and cooperation than ever before. Agreement over equitable pricing and use of the Arab world's oil resources, water resources, the gradual transition from autocracies to democracies, and the future economic status of the non-oil states all will require careful attention. They are all volatile issues and involve potential charges of "imperialist" intervention, and differences between global haves and have-nots.

Through multilateralism the United States, in particular, will find it easier to avoid some of the political "baggage" that its unilateral actions in the region have invariably created in the past. Hopefully, joint military operations and broad international economic action, as witnessed in the Gulf War against Iraq, are the first steps towards a new regional order in the region. A just solution of the

Palestinians' political aspirations to statehood and Israel's search for permanent security and integration into the region will help clear the decks for a more rational approach to solving these new kinds of problems in the next decade.

PART TWO

Theoretical Underpinnings

3 Preventing War in the Middle East: When Do Deterrence and Reassurance Work?

Even though the Cold War had ended, the Middle East and the international community faced a serious crisis in August 1990 with dangerous short-term risks and troubling long-term consequences. Before dawn on August 2, Iraqi troops poured across the border into Kuwait. Within three hours, the army had accomplished its objectives: the overthrow of the government of Kuwait and control of Kuwait's oilfields. Worldwide condemnation, an international embargo, and the deployment of American air and ground forces to Saudi Arabia and naval forces to the Gulf did not succeed in compelling Iraq to withdraw. A week later, Iraq formally annexed Kuwait.

The use of force by one Arab government to annex another is unprecedented in the modern Middle East. Could this use of force have been prevented? Once crisis prevention failed, the United States deployed forces to Saudi Arabia and the Gulf to deter Iraq from using force against other Gulf states, and the international community approved economic sanctions to compel Iraq to withdraw from Kuwait. Could the crisis have been managed without resorting to major war? Could compellence have succeeded without dangerous escalation? The crisis created by the Iraqi annexation of Kuwait dramatically underlines the dilemmas and difficulties of international crisis prevention and management.

The authors of this chapter acknowledge the generous support of the Canadian Institute for International Peace and Security and the United States Institute of Peace.

To develop strategies to prevent war and manage crises, analysts of international crisis management have drawn on two quite different analogies. Heavily influenced by Munich and the failure to prevent German aggression, post-war analysts preoccupied with a putative threat from the Soviet Union refined strategies of nuclear and conventional deterrence designed to prevent wars of opportunity and aggression. Deterrence seeks to prevent undesired behavior by convincing those who might contemplate such action that the probable cost will exceed the anticipated gain. Deterrence can take two forms: general and immediate. General deterrence is based on the existing balance of capabilities between the parties and attempts to prevent an adversary from seriously considering any kind of military challenge because of its expected adverse consequences. Immediate deterrence is specific: It is designed to forestall an anticipated challenge to a well-defined and publicized commitment.[1] The strategy of immediate deterrence manipulates threats to prevent unwanted action by an adversary. It requires that leaders define the behavior that is unacceptable, publicize their commitment to punish or deny transgressors their objectives, possess the capability to do so, and communicate their resolve to implement their threats. Central to all theories of immediate deterrence is an emphasis on commitment, reputation and resolve to reinforce commitment, and the development of the military capabilities necessary to make commitments credible. Critics of immediate deterrence as a strategy of crisis prevention and management have pointed to its limited assumptions and unrealistic requirements. Theories of deterrence assume an adversary that is largely motivated by the opportunity for gain rather than by the fear of loss. When it is used against an adversary who is vulnerable or frightened, it intensifies the pressure to act and can provoke the use of force it is designed to prevent.[2] When leaders are pessimistic about the future, feel threatened or vulnerable, and consider the costs of the status quo unacceptable, they are motivated to discount evidence that their strategies will encounter opposition and, therefore, are especially likely to resort to confrontational strategies to use force. Aggressive behavior has frequently occurred, not as much as the "realist" theory predicts when leaders feel strong and confident, but rather when they are pessimistic and vulnerable, either at home or abroad.

Even when deterrence does not provoke war, it can prolong and exacerbate conflict. The heavy emphasis on deterrence as a strategy had pernicious consequences in the relationship between the two superpowers. It led to a massive build-up of tightly coupled strategic arsenals by Washington and Moscow, and to an extension of competition in areas of peripheral interest because commitments were seen as interdependent. A failure to respond to a challenge anywhere, Thomas Schelling argued, would lead to a challenge everywhere.[3]

Others worried not primarily about unprovoked aggression, but rather about the risk of inadvertent or accidental war between the two superpowers in a tightly interlocked strategic environment. Analysts preoccupied by the risk of nuclear war between the United States and the Soviet Union drew an analogy not to World War II, but to World War I. The challenge is to prevent war through loss of control of complex strategic systems, through miscalculated escalation by leaders who practice brinkmanship, or through preemption of an anticipated attack.[4]

To address these dangers of unplanned and unwanted escalation, analysts have written extensively on the political, operational, and technical requirements of managing crises so that war is avoided. Alexander George has underlined the complex trade-offs between achieving important objectives and avoiding war. He has emphasized the contradictions between military and political logic, and the consequent importance of limiting political objectives as a crisis escalates.[5] He and others have stressed the importance of political control and of effective command, communication and control of armed forces to prevent accidental escalation that can occur without the knowledge of central policy-makers.[6]

These analyses are helpful in identifying important obstacles to effective crisis prevention and management. The obstacles that are identified, however, are often strongly resistant to management and manipulation. Complex and tightly coupled strategic systems are highly vulnerable to loss of control despite the best efforts of leaders at the top. Leaders may be so sensitive to domestic political pressures that they are unable to limit their objectives as a crisis develops. The stress created by high levels of uncertainty and threats have frequently degraded leaders' capacities to perform effectively in a crisis. Case studies of international crisis management have demonstrated that when leaders' processes of perception and spans of attention become impaired, they become rigid in their thinking and insensitive to information that challenged their beliefs, and that their capacity to consider a wide-range of consequences is limited.[7] These are generic responses to high levels of stress. In this sense, if it inflates leaders' expectations of their capacities to craft and calibrate strategies of crisis management once a crisis erupts, the promise of effective crisis management is a dangerous illusion.[8]

Crisis Prevention and Management
in the Middle East

The analysis of obstacles to and strategies of crisis management is directly relevant to the Middle East. In the Arab-Israeli conflict, deterrence has been an important strategy of conflict management at least since 1956. A status quo power after the war in the Sinai, Israel attempted to deter Arab attacks against its territory by specifying a series of *casus belli*, developing a reputation for resolve, and acquiring the military capabilities necessary to make its threats credible against a coalition of Arab adversaries. Egypt and other Arab countries also attempted to deter Israel from launching punitive attacks in retaliation for *feda'yeen* raids across its borders. In the Arab-Israeli conflict, as in the superpower conflict, the strategy of deterrence has had a mixed record. Although it is impossible to review the multiple cases of deterrence in the Arab-Israeli relationship over time, the relationship between Egypt and Israel illustrates the complex impact of general and immediate deterrence on crisis prevention, crisis management, and conflict resolution.

The war in 1967 was an inadvertent war, one that no leader planned or wanted. Ironically, it grew out of the successful attempt by Egypt to deter Israel from punishing Syria for its support of raids across Israel's borders. The success of extended deterrence, however, set in motion a political process which Egyptian President Gamal Abdel Nasser could not control. Even though Egyptian troops sent across the Suez Canal into the Sinai peninsula succeeded in deterring Israel, their presence then unleashed a set of demands which the president was unable to resist. He faced an aroused domestic public, the taunts of regional adversaries, and pressures from regional allies. His leadership challenged in the Arab world, Nasser moved incrementally through a series of escalatory steps which challenged Israel's deterrent strategy and broadened the scope of the conflict. Under political pressure, Nasser was unable to limit his objectives; instead he escalated the stakes for Israel. Although the Egyptian extension of deterrence succeeded in its immediate objective of protecting a weaker ally, its success simultaneously provoked a wider war through its unintended impact on Egypt's domestic public, its Arab allies and adversaries, and the consequent pressures on President Nasser.

The failure of Israel's deterrent strategy against Egypt prompted a redefinition of the issues at stake, raised the consequences of concession, facilitated miscalculation of Egyptian intentions, and worked heavily in favor of a decision to use force. This was so whether or not Israel's leaders believed that Egyptian leaders were preparing to strike first. While the logic of force deployments was a component of the process of escalation, it was not the most important part. In the strategic thinking of Israel's leaders, the logic of their deterrent strategy blurred the distinction between preemption and prevention. The failure of Israel's deterrent strategy dictated a military response, sooner or later. The crisis was unmanageable short of war.[9]

At the end of the war, the intelligence services of the United States, the Soviet Union, Egypt, and Israel all agreed that Egypt's military capability was inferior to that of Israel: Egypt could not succeed in recapturing the Sinai lost in the 1967 war. A necessary condition for the success of general deterrence and crisis prevention was in place.

Israel's continuing occupation of the Sinai was, however, an intolerable humiliation for Egyptian leaders. Despite Israel's acknowledged military superiority, deterrence failed again as a strategy of conflict management when Nasser launched the War of Attrition in March 1969 along the Suez Canal in an attempt to compel Israel to withdraw its forces. Nasser challenged deterrence because of the high political costs of inaction that motivated his miscalculation of the relative balance of capabilities.[10]

During the fighting which continued for 18 months, Moscow sent 20,000 combat and support personnel to Egypt. Also, Soviet forces assumed responsibility for the defense of Egyptian air space and engaged in combat with Israel's pilots over the Suez Canal. The war ended only as a result of American diplomatic intervention when both sides acknowledged the high costs of the stalemate.

The protracted and costly war settled little and the lines of conflict were, if anything, more clearly drawn. Egypt and Israel read the results of the war quite differently. Both sides claimed victory even though both sides had suffered serious losses. Although Egypt had failed to compel even a partial withdrawal by Israel, its leaders insisted that they had won a significant victory because they had neutralized Israel's air superiority over the canal zone. Nevertheless, the high political, economic, and psychological costs of the continued occupation of the Sinai led Nasser's successor, Anwar el-Sadat, to search desperately for a strategy to compensate for Egypt's military inferiority.[11]

In February 1971, the new president departed from past practice and offered to sign a peace agreement with Israel in return for a full withdrawal of Israel's forces.[12] Although Sadat explicitly rejected the normalization of relations between Egypt and Israel, he expressed interest in a diplomatic resolution of the conflict. Two years of indirect bargaining with Israel through the United States produced no tangible results. Israel's leaders saw little reason to make concessions.

Israel's civilian and military leaders, with only one or two exceptions, insisted that they had prevailed in the War of Attrition.[13] Israel had shown itself capable of withstanding significant military pressure in a long war and had resisted Egyptian as well as international pressure to withdraw from the Sinai without compensating political concessions. Some of Israel's leaders recognized the growing frustration of Arab governments, but, in response, placed even heavier emphasis than they had in the past on the importance of military superiority as the basis of deterrence and crisis prevention. Their confidence in the effectiveness of deterrence blinded them to the intense pressures on President Sadat and to his growing desperation. Israel's leaders did not use the time provided by deterrence to push the process of negotiation forward. Rather, deterrence became a substitute for diplomacy.

By 1972, President Sadat anticipated that if the military and diplomatic stalemate were not broken, the ceasefire along the canal would become permanent and Egypt would be unable to reverse the status quo. He worried that the postponement of military action month after month would lead to explosive domestic consequences, an alarming deterioration of Egypt's position in the Arab world, and serious deterioration in domestic morale.[14] Pessimistic about the prospects of negotiation, and alarmed by the growing costs of inaction, President Sadat turned his attention to the creation of a military option that would compensate for Egypt's military inferiority. In consultation with his generals, the president designed a limited military attack which had as its larger political purpose the deliberate creation of an international crisis. Deterrence and crisis prevention failed again because of the desperation and vulnerability of the Egyptian president.

This cursory review of immediate deterrence as a strategy of crisis prevention suggests several important propositions which are directly relevant to the future management of conflict in the Middle East. The strategy of deterrence failed because of factors outside the scope of the theory: leaders did not resort to force because they were confident of their military superiority, but rather because they considered the costs of the status quo to be intolerably high. The costs they considered, moreover, were not only the obvious strategic losses but the domestic political and economic consequences of inaction. Strategic behavior cannot be explained without considering the impact of economic and political factors.

Nevertheless, leaders learned from the failure of deterrence as a strategy for crisis prevention. Egyptian leaders learned the lessons they did because of the robustness of general deterrence, while Israel's leaders learned from the failure of immediate deterrence. In large part because of the lessons they learned, Arab and Israeli leaders began to experiment with alternative strategies of conflict management that we call "reassurance."

Reassurance as a Strategy
of Conflict Management

Strategies of reassurance begin from a different set of assumptions.[15] Like deterrence, they presume ongoing hostility but root the source of that hostility in adversaries' feelings of acute vulnerability. Whereas deterrence attempts to discourage the resort to force by persuading adversaries that such action would be too costly, reassurance seeks to reduce the incentives adversaries have to use force. In the broadest sense, reassurance tries to ameliorate adversarial hostility by trying to reduce the fear, misunderstanding, and insecurity that are so often responsible for escalation to war. Reassurance dictates that defenders try to communicate both their benign intentions and their interests in alternative ways of addressing the issues in dispute.

Reassurance, like deterrence, can be divided into immediate and general reassurance. General reassurance is designed to alter an adversary's calculations of the relative advantages of the use of force in comparison to other alternatives. It attempts to shift the trajectory of a conflict and to encourage an adversary to restructure and reframe a problem by creating alternatives to the use of force. Immediate reassurance, like immediate deterrence, seeks to prevent an anticipated challenge to a specific commitment. It attempts to reduce adversarial perceptions of hostility, the domestic pressures to act, the workings of the security dilemma abroad, and the likelihood of miscalculation.

When leaders anticipate a deliberate challenge to a specific commitment or consider a miscalculated challenge likely, they can in the first instance use strategies of immediate reassurance to compensate for some of the obvious risks of deterrence. They can attempt through self-restraint to avoid exacerbating the pressures and constraints that may operate on an adversary who may choose force because of the costs of inaction. They may attempt to communicate to an adversary the limits of their intentions in an effort to avoid a miscalculated use of force by their adversary. To reduce the likelihood of a miscalculated challenge, they can also develop "norms of competition" to regulate their conflict and signal the limits of their intentions. In a closely related strategy, leaders can attempt to put in place informal or formal regimes designed specifically to build confidence and reduce uncertainty. These strategies have been very effective in managing the ongoing conflict between Israel and Syria, even though the communication has almost always been tacit or through third parties.[16]

The more ambitious strategies of reassurance seek to shift the trajectory of the conflict and create alternatives to a use of force. A strategy of reciprocal concessions can be used to initiate tacit or explicit communication between adversaries in an effort to signal an interest in moving away from a use of force and toward negotiation. To compensate for some of the weaknesses of reciprocal strategies, leaders can also try to break out of habitual conflict through less conventional methods of unilateral and irrevocable commitments. This kind of strategy tries to send a credible signal of leaders' interest by addressing the issues in conflict and by offering alternatives to the use of force. We classify these kinds of strategies as general reassurance.

Reassurance in the Arab-Israel Conflict

The most striking example of the effective use of reassurance was President Sadat's visit to Jerusalem in November 1977 to speak to Israel's Knesset. Like deterrence, the use of the strategy was rooted as much in the domestic political economy of Egypt as in its strategic environment. We first assess the reasons for the effectiveness of Sadat's strategy and then examine why he chose to reassure.

In considering a dramatic visit to address Israel's Knesset personally, Sadat hoped to create a constituency for negotiation with Egypt by reassuring Israel's leaders and public of his benign intentions. The Egyptian president also hoped to influence American public opinion and help President Carter to compensate for his self-professed political weakness. Sadat's strategy of reassuring through irrevocable commitments succeeded brilliantly. Egyptian demands for withdrawal from captured Arab territory were unchanged, but Israel's leaders and public paid attention to the deed rather than to the words. In large part through this single, dramatic act, Sadat changed Israel's incentives to negotiate. Why did the strategy succeed in reshaping domestic constraints in Israel? Several factors were at play, some general and some specific to the historical context.

The initiative was irreversible; once the president of Egypt travelled to Jerusalem, he could not undo the deed. Because it could not be reversed, the action was treated as a valid indicator of Egyptian intentions rather than as a signal that could be manipulated.[17] Israel's leadership and public recognized the irreversibility of the action and, consequently, gave it great weight.

The substantial political cost to President Sadat of breaking the long-standing Arab taboo of not negotiating directly with Israel was also apparent to Israel's leaders. Dissension within the Egyptian government was pronounced and a tidal wave of criticism from the Arab world engulfed the Egyptian leader. Israel's leaders reasoned that Egypt's president would not incur such heavy costs were he not sincere.

Sadat's arrival in Jerusalem also challenged the most important set of beliefs about Arab goals among Israel's leadership and public. A broad cross section of Israelis had assumed that Arab leaders were unrelentingly hostile, so much so that they were unprepared to meet Israel's leaders face-to-face. Once these core beliefs were shaken, it became easier for Israelis to revise associated assumptions and expectations.

Finally, President Sadat spoke over the heads of Israel's leadership, speaking directly to Israel's public and, indeed, to the American public. With his flair for the dramatic, he created the psychological and political symbols which would mobilize public opinion to press their more cautious and restrained leaders. In so doing, he removed constraints on leaders in Israel and the United States and created political inducements for action. Sadat's action reverberated through multiple audiences and multiple constituencies.

Why did President Sadat choose a strategy of reassurance? His strategy can best be explained by the intersection of crises in Egypt's domestic political economy and in its strategic environment. Egypt faced a domestic crisis and threatening strategic uncertainties which were amplified by their simultaneity. Moreover, President Sadat saw the two crises as tightly interlinked: economic and political problems at home delimited the set of strategies that could be used internationally.

Historically in Egypt, a domestic strategy of mobilization to create a command economy was associated with a strategy of confrontation against regional states with traditional political economies as well as against Israel. Even before President Nasser's death in 1970, Egypt began tentative experiments with an "open door" investment policy in order to address a growing crisis in the economy that had been badly exacerbated by the wars in 1967 and 1969-70. In 1973, student and worker demonstrations, rapidly falling foreign exchange reserves, and pessimism about the prospects of diplomacy mediated by the United States converged to persuade President Sadat that the only alternative to an intolerable economic and strategic status quo was a limited war with Israel. In the aftermath of the war, Egypt accelerated the pace of economic liberalization. The quasi-liberal experimentation, *al-infitah al-iqtisadi*, was consistent with Sadat's regional strategy: closer reliance on Arab oil-producing states and an end to confrontation with traditional regimes. Sadat looked to the oil-producing states to provide the capital and investment needed to push the Egyptian economy forward.

Egypt's international strategy was consistent with its strategy of limited economic and political liberalization at home and rapprochement with traditional oil-producing states in the region. President Sadat relied heavily on the United States to mediate between Egypt and Israel in order to secure the withdrawal of Israel's force from the territories it had occupied in 1967. He did so in part because of the lessons learnt from the war in 1973.

Egyptian generals recognized that Egypt had fought the war under optimal conditions; a military alliance with Syria had permitted a coordinated two-front attack for the first time. Arab oil-producers had joined in the accompanying diplomatic offensive, and Egypt had the strategic advantage of surprise. Yet, even under those conditions, Egypt had come perilously close to a strategic defeat after important initial military successes in crossing the Suez Canal. In this context, Sadat was reluctant to risk the limited gains he had achieved through phased disengagement by renewed warfare.

By the autumn of 1977, President Sadat had decided that the ongoing process of multilateral negotiation under Carter's leadership would fail and that a dramatic change in strategy was necessary if a negotiated agreement were to be reached.[18] In Egypt the domestic political and economic crisis had also intensified in the first nine months of 1977, shortening the time available for a negotiated agreement.

On the night of January 17, official prices of subsidized commodities were increased by administrative decision, without consultation, debate, or vote by the Assembly. Immediately, Egypt experienced its worst riots in 25 years. From Aswan to Alexandria, with the police and government as their primary target, workers in the urban and industrial areas rioted; the army was forced to fire on demonstrators and a curfew was imposed. Although the increased cost of basic commodities was the spark, the political weakness of the regime among urban residents, industrial workers, and public-sector employees combined to produce the most acute political crisis Egypt had experienced in a quarter of a century.

President Sadat quickly attempted to shore up the legitimacy of his regime by organizing a nation-wide referendum. At the same time, Sadat began a sustained attack against the left, whom he held responsible for the riots, and rehabilitated the right as a counterweight.[19] That summer, Sadat halted exports of cotton to Soviet Union and in September, postponed scheduled repayment of the $4 billion owed to the Soviet Union. At the same time, he accused Moscow of fomenting dissent within Egypt. The changing political and economic context made even more imperative an agreement brokered by the United States and the exclusion of the Soviet Union from the diplomatic process.

There were, of course, potential regional costs to such a dramatic shift in strategy.[20] Foremost among them was a decline in capital investment and aid from the oil-producing countries. But Arab aid to Egypt, which had reached a high of $1,264 million in 1974 in the aftermath of the October War, had declined to $625 million in 1976. Moreover, as Boutrus Ghali, a senior foreign policy adviser to President Sadat observed:

Arab states have often made some impressive offers of aid, but when it comes down to it, they set unacceptable conditions. I mean, you will have the Saudi government calling and threatening to cut off aid to us, because one of our magazines wrote an unfavorable story about a given prince. That is unacceptable. American aid is stable and predictable.[21]

In the absence of a peace settlement, defense expenditures remained at approximately 50% of total GNP, and Egypt continued to forego the estimated $1 billion of revenue from the oil fields in the Sinai. Egypt desperately needed a resolution to the strategic crisis; only if it were resolved would it receive the materials, factories and food, quickly and cheaply on predictable terms, which it needed to revitalize the economy. Only the United States could meet both these needs. The cost of the loss of Arab support was dwarfed by the losses imposed by the absence of an agreement. President Sadat considered that a strategy of reassurance was most likely to avoid the political and economic costs of a failure to agree.

Reassurance and Conflict Resolution

Analysis of this case points to the positive relationship between the intensifying crisis in the Egyptian political economy, an unstable and threatening security environment, and agreement through reassurance. It suggests that in a context of uncertainty about security and a political-economic crisis, a bias toward agreement on security issues in a hostile international environment is partly a function of the capacity of an agreement on security to effect structural transformations at home.[22]

This argument needs an important qualification. Leaders' preferred strategies of domestic reconfiguration may critically affect their assessment of the linkages between strategies of conflict management and their political economies. In the nineteen-sixties, when Egyptian leaders attempted to reconfigure their political economy in a hierarchical command structure, even though they depended heavily on international resources to effect that transformation, they were strongly biased against agreement and chose to manage their security crisis through confrontation. It was only when Egypt turned toward a strategy of economic and political liberalization that its leaders focused on the importance of reducing the intensity of the security crisis as a prerequisite to successful liberalization and on the absolute costs of non-agreement.

The argument depends on the specification of the causal sequence of domestic and strategic variables in changing strategic behavior. It gives primacy to political and economic variables, broadly defined, and their impact on strategic behavior. It is extraordinarily difficult, however, to disentangle the impact of the two sets of variables when security and domestic crises intersect, as they did in the case of Egypt. Two indirect streams of evidence are suggestive, however, about the sequencing of domestic and security variables in this process toward agreement.

Indirectly, there is no evidence of covariation between President Sadat's estimate of Egyptian military capabilities from 1977 through to Camp David and his strategies of conflict management. After the October War, Sadat began to seriously explore agreement as an alternative to war in its capacity to resolve the crisis with Israel as well as to ameliorate the economic crisis at home. The lessons learned from the last war, however, can be treated as a constant rather than a variable throughout the period under analysis, when Sadat's strategies varied substantially. Moreover, from the onset of negotiations through to their conclusion, Egyptian military capabilities did not decline nor did President Sadat display increased pessimism about Egypt's military option. The intensity of the crisis in Egypt's political economy, however, did intensify dramatically during the process of negotiation.

More directly relevant, in both cases of domestic reconfiguration in Egypt, first toward a command economy in the sixties and then toward a liberalized political economy in the seventies, efforts at domestic restructuring preceded the changes in behavior on security issues. If this is indeed the correct sequencing, the *kind* of domestic reconfiguration Egyptian leaders attempted appears, at least indirectly, to have shaped their evaluation of alternative strategies of conflict management. It did so by delimiting the kinds of international strategies that would create the benefits they needed at home. Analysis of both deterrence and reassurance between Egypt and Israel suggests that leaders' attempts to reconfigure their domestic as well as their strategic environments, and the interactive linkages they identify across the international-domestic divide, are crucially important to the kinds of strategies of conflict management they choose and to the effectiveness of these strategies. As we have seen in the analysis of Sadat's strategy of reassurance, the choice among strategies of international conflict management is partly determined by the linkages leaders identify with domestic politics and economics. Once persuaded that the military option was both limited in what it could accomplish and costly, Sadat, anticipating important domestic benefits from a resolution of the conflict with Israel, moved to reassure his adversary of Egypt's benign intentions. As we argued in the analysis of deterrence, the effectiveness of these strategies is similarly determined in part by political and economic constraints. The same set of propositions is also very helpful in explaining the propensity of the superpowers to cooperate in the Middle East.

Cooperation Between the Superpowers: A Speculative Analysis of Its Impact on the Middle East

Conflict management in the Middle East will be affected in part by the role of the two superpowers in the future. Two questions are directly relevant: What is the probability of future tacit or explicit cooperation between the superpowers in the Middle East, and, closely related but distinct, what impact is superpower cooperation likely to have on crisis management, crisis prevention, and conflict management in the region?

In a forthcoming analysis of Soviet-American relations under Stalin, Khrushchev, Brezhnev, and Gorbachev, we have examined the ways in which four contextual variables shaped these leaders' propensity to cooperate with the West. These four are (1) leaders' optimism or pessimism about the future; (2) their assessment of their adversary's intentions; (3) their foreign policy objectives; and (4) the nature of the links between these objectives and important domestic goals. Our analysis suggests that the change in Soviet foreign policy toward accommodation with the West is deeply rooted in the domestic economics and politics of the Soviet Union. The shift toward cooperation provides an unprecedented opportunity; however real dangers exist if the West does not reciprocate and Soviet expectations of the domestic benefits from international cooperation are not met.

The linkages across the domestic-international divide are particularly important. Central are the kinds of linkages leaders identify and the direction in which the arrow of influence points. For Stalin, the Soviet state was a resource to be exploited for foreign policy objectives. Khrushchev, on the other hand, tried to use foreign policy to support his agricultural, industrial, and political reforms. The subordination of foreign policy to domestic objectives by Khrushchev--and later, by Gorbachev--made these two leaders both more vulnerable and accommodating to the West. This is the most promising and most dangerous context for Soviet-American relations; conciliatory policies are most likely to be reciprocated, and confrontational policies are most likely to provoke. When Khrushchev's cooperative actions were not reciprocated and détente failed, the most dangerous confrontation of the Cold War, the Cuban Missile Crisis, followed quickly.

Many analysts explain Gorbachev's accommodating policies as a necessary response to the country's economic stagnation. This interpretation is apolitical. It ignores the fact that the Soviet economy experienced a decade of decline under Brezhnev and that neither he nor his two immediate successors changed their domestic or foreign policies. Radical changes in domestic, foreign, and military policy came only with Gorbachev. In a pattern strikingly similar to that of Sadat, Gorbachev's shift to accommodation with the West was closely tied to the anticipated domestic benefits of this new strategy. He expected the Soviet economy to benefit from resources and manpower formerly reserved for the military and from greater access to western capital and technology.

The shift toward accommodation was driven not only by anticipation of the domestic benefits from international cooperation but also by Gorbachev's deep pessimism about the future if the

Soviet domestic system was not reformed. Convinced of the gravity of the failures in the economy and in foreign policy under Brezhnev, Gorbachev recognized the inability of existing institutions to address these problems. He was therefore willing to consider radical political and economic changes to the Soviet system. *Perestroika* and *glasnost* were motivated by a much broader political vision that sought to restructure the Soviet Union politically as well as economically, and to integrate it into the international political economy. Gorbachev's estimate of Western intentions facilitated the change to a strategy of accommodation. Gorbachev was much less pessimistic about Western intentions than his predecessors and consequently less worried that the United States and its allies would exploit Soviet concessions.

Anticipation of significant benefits to domestic politics and economics from a strategy of international cooperation, deep pessimism about the future of the Soviet Union unless its political and economic system were restructured, and a reduced fear of exploitation by the West converged to produce a significant shift in Soviet foreign policy toward international cooperation. In response, the Western world has reassured Soviet leaders that it does not intend to exploit these changes and it has reciprocated. Recently, the West has begun to provide some of the tangible economic benefits anticipated by Soviet leaders. In so doing, the structure of cooperation between the two superpowers is reinforced and deepened.

If the pattern of reciprocation continues and Soviet leaders realize some of the benefits they have anticipated, their post-war pattern of competition in the Middle East is likely to undergo significant change. In the recent crisis created by Iraq's invasion and annexation of Soviet-American interaction could not be more dramatically different than it was during the last crisis in the Gulf in 1987-88. Then the United States decided to reflag Kuwaiti tankers in large part to preempt Soviet involvement in the Gulf.[23] In August 1990, Foreign Minister Eduard A. Shevardnadze and Secretary of State James Baker jointly called for a world-wide embargo against Iraq, the Soviet Union halted the sale of arms to Iraq, and both nations supported tough economic sanctions at the United Nations. Even more striking, the United States invited

Soviet naval participation to enforce the international embargo against Iraq.[24] As Maksim A. Yuzin, the correspondent for *Izvestiia* observed:

> True, you cannot say that Soviet and American interests coincide in the Middle East. But I think we have passed a critical moment: now we cannot say that our interests and American interests there are opposed.[25]

Although the convergence of Soviet and American interests in the Gulf should not be overexaggerated, both center on the wish to prevent "extremism" or "destabilization."

The impact of the changed Soviet-American relationship on conflict management, crisis prevention, and crisis management in the Middle East should not be overstated. Analysis of past superpower attempts to prevent crises in the Middle East finds that the United States and the Soviet Union were less managers than managed by their local allies.[26] Their regional allies had surprising autonomy and were able to create crises despite the opposition of those who provided military, economic, and diplomatic support. Indeed, Sadat's concern in 1973 about the impact of Soviet-American détente on the Arab-Israeli conflict was a contributing factor to his decision to intentionally and deliberately create a crisis. Conflict management and crisis prevention in the Middle East will not become much easier as a result of the ending of the Cold War. We can speculate that as the superpowers disengage from their competition for allies, the limited restraint the superpowers were able to exercise on their allies will disappear.

In contrast to crisis prevention, crisis management should become somewhat less dangerous and more effective. The new relationship between the superpowers should reduce some of the most serious risks of the past. Most important, the risk of a nuclear confrontation between the United States and the Soviet Union as they supported allies locked in bitter conflict has been significantly reduced, if not eliminated. The Middle East is no longer the Balkans of the twenty-first century. It should also be easier to initiate and enforce international action through the United Nations and to control the supply of arms to local belligerents.

Nevertheless, the risks of compellence and deterrence as strategies of crisis management remain serious. The recent crisis is unfolding in a Middle East armed with chemical and nuclear weapons, and ballistic missiles. The possibility of chemical warfare has replaced the earlier fear of nuclear war. It is a distinction with little difference.

Deterrence and Reassurance:
The Inherent Dilemmas
of Crisis Prevention and Management

Deterrence and reassurance can elicit a range of responses. Deterrence can restrain or provoke an adversary. It can also be exploited by its targets to buttress their domestic authority or justify an expansionist foreign policy. Reassurance can also be reciprocated, exploited, or ignored. Reciprocal reassurance between China and the United States in the 1960s, and Egypt and Israel following the war in 1973 helped to transform active hostility into relationships where conflict was managed without the threat of or resort to force. The attempted appeasement of Hitler's Germany in the 1930s remains the paradigmatic example of the exploitation of reassurance.

The crucial task for those who seek to prevent and manage crises is to determine whether deterrence or reassurance is appropriate. The available evidence suggests that deterrence and the related strategy of compellence are appropriate when an adversary is opportunistic and motivated largely by the prospect of gain. Against such an adversary, deterrence and compellence are most likely to succeed when an adversary has the political and strategic freedom to exercise restraint, is not misled by grossly distorted assessments of the political-military situation, and is vulnerable to the kinds of threats a deterrer is capable of making credible. The timing of deterrence may also be important. The effectiveness of deterrence is likely to be enhanced if it is used early, before an adversary becomes committed to a use of force and becomes correspondingly insensitive to warnings and threats. Insofar as these strategic, political, and psychological conditions are not met, deterrence is increasingly likely to become ineffective, irrelevant, or even provocative.

When adversaries are vulnerable at home or abroad, and are motivated largely by the fear of loss rather than by the prospect of gain, reassurance is appropriate, alone or as a complement to deterrence. Strategies of reassurance are most likely to succeed against an adversary who is concerned largely about its own security and does not seek primarily to exploit the weakness of others.

Determining whether an adversary is aggressive and motivated primarily by the desire to exploit, or vulnerable and driven primarily by the fear of loss is extraordinarily difficult. Although "opportunity" and "need" are theoretically distinct concepts, in practice they are frequently not mutually exclusive. The dichotomy between the two is almost always blurred in specific historical cases. In most cases, both are likely to be present to different degrees.

Analysis across the political spectrum in the West considers President Saddam Hussein an opportunity-driven aggressor, but a plausible argument can be made that Iraq's leader was motivated in part by vulnerability when he decided to invade Kuwait. Most of the available evidence sustains the interpretation that Saddam Hussein identified a long-awaited opportunity to assert Iraq's claim to Kuwait and to establish a commanding position in the international oil market. In large part because the United States failed to warn of the consequences of an invasion, Iraq's president was convinced that Kuwait would not be able to mobilize the assistance of powerful outsiders. In addition, Iraq's military capabilities were overwhelmingly superior to any coalition of regional adversaries. These are ideal conditions for a war of opportunity.

It is also possible that President Hussein was driven in part by the growing vulnerability of Iraq's economy. Foreign Minister Tariq Aziz, in an interview after the invasion, explained that Iraq was stunned by Kuwait's insistence that Iraq's debt be repaid; the debt had accumulated during the war with Iran, a war fought to defend the Gulf states as well as Iraq. He then drew an explicit linkage between Iraq's deteriorating economy and the invasion of Kuwait:

The economic question was a major factor in triggering the current situation. In addition to the forty billion dollars in

Arab debts, we owe at least as much to the West. This year's state budget required seven billion dollars for debt service, which was a huge amount, leaving us with only enough for basic services for our country. Our budget is based on a price of eighteen dollars a barrel for oil, but since the Kuwaitis began flooding the world with oil, the price has gone down by a third. When we met again--in Jidda, at the end of July--Kuwait said it was not interested in any change. We were not interested in any change. We were now desperate, and could not pay our bills for food imports. It was a starvation war. When do you use your military power to preserve yourself?[27]

To the extent that Iraq was motivated principally by opportunity, only a clear and unequivocal commitment combined with an explicit threat of the consequences of the use of force stood any chance of preventing Iraq's massive use of force against Kuwait. Deterrence had to be forcefully executed. If President Hussein was driven primarily by Iraq's economic vulnerability, then a strategy of reassurance had to address the issues that were central to ameliorating its acute economic problems. If the United States was uncertain of Iraq's motives and intentions, as is so often the case, then it could have used a mixed strategy of a strong and unequivocal commitment to come to Kuwait's defense and reassurance to address Iraq's pressing economic concerns. Although it is far from certain that a mixed strategy of deterrence and reassurance would have succeeded had it been tried, Washington neither deterred nor reassured effectively. Rather, it distanced itself from an "inter-Arab dispute" and did not address Iraq's concerns about its growing debt and debt-servicing charges. Under these conditions, crisis prevention stood little chance of success.

No hard and fast decision-making rules exist to help leaders determine the mix of need and opportunity motivating an adversary's strategic choice. Yet this determination is critical because it speaks to the appropriate mixture and sequencing of deterrence with strategies of reassurance. On this judgment rests the choice of strategies of crisis prevention and management.

50

Designing strategies of conflict management that combine components of deterrence and reassurance in appropriate mixtures and sequences is no easy task. There are formidable obstacles to the success of these strategies, used alone or in tandem, and the risks of one are often the benefits of the other. No single strategy is likely to work across cases under different strategic, political, and psychological conditions. Nevertheless, sensitivity to the limiting conditions of each strategy, to its relative strengths and weaknesses, and to its interactive effects is essential to the prevention and management of international conflict short of war.

Notes

1. This distinction is developed by Patrick M. Morgan, *Deterrence: A Conceptual Analysis* (Beverly Hills: Sage Library of Social Science, revised edition, 1983).

2. Robert Jervis, Richard Ned Lebow, and Janice Gross Stein, *Psychology and Deterrence* (Baltimore: Johns Hopkins University Press, 1985).

3. Thomas Schelling, *The Strategy of Conflict* (Cambridge: Harvard University Press, 1960).

4. See Richard Ned Lebow, *Nuclear Crisis Management: A Dangerous Illusion* (Ithaca: Cornell University Press, 1987) and Lawrence Freedman, *The Evolution of Nuclear Strategy* (New York: St. Martin's Press, 1981).

5. Alexander L. George, *Managing U.S.-Soviet Rivalry: Problems of Crisis Prevention* (Boulder, CO: Westview Press, 1983); "Crisis Management: The Interaction of Political and Military Considerations," *Survival* 26, 5 (September/October 1984), pp. 223-234; "Political Crises," in Joseph S. Nye Jr., ed., *The Making of America's Soviet Policy* (New Haven: Yale University Press, 1984); and *Avoiding War: Problems of Crisis Management* (Boulder, CO: Westview Press, 1991). See also Gilbert R. Winham, ed., *New Issues in International Crisis Management* (Boulder, CO: Westview Press, 1988).

6. John Steinbruner, "Nuclear Decapitation," *Foreign Policy* 45 (Winter 1981/82), pp. 16-28; Desmond Ball, *Can Nuclear War Be Controlled?* Adelphi Paper 169 (London: Institute of Strategic Studies, 1981).

7. Alexander L. George, "The Impact of Crisis-Induced Stress on Decisionmaking," paper prepared for the Institution of Medicine Symposium on the Medical Aspects of Nuclear War, National Academy of Sciences, Washington, D.C., 20-22 September 1985.

8. See Lebow, *Nuclear Crisis Management.*

9. See Janice Gross Stein, "The Arab-Israeli War of 1967: Inadvertent War Through Miscalculated Escalation," in George, ed., *Avoiding War: Problems of Crisis Management, pp. 126-159.*

10. Janice Gross Stein, "Calculation, Miscalculation, and Conventional Deterrence I: The View from Cairo," in Jervis, Lebow, and Stein, *Psychology and Deterrence*, pp. 34-59.

11. *Ibid.*

12. Anwar el-Sadat, Speech to the People's Assembly, February 4, 1971, *Al-Ahram*, February 5, 1971. See also Anwar el-Sadat, *In Search of Identity* (New York: Harper & Row, 1977), pp. 279-280.

13. The exception was Ezer Weizmann, a former commander of the Israel Air Force and a member of the Israeli cabinet during the War of Attrition, who argued that Israel had lost the war. See *On Eagles' Wings* (Jerusalem: Steimatzky's Agency, 1976).

14. Anwar el-Sadat, Speech, Cairo, May 1, 1973, *Al-Ahram*, May 2, 1973.

15. We treat reassurance and its relationship to deterrence in Janice Gross Stein, "Deterrence and Reassurance," in Philip E. Tetlock, Jo L. Husbands, Robert Jervis, Robert C. Stern and Charles Tilly, eds., *Behavior, Society, and Nuclear War* (New York: Oxford University Press, 1991), pp. 8-72.

16. Yair Evron, *War and Intervention in Lebanon* (Baltimore: Johns Hopkins University Press, 1987).

17. Robert Jervis, *The Logic of Images in International Relations* (Princeton: Princeton University Press, 1970).

18. For a detailed discussion of the impact of the process of "prenegotiation," see Janice Gross Stein, "Prenegotiation in the Arab-Israel Conflict: The Paradoxes of Success and Failure," in Janice Gross Stein, ed., *Getting to the Table: Processes of International Prenegotiation* (Baltimore: Johns Hopkins University Press, 1989), pp. 174-205.

19. John Waterbury, *Egypt: Burdens of the Past/Options for the Future* (Bloomington: University of Indiana Press, 1978), p. 202; Munir K. Nasser, *Press, Politics, and Powers: Egypt's Heikal and Al-Ahram* (Ames: The Iowa State University Press, 1979), pp. 100-102; Melvin A. Friedlander, *Sadat and Begin: The Domestic Politics of Peacemaking* (Boulder, CO: Westview Press, 1983); and R. Michael Burrell and Abbas R. Kelidar, *Egypt: The Dilemmas of a Nation 1970-1977* (Beverly Hills: Sage Publications, 1977), p. 38.

20. Ehud Ya'ari, "Sadat's Pyramid of Power," *Jerusalem Quarterly* (Winter 1980), pp. 113-114; Friedlander, *Sadat and Begin: The Domestic Politics of Peacemaking*; and P.J. Vatikiotis, *The History of Egypt* (Baltimore: Johns Hopkins University Press, 1980, second edition).

21. Interview by Shibley Telhami of Butrus Ghali, Cairo, August 28, 1983, cited in Shibley Telhami, *Power and Leadership in International Bargaining* (New York: Columbia University Press, 1990).

22. These linkages are discussed in detail in Janice Gross Stein, "The Political Economy of Strategic Agreements: The Linked Costs of Failure at Camp David," in Peter Evans, Harold Jacobsen and Robert Putnam, eds., *International Bargaining and Domestic Politics: An Interactive Process* (Berkeley: University of California Press, in press).

23. See Janice Gross Stein, "The Wrong Strategy in the Right Place: The Escalation of American Commitment in the Gulf," *International Security* 13, 3 (Winter 1988-89), pp. 142-167.

24. Thomas L. Friedman, "U.S. Is Ready to Ask Soviets to Help with Naval Blockade of Iraq," *The New York Times*, August 8. 1990, A6, citing a "senior Administration official."

25. *Izvestiia*, August 7, 1990.

26. Janice Gross Stein, "The Managed and the Managers: Crisis Prevention in the Middle East," in Winham, *New Issues in International Crisis Management*, pp. 171-98.

27. Cited by Milton Viorst, "Report from Baghdad," *The New Yorker*, September 29, 1990, p. 91.

4   Crisis Avoidance and Conflict Resolution: The Superpowers and the Middle East

The Nature of Crisis Avoidance and Conflict Resolution

Though aware of the importance of cooperation for mutual security, the United States and the Soviet Union remained locked in a globalized, nuclearized political rivalry for the four decades of the Cold War. This rivalry, which has only recently begun to abate, was the dominant feature of the post-war international system, and its two-fold character explains the central policy dilemma of superpower decision-makers throughout that era: how to promote or defend interests that extended around the world while avoiding war with each other. Because the rivalry was globalized, all issues were seen as vital; because it was nuclearized, none of them was worth a war. In other words, there was a fundamental contradiction in the evaluation of the stakes of the rivalry, and from this contradiction flowed the two mutually exclusive behavioral injunctions--don't surrender and don't fight--that succinctly describe the horns of the superpower dilemma.

Conventional wisdom holds that the most difficult theater in which to maneuver between the horns of this dilemma was the Third World, because engagement there usually involved commitment without a corresponding degree of control. Consequently, both practitioners and analysts of superpower policy in the Third World were concerned with the danger that regional conflict would somehow be transformed into a superpower crisis culminating in a direct clash, i.e., that unplanned escalation would result in an inadvertent Soviet-American war. Indeed, the triggering of this putative transformation mechanism underpinned most discussions about nuclear force postures, C^3I and arms control, all of which focused on the problem of crisis stability.

In their distillations of this historical experience, academic analysts have posited three basic strategies for warding off great power confrontation stemming from conflicts in the Third World: crisis management, conflict resolution, and crisis avoidance. A great deal of conceptual confusion surrounds these strategies, with profound implications at both the policy and the theoretical levels. The purpose of the following analysis is to disentangle the premises and perspectives of these different strategies, and particularly to show that while crisis management and conflict resolution proceed from the traditional logic of Soviet and American behavior, crisis avoidance is grounded in a different, indeed opposite type of policy logic. In view of the changes that hold out the promise of eliminating intense bipolar-confrontational elements from the structure of the international system, an attempt will also be made to analyze alternative modes of superpower conflict-reduction conduct in terms of the emerging parameters of the post-Cold War era.

Crisis management and conflict resolution can be viewed as complementary, consecutive sequences of activity to which superpowers resort in order to constrain and then mitigate acutely threatening "adversary crises of the local balance."[1] There are, of course, significant differences in the implementation of these strategies; crisis management merely requires the superpowers to constrain third parties in adversarial situations, whereas conflict resolution implies the more ambitious objective of persuading local protagonists to abandon ideological passions or irreconcilable aims in favor of more pragmatic and accommodative policies. Nevertheless, both approaches are essentially interventionist, though at different points on the spectrum of involvement.

Crisis avoidance, on the other hand, is driven by the logic of non-involvement. While this posture does not presume to address regional conflicts *per se*, it is, as long as the competitive dimension of superpower relations predominates, a potentially more promising approach to the problem of avoiding inadvertent central war.

Crisis Management in the Cold War Era

The need to regulate and manage "adversary crises of the local balance" in third areas of disputed symmetry reflected a duality of purpose in superpower behavior during the Cold War era. On the one hand, both Washington and Moscow consistently sought to compete for bases of influence in areas where no clear-cut demarcation lines or well-defined, mutually acceptable spheres of influence existed. This competition was pursued by providing economic, military, and political support to regional allies and proxies. On the other hand, the superpowers were acutely aware of the dangers to global stability inherent in the failure to terminate local disputes, to reach agreement on refraining from unilateral action, to limit arms transfers to third areas, or to define more explicitly various interests and types of involvement. To minimize these dangers, the superpowers resorted to certain behavioral patterns that would prevent their being drawn into dangerous confrontations and military clashes. This cluster of attitudes and actions--crisis management--was designed to control the risks of escalation and deterioration, i.e., to reconcile continued competition with the need to prevent its most extreme consequences, especially the transformation of adversary crises of the local balance into adversary crises of the central (global) balance.[2]

Crisis management refers to functional limitations on superpower competition through a highly fragile structure of thresholds or demarcation lines. This structure, itself an analytical abstraction rather than a formal framework, incorporated rules of engagement, norms of behavior or patterns of conduct that recognized the inevitability of superpower involvement in Third World conflicts but aimed to make it safe by limiting the intensity, minimizing the stakes, or lengthening the decision time. Two types of rules were normally recalled: explicit rules codified in formal agreements, and implicit or customary rules evolved from experience. The first type, exemplified by the 1972 Basic Principles Agreement and the 1973 Agreement on the Prevention of Nuclear War, operated at the highest level of generality. In the 1972 agreement, for example, "Both sides recognize that efforts to obtain unilateral advantages at the expense of the other, directly or indirectly, are inconsistent with these objectives [i.e., avoiding military confrontations and preventing the outbreak of nuclear war]." But since no superpower would commit itself *a priori* to accepting any outcome of any Third World conflict, explicit agreement was possible only on such vague principles; it should not be surprising that these were subject to differing interpretations and did not provide a very reliable basis for predicting behavior in specific situations.[3]

The second type of rules was commentary on the theme of prudence, such as the need to communicate interests as clearly as possible to the other superpower in order to reduce the risks of misunderstanding and the attribution of hostile intentions that did not really exist. There is an extensive literature on "rules of the game."[4] The prescriptive conclusions of this literature can be summarized in a number of injunctions, essentially derived from the classical realist theory, which together form a system of controlled superpower competition. The most basic and essential of these is that neither superpower shall initiate military action against the forces of the other superpower.[5] The corollary of this notion is that neither superpower shall permit his ally to place the other superpower in a position where it is forced to choose between fight and surrender, i.e., each superpower shall prevent the overwhelming defeat of the other's regional ally by pressuring its own ally "to stop short of inflicting such a defeat on its local opponent."[6]

If an established regional ally is nevertheless faced with an acute threat to its very survival because of imminent military defeat by an ally of the other superpower, intervention becomes legitimate and should not be contested. In such circumstances, each superpower "shall accept military intervention of the other superpower in a regional conflict."[7] Even then, however, intervention should only be in a defensive mode, on one's "own" side of the line, and no higher up on the escalation ladder than is absolutely necessary to stave off disaster. Graduated intervention means the following:

- verbal threats or warnings of support should precede demonstrations of support;
- demonstrations of support should precede actual provision of support;

- unobtrusive non-combat support (e.g., intelligence, EM/ECM) should precede obtrusive non-combat support (arms supplies);
- non-combat support should precede combat support;
- combat support by proxies is preferable to combat support by superpowers;
- passive defense or interposition is preferable to active defense or intervention;
- intervention by naval and/or air forces is preferable to intervention by ground forces.

In applying these rules of conduct to the Middle East, the success of the superpowers in avoiding a direct clash should not obscure the fact that their asymmetrical objectives and policies sometimes brought the crisis management system perilously close to breakdown. Indeed, one Soviet analyst argues that because of developments in the Middle East, the world stood on the brink of global nuclear catastrophe on four occasions.[8] Nor were the superpowers unaware of the potential dangers. During the War of Attrition, the Soviet leadership was extremely reluctant to intervene in the defense of Egypt. Brezhnev reportedly responded to Nasser's request for active assistance by pointing out that this "would be a step with serious international implications. . . . It would provide all the makings of a crisis between the Soviet Union and the United States, and I don't know if we are justified in taking it."[9] Nevertheless, a tacit Egyptian threat to "defect" to the United States was enough to tip the balance in favor of intervention. This is perhaps the most graphic example, but by no means the only one, of the general tendency of the superpowers to permit the competitive dimension of their involvement in the Middle East to overshadow any urge or perceived need to cooperate.

Short-term Soviet and American behavior rarely converged until some adversary crisis of the local balance, to which they were inextricably linked as patrons of the belligerents, brought them to the brink of a direct confrontation. Of course, nothing concentrates the mind so much as an imminent superpower clash, but it was only then that system-wide considerations (bilateral cooperation to avoid a confrontation) took priority over alliance considerations (supporting the regional ally). At that point, however, the innate contradiction between their roles as patrons of allies in the Middle East subsystem and their roles as superpowers concerned with the global international system was resolved in favor of global-systemic concerns.

This preference was most clearly manifested during the climactic phases of the 1967 and 1973 crises, when the United States was induced to curb its ally Israel for the sake of reducing the risk of global instability.[10] Thus, alliance considerations were sacrificed in order to avert the direct superpower confrontation that might have ensued from the humiliating defeat of a regional client.[11] In the final analysis, the superpowers assigned priority to the requirements of prudent crisis management when they were intimidated by the potential for escalation; containing the global crisis made it necessary to manage the local crisis.

Nevertheless, it is extremely difficult to demonstrate the robustness of this rather diffuse cluster of superpower rules or norms. While superpower crisis management appears to have been effective in defusing acutely threatening regional conflagrations, it is not altogether clear, even in retrospect, how the danger was actually avoided.[12] And we can only speculate about how an escalation scenario might play out in the absence of the coercion of regional allies; efforts to examine the operation of the transformation mechanism by gaming the spiraling of Third World crises into superpower war are generally unconvincing.[13]

What is clear, however, is that whatever coordination or convergence of expectations underlay superpower conduct in specific crisis episodes, it was insufficient to prevent the recurrence of crisis. In other words, the challenge of proceeding beyond the narrow parameters of crisis behavior in order to implement the second strategy of crisis aversion--conflict resolution--was not met.

Efforts to apply the techniques of conflict resolution during the Cold War were noticeably rare because they entailed persuading allies to abandon important objectives, policies or actions. Persuasion could include positive incentives, i.e., inducements to compensate the ally for whatever concessions it was called upon to make; and this almost certainly means new political, military or economic commitments for the superpower. For example, the Ford

Administration offered Israel a wide range of incentives in order to coax it into abandoning most of its objections to the second Sinai Agreement with Egypt. In August 1975, the United States agreed to provide Israel with advanced weapons systems and large-scale financial assistance (approximately $1.5 billion in military credits and about half that amount in economic aid for fiscal years 1975/76). Several far-reaching guarantees of a strategic-political nature were also incorporated into the U.S.-Israel Memorandum of Agreement initialed on September 1, 1975. The United States undertook to consult with Israel in the event of any threat to it from "a world power," to supply oil "if the oil Israel needs to meet all of its normal requirements for domestic consumption is unavailable for purchase," to maintain Israel's defensive strength through the transfer of advanced equipment such as F-16 aircraft, to adhere to the U.S. policy of not recognizing the PLO as long as that organization did not recognize Israel's right to exist and accept UN Security Council Resolutions 242 and 338, "to consult fully and seek to concert its position and strategy at the Geneva peace conference on this issue with the Government of Israel," and "to join in and seek to prevent efforts by others to bring about consideration of proposals which it and Israel agree are detrimental to the interests of Israel."[14]

However, even such "positive sanctions" rarely sufficed unless they were coupled with at least the implied threat of negative sanctions; therefore, conflict resolution also required the exercise of existing influence in a way that was likely to jeopardize that influence. As we have already argued, superpowers were ordinarily willing to do that only under the shadow of an imminent bilateral confrontation, i.e., only when the crisis had already arrived.

Historically, the structural realities of the Middle East were conducive to "influence parity" relationships between the superpowers and their regional allies.[15] These militated against any progression from crisis management to the more ambitious objective of conflict resolution. Since there was no organic link between the two categories, extending the domain of rules to the latter category required making normal and routine that which was exceptional and rare.

One major obstacle to the institutionalization of conflict resolution rules was the paradoxical relationship between crisis management and conflict resolution. As Coral Bell observes, "though crises grow out of conflicts, some apparent successes for crisis management may actually have the result of helping to perpetuate the conflict."[16] The inability of crisis management to deal with the deep-rooted origins of a given conflict stemmed from its basic premises, specifically, the notion that a drastic disruption of the regional balance of power had to be avoided and that intervention by the superpowers to prevent the collapse of a regional ally was therefore legitimate. Thus, the norms of crisis management actually preserved the position of the weaker party in a conflict by providing it with a "safety net" against the ultimate dangers of military defeat and loss of power.[17]

Furthermore, the effectiveness of crisis management procedures and techniques derived from the emotion-laden atmosphere in which they were applied. When the dangers of escalation were immediate and palpable, the logic of "nuclear egotism" switched on and the superpowers acted to preserve their essential national interests against threats by minor (or even major) allies.[18]

However, while coercion of allies was seen as acceptable and legitimate during a war, incorporating such an approach into any joint non-crisis attempt at conflict resolution was bound to provoke strong opposition, both external and domestic. And the more ambitious the superpower collaborative design, the more determined this opposition was likely to be. Forging a superpower bloc in order to tackle the basic sources of turbulence and conflict in a given area required a broad base of external and internal support. But a review of some of the non-crisis superpower peacemaking initiatives in the Arab-Israeli arena demonstrates that when the two sides did manage to set aside most of their differences and define together the parameters of a Middle East settlement they were unable to control their allies' behavior or to persist in their efforts to impose a settlement.

These obstacles are particularly evident in the case of the joint U.S.-Soviet communiqué of October 1977. The regional setting at the time was highly recalcitrant. The major Middle Eastern actors were adamantly opposed to the superpower initiative, and Israel's opposition was especially resolute because its rejection of PLO participation in the peace-making process had long been defined as a "core" or cardinal issue. In this case, asymmetry of interest overrode asymmetry of power; Israel was prepared to risk an open confrontation with the United States, and Washington was eventually forced to reassess its policy and abandon the "superpower scenario" as a short-term policy option. In George's terminology, the disutility of the action demanded from the local partner (in this case, Israel's *de facto* recognition of the PLO) far exceeded the disutility of the possible consequences (such as the withholding of economic and military aid) of an intensified crisis in relations with its superpower ally.[19] Given the asymmetry of motivation, the concerted drive to redefine the parameters of a settlement could not override Israel's refusal to negotiate with the PLO.

This was true even though Israel was in a comparatively weak bargaining position vis-à-vis its superpower ally. Unlike most Third World actors, Israel lacked a credible threat to defect to the superpower rival. Thus, the Administration would logically be less concerned about the direct consequences for the global balance of "excessive" pressure on this particular regional ally, although the possible effect of such action on the calculations of other allies which did have more diplomatic flexibility might well have been an inhibiting factor. Moreover, the internal setting was particularly relevant to the Administration's willingness to pursue a confrontation with Israel. Indeed, President Carter and his advisers faced a storm of domestic protest. One hundred and fifty Congressmen expressed "grave concern" about the document and about what was regarded as an unwise and unnecessary invitation to the Soviet Union to re-enter Middle East negotiations.[20] The Jewish community leadership reacted equally swiftly and unequivocally with an avalanche of angry telephone calls and telegrams to the White House.

Although perceived by Israel as a highly menacing drive to change the rules of the game in American-Israeli relations, the October 1 initiative was in fact a fairly modest design. It fell well short of a superpower condominium, which would have entailed "a comprehensive, harmonious and collusive definition of interests, geared toward jointly imposing on weaker states terms for conflict resolution that the superpowers have worked out on their own."[21] Premised on a hierarchical division of labor among the various parties to a regional dispute, condominium is a maximalist model of superpower collaboration which assumes that unity among the central global entities permits the effective definition and implementation of a settlement. In this design, at least some of the local adversaries are reduced to impotence and compelled to submit in the face of big power cohesion and resolve. Though not nearly so ambitious as that, even the October 1 initiative failed dismally, simply because of the immense difficulties inherent in any effort to proceed beyond the narrow parameters within which crisis management collaboration takes place.

Although the clusters of domestic and external constraints which aborted that design have changed, any effort to reactivate the "superpower option" for resolution of the Arab-Israeli conflict still faces very serious obstacles. It is true that a more receptive domestic environment for the collaborative pursuit of conflict resolution has emerged in recent years. In the United States, there is mounting evidence of a growing public willingness to endorse a joint superpower strategy on a variety of regional and arms control issues in order to avoid dangerous confrontations. Even Ronald Reagan endorsed the idea of "periodic consultations at the policy level about regional problems," and regional conflicts have been on the agenda of virtually every high-level Soviet-American meeting during the past ten years. Insofar as the Arab-Israeli conflict is concerned, the prospect of collaboration has presumably been strengthened by findings that American public opinion has become increasingly critical of Israel in recent years and has even sustained certain *ad hoc* punitive measures whenever Israeli conduct was perceived as deviating from "legitimate security needs" (which the public continued to support).[22]

A similar trend, though less pronounced, also characterizes the external environment. Israel, which in the past comprised an essential element of the "external legitimacy constraint," has undergone profound changes since the 1977 crisis, making it more receptive to at least some of the tenets of any superpower design. In other words, the unanimity of purpose and approach which linked all the major political parties (as well as most strata and segments of Israeli public opinion) in their staunch opposition to the idea of PLO participation in the peace process has been eroding since 1977. During this period, the Israeli political scene has become more fractious, with an ever growing percentage of the public opting out of the consensus that previously excluded the PLO as a legitimate partner in any negotiations.

Notwithstanding these changes, however, the Soviets and the Americans have themselves not yet set aside all their differences concerning both the structure and the substance of the peace process. Although some of these differences have been narrowed in recent years (the Soviet Union, for example, no longer insists on a coercive international conference nor categorically rejects all elements of the Israeli initiative of May 1989), Washington and Moscow have yet to reach an understanding on the substance or even the desirability of the "superpower scenario."

However, even if the two ultimately succeed in bridging the gaps which still separate them (particularly on such cardinal issues as a Palestinian state), they will encounter a different set of problems related to implementation of any plan on which they agree. More specifically, although the American public supports the conclusion of Soviet-American agreements in order to avoid dangerous confrontations, it is highly skeptical of the costs--guarantees, economic support, long-term security commitments and perhaps permanent large-scale military presence--which a Middle East agreement under superpower auspices would entail. This is especially true in the case of the "noninternationalists" who are:

> predisposed against American involvement in other countries' affairs unless a clear and compelling issue of national interest or national security is at stake . . . Noninternationalists see no point to American involvement in most of the world. They are against foreign aid, against troop involvement, against anything that smacks of foreign entanglement.[23]

Similar sentiments, while harder to document, have apparently become widespread in the Soviet Union in the aftermath of Afghanistan. One example of a kind of "Russia First" ideology is the assertion by academician Igor Malashenko that improving domestic living standards is far more important for national security "than the course developments may take in some exotic country that many of us can barely find on a map of the world."[24]

The reluctance to become engaged indiscriminately in Third World areas obviously implies that future security commitments by both superpowers will be limited to the indispensable minimum. At the same time, persistent budgetary deficits will erode American willingness to assume additional financial commitments in the Middle East, while the Soviet capacity to underwrite a settlement will be highly constrained under almost any foreseeable circumstance. In short, both the United States and the Soviet Union, though not to the same degree, are probably unwilling and/or unable to pay the price of any settlement they might be tempted to try to impose. Regardless of the environmental constraints, this consideration alone suggests that cooperative conflict resolution is not a promising method for resolving the basic dilemma of superpower involvement in the Middle East. However, the growing tendency of the Soviet Union to disengage unilaterally from many of its regional commitments creates an asymmetry in the character of superpower involvement in the region. The change in the bilateral relationship eliminates many of the traditional hurdles to cooperation and suggests new possibilities for conflict resolution based on different premises.

Crisis Avoidance as an Alternative
to Crisis Management and Conflict Resolution

While the danger of a Soviet-American clash stemming from Middle Eastern conflicts has subsided because of the overall reduction in superpower tensions, the techniques of crisis management and conflict resolution do not inspire much confidence. Since both these approaches assume some degree of superpower involvement, it is worthwhile considering whether the strategy of crisis avoidance, which proceeds from an entirely different conceptual base, might not be a more stable and enduring solution to the problems associated with superpower involvement in the Third World.

Crisis avoidance essentially means geographical limitations on superpower competition through agreed neutralization or demarcation of spheres of influence, i.e., a mutual decision to minimize the presence and commitments of one or both superpowers in a given area. As opposed to the restraint of allies, which characterizes both crisis management and conflict resolution, the issue here is self-restraint: voluntary disengagement based on a conscious decision not to compete. Peculiar local circumstances have made it possible to decouple local issues from the central balance in a limited number of instances (such as Austria or Laos), but a generalized adoption of this strategy, especially in so prominent an area as the Middle East, would entail renunciation of the last remnants of the logic governing American and Soviet involvement in the Third World since the end of World War II.

That logic consisted of two elements: the extension of a pre-1945 geo-strategic calculus into the nuclear era, and the post-1945 application of this calculus to the entire globe. At the risk of some oversimplification, transactions between superpowers and Third World regimes can be conceived of as market relations in which the commodity is power; the superpowers sell or loan it, and local regimes buy or borrow it.[25] Third World actors usually need this power because they cannot generate enough of their own to wage the domestic or regional struggles in which they are involved. This need creates the demand for superpower support of one sort or another. The supply is explained by superpower desire for the currency of exchange in this transaction--namely, influence, as symbolized by some kind of economic, cultural or military presence. In the marketplace where power is traded for influence, superpowers are competing with each other for the alignment, allegiance and sympathy of Third World regimes, a kind of twentieth century equivalent of the historical rivalries for overseas empires.

In practice, the utility of these interest transactions for the superpowers has usually turned out to be even more dubious than was the utility of colonies. Whatever the economic rationale of imperialism may have been (and it has been subjected to serious criticism), contemporary trade relations are normally governed by economic considerations unless the superpower chooses otherwise. The United States, for example, "lost" Cuba but lost access to Cuban markets only because it chose to boycott them; it "lost" Angola but kept on buying Angolan oil. And even when trade does follow the flag, the outcome is at least as likely to be a liability as an asset for the superpower partner. The expansion of the Soviet presence in the Third World during the 1970s saddled the Soviet Treasury with a collection of basket cases, resentment of which has become an important factor in popular Soviet support for disengagement from Third World commitments.

The geopolitics of superpower competition appear, if anything, to be even more anachronistic. Gaining access to bases and military facilities in some country or denying such access to the superpower rival bears directly only on the security of that country or other allies. In other words, it may provide "extended security," but it has no direct impact on the core security of nuclear-armed superpowers with assured second-strike capability. Expanding the security perimeter therefore means giving security to others, not getting it from them. In all but the most farfetched scenarios of protracted conventional war--a replay of World War II--alliances with Third World countries have virtually no impact on the bilateral balance of military power between the Soviet Union and the United States.

But whatever the importance of such material calculations, a major force driving the rivalry has been psychological: the assumption that deterrence is indivisible. In the language of software menus, this was always the "default" rationale for superpower engagement. Even when there was no intrinsic interest at stake, maintaining influence was important, in and of itself, because acquiescing in its loss was expected to redound to the advantage of the other superpower and reverberate throughout the entire system. Consequently, foreign policy desiderata were translated into questions of national survival, and the range of threats became limitless. This is the logic that placed such a premium on demonstrating firmness, maintaining credibility, and upholding principles of behavior--in short, the logic of the domino theory. And this logic explains why the superpowers were so concerned about the balance of influence in the Third World, why they worked so hard to prevent damage to or loss of position, and why they frequently found themselves drawn into conflicts with potentially dangerous ramifications at the bilateral level.

In this paradigm, the most common threat to the superpower position is the defection or overthrow of an allied regime. To avoid the first outcome, superpower patrons must avoid alienating local allies. In practice, this limits the superpowers' ability to prevent local allies from using the power they bought or borrowed, or even to deny giving them more. Herein resides the central paradox of patron-client relations (wherever the possibility of defection to the superpower rival exists): influence can be retained only if it is not exercised. Consequently, superpowers are rarely willing to restrain determined allies from acting in ways that provoke or exacerbate violent hostilities. Thus, for all their vastly superior military and economic capabilities, they have little control over crisis-producing behavior.[26]

To avoid the overthrow of local allies, superpowers have to support their allies when they are threatened by domestic or regional adversaries, regardless of how or why these allies got into trouble. Such commitments, even if they were assumed involuntarily or unconsciously, must nevertheless be honored unless the superpower is prepared to write the ally off as sunk cost. As Snyder and Diesing observe, "Since they can be quite sure that the structurally ordained chasm between the superpowers themselves can never be entirely bridged," allies can independently pursue their own agendas, secure in the knowledge that they "will be protected whatever happens."[27]

This combination of commitment and non-control creates the danger that Third World conflicts, which originally explained the demand for Soviet or American power, will be transformed into superpower crises leading to a direct clash. Given the inadequacies of crisis management and conflict resolution, there is much to recommend the alternative strategy of conflict avoidance through disengagement by agreement, i.e., through minimization of superpower presence and commitment in the area. For such a posture to emerge, however, both superpowers must recognize that the competition is an atavism from earlier times and that commitments should be limited to areas and contingencies in which truly vital geo-strategic interests are at stake.

Even before the outbreak of the Gulf Crisis in the summer of 1990, there was evidence of a shift in superpower attitudes towards the Third World in general, and the Middle East in particular. American spokesmen, for example, expressed annoyance on several occasions with the excruciatingly slow pace of the Arab-Israeli peace process and they threatened indirectly, without any reference to Soviet actions, simply to disengage from the entire issue. More dramatically, President Gorbachev had explicitly denounced the "zero-sum" thinking that governed superpower behavior in the Third World, and some analysts had detected, soon after his accession to power, at least the beginning of unilateral Soviet retrenchment.[28] In the Middle East, Soviet spokesmen repeatedly warned Syria against using military means to settle its conflict with Israel, and the Soviet ambassador in Damascus pointedly remarked that the Soviet-Syrian Treaty of Friendship and Cooperation does not oblige the Soviet Union to take part in Syria's wars.[29]

Nevertheless, neither superpower has made the break from past logic necessary to convert these conceptual probes into a dominant strategy. For example, although basic superpower interests in the Iran-Iraq war converged (or at least ran parallel), American and Soviet policies seemed to be driven largely by the fear of short-term tactical advantage for the superpower rival; the traditional logic of competitive involvement informed both the American decision to "reflag" Kuwaiti tankers and the Soviet refusal to endorse an American-sponsored embargo of arms sales to Iran.

The reactions to the Iraqi invasion of Kuwait in August 1990 seemed to reflect quite different principles of behavior, so much so that many observers termed this "the first post-Cold War crisis." The massive American deployment of forces and the provision of other military assistance to Saudi Arabia, though hardly compatible with the principle of disengagement, was motivated by an acute local threat to core interests rather than by any concern with the Soviet-American balance; indeed, the United States consulted with the Soviet Union and actively sought its cooperation. Similarly, the Soviet Union, rather than aligning itself with a regional ally of long standing, denounced the Iraqi action, cut off arms sales, and supported the institution and enforcement of economic sanctions; traditional Cold War logic would have dictated mechanical support for Iraq and vigorous condemnation of American imperialism.

Even in this case, however, the positions of the superpowers were not completely congruent. The Soviets did not immediately withdraw their military advisers from Iraq, they continuously exhorted the American government not to act unilaterally, they were much more categorical in rejecting the use of military means against Iraq (and themselves refrained from helping to enforce the embargo), they tended to depict extra-regional intervention as a regrettable and a temporary expedient until such time as an "Arab solution" to the problem could be found, and they were much more receptive to the idea of establishing procedural and substantive links between the Gulf Crisis and the Israeli-Palestinian conflict. There are a variety of possible explanations for the Soviet unwillingness to the become completely identified with the American position. Stated suspicions about the long-term impact of the American buildup in the Gulf, for example, may reflect institutional interests or traditional perspectives of the Soviet military establishment. Nor were such positions unique to the Soviet Union; many of America's allies in the West expressed similar reservations. The impression nevertheless emerged that the Soviet Union was trying to leave itself better positioned than the United States to cultivate preferred relations with the Arab world (including Iraq) after the crisis ended. But even if this impression was accurate, the situation was still a far cry from traditional Cold War patterns, in which Soviet political-security commitments to a Third World partner confronting the United States or an American ally raised the prospect of escalation into a direct superpower clash.

While that traditional pattern of symmetrical involvement prevailed, mutual disengagement was the only truly effective insurance against the ultimate danger of global nuclear war. The drawback of such a posture was that it would provide no immediate impetus to conflict resolution in the region. Indeed, decoupling could convince local actors opposed to the status quo that there was no longer any prospect of effective external political intervention and actually strengthen their determination to pursue their objectives by military means. By most accounts, this was precisely Egyptian President Sadat's response to the Soviet-American détente summits of May 1972 and June 1973, which he interpreted as tacit superpower affirmation of the status quo.[30]

A crisis avoidance strategy of mutual disengagement essentially meant neglect of local conflicts, and this was something which the United States, because of various interests in the Middle East beyond the Soviet factor, was reluctant to do. As long as intense superpower competition implied the danger of escalation to a Soviet-American crisis, the United States was inevitably tempted to combine elements of both approaches, even though this meant ignoring the logical contradiction between more superpower involvement demanded by conflict resolution (and crisis management) at the local level, and less superpower involvement required by crisis avoidance at the global level.

However, the tendency of the Soviet Union to disengage unilaterally in a military/security sense, i.e., to become a "normal" major international actor like France or Japan, promises to eliminate this contradiction by terminating the bipolar system that coupled regional conflicts to superpower relations, thereby making the region "safe" for conflict resolution. In other words, the transformation of the international system will permit the United States, freed from its traditional preoccupation with the global ramifications of alliance politics, to take a more active role in promoting the settlement of Middle Eastern disputes.

Notes

1. Coral Bell, "Crisis Diplomacy," in Lawrence Martin, ed., *Strategic Thought in the Nuclear Age* (London: Heineman, 1979), p. 152.

2. *Ibid.*

3. Alexander L. George, "The Basic Principles Agreement of 1972: Origins and Expectations," in George, ed., *Managing U.S.-Soviet Rivalry: Problems of Crisis Prevention* (Boulder, CO: Westview Press, 1983), pp. 107-117.

4. See, for example, Alexander L. George, *Managing U.S.-Soviet Rivalry*, *passim*; "Mechanisms for Moderating Superpower Competition," *AEI Foreign Policy and Defense Review*, 6, 1 (1986), pp. 5-13; and (with Philip J. Farley and Alexander Dallin) *U.S.-Soviet Security Cooperation: Achievements, Failures, Lessons* (New York: Oxford University Press, 1988).

5. George, "U.S.-Soviet Efforts to Cooperate in Crisis Management and Crisis Avoidance," in George, et al., *U.S.-Soviet Security Cooperation*, pp. 583-84.

6. *Ibid.*

7. Yair Evron, "Great Powers' Military Intervention in the Middle East," in Milton Leitenberg and Gabriel Sheffer, eds., *Great Power Intervention in the Middle East* (New York: Pergamon, 1979), pp. 30, 33, 38-39; Uri Bar-Joseph and John P. Hannah, "Intervention Threats in Short Arab-Israeli Wars: An Analysis of Soviet Crisis Behavior," *The Journal of Strategic Studies* 11, no. 4 (December 1988), pp. 438, 461.

8. Igor Belaev, "Middle East Conflicts and Proposed Solutions," *Mezhdunarodnaia Zhizn* 5 (May 1988).

9. Muhammad Heikal, *The Road to Ramadan* (London: Collins, 1975), p. 86.

10. Alexander L. George, "Political Crises," in Joseph S. Nye, Jr. ed., *The Making of America's Foreign Policy* (New Haven: Yale University Press, 1984), p. 135.

11. Janice Gross Stein, "Proxy Wars--How Superpowers End Them: The Diplomacy of War Termination in the Middle East," *International Journal* 35, 3 (Summer 1980), pp. 479, 489, 494-95.

12. The defusing of the 1970 Jordan Crisis is analyzed in a double article by Henry Brandon and David Schoenbaum entitled "Were We Masterful . . . Or Lucky?" in *Foreign Policy* 10 (Spring 1973), pp. 158-81. Given the opaqueness of decision-making on all sides, both contentions are persuasive.

13. See, for example, Bruce G. Blair, David S. Cohen, and Kurt Gottfried, "Command in Crisis: A Middle East Scenario," *Bulletin of Peace Proposals* 17, 2 (June 1986), pp. 113-20, in which the authors try to implicate the superpowers directly in a Syrian-Israeli clash and admit (p. 119) that "it was remarkably difficult to escalate the simulated crisis."

14. Citations from Edward R.F. Sheehan, *The Arabs, the Israelis and Kissinger* (New York: Crowell, 1975), pp. 254-57. See, also, David Pollock, *The Politics of Pressure: American Arms and Israeli Policy Since the Six-Day War* (Westport, CT: Greenwood Press, 1982), p. 191.

74

15. Christopher C. Shoemaker and John Spanier, *Patron-Client State Relationships: Multilateral Crises in the Nuclear Age* (New York: Praeger, 1984), pp. 33-34.

16. Bell, "Crisis Diplomacy," p. 163.

17. Bar-Joseph and Hannah, "Intervention Threats," p. 462.

18. *Ibid.*

19. Alexander L. George, "The Development of Doctrine and Strategy," in George, David K. Hall, and William E. Simons, *The Limits of Coercive Diplomacy: Laos, Cuba, Vietnam* (Boston: Little, Brown & Co., 1971), p. 27.

20. Abraham Ben-Zvi, *Alliance Politics and the Limits of Influence: The Case of the U.S. and Israel, 1975-1983* (Tel Aviv: Jaffee Center for Strategic Studies, 1984), pp. 30-31.

21. George W. Breslauer, "Why Detente Failed: An Interpretation," in George, *Managing Superpower Rivalry*, p. 330. See, also, Carsten Hollbraad, *Superpowers and International Conflict*, p. 10.

22. For early indications of this trend, see Nimrod Novik, *The U.S. and Israel: Domestic Determinants of a Changing U.S. Commitment* (Boulder, CO: Westview Press, 1986), p. 32.

23. William Schneider, "Conservatism, Not Interventionism: Trends in Foreign Policy Opinion, 1974-1982," in Kenneth Oye, Robert J. Lieber, and Donald Rothschild, eds., *Eagle Defiant: U.S. Foreign Policy in the 1980s* (Boston: Little, Brown, and Co., 1982), pp. 41-42.

24. "Ideals and Interests," *New Times* 45 (November 1988), p. 28.

25. I. William Zartman, "The Strategy of Preventive Diplomacy in Third World Conflicts," in George, *Managing U.S.-Soviet Rivalry*, p. 362.

26. The dynamics of patron-client relationships are also examined, *inter alia*, in Robert Keohane, "The Big Influence of Small Allies," in *Foreign Policy* 2 (Spring 1971), pp. 161-82; Michael I. Handel, "Does the Dog Wag the Tail or Vice Versa?: Patron-Client Relations," *Jerusalem Journal of International Relations* 6, 2 (1982), pp. 24-35; and Robert L. Rothstein, *The Weak in the World of the Strong* (New York: Columbia University Press, 1977), pp. 119-247.

27. Glenn H. Snyder and Paul Diesing, *Conflict Among Nations: Bargaining, Decision-Making, and System Structure in International Crises* (Princeton: Princeton University Press, 1977), pp. 441-42.

28. Mikhail S. Gorbachev, *Perestroika: New Thinking for Our Country and the World* (London: Collins, 1987), pp. 176-89. The retrenchment theme is skillfully expounded in Elizabeth Krindl Valkenier, "New Soviet Thinking about the Third World: A Hands-Off Approach to Radical Change," *World Policy Journal* 4, 4 (Fall, 1987).

29. *Ha-Aretz*, January 19, 1990.

30. Bernard Reich, *Quest for Peace: United States-Israel Relations and the Arab-Israeli Conflict* (New Brunswick, NJ: Transaction Books, 1977), p. 204; and, Heikal, *The Road to Ramadan*, p. 174.

5 A Theoretical Analysis of U.S.-Soviet Conflict Management in the Middle East

Surprises, Accomplishments, Limitations and Changes from the Cold War to the Post-Bipolar Era

A common impression of the superpower role in Third World conflicts is that their keen competition all over the globe until the mid-1980s, and their consequent intervention in faraway regions, contributed to instability and brought about the escalation of local conflicts into global crises.   Another view maintains that, due to their superior capabilities and presumed "responsibility" for world stability, the superpowers, especially if they collaborated, could bring peace and order to unstable Third World regions.

This chapter argues that neither of these views is correct. Rather, the record is mixed, notably in the Middle East. Not only did the superpowers avoid escalation of local crises into global wars, but they tacitly cooperated in the termination of regional wars. Yet, although they attempted conflict resolution, they failed to concert their diplomacy for such purposes. Through their successful crisis management, the superpowers helped to maintain the status quo and the regional balance of power.   Their inability to concert their diplomacy undermined efforts at accomplishing peaceful change in the Middle East.

The successful crisis management by the Cold War adversaries can be accounted for by systemic factors such as the bipolar distribution of capabilities during the post-war era and the stabilizing effects of the nuclear revolution on the superpowers. The failure to cooperate in conflict resolution, for its part, can be explained by non-systemic elements such as the ideological differences between the superpowers and the effects of domestic politics and leaders' beliefs.

The rationale of my model is, in brief, that in times of crisis, when international pressures on the state are extremely strong, systemic elements logically exert greater effect than usual on the conduct of great powers, especially for the purposes of crisis management. Conversely, causal factors "below" the system level (internal constraints and ideological beliefs) are more consequential for understanding the somewhat less intense non-crisis collaboration, especially when it aims at conflict resolution. Indeed, the higher the level of cooperation, the lower the level of analysis (state and individual) at which supportive factors are required for the emergence and endurance of cooperative arrangements (i.e., concerted diplomacy).

A structural explanation and the closely related balance of power perspective,[1] I propose, will be most useful for comprehending "spontaneous" or avoidance-type collaboration, which takes place, notably, during the successful management of international crises. In the post-war system, nuclear deterrence has reinforced the tendency in bipolar systems to create tacit "rules" for regulating the use of force.

A major point that will emerge is that although structurally ordained tacit rules may be effective for crisis management, they will not constitute a sufficient basis for longer-term peaceful change. Such change would require a shared vision of the international order, or at least a convergence of leaders' perceptions and related cognitive learning by elites. In other words, unit-level factors must come into play here. Indeed, compatibility of state attributes and explicit legitimation of the status quo (or of an acceptable means for revising it) by the powers should help to resolve conflicts and thus minimize the probability of crises and wars.

Patterns of Conflict Management:
Crisis Management/War Termination vs.
Crisis Prevention/Conflict Resolution

A major distinction in the area of conflict management was developed by Alexander George between crisis management and crisis prevention.[2] In crisis management the cooperation starts after the parties have already been drawn into a war-threatening confrontation. The collaboration is reflected in an effort to prevent the outbreak of a major war and, especially in third areas, an attempt is made to control escalation of the local conflict into a global war. In their landmark study of crises, Snyder and Diesing conceived of crisis management as reflecting the tension between the competitive aspect in a crisis (namely, how is it possible to advance or protect one's interests by coercive threats and maneuvers, which necessarily require posing the prospect of war) without actually raising the risk of war to an intolerable level.[3] In contrast, in crisis prevention, the collaboration should begin before the participants find themselves in a crisis situation.

Yet crisis management on the global level would necessitate, in fact, termination of the regional war if and when the war escalates to the point of involving the military forces of one or more of the great powers. At that point, the local war would not only be confined in its scope but terminated by the intervention of the great powers. Such intervention would occur when the existence of a key ally of one of the superpowers is threatened and consequently the regional balance of power is endangered. The outcome of the superpower intervention would be the preservation of the balance by checking those regional powers that threaten the territorial status quo.

The more specific dependent variable here is the emergence of tacit rules that address the two dimensions of crisis management through the regulation of the threat and the use of force by the powers, their military intervention, and the nature of "legitimate" responses to threats of use of force by the other powers. The tacit rules establish the range of acceptable conduct each state will tolerate from the other in the absence of a world authority. Evidence for the existence of such rules can be gleaned from regularities in the participants' actual behavior; this does not indicate that the decision-makers are necessarily aware of these rules and it certainly does not suggest that they have reached an explicit agreement on adherence to them.

The Tacit Superpower Cooperation in War:
Termination of Arab-Israeli Wars

At first glance, superpower behavior in the Middle East during the Cold War looks neither cooperative nor stabilizing. For example, the superpowers delivered sophisticated arms to their respective clients without modifying in a significant way the latter's uncompromising positions (apart from the U.S. success under Kissinger and Carter in the Israeli-Egyptian peace process in the aftermath of the 1973 war). Moreover, the superpowers became involved in all Arab-Israeli wars through naval and aerial activities; particularly the Soviets, who threatened military intervention, most notably toward the end of the 1956 Suez Crisis, in the June 1967 Six Day War, and in the 1973 Yom Kippur War. Moscow also deployed military advisors in three crises and even combat forces, primarily air-defense crews, during the 1970 War of Attrition between Israel and Egypt, and in Syria following the 1982 Lebanon War.

Yet, a second look suggests that superpower interaction in Arab-Israeli wars during the Cold War showed patterns of restraint that might approximate tacit rules of the game, or unwritten understandings.[4] These "rules" established when it was "legitimate" for a superpower to intervene militarily on behalf of its local ally, how the intervention was to be carried out, and what ought to have been the other superpower's reaction. These tacit rules responded to the need to find a delicate balance in superpower behavior between resolve and restraint or, more specifically, between the commitment to an ally on the one hand and the desire to avoid an armed conflict with the rival superpower on the other. In Snyder and Diesing's terminology, this dilemma corresponds to the problem of how "to find the optimum mix or trade-off between coercion and accommodation."[5]

In the initial stages of these Arab-Israeli wars, the great powers demonstrated their resolve mainly by supporting their clients diplomatically, tailoring their positions with respect to cease-fires and to the fortunes of their clients on the battleground.[6] Occasionally, as in 1973, they also resupplied their proteges militarily. Moreover, at that stage of the game the superpowers neutralized each other[7] through mutual deterrence, both of them behaving cautiously and neither of them threatening to intervene militarily.

This symmetry changed, however, once "red lines" were trespassed.[8] The most significant "red line" was the high probability of a complete military defeat of a key regional ally of a superpower which jeopardized the existence of the losing regime. Since, in terms of the global balance of power, the collapse of an allied government meant a "loss" to its patron, the balance of motivation--or stakes--clearly shifted, at this point, in favor of the patron supporting the loser. The rules of the game suggested that this asymmetry in the balance of interests made it both "legitimate" and credible for the patron of the loser to threaten to use force in order to prevent the loser's collapse. The patron of the winner was expected to restrain its client while, at the same time, deter the other superpower from military intervention. As long as the intervention remained defensive, it should have been "acceptable" to the patron of the winning regional party. Thus, the United States could tacitly accept the "legitimacy" of the Soviet intervention in Egypt during the War of Attrition as long as it was confined to saving Nasser's regime. The more Soviet forces became involved in the Canal Zone itself, however, the greater became the United States' willingness to provide sophisticated electronic countermeasures to the Israelis and, thus, to signal non-verbally its disapproval of the expanded and more offensive form of Soviet engagement.

The Soviets issued most of the intervention threats; this was "acceptable" according to the "rules" because in most of the crises the survival of their Arab clients was at stake. Moreover, by restraining Israel, the United States implicitly recognized the "legitimacy" of the Soviet threats so long as the purpose was to save their major clients in the Middle East (Egypt and Syria) from strategic defeats by the Israelis, as was the case, most notably, toward the end of the 1956, 1967 and 1973 wars. The U.S.S.R.

threatened to intervene in the 1967 war, for example, only when the road to the capital was in jeopardy[9] which could have brought down the pro-Soviet government. Before that stage of the Six Day War, however, the Soviets did not threaten to intervene and did not provide much help to their Arab allies, despite the humiliating defeats that they suffered,[10] and despite the Arabs' outrage at the Soviets' nonintervention.[11] On the Egyptian front, the Israelis stopped at the Suez Canal and did not make any threatening moves toward Cairo. But on the Syrian front, on June 10 Israel could easily have advanced on Damascus since Syrian defenses on the nearby Golan Heights had collapsed.[12] There were also indications that the Israelis were more inclined to overthrow the radical Syrian regime.[13] The United States, for its part:

> would probably not have acted on her own to prevent Israel from cutting the three main highways to Damascus (the presumed operational plan) and thus humiliating the Syrian regime . . . it was only when the Soviet Union threatened independent action that the U.S. decided, if she could, to exercise a moderating influence on Israel.[14]

U.S. pressures, indeed, probably helped to stop the Israeli advance.[15]

Thus, the superpowers in fact tacitly agreed that the overthrow of Middle Eastern governments through external military pressure should be avoided. In an interview with A.R. Wells, Dean Rusk, then Secretary of State, recalls that he and President Johnson were extremely concerned about Israeli actions in that war, which in their view gave the Soviets a "legitimate" reason for intervention. On the whole, both superpowers demonstrated caution. Whereas the United States showed sensitivity to Soviet interests in Syria, the U.S.S.R. did not back up its intervention with any military moves; nor did the Fifth Eskadra behave as if a Middle East war were under way.[16]

Instead of a tendency to try to maximize gains, the rules manifest an inclination by the superpowers to minimize losses.[17] In fact, they have defended the status quo: the loser's patron by preserving its client, and the other superpower by tacitly accepting the "legitimacy" of the intervention as well as by staying on guard to keep the first superpower from going beyond reducing losses. Hence, as

McConnell puts it, "this is no zero-sum game."[18] Their failure to prevent local wars notwithstanding, by observing the tacit rules and by being restrained in crises, the United States and the Soviet Union have shown little inclination to provide "blank checks" to their allies. Instead, they have demonstrated a strong desire to avoid armed hostilities between themselves, a desire which has induced them to cooperate in the limitation and relatively early termination of these local wars.

Obviously, the Soviets did not fully control the behavior of their Arab clients. There were lapses of time before their clients accepted the Soviet position; moreover, developments on the battlefield played a greater role in Arab acceptance of cease-fires than the Soviet pressures. As their primary arms supplier, however, the Soviets could exercise restraining influence and, more specifically, could limit the ability of their proteges to fight protracted wars. Thus, lack of Soviet support for continuation of the fighting probably helped lead to earlier termination of the wars than would otherwise have been the case. It is true that Moscow failed in its efforts to prevent the outbreak of the 1967 and 1973 wars. Such failures indicate the limits of superpower influence on determined clients who have greater stakes, at least initially, than the external powers in the outcome of local conflicts.

Through their diplomacy of force the Soviets also exerted a restraining influence on the military conduct of American allies. Occasionally this was done directly, as when their involvement in the War of Attrition halted the Israeli deep-penetration raids. More important, however, was the indirect effect of the Soviet threats exerting pressure on the United States Soviet intervention was instrumental even in those cases in which the United States shared the same operational goal of containing the hostilities. At the very least, Soviet threats increased the effectiveness of U.S. restraining efforts toward its own allies. Hence, Moscow's threats lent greater credibility to American pressures on the Israelis in 1956 and 1973 (and also on the British and the French in 1956) to stop their advances, for fear they would trigger World War III. On the other hand, in 1967, in the War of Attrition, and to a lesser extent in 1983, the Soviets fulfilled even more important roles by defending regimes that the United States and Israel might have wanted to topple. On a more general level, by conferring identical "rights" and "duties" on both superpowers, the unspoken rules connoted a sense of great power parity, and fostered international order through this parallelism of great power responsibilities. The great powers have been conscious of their common interests, most notably the avoidance of any violence between themselves. Closely related has been their desire to contain and end local wars and sometimes also to prevent them. The awareness of common interests gave rise to shared rules and a joint "institution." The rules have been discussed; the "institution" refers to the methods and practices of crisis management. Specifically, throughout the post-war period the United States and the Soviet Union demonstrated readiness to concert their restraining efforts through direct negotiations with each other. This was true regarding both their own activities as well as their pressures on third parties directly involved in the conflict.

Thus, in the Arab-Israeli sphere, as soon as large-scale violence broke out in 1967 and in 1973, the superpowers managed to communicate with each other about their intention not to intervene directly. Kosygin's reply to Secretary Rusk's message on June 5, 1967, was the first use of the hot line in a crisis. In the ensuing exchange, the Soviet Premier and the U.S. President agreed on mutual non-intervention.[19] And on October 7, 1973, a day after the Yom Kippur War had started, Nixon sent Brezhnev a letter urging reciprocal caution; Brezhnev's reply was conciliatory and encouraging.[20]

An interesting example of prompt crisis communication to avoid escalation involved an American intelligence ship, the *USS Liberty*, that was operating off the Sinai coast during the Six Day War. On the fourth day of the war (June 8, 1967) the ship was attacked by unidentified aircraft and torpedo boats, which later proved to be Israeli. What is most relevant here is the great sensitivity that the administration exhibited toward Moscow in handling the affair. Initially, Johnson and McNamara were worried that it might have been a Soviet attack, "and dark predictions of 'World War III' were briefly heard in the White House situation room."[21] As soon as the administration learned the identity of the attackers, however, Johnson cabled Kosygin on the hot line to inform the Soviets of the incident and of the dispatch of aircraft from the Sixth Fleet to the scene of the attack. The incident is an indication, as William Quandt comments:

> of the extraordinary degree to which Johnson was attuned to Soviet behavior once the war actually began. If during the May crisis he had been prepared to see the conflict primarily in terms of Arabs and Israelis, once hostilities were under way the main focus of his attention was the Soviet Union. With Israel secure from defeat by the Arabs, only Soviet behavior could trigger a direct American military response. The regional dispute paled in significance before the danger of superpower confrontation.[22]

Thus, the same administration that was blamed by many for irresponsible behavior in escalating U.S. involvement in Vietnam showed great restraint and caution in an arena where Soviet capabilities and interests were heavily involved. Indeed, rather than differences of personality, a structural factor--namely, the degree of Moscow's engagement in a certain area--goes a long way toward explaining the differences in American behavior in Vietnam and in the Middle East. Eugene Rostow, then the Undersecretary of State for Political Affairs, stated in late 1968 that the President "feels in many ways [the Middle East] is a more dangerous crisis than Vietnam, because it can involve a confrontation with the Russians, not the Chinese."[23]

In some ways, the United States and the Soviet Union have behaved as responsible great powers and have contributed to the international order. They have tried repeatedly, although unsuccessfully in 1967 and 1973, to prevent the eruption of local wars. And they have limited the duration, outcome, and scope of regional wars that have broken out, even if it has taken some time to reach a cease-fire and then to implement it on the battlefield (six days in 1967, eighteen days in 1973). Moreover, by lending, in the Arab-Israeli sphere, more effective and credible support to the defensive operations of their clients than to their aggressive designs, the superpowers helped to preserve the independence of small states in this region, in the process upholding international norms against the aggressive use of force. The United States and the Soviet

Union have been most successful in regulating their own military engagement in Third World conflicts, thereby minimizing the chances of globalization of these conflicts. But in the process they also tacitly recognized the stakes of the rival superpower, its sphere of influence and co-equal status.

This superpower cooperation in post-war crises, however, had its limitations. The superpowers faced recurrent dilemmas and frequent trade-offs between their global role as co-managers of the international system and their regional role as alliance leaders and protectors.[24] They tried to reconcile the resulting inevitable conflicts by maintaining a delicate balance between resolve and restraint, by coercing prudently or accommodating cheaply or by some combination of both.[25] But as patrons they were committed to minimizing losses by their clients, even if that entailed coercive diplomacy that might lead to confrontations with the other superpower.

Thus, despite their concerted crisis diplomacy in 1967 and 1973, Washington and Moscow stumbled into confrontations toward the end of both wars--confrontations in which "shows of force" played a key role. The recurrence of confrontations in the post-war era, and the frequent need to threaten the use of force in order to manage crises, demonstrate that the tacit rules were not self-enforcing; they did not come into play automatically. Threats of intervention backed by short-of-war procedures were essential in order to activate the unspoken norms.[26] As Janice Stein put it:

> Only when the patron of the loser deliberately and self-consciously manipulated the risk of confrontation through threat of intervention, did the other patron exert sufficient pressure to force an end to the fighting.[27]

Threats to intervene, guided by diplomatic rather than military "logic" were used primarily for bargaining purposes. During crises, the superpowers usually focused on the signalling, bargaining, and negotiating character of the use of military power and not on the actual negation of the rival's military capabilities. Signalling for political purposes was, indeed, an important function of the superpower nuclear and power-projection forces.

Thus, Soviet threats in 1967 and 1973 were designed to activate U.S. pressure on Israel to comply with the cease fires. In other words, the threats were, as Phil Williams points out, designed specifically to ensure that intervention would be unnecessary.[28] The Soviet alert of four airborne divisions on October 24, 1973, which "appeared as vigorous preparation for military action, was probably intended as a substitute for it."[29] This is also true for Soviet threats in 1956 and 1967, and probably in 1970 (before the actual Soviet deployment in Egypt during the War of Attrition). Similarly, the U.S. show of force in September 1970 was intended to avoid the necessity of use of force, as was the case with the 1973 alert.

Puzzles and Surprises in Superpower Crisis
Behavior During the Cold War

The crisis behavior of the superpowers during Arab-Israeli wars in the post-war era, beginning with the 1956 Suez Crisis, presents some major puzzles and surprises. First, their engagement in these crises never escalated to a global armed conflict; moreover, in contrast to past experience of earlier great powers in similarly intense regional conflicts, the superpowers avoided any actual use of force against each other.

Second, despite the superpowers' intense political-ideological rivalry and the popular wisdom about the Cold War, the Arab-Israeli crises were part of a larger pattern of cooperation between Moscow and Washington in regulating local conflicts.   This pattern contradicts what we would expect from unit-level theories that suggest the prevalence in foreign policy-making of non-systematic factors such as domestic politics, bureaucratic politics, crisis-induced stress, and ideology. Indeed, in the case of the Cold War, these theories should have led us to expect severe problems in superpower crisis management.   Such problems should have been supposedly derived from the ideological differences between the superpowers, the widely expected adverse effects of public opinion and bureaucratic politics on crisis management by modern societies, and from the special intensity of crisis-induced stress in nuclear crises.

Third, the superpowers' mutual restraint persisted despite changes in the balance of their military forces due to the rising power-projection capability of the Soviet Union and its achievement of a nuclear second-strike capability. In previous eras such changes, especially the growing military capabilities of a "revisionist" power, have led to instability and major wars. Most interestingly, this cooperation occurred in an era of decolonization, which, together with the Cold War, supposedly should have made it possible for small states to manipulate both the United States and the Soviet Union.

Finally, despite the absence of an explicit agreement on the superpowers' balance of interests in the Middle East, in times of crisis that balance, as a matter of fact, has informed the tacit rules for regulation of the use of force. The Middle East, however, has been characterized by what George called "disputed interest symmetry."[30] The United States has claimed to possess paramount interests because of two particular objectives it has in the region.[31] The first is to guarantee the free flow of oil from the region, especially in light of the dependence of major U.S. allies--Western Europe and Japan--on Gulf oil. The second is the U.S. moral commitment to the survival of the state of Israel. The Soviets, for their part, have persistently rejected the American claims of superior stakes, asserting that they have special security interests in a region that almost adjoins the U.S.S.R.'s own southwestern borders, its "soft underbelly"; indeed, much of the Middle East is far closer to the Soviet border than Grenada is to the United States. But most U.S. administrations did not recognize the equality or even the legitimacy of Soviet security interests in the Middle East, perceiving Soviet motives as "offensive" rather than "defensive." Accordingly, many, though by no means all, U.S. policy-makers denied that Moscow deserved an equal voice in Middle East diplomacy.

But in times of crisis, superpower interaction was guided by the balance of resolve. Thus, a patron defending the survival of its client, an interest that was in its possession, had the edge in the balance of resolve. As a result, by adhering to the tacit rules, the United States, at least in periods of crisis, recognized Soviet interests in the Middle East, notably with respect to the preservation of its clients by intervening to prevent their strategic defeats.

Systemic Explanation of the Tacit Rules

These kinds of surprises suggest that a structural explanation could be useful in accounting for the tacit rules of crisis management. Indeed, a systemic explanation is useful where intentions and results do not coincide. According to such an explanation, the structure of the international system conditions how actors behave.[32] Due to external pressures, the outcomes of states' interactions often will not correspond to the actors' ideological desires and domestic or bureaucratic characteristics. Thus, the bipolar structure of the post-war era generated some outcomes that were more moderate and stabilizing than one might have expected from the ideologies and internal characteristics of Moscow and Washington.

Indeed, a bipolar structure can restrain the behavior of immoderate players, especially during international crises. Thus, despite their intense ideological and geopolitical rivalry, the United States and the Soviet Union were able to cooperate tacitly in times of crisis, more from necessity than by choice. As structural theory would lead us to expect, the absence of a shared vision of world order did not jeopardize the emergence of tacit arrangements for crisis management, once the appropriate systemic conditions were in place. More specifically, the tacit rules constituted "unintended outcomes" in that whereas during normal periods the superpowers desired to revise the status quo in their favor, their crisis behavior, in fact, helped to consolidate it. Similarly, while both the United States and the U.S.S.R. fundamentally rejected the idea of spheres of influence, the tacit rules did acknowledge in practice the "legitimacy" of such spheres even in the Third World. Ideological rivalry and cultural heterogeneity, in contrast, were able to constrain the construction of long-term security regimes with explicit norms and principles.

The fear of World War III in the nuclear age created the need for a means of exercising power in a crisis that would be more powerful than mere verbal threats, yet short of large-scale violence. The various signals of a "show of force," which became more common in the post-war era, provided these means, as we have seen in Middle East crises. Indeed, short-of-war options enabled the

United States and the Soviet Union to demonstrate resolve in defending their interests and yet avoid war by showing self-restraint. Hence, crises became a surrogate for war in the post-1945 era and a means for demonstrating resolve.[33]

The transition to bipolarity, for its part, made possible the emergence of tacit norms that were not only necessary for effective coordination between adversaries during crises, but were also important for the superpowers in regulating the Middle East crises. Indeed, the bipolar structure facilitated the communication of the show-of-force signals and helped to make them more credible and effective. In a world of several big powers, on the other hand, it would be more difficult to identify the balance of forces and interests and to communicate nonverbally to adversaries the relative stakes during times of tension.

And when push came to shove, the limited significance of allies for the global balance of capabilities in a bipolar world encouraged the superpowers to be restrained in their support of clients. In a world in which so powerful a state as China could switch alliances twice since 1945 without bringing about a major change in the global balance of forces, no "loss" in the Middle East could have caused a decisive shift in the East-West balance, despite the significance of such states as Iran, which the United States "lost" in 1979, or Egypt, which the Soviets "lost" between 1974 and 1976. Moreover, the high dependence of clients on the superpowers' economic assistance, arms transfer, and diplomatic support made it easier for Moscow and Washington to restrain their allies, at least at the time when such structural asymmetries in relative capabilities should play the most critical role--times of crisis.

No less important for the avoidance of a general war, however, was the resolve that the superpowers repeatedly demonstrated in defending their important interests. At first glance, this determination seems to have been destabilizing since it brought about frequent superpower crises. Nevertheless, the frequency of crises in the initial period of the Cold War gave the global antagonists the opportunity to delineate their "red lines" and to "learn" the implicit rules through a process of signalling threats and promises. Hence, precisely because of their recurrent willingness to protect vital assets, it became easier for each superpower, in a world of only two great powers, both to identify and to respect the interests and spheres of influence of their rivals in crisis situations.

The type of cooperation discussed thus far, however, was primarily tacit and "spontaneous"--the "unintended outcome" of unilateral moves. The crisis behavior described in this paper fits the expectations of systems theory regarding cooperation in a bi-polar world; we have seen how, in the sphere of Arab-Israeli conflict with superpower involvement, even seemingly aggressive, unilateral moves lead to "partisan mutual adjustment," tacit bargaining, and "unintended" collaboration.[34]

The systemic factors that were so helpful for the emergence of the tacit rules were not, however, sufficient for producing a higher-level of cooperation. Indeed, factors below the systems level exert a critical influence on normal diplomacy and joint attempts not only to manage crises but also to resolve conflicts. We will now turn to a brief analysis of such attempts by Washington and Moscow to collaborate in settling the Arab-Israeli conflict.

Superpower Cooperation in Conflict Resolution

When we look at the record of superpower diplomacy in the Middle East two puzzles confront us. First, the intensity of the global U.S.-Soviet competition during the Cold War, which was sharper in the Middle East than in other areas, should ostensibly lead us to expect the likelihood of explicit superpower cooperation in normal Middle Eastern diplomacy to be very low. Yet, surprisingly, the record of U.S.-Soviet interaction in non-crisis situations in this region shows that on various occasions both superpowers have tried to construct common diplomatic initiatives. These initiatives include Security Council Resolution 242 of November 22, 1967, the Big Two talks (1969-70), the Brezhnev-Nixon Summits of 1972-73, the Geneva Conference (1973), the joint statement of October 1, 1977 during the initial phase of the Carter administration, and the attempts to convene an international conference on the Middle East during the 1980s. At the least, the superpowers have shown some willingness to behave responsibly and, at times, to take positions at some distance from their respective allies in order to promote conflict resolution in the Middle East. In other words, the bipolar structure of the post-war system at least did not prevent recurrent attempts at superpower cooperation in this region.

Yet, in contrast to the repeated success of superpower crisis management, the record of joint superpower conflict resolution in the Middle East was, at least until recently, poor. In other words, on the one hand the superpowers made more attempts at cooperation than should ostensibly have been expected; on the other, these attempts bore little fruit. Despite large differences in capabilities between the superpowers and their clients, Moscow and Washington did not succeed in imposing a settlement in the Middle East or even in radically changing their allies' positions, as we supposedly should have expected from a structural analysis. Indeed, though the positions of the superpowers have at times been closer than at other times, they have never succeeded in sustaining a collaboration long enough to decisively propel the region toward conflict resolution. Moreover, in contrast to the continuity and similarity of superpower crisis behavior, their attempts at conflict resolution have been characterized by discontinuity and dissimilarity. And to understand the reasons for this, we must focus on ideological, cognitive, and domestic factors that are not treated in a systemic, balance of power perspective. These factors include differences in U.S. and Soviet approaches toward the Arab-Israeli conflict, U.S. domestic and bureaucratic politics, and the beliefs of key American and Soviet policy-makers.

This paper will not be able to go into detail with respect to analyzing these factors, but it will review especially the ideological rivalry between communism and capitalism which severely constrained U.S-Soviet cooperation by reinforcing mutual images of "enemies" rather than of "limited adversaries."[35] Strong commitments to their respective visions of the international order made it difficult for Washington and Moscow to agree about the legitimacy of the status quo,[36] to accept each other's spheres of influence, and to recognize each other's equal status. This was particularly true regarding the Third World, where the Soviets were committed to support the "progressive forces" and national liberation movements whereas the United States was obligated to promote democracy and free enterprise, or at least to oppose the rise of pro-communist regimes. The lack of consensus on their balance of interests was especially notable in the Middle East. The combination of (generally) negative images of each other (images shaped by ideology) and the specific content of their ideologies (i.e., rejection of spheres of influence) undermined attempts at concerted diplomacy. Moreover, ideological or "moral" affiliation with at least some of their allies (Moscow to the Arab radicals such as Syria and Iraq and the United States to democratic Israel and to Arab conservatives such as the Gulf states) made their commitment to these allies stronger than if it had been just another case of traditional great power patronage.

The power-politics perspective appears to go a long way toward explaining the failure of non-crisis superpower cooperation in the Middle East. More often than in times of crisis, the United States and the Soviet Union have, during normal periods, sought unilateral advantages. Indeed, every attempt at collaboration was followed by unilateral policies, each power using its respective comparative advantages in order to build up its influence. The great powers did not, moreover, persist in maintaining a distance between their own diplomatic positions and those of their clients; in the aftermath of the collaborative episodes, they were quick to return to supporting their proteges' stances. At any rate, neither superpower managed to persuade the other that it was willing and/or able to restrain its client(s). The "collective goods" of an international society--(local) war avoidance, (global) crisis prevention, (regional) arms control and conflict resolution--seemed to take a back seat to the particular interests of each superpower in its role as protector of local proteges.

An examination of the historical record may seem, indeed, to suggest the dominance of competitive, or at best mutually balancing, policies. On the whole, Washington helped to maintain Israel's military advantage. It also tended to exclude the Soviets from participation in the peace process, and to reject Moscow's offers of collaboration in settling the Arab-Israeli dispute. It seems that Moscow, for its part, focused on arming the Arabs, especially those who opposed peacemaking efforts, in order to spoil American diplomacy in the region. The general consequences of these superpower policies (on top of regional dynamics) have been an accelerated arms race in the Middle East, the outbreak of a number of regional wars, and the failure of attempts to achieve a comprehensive peace settlement. Thus, at least partly as a result of such superpower behavior (in addition to local animosities and regional intransigence), the Arab-Israeli conflict has continued to pose grave risks to the stability of the region and to the peacefulness of the world.

For example, in the wake of the superpower cooperation in reaching Security Council Resolution 242, the United States and the Soviet Union reverted, in 1968, to a focus on arming their respective allies without substantial efforts to ameliorate the conflict. In the following year, during the two-power talks, the Soviets backtracked twice just as an agreement on a settlement seemed to be close: in June 1969 when the Soviets withdrew previous concessions which included acceptance of a lasting peace agreement and Arab recognition of Israel,[37] and, most notably, six months later, when on December 23 the Soviets formally informed the United States of their objection to the first Rogers Plan, although the plan was, in fact, identical to the joint U.S.-Soviet brief of October 28 of that year.[38] The major, if not the only, reason for such Soviet about-faces appears to have been Arab opposition to progress in the peace process with Israel.

On top of these diplomatic retrogressions, Moscow deployed air-defense systems in Egypt during 1970. Thus, it does not seem surprising that Washington started to move away from the cooperative path in spring 1970, or that following the Soviet role in the Egyptian violations of the cease-fire in August 1970, the United States formally disengaged from the two-power talks. Finally, the shipment of major Soviet military hardware to Egypt and Syria, beginning in February 1973, enabled those countries to attack Israel on October 6, 1973, probably with some kind of Soviet approval for the use of the military option, if necessary, to take back the Occupied Territories.

Nevertheless, the Soviets were not the only great power that played power politics by preferring patrons' commitments to larger "managerial responsibilities." During the period before the 1973 war, the United States helped Israel to maintain its qualitative military edge, especially in air power, over the Arabs, and did not lean too forcefully on Israel in the diplomatic arena. Keeping Israel predominant and avoiding strong pressures on it (especially in the context of superpower collusion) were deliberate steps. As Kissinger makes clear in his memoirs, these policies were two components in his strategy to establish a *Pax Americana* in the Middle East and to drastically reduce Soviet influence in the region. Kissinger aimed to accomplish these objectives by excluding the Soviets from real participation in the diplomatic process, which would, he hoped, be arbitrated exclusively by the United States.

The Effect of the Recent Changes in the
Soviet Union on the Prospects for Cooperation
in Conflict Resolution

Only in the second half of the 1980s did superpower cooperation in conflict resolution become feasible in the Middle East, as was the case in some other regional conflicts in the Third World. This was closely related to the much greater flexibility and moderation of Soviet foreign policy under Gorbachev, including the openness toward Israel and to the reciprocal response by the Reagan administration and later the Bush administration. Yet, what underlay these policy changes was cognitive learning, at the leadership level, about the limits to and the costs of unilateralism; and a convergence, as the great powers become more moderate (externally) and more similar (internally), in outlook and aims that enhance the prospects for the emergence of a great-power concert for the purposes of conflict resolution. Thus, on the one hand, the translation of the Soviet "new thinking" into policy actions has increased the Soviet capability to contribute constructively to peacemaking, while on the other hand Gorbachev's domestic reforms have made Moscow a much more acceptable partner in American eyes for joint diplomacy in conflict resolution.

From 1967 to the Gorbachev era, the Soviets tried to either construct joint peace initiatives with the United States or to obstruct U.S. exclusionary moves by supporting Arab radicals in the Middle Eastern sphere. Gorbachev, however, as part of his "new thinking" in foreign policy and his new approach to regional conflicts in particular, initiated two important changes in this strategy. On the one hand, since 1985 Moscow broadened its options by opening a dialogue with a greater variety of Middle East actors beyond the members of the "radical club." On the other hand, Gorbachev demonstrated greater willingness than his predecessors to forcefully press traditional Soviet allies toward moderation.

These policy changes reflected greater ideological flexibility and moderation. The "new thinking" suggested, in fact, the de-ideologization of foreign policy. It advocated improving Soviet relations with a wider range of states, including good ties with Third World countries having a capitalist orientation.[39] In the Middle East, this new doctrine was expressed by overtures toward conservative Arab states and increasing contacts with Israel. Gorbachev indeed succeeded in upgrading relations with the Arab Gulf states, Egypt, and Jordan; this, in turn, solidified their support for the idea of an international conference. Even more innovative were the overtures in recent years towards Israel after two decades of estranged relations in diplomatic and other fields with the Jewish state. These moves included cultural exchanges, opening of consular relations, intensified diplomatic contacts, initiation of economic relations, and, not least, allowing unlimited Jewish emigration to Israel.

At the same time, Gorbachev publicly distanced himself from the positions of his closest ally in the Middle East. At a state dinner in honor of President Assad of Syria, he remarked, "the reliance on military force has completely lost its credibility as a way of solving the Middle East conflict."[40] A year later Gorbachev suggested, "recognition of the State of Israel [and] consideration of its security interests . . . is a necessary element for the establishment of peace and good neighborliness in the region based on the principles of international law."[41]

Although the Soviets continued to supply Syria with sophisticated weapons, the Soviets failed to meet some of the Syrians' quantitative and qualitative requests and slowed their arms shipment.[42] In this spirit, the Soviet ambassador to Syria stated in November 1989 that his country no longer supported the declared Syrian objectives of reaching "strategic parity" with Israel.

The Soviets were also instrumental in moderating the positions of the PLO in winter of 1988. They pressured the Palestinian organizations to accept UN Resolutions 242 and 338, renounce terrorism, and recognize Israel's right to exist. Since the main short-term outcome of this PLO moderation was the launching of a U.S.-PLO dialogue, the Soviets, in fact, helped to make it possible. This stands in marked contrast to the Soviets' anxieties earlier in the 1980s that talks between a joint Palestinian-Jordanian delegation and the United States would eventually lead to a *pax Americana.*

A related change has recently taken place in the softening of the Soviet position regarding the procedures and the authority of an international conference for the resolution of the Arab-Israeli conflict.

Such shifts in Moscow's position can be accounted for by the desire to have better relations with the United States (a desire which is closely related to the enormous economic needs of the Soviet Union). Another motivation for the greater moderation implied by the "new thinking" and the associated desire to promote peaceful resolution of regional conflicts is the growing Soviet interest in stabilizing turbulent regions proximate to its southern "soft underbelly" with its increasingly mobilized Islamic populations. Such stability should not only help to prevent dangerous crises but could also make it possible for the Soviets to invest scarce resources in economic development at the expense of the military and assistance to unreliable and unstable radical Third World clients with basket-case economies.

The new Soviet leadership also seemingly realized that it would be extremely difficult for any one of the superpowers to permanently exclude the other superpower from such a turbulent and important region as the Middle East. But by the same token, they also understood that in order to stay in the diplomatic picture, let alone advance Middle East stability and reduce the risk of escalation, they had to show flexibility, moderation, and willingness to cooperate with the United States.

The American Response to Gorbachev's Moderation

Because of Reagan's vehemently anti-Communist views, he was even less inclined than his predecessors to involve the Soviets in Middle East diplomacy. Yet, two kinds of changes, one regional and the other global, brought about a new stage, in which there seemed to be a greater (although by no means unqualified) U.S. willingness to include Moscow in the peace process. The first was a new Middle East crisis which erupted in late 1987. As we have seen, crises have usually triggered some kind of superpower cooperation. This time, however, it was not the traditional type of regional crisis with the accompanying risk of escalation to an interstate war, but rather the uprising, or intifada, of the Palestinians in the territories occupied by Israel. Thus, forceful superpower intervention was not as urgent as in preceding crises; yet, at the same time the prolonged nature of the crisis lent itself to the emergence of diplomatic initiatives aimed not just at ending the immediate violence, but also at resolving the Arab-Israeli conflict, or at least its critical Palestinian dimension.

The second change was the great improvement in superpower relations with the progress made in the negotiations on the INF agreement in late 1987 and the signing of the treaty that December. Throughout 1988 not only did the bilateral relations continue to warm up (a summit took place in May-June 1988 during which the life-long communist-baiter Reagan visited Moscow), but the accelerating domestic reforms in the Soviet Union markedly improved the image of the Soviets, and in particular that of Gorbachev personally, in the eyes of Americans.

But the change in the U.S. position was limited, at least partly because there were still misgivings in the Reagan administration about full-blown and influential Soviet participation in delicate Middle East diplomacy. By the time the Reagan administration completed its term in office, the most important change was not any specific transformation in the parties' respective policy positions. Rather, it was the diplomatic legacy that the Reagan team left to its successor, that is, the removal of some important taboos in American public opinion concerning U.S. policy in the Middle East. One was the negotiations with the PLO; the other was the talks with the Soviets about Middle East problems and the related notion that some form of international framework was necessary for resolving conflicts in the region, notably the Arab-Israeli dispute. Especially significant was the fact that the removal of the taboos was carried out by an administration with an unprecedented record of support for Israel and (initial) hostility toward the Soviets. This could provide important domestic legitimacy for potential superpower cooperation in the next administration.

The accelerated pace of revolutionary changes in the Soviet domestic affairs, in Eastern Europe, and in Soviet policies in the Third World under the leadership of Gorbachev in 1989-90 made the Bush administration more receptive to Soviet participation and to ongoing diplomatic consultations with Moscow about the Middle East. The changing attitude saw its most public manifestation in the Malta Summit of late 1989, where President Bush stated that the Soviets could play a constructive role in the Middle East and that he did not think there was a great distance between the superpowers on the questions of Lebanon and the West Bank.

During 1989-90 some concrete elements of superpower cooperation emerged, although they fell short of a call for a full-blown international conference or a joint statement on the resolution of the Arab-Israeli conflict. These practical steps included: a joint action to prevent UN recognition of a declared Palestinian state; some degree of pressure on their respective allies (the United States on Israel; the Soviets on the PLO) to moderate their positions concerning the Israeli initiative to hold elections in the Occupied Territories; a joint declaration in the June 1990 summit in Washington against the settlement of new immigrants (mostly from the Soviet Union) in the territories held by Israel; and talks on arms control and non-proliferation of non-conventional weapons in the Middle East.

During summer and fall of 1990, U.S.-Soviet cooperation peaked in confronting Saddam Hussein's aggression against Kuwait by making possible Security Council resolutions imposing economic sanctions, and in late November, authorizing the use of force against Iraq. The superpowers also agreed that following the resolution of the Gulf Crisis, a major effort should be made to resolve the Arab-Israeli conflict and that they should cooperate in this enterprise.

Indeed, in the aftermath of the Gulf War, the United States, as the widely recognized leading power, initiated precisely such an effort. The logic of the model presented here suggests that Soviet participation in the peace process depends on the future of the internal reforms and the outcome of the domestic struggle between conservatives and liberals inside the Soviet Union. As the conservative forces become more powerful, the likelihood of Soviet restraining pressures on Syria to make concessions in the negotiations and of limitations on Soviet arms sales to the Middle East declines. In turn, U.S. willingness to involve the Soviets in the diplomatic process will depend heavily on the nature of the emerging Soviet domestic system; the more it continues with liberal reforms, as well as with implementing the "new thinking" in its foreign policy, the greater the American support for Soviet participation will be and vice versa.

Structural Changes and Crisis Management

With the growing economic and nationalities problems in the Soviet Union in 1989-1990, and its disengagement from Eastern Europe, the bipolar structure of two leading superpowers, which dominated world affairs since the late 1940s, started to decline. What were the effects of this structural change on patterns of crisis management? On the one hand, it brought about some degree of destabilization and increased the likelihood for the actual use of force. On the other, the prospects for a *pax Americana* seemed to increase, although they generated some Soviet resistance.

A major manifestation of the destabilizing implications of the new world order was Saddam Hussein's invasion of Kuwait which, in turn, could be accounted for by his (mis)perceptions of the emergence of a "power vacuum" in the Persian Gulf with the seeming disengagement of the superpowers from the Third World. Because of the Soviet withdrawal from Eastern Europe and from some parts of the Third World, Hussein perceived Moscow as a power in decline,[43] and thus was less of a constraint on his actions. Thus, he probably felt less constrained with respect to the invasion since he could now more easily discount Moscow's tendency even during the Cold War, to oppose "naked" cross-border aggression by its clients. Moreover, Hussein was also not deterred by the United States because he thought the United States would see no Soviet military threat behind his invasion,[44] and thus he did not believe, until it was too late, that Washington would actually use its military power against him.

At the same time, because of Soviet decline and disengagement, the United States was less constrained by its old-time adversary, and thus could afford to deploy a massive force not far from Soviet frontiers, which included withdrawing some forces from the European front--moves which were much less conceivable during the Cold War. In a world in which Soviet military action became much less likely, and as a consequence the danger of escalation to a global confrontation decreased drastically, the United States could allow itself not to compromise with Saddam Hussein and to contemplate and eventually carry out a massive use of force in a region considered vital to the Soviets. Thus, the decline of bipolarity made possible the outbreak of a war in the Middle East with the massive participation of a superpower--in fact, the only superpower in the international system.

By turning down Soviet proposals for a cease-fire prior to the defeat of Iraq, the United States established its predominant role in the Middle East, at least as a temporary "stabilizing hegemon." By contrast, in the bipolar era there was a tendency on the part of the United States, at least tacitly, to recognize the equal status of the Soviets in times of crisis, even though after the war, it would try to establish pax Americana by unilateral-exclusionary diplomacy in the Arab-Israeli conflict. This difference reflects the declining power of the Soviet Union in the post bipolar era and, as usual, times of crisis expose most clearly the basic distribution of power in the international systems as well as the extent of the geo-strategic rivalry between great powers.

Despite the reduction in their power, the Soviets continue to be important players in the international politics of the Middle East both because of their interests in a proximate region and because of their leading role as arms suppliers. Indeed, in order to be effective, every arms control regime must involve them. But beyond arms control, the Soviets could contribute constructively to the broader peace process by encouraging their allies, notably the Syrians and Palestinians, to make concessions parallel to steps the United States should encourage Israel to take in order to advance the cause of peace in a region which has known in recent decades less tranquility than most other regions.

Conclusion

This chapter shows the utility of structural-balance of power theory for explaining crisis management outcomes, especially the emergence of tacit rules for the regulation of the use of force between antagonists such as the superpowers in the post-war era. Indeed, as structural theory predicts, the bipolar structure of the post-war system (and the presence of nuclear weapons) helped to stabilize superpower interaction and to generate a higher degree of cooperation, especially in times of crisis, than what we could expect from focusing only on the internal attributes and objectives of the United States and the Soviet Union. Superpower intervention in Arab-Israeli wars is a major manifestation of this logic, and it thus affected war termination in these conflicts, helping to maintain the regional status quo and balance of power.

In accordance with the logic of the model presented here, the recent changes in the international structure and the weakening of the Soviet Union affected the nature of superpower interaction during the Gulf Crisis. These structural changes also influenced the outbreak of the crisis (Iraq's invasion of Kuwait) and the war (U.S. employment of massive force) as well as the leading role of the United States in determining the outcome of the conflict.

Domestic and ideological factors severely constrained superpower cooperation for the purposes of conflict resolution during the Cold War. Yet, as this chapter indicates, the internal reforms in the Soviet Union have paved the way for a higher level of cooperation between Washington and Moscow in resolving the Arab-Israeli conflict. But the same rationale points out that if a conservative backlash takes place in the Soviet Union, it may reduce, once again, the prospects for an enduring and effective collaboration between

Washington and Moscow in helping to construct a new regional order in the Middle East.

Notes

1. Kenneth Waltz, *Theory of International Politics* (Reading, MA: Addison-Wesley Publishing Company, 1979).

2. Alexander George, *Managing U.S.-Soviet Rivalry: Problems of Crisis Prevention* (Boulder, CO: Westview Press, 1983), pp. 365-369; and "Political Crises," in Joseph Nye ed., *The Making of America's Soviet Policy* (New Haven: Yale University Press, 1984), ch. 6. See also Alexander George, et. al., eds., *U.S.-Soviet Security Cooperation: Achievements, Failures, Lessons* (New York: Oxford University Press, 1988), especially ch. 23.

3. Glenn Snyder and Paul Diesing, *Conflict Among Nations* (Princeton: Princeton University Press, 1977), p. 451.

4. This section draws on the works of a number of observers of the international politics of the Middle East who have addressed the regularities of U.S.-Soviet interaction during Middle Eastern wars. See Yair Evron, "Great Power Military Intervention in the Middle East," in M. Leitenberg and G. Sheffer, eds., *Great Power Intervention in the Middle East* (New York: Pergamon, 1979) pp. 17-45; George, *Managing U.S.-Soviet Rivalry*, ch. 15; Alexander George, "Mechanisms for Moderating Superpower Competition," in *AEI Foreign Policy and Defense Review* 6, no. 1 (1986), pp. 5-13; James McConnell, "'The Rules of the Game': A Theory on the Practice of Superpower Naval Diplomacy," in B. Dismukes and J. McConnell, eds., *Soviet Naval Diplomacy* (New York: Pergamon, 1979); Janice Stein, "Proxy Wars-How Superpowers End Them: the Diplomacy of War Termination in the Middle East," *International Journal* 35, no. 3 (Summer 1980), pp. 478-519; Lawrence L. Whetten, "The Arab-Israeli Dispute: Great Power Behavior," in G. Treverton, ed., *Crisis Management and the Superpowers in the Middle East* (Farnborough, England: Gower, 1981).

5. Snyder and Diesing, pp. 207-281.

6. See Stein, "Proxy Wars."

7. McConnell, p. 249.

104

8. See Evron, "Great Power Intervention."

9. P. Jabber and R. Kolkowicz, "The Arab-Israeli Wars of 1967 and 1973," in S.S. Kaplan, *Diplomacy of Power* (Washington, D.C.: Brookings Institute, 1981), p. 434; and A.R. Wells, "Superpowers Naval Confrontations: The June Arab-Israeli War," in Bradford Dismukes and James McConnell, *Soviet Naval Diplomacy* (New York: Pergamon, 1979), p. 165.

10. Wells, p. 165; Mohammed Heikal, *The Sphinx and the Commissar* (New York: Harper and Row, 1978), pp. 181, 185, 191.

11. Jabber and Kolkowicz, p. 436.

12. Wells, p. 165; and Jabber and Kolkowicz, p. 434.

13. Shlomo Aronson, *Conflict and Bargaining in the Middle East: An Israeli Perspective* (Baltimore, MD: The Johns Hopkins University Press, 1978), p. 388, n. 85; Whetten, p. 47; and Mahmoud Riad, *The Struggle for Peace in the Middle East* (London: Quartet Books, 1981), p. 17.

14. Whetten, "The Arab-Israeli Dispute," p. 54.

15. *Ibid*.

16. Jabber and Kolkowicz, pp. 436-437; Whetten, "The Arab-Israeli Dispute," p. 54.

17. Stein, p. 495; McConnell, p. 277.

18. *Ibid.*

19. L.B. Johnson, *The Vantage Point: Perspectives on the Presidency 1963-1969* (New York: Holt, Rinehart and Winston) pp. 297-98; William Quandt, *Decade of Decisions: American Policy Toward the Middle East Conflict, 1967-1976*, (Berkeley: University of California Press, 1977), p. 62; Stein, pp. 488-89.

20. Bernard Kalb and Marvin Kalb, *Kissinger*, (New York: Dell Publishing, 1975) p. 524.

21. Quandt, *Decade*, p. 62.

22. Quandt, *Decade of Decisions*, p. 63.

23. Cited in Steven L. Spiegel, *The Other Arab-Israeli Conflict: Making America's Middle East Policy, from Truman to Reagan* (Chicago: The University of Chicago Press, 1985), p. 151.

24. Snyder and Diesing, pp. 447; Stein, pp. 488-489, 513.

25. Snyder and Diesing, pp. 207-208; see also Phil Williams, *Crisis Management: Confrontation and Diplomacy in the Nuclear Age* (London: Martin Robinson, 1976), pp. 52-55.

26. George, "Mechanisms," p. 9.

27. Stein, p. 496.

28. Phil Williams, *Crisis Management: Confrontation and Diplomacy in the Nuclear Age* (London: Martin Robertson, 1976), p. 109.

29. *Ibid.*

30. George, "Mechanism for Moderating," p. 7.

31. On U.S. interests in the Middle East, see Quandt, *Decade of Decisions*, pp. 9-15; and Harold H. Saunders, ed., "The Superpowers in the Middle East," in *AEI Foreign Policy and Defense Review* 6, 1 (1986), pp. 16-20.

32. See Waltz, *Theory*.

33. Waltz, "Stability"; Coral Bell, *The Conventions of Crisis: A Study in Diplomatic Management* (Oxford: Oxford University Press, 1971); and Snyder and Diesing.

34. The term "partisan mutual adjustment" is Charles E. Lindblom's, from Lindblom, *The Intelligence of Democracy* (New York: Free Press, 1965).

35. See Michael Mandelbaum, *The Fate of Nations* (New York: Cambridge University Press, 1988), p. 29.

36. Joseph Nye, "Nuclear Learning and U.S.-Soviet Security Regimes," paper delivered to the annual meeting of the American Political Science Association, (Washington, D.C.: 1986), pp. 26, 29.

37. See Whetten, *Canal War*, p. 73.

106

38. Whetten, pp. 79-80; George Breslauer, "Soviet Policy in the Middle East, 1967-1972: Unalterable Antagonism or Collaborative Competition?" in Alexander George, *Managing U.S.-Soviet Rivalry: Problems of Crisis Prevention* (Boulder,CO: Westview Press, 1983), p. 84.

39. Galia Golan, "The Soviet Union and the Palestinian Issue" and "Gorbachev's Middle East Strategy" in G. Breslauer, ed., *Soviet Strategy in the Middle East* (Winchester, MA: Unwin Hyman, 1990), pp. 157-58.

40. Quoted in *Pravda*, 25 April 1987.

41. Quoted in *The New York Times*, April 11, 1988.

42. *The New York Times*, June 12, 1988; Golan, pp. 160; Breslauer, pp. 311; *Ha'Aretz*, January 30, April 29, 1990.

43. See his Amman speech of February 24, 1990, *International Affairs*, FBIS-NES-90-039.

44. See Craig R. Whitney, "The Next Step Will be Building a Solid Future On the Shifting Sands," *The New York Times,* March 3, 1991, p. IE 3.

PART THREE

Historical Cases

The Crisis Experience

6 The Superpowers, Crisis, and the Middle East: Moments of Tension, Moments of Promise

Introduction

The manner in which both superpowers perceived their core and secondary interests in the Middle East has had a clear impact on their management of the region's crises. Of course, different factors have influenced the superpowers' perception of their interests during each of the region's crises--factors such as ideology, the development of the international system, the evolution of bilateral Soviet-U.S. relations, domestic politics, and the politics and policies of regional powers. The influence of each factor has varied from time to time and from one crisis to another. Although the superpowers' interests in the Middle East have generally been consistent during the post-World War II period, management of the region's crises varied in terms of policies, positions and bargaining tactics. These tactics have ranged from coercion to cooperation and have included acts of persuasion, accommodation and collaboration.

The Middle East is approaching a new era in which the map of its conflicts and crises will be subject to substantial changes. In the meantime the international system is undergoing profound transformations. Therefore, it is wise to draw lessons from the past crisis experience of the region, on the level of crisis avoidance, crisis provocation, crisis management and/or crisis termination, and to assess the relevance of such lessons for future crisis management.

112

The Superpowers and Middle Eastern Crises:
The Early Stage, 1947-1956

The first two crises in the Arab-Israeli conflict took place in 1947 and 1948. The first concerned the UN plan for partitioning Palestine into two states: one Jewish and the other Arab; the second erupted as a result of the establishment of the state of Israel on May 15, 1948. Both superpowers approved the UN partition plan, immediately recognized the state of Israel, condemned the entrance of Arab armies into Palestine, and co-sponsored a draft resolution imposing a permanent cease-fire. The resolution was adopted by the Security Council on July 15, 1948.[1]

U.S.-Soviet cooperation in dealing with the crises of 1947 and 1948 can probably be explained in view of several factors: 1) the absence of the Cold War spirit in the region; 2) American and Soviet sympathy with Jewish national aspirations in compensation for the bitter sufferings inflicted upon the Jews by the Nazis; and 3) the recognition that the emergence of Israel could serve the purpose of terminating the British presence in the Eastern Mediterranean.[2] Moreover, in the United States, the Jewish community was influential in convincing President Truman to recognize the state of Israel immediately after its establishment. In addition, each superpower recognized the potential that the establishment of a Jewish state in the Middle East held. For the Soviet Union, such a Jewish state might have been regarded as a source of support for socialism. On the other hand, the United States might have believed that the loyalty of the new Jewish state was guaranteed in view of the role of the American Jewish community in U.S.-Israeli relations.

During the early stage of their involvement in the region (by the time of the Suez crisis of 1956), the superpowers gradually expanded their competing global interests into the Middle East. The quarrel over the arms deal in 1955 and particularly the episode of the Aswan "High Dam" in July 1956 were both clear examples of this. When Nasser retaliated against the withdrawal of the U.S. offer to finance the High Dam by nationalizing the Suez Canal company, the United States took a firm stand against the Egyptian move and coordinated its coercive policy with other maritime powers in the

West. The Soviet Union, on the contrary, strongly supported Nasser's position on the grounds that Western interests in Egypt should not be maintained by force or threat of force. The Cold War was partly responsible for the differing positions of the Soviet Union and Western powers after July 26, 1956.

The United States took a resolute position on aggression against Egypt in October 1956. It managed to compel the combatants to accept a cease-fire and then to pull the foreign forces out of Egypt. It took the lead in passing the UN resolutions in that context. The American stance during the 1956 crisis, and particularly after October 29, was often explained as a strategic maneuver aimed at eliminating the last remnants of British and French colonial influence and replacing them in leading the Western bloc in the Middle East. Such an explanation draws attention to the fact that the aggressors did not consult with the United States beforehand.

During the 1956 crisis the Cold War did not always have a negative effect on the superpowers' communications and relations. In the first stage of the crisis--July 26 through October 29--they pursued diverging policies. But after the incident, they joined each other in the UN to oppose Britain and France. In addition, the United States adopted an accommodative posture to the Soviet ultimatum of November 5, 1956, in which the latter state threatened to shoot missiles into London and Paris. The British prime minister called Washington and asked for President Eisenhower's assessment of the Soviet threat. Eisenhower declined to reply. Sherman Adams bluntly told Eden that the President had been aware of the Soviet message and that he did not regard it as directed towards the United States. Adams added that "those who acted independently without the explicit consent of the United States had to face the repercussions of their action."[3] Moreover, Eisenhower refused to set up appointments for Mollet and Eden to meet with him in Washington.

However, it seems that the Hungarian crisis of 1956 had partially overshadowed the U.S. position towards the Suez crisis. The United States wanted to convey a message to the people of Eastern Europe that, in principle, it was against all acts of violent aggression regardless of who the aggressor was. But when the Soviets suggested dispatching joint U.S.-Soviet air and naval forces to Egypt in order to end the aggression, the United States rejected the idea, put its Strategic Air Command on alert and posed the threat of nuclear retaliation if the Soviets attacked London and Paris.[4] Thus, the United States reacted coercively, making it clear that the presence of Soviet troops in the Middle East was against its interests in the region and would not be accepted. Objecting to Soviet military presence constituted a permanent pillar in U.S. policy thereafter. This was a further indication of the effect of the Cold War on the superpowers' management of the region's crises.

On the Soviet side strong statements condemning "imperial aggressors" constituted the substance of Moscow's position until November 5, 1956. The Soviets were very much interested in avoiding nuclear confrontation with the United States. Khrushchev told Syrian President Kwatly, who was visiting Moscow, that the Arabs should not count on anybody but themselves.[5] In response to the Israeli invasion of the Sinai on October 29, the Anglo-French ultimatum of the next day, and the Anglo-French military action against Egypt, the Soviets did not commit themselves to actually defending Egypt. They focused on supportive diplomatic and propaganda moves.

However, after the adoption of the UN General Assembly resolution which imposed a cease-fire on the aggressors and stipulated a complete withdrawal of the invading forces on November 5, the Soviet government sent letters to the governments of the U.K. and France hinting that it considered launching missiles against them. A simultaneous message was sent to Israel threatening outright annihilation. In case of the belligerents' non-compliance with the UN resolution demanding an immediate cease-fire and withdrawal of foreign troops from Egypt, Premier Bulganin proposed a joint U.S.-Soviet armed intervention.[6]

The credibility of Soviet communications of November 5th was found suspect by the United States and also by Egypt. However, such maneuvers affected the perceptions and actions of the British and the French. They probably regarded the Soviet moves as grave, since they added a nuclear dimension which increased the complexity and the gravity of the conflict.[7] The psychological impact of the Soviet nuclear threat posed to London and Paris was mainly due to the United States warning that such a threat had to be interpreted correctly and taken seriously. The U.S. maneuvering which took advantage of the Soviet verbal threat was quite successful in persuading London and Paris to comply with the UN resolutions.

It might be argued that the Soviet involvement in the Hungarian crisis prevented the Soviet Union from taking a truly firm stand against the aggressors in the Suez Crisis of 1956. However, it is evident that the Soviet threat to the aggressors appeared only when it was clear that the U.S. pressure was effective in imposing a cease-fire and withdrawal of foreign troops from Egypt. This was the first case which indicated that the Soviet Union's ability to pursue coercive diplomacy in the management of Middle East crises was quite limited.

The U.S.-Soviet Rivalry and Middle Eastern Regional Crises: 1957-1972

During the late 1950s and early 1960s, the U.S. interests in the Middle East--and particularly its interests in oil--became increasingly salient. During that period the Arab world was becoming more and more radical. Powerful Arab nationalism and emerging socialism within significant Arab countries were the main driving forces of radicalization in the Arab world. The old dream of Arab unity started to materialize, in part by the emergence of the United Arab Republic from 1958 to 1961. The United States felt quite uneasy about the spread and influence of Arab nationalism in significant Arab countries. Socialist practices within such countries also did not please Western powers. Nationalist and socialist regimes, movements, and policies were seen by the United States as sources of potential threat to its interests in the region. The region's oil supplies to the West might have been menaced by such regimes, policies, and movements. The survival of the United States allied regimes in the region was at stake if nationalist and socialist attitudes were to prevail.

This was why the Iraqi "revolution" of 1958 initiated a new stage in the evolution of the Lebanese crisis of 1958. The Iraqi revolution toppled the regime which hosted the "Baghdad Pact." It also caused a substantial political and ideological change in a strategically significant oil producing region. Following the Iraqi revolution, the United States put its bases in the Mediterranean and Europe on alert. Since the Soviets were not the targets, the United States decided to notify the Soviet Union of this decision. This meant that American involvement in the Lebanese crises of 1958 was not seen by Washington as a part of the Cold War competition. Rather, the main objective of the U.S. involvement was to strike against the dream of Arab unity. Some U.S. Marines were placed in Lebanon to serve that purpose. The position of Congress focused on the following points:[8]

a.   The search for legal pretexts to justify intervention.
b.   Careful assessment of Soviet reaction.
c.   No expansion of U.S. involvement elsewhere outside Lebanon, i.e., Jordan.
d.   Rejection of British participation in Lebanon: fear of recalling the Suez experience.
e.   Implicit U.S. assistance to the British presence in Jordan.

The Soviet Union believed that the 1958 crisis was brought on by threatened Western oil interests in the wake of the Iraqi revolution. However, the Soviet perception was that the crisis would cause a politico-psychological, rather than military confrontation. Moscow stuck to its policy of not taking measures which might cause a nuclear confrontation. However, its military maneuvers on its borders with Turkey aimed at creating a psychological effect.[9]

The actual articulation of U.S. interests and objectives became more obvious during the 1967 crisis. The Soviet Union developed strong relations with the Arab world and managed to have a significant foothold in the region in view of the independence of some Arab countries (Algeria), the change of political regimes in some others (Iraq and Yemen), and the resulting adoption of radical policies. Consequently, the Middle East's strategic significance increased considerably for both superpowers in the 1960s. Moreover, economic transactions and arms trade between the superpowers and Arab countries had obviously been on the rise. In its endeavor to achieve global strategic parity with the United States, the Soviet Union paid more attention to regions outside Europe, and particularly to Southeast Asia and the Middle East. The war in Vietnam and the superpowers' involvement in it influenced their rivalry in the Middle East. This is to say that the Cold War became an increasingly large part of the superpowers' policy calculations in the region in the late 1950s and the 1960s.

However, the U.S.-Soviet Cold War in the Middle East was, in the 1960s, restricted by two factors. First, after 1963 (i.e., following the Cuban missile crisis), the superpowers began to strive for an international system whereby they would be committed to crisis prevention, avoiding nuclear confrontation, cooperating in disarmament programs and the establishment of détente.[10] Consequently, both superpowers were keen not to let the 1967 crisis drag them to the brink of nuclear confrontation. The second factor relates to the different types of relationships between each superpower and its regional ally (allies). The U.S.-Israeli relationship did not undergo the ideological and cultural differences and/or strategic sensitivities that the Soviet-Arab relationship suffered in the 1960s. Such differences in the nature of the "patron-client" relationship explain the ambivalence which characterized some Soviet moves during the 1967 crisis.

The most questionable Soviet move during that crisis relates to the Soviet message to Egypt during the first half of May. It warned Egypt that Israel had mobilized an unusual number of troops on the border with Syria in order to strike the latter.[11] Several sources, international and regional, concluded that such information was incorrect.[12]

The important question to raise in this regard is what was the motive behind that Soviet move? There are several explanations in response to this question.[13] Some in the Arab world, including Egyptian President Sadat, tend to believe in a conspiratorial role played by the Soviet Union to drag Nasser into the trap in order to strike the Egyptian army. Others said that Soviet intelligence regarding this piece of information might have counted on ill-informed or distorted sources.[14] A third and most reasonable interpretation is that Moscow wanted to utilize such information to induce Nasser to take a firm deterrent position that could defend and protect the survival of the Syrian "progressive" regime vis-à-vis Israeli threats. This maneuver, along with other factors, convinced

Nasser to move his troops into the Sinai. This step started the second stage of the crisis, i.e., the stage of escalation. For Egypt, such a move was extremely costly.

Nasser employed a series of measures to deter Israel in response to Soviet information, Arab pressure and his miscalculation of both the potential consequences of pursuing an escalatory offensive policy and of the regional balance of power. He requested the withdrawal of the UN Emergency Force (with the exception of the troops serving both in Gaza and in Sharm El Sheikh), and closed the Gulf of Aqaba and Tiran Straits to Israeli ships. These moves followed an explicit mobilization of the Egyptian armed forces and their entrance into the Sinai.[15]

The Soviet Union adopted a cautious position in response to Nasser's request for the United Nations Emergency Force (UNEF) withdrawal and his closure of the Straits of Tiran, on the grounds that these two cards could stimulate unpredictable regional and international reactions. In addition Moscow tried persistently after May 23 (the day of the closing of the Gulf and the Straits) to prevent the eruption of a total war. The Soviet Union put pressure on Egypt to de-escalate the crisis and refrain from initiating the first strike. In persuasive communication with Egypt, the Soviet Union made the argument that the political profit that Egypt had gained up until that point was quite sufficient.

Meanwhile, the Soviet Union tried to influence Israel by calling upon it to perform the utmost self-restraint and to take all measures necessary for avoiding the eruption of armed conflict. Moscow also addressed threatening verbal statements, but such Soviet moves failed to prevent Israel from launching the war since the Soviets at that time had minimal leverage, if any, on Israel.[16]

Moscow utilized the hot-line to communicate with Washington in order to reach an understanding that both superpowers should exert mutual influence on their local allies to prevent them from using force and that Soviet forces would be kept away from the battlefield in case war erupted in the region.[17]

Soviet cautionary behavior from May 23 to June 4, 1967, is understandable. The Soviet Union did not want a war emanating from the 1967 crisis since the outcome of such a war would not be in its favor. A clear Arab victory would have given the Arab countries a much better chance to become more powerful and independent and consequently capable of ridding the region of the influence of intrusive powers, including that of the Soviet Union. A humiliating complete defeat of the Arabs would undermine Soviet interests in the Arab world. While the defeat of the Arab countries in 1967 led to unprecedented direct Soviet military presence in the region (i.e., an increase in Soviet influence in the region during the War of Attrition), such Soviet presence along with the bad memory of the 1967 episode contributed later to Sadat's expulsion of Soviet advisors and experts and to the undermining of Soviet influence in the region. In addition, Moscow rightly perceived that the strategic balance in the Middle East was not to its advantage. This perception exacerbated Soviet fears and concerns regarding the outcome of any confrontation with the United States over the Middle East. Furthermore, it was in the interest of the Soviet Union, as a superpower, to secure free passage for its naval forces through the world's waterways. In other words, the Soviet Union should not have been expected to be pleased with the closing of any waterway and the prevention of ships and other naval vessels from passing through such waterways. The geopolitical position of the Soviet Union and the unusual importance of the Turkish straits connecting the Black Sea with the Mediterranean affect to a great extent the Soviet stance regarding issues of free passage through waterways. Similarly despite close relations with Libya at the time of the U.S.-Libyan confrontation in April 1986, the Soviet Union maintained an ambivalent stand. Moscow kept silent in the dispute between the United States and Libya over the legal position of the Gulf of Sidra. The Soviets could not support the Libyan stance. Such a Soviet position is a further indication of the Soviet policy towards the whole issue of waterways and the Law of the Sea. Finally the Sino-Soviet dispute in the 1960s, the nature of Soviet-Arab relations and Soviet emphasis on domestic developmental affairs were possible factors that limited Soviet support and increased Soviet caution in dealing with the 1967 crisis.

On its part, the United States declared frequently its commitment to preserving peace in the region and called upon the regional parties to practice self-restraint. However, the United States explicitly opposed Egypt's mobilization of troops in Sinai, its request for the withdrawal of UNEF and the closure of the Straits of Tiran. In conjunction with the U.K. and Canada, the United States believed that certain measures had to be taken by the UN, by the Big Four or by a joint naval force to reopen the Straits of Tiran to Israeli navigation. More importantly, the United States had taken a mixture of persuasive, accommodative and its coercive moves in its contacts with Egypt and the Soviet Union. Johnson's letter to Nasser on May 25, 1967, reiterated that avoidance of war was the supreme goal and proposed that U.S. Vice-President Hubert Humphrey visit Egypt and Israel to achieve this goal. On May 26 the State Department asked the Egyptian ambassador to the United States to urge the Egyptian government not to make war, thus forcing the United States to take a militant stand. In the meantime Robert Anderson visited Cairo. During their talks, he and Egyptian leaders agreed to a June 6, 1967, visit to Washington by the Egyptian Vice-President Zakarrya Mohey El-Din. However, Washington moved the Sixth Fleet to the Eastern Mediterranean in a deterrent move directed at the Soviet Union to prevent the latter from intervening.[18] The U.S. actions between May 23 and June 5, 1967 created a remarkably favorable setting for a harshly coercive Israeli response to Nasser's moves of May 14 to May 23, 1967. This manifested itself in an Israeli-initiated air strike on the morning of June 5, 1967.

According to a Congressional report undertaken by a study mission in Greece, the United Arab Republic (UAR), Jordan and Israel in 1967, Nasser's unlimited aspirations posed a threat to his neighbors' security and to international security as well. Nasser's disappearance, concludes the report, would lead to the elimination of the region's problems since other Arab countries were weak.

Thus, the termination of Nasser's influence in the Arab world and the values, attitudes and thoughts that he represented, was the objective of both the United States and Israel. The 1967 crisis was the ideal chance to achieve this goal. Nasser's hasty moves and irrational management of the crisis created that chance. The trap was very carefully and skillfully planned. Egypt was smoothly dragged into the trap; in fact, it placed itself inside it.

When war erupted, the Soviets reassured Washington through the hot-line that they sought no military confrontation with the United States in the Middle East. They also tried to work with the

Americans to reach a cease-fire. Moscow made no threats at that time but only tried to use persuasion to gain cooperation. Johnson sent a hot-line message to Kosygin telling him that the United States received the news of the eruption of war in the Middle East with great concern and that the United States was committed to cooperate with all members of the Security Council to end that war. The Soviet Union introduced a draft resolution calling for an immediate cease-fire and the unconditional withdrawal of Israeli forces. The United States presented a counter draft resolution merely requesting an immediate cease-fire. The Soviet Union dropped its draft and the American one was adopted on June 6. A second version of that draft was adopted on the 7th and accepted first by Jordan, then by Egypt on the 8th and by Syria on the 9th. Dropping of the Soviet draft resolution reflected what was going on the battlefield. But Israel disregarded the Security Council cease-fire resolutions. Consequently, the Soviet Union made strong coercive moves to support its Arab allies and particularly to protect Syria and ensure its survival. On June 9, it convened a summit conference of communist party leaders in Moscow. Communist leaders threatened decisive action and the imposition of sanctions if Israel did not immediately accept the UN cease-fire. The conference pledged immediate military aid to the Arabs and decided to break diplomatic relations with Israel. Kosygin called Johnson on June 10 and warned that if Israel did not immediately accept a cease-fire, the Soviet Union might have to take independent action, including military operations. The U.S. response was twofold: a) informing Israel of the Soviet threat and advising it to take it seriously if Damascus were threatened; and b) moving the Sixth Fleet closer to the Syrian coast. It was a mixed (accommodative and coercive) response.[19]

The 1967 war did not lead to the surrender of the Arabs. However, it put at stake the first and foremost interest of Arab national security, i.e., survival of the Arab nation. Therefore, Egypt decided to reconstruct its armed forces by cooperating closely with the Soviet Union. The Soviets resupplied Egypt with arms and provided it with military advisers and experts for training and maintenance purposes. The United States responded by providing massive supplies of sophisticated arms to Israel in order to ensure its superiority in the Middle East balance of power.

From June 1967 to April 1969, and also during the War of Attrition, efforts were exerted and talks held in order to reach a peaceful settlement of the Arab-Israeli conflict. There were a variety of formulae and modalities for such international efforts in which both superpowers took part and/or had influence: talks among the Big Four, talks between the two superpowers, and indirect negotiations between the Arabs and the Israelis through the UN representative Mr. Gunner Jarring. "The Soviets were pushing for a peace settlement during those years."[20] Meanwhile the U.S. State Department held the view that "the root of U.S. difficulties in the Middle East was the Arab-Israeli conflict over territory. Accordingly, once that was resolved the influence of radical Arabs would dwindle and with it the Soviet role in the Middle East."[21] This view was reflected in a number of specific U.S. proposals for a comprehensive settlement. The superpowers collaborated with each other in different negotiating forums. They tried to reach an agreement or at least an understanding on some points of a settlement and when failing this, narrowed the gap which separated their positions. However, they differed on the form of Arab-Israeli negotiations (direct versus indirect negotiations) and on the scope and time of Israeli withdrawal. But it could be argued that the failure of Middle East peace talks between the superpowers was mainly due to substantive reasons which went beyond their differences over modalities and formalities of negotiations. Such reasons were related to the goals and philosophy that stood behind the moves of each party and also to the nature of each superpower's relations with its regional client and its willingness and ability to pressure such clients in order to reach a settlement.

In 1970, Soviet military assistance to Egypt increased rapidly. Such assistance took the form of expanded arms deliveries and a massive influx of Soviet military advisers and combat personnel as well. The enormous increase in the Soviet military presence in Egypt occurred at a time when Egypt was in dire need of a direct Soviet presence to assist it in defending Egyptian urban centers, vital economic and military facilities, and installations against Israeli air strikes. Soviet military involvement in Egypt could be viewed from two angles. The first is the view that the Soviets were interested in keeping the Middle East as unstable as possible; such instability was to the advantage of the Soviets because of the arms trade revenues and political influence they gained as a result of such a presence. According to this view, the Soviet military presence in the region paid off well.

On the other hand, a massive Soviet presence could be seen as a protective move aimed at defending the survival of a friendly and strategically significant state for the Soviet Union. Before dispatching its massive combat force to Egypt, Moscow contacted Washington in a persuasive move to explain the seriousness of the new military situation resulting from Israeli attacks against Egypt; which was vulnerable to strategic bombing. The Soviet Union made it clear that if the United States could not restrain Israel and confine hostilities to the tactical battlefield, the Soviet Union would have no alternative but to supply new arms to Egypt.[22]

The U.S. administration was divided as to the best response to the Soviet message of January 31, 1970. Secretary of State Henry Kissinger held the militant view and the State Department a more moderate one. Although Nixon leaned toward the Department's views that Israel's policies were the basic cause of the difficulty, he nonetheless ordered the supplying of Israel with sophisticated arms.[23]

To conclude, both superpowers pursued a dual policy towards the War of Attrition: massive arms supplies to regional clients on the one hand and engagement in peace talks on the other. Both tried simultaneously to maintain and develop their influence in the region while reinforcing efforts of building peace and preserving and enhancing international détente. Both tried to keep the balance between two poles that could hardly be merged together, particularly if regional clients were intransigent, if the superpowers' ability to pressure them was limited and/or if willingness to pressure was not reciprocated. The superpowers tried to increase their influence by being committed to massive military assistance and/or presence. Meanwhile they were keen that such commitment would not lead to the destruction of the emerging détente. What was the result of such policies? The result was threefold:

a. Failure of talks aimed at a settlement. This reflected a deviation from the general course of U.S.-Soviet détente;

b. An early beginning of a much more active American role in the Middle East: The Rogers plan and its acceptance by regional powers after suffering from the War of Attrition led to a contradiction: a massive Soviet military presence along with effective U.S. diplomacy;

c. And the reaching of an understanding or agreement regarding the situation in the Middle East within the general content of détente. In their summit conference in Moscow (May, 1972) and in Washington (June, 1973) they tried to impose a state of military relaxation in the Middle East. Paradoxically, regional actors revolted against such a U.S.-Soviet agreement and rejected it through the October 1973 War.

The Middle East is a world of complexities and contradictions. Suffice it to refer in this context to the experience of the War of Attrition.

The October 1973 Crisis

In their endeavor to establish the basis of the first U.S.-Soviet détente in the early 1970s, Nixon and Brezhnev held two summit conferences--in Moscow (May 1972) and in Washington (June 1973). Among other accomplishments, the "Basic Principles Agreement" (BPA) was concluded in the first conference and the "Agreement on Prevention of Nuclear War" (APNW) was concluded in the second. In the first conference of May 1972, the superpowers agreed upon the imposition of a state of military relaxation in the Middle East.

It seems that the problem for Nixon and Kissinger in 1972 was that of maintain the status quo in the Middle East, while at the same time working at completing an agreement on U.S. withdrawal from Vietnam and conducting the political campaign for Nixon's reelection.[24] In the meantime, the difficulties in Soviet-Egyptian relations (namely, the expulsion of thousands of Soviet personnel from Egypt in April) impacted the Soviet position towards the Arab-Israeli conflict through constraints on arms deliveries.

The eruption of the October War brought into question the effectiveness of the BPA and the whole framework of détente. That war was, quite definitely, a successful challenge to the joint will of the superpowers on the part of smaller countries capable of making their own decisions on peace and war.[25] The 1973 war proved that détente could not constitute a U.S.-Soviet condominium capable of ruling the world.[26] According to the rules of détente, the superpowers were to consult with each other if a crisis threatened to erupt. Brezhnev warned Nixon during the June 1973 summit conference of the danger of war. Nixon did not regard the warning as credible. Three days before the war started the Soviets began evacuating Soviet civilian personnel from Egypt and Syria in an indirect warning of the imminent war. A hot debate erupted in the United States over what had been regarded as irresponsible Soviet behavior in taking advantage of détente, which was then suspended in its entirety.[27]

In managing the 1973 crisis, the superpowers resorted to the whole spectrum of crisis-bargaining tactics ranging from persuasion to accommodation, cooperation and/or coercion. At the very beginning of the crisis both made persuasive communications and took accommodative positions. They expressed their interest in maintaining détente, their commitment to avoiding nuclear confrontation, and their willingness to cooperate and to work together in order to prevent their direct involvement in the conflict. Notably, they did not exchange accusations. In addition, they talked about the necessity of mutual self-restraint and the need for pressuring their regional allies to practice similar self-restraint. Nevertheless, before the end of the first week of the crisis both superpowers had taken coercive steps. They differed on their interpretation of the substance of a UN resolution dealing with a cease-fire. While the Soviet Union proposed a cease-fire-in-place, the United States insisted on a cease-fire with a return to the lines of 5 October. On October 8, Kissinger warned that if the Middle East order disintegrated, there would be no U.S.-Soviet détente. On October 12, he made it clear that Soviet intervention (referring to a Soviet alert to some airborne divisions) would be countered with a harsh reaction that might devastate U.S.-Soviet relations. More importantly, coercive military measures had been taken. Massive airlifts transferred very sophisticated weapons, sometimes directly to the battlefield. Also, the fleets of both sides were entering the Mediterranean and moving eastward in a deterrent show of force in order to secure the route of airlifts.[28] By such coercive moves and communications, each superpower was trying to consolidate its influence in the region and to support its ally in order that it could maximize profit or minimize loss. Thus the détente relationship was put in the balance.

When the situation in the battlefield became more complex the superpowers moved from coercion to persuasion, accommodation and even cooperation to produce a cease-fire resolution. Kissinger spent two days in Moscow working with Soviet leaders on a joint draft resolution which was the basis for Security Council Resolution 338 on October 22. It called for a cease-fire, a negotiated settlement of the conflict on the basis of the Security Council Resolution 242 and U.S.-Soviet co-chairmanship of a peace conference to follow the war.

However, because of the continuing violation of the cease-fire on the part of Israel, the Soviet Union increased its naval presence in the Mediterranean and alerted seven airborne divisions. Additionally, it requested a joint U.S.-Soviet force be sent to Egypt to impose the implementation of the Security Council resolution, warning that if they were not sent the Soviet Union would think about appropriate unilateral measures. At that point the relations between the two superpowers reached the brink of a nuclear confrontation as the United States responded by 1) firmly rejecting Soviet ideas on joint forces in the Middle East; 2) raising the status of alert of all U.S. nuclear forces and bases around the world to the Def Con 3; 3) ordering the 82nd Airborne Division to be ready to move any time; and 4) warning Egypt that Soviet troops would be fought against on Egyptian land.[29] The U.S.'s firm, coercive moves made on October 24 could be understood in light of the pivotal role played by Kissinger in making those decisions, especially in light of the limited role played by Nixon who was suffering from the backlash from the Watergate scandal.[30]

However, the superpowers managed to survive the crisis. Egypt withdrew its request for joint U.S.-Soviet troops, the Soviet Union ceased to raise the idea and, instead, was satisfied with sending a few observers to the region to watch the implementation of the

Security Council resolutions. Consequently, the U.S. alert was terminated.

At this point, an important question could be raised: was the U.S.-Soviet détente the factor that enabled them to avoid a nuclear confrontation in October 1973? Some may argue that "despite strains, difficulties and momentary confrontation, détente survived and was used to solve the crisis."[31] Others may see the relationship between the 1973 crisis and U.S.-Soviet détente differently. Alexander George is of the view that "the war and its aftermath strengthened suspicions on each side that the other side defined détente differently and would ignore or misuse détente when the opportunity arose to advance its own interest."[32] It appears that détente could not prevent the eruption of the 1973 war. In addition, for the U.S. and Soviet positions in the 1973 crisis the advancement of national interest in the region outweighed and overwhelmed the development of a common interest in détente.

I believe that it was not détente which made possible the prevention of a nuclear confrontation between the superpowers in 1973. It suffices that we remind ourselves, in this connection, that the superpowers encountered a more severe and much more dangerous crisis in October 1962 (the Cuban Missile Crisis). They managed to get out of that crisis and prevent nuclear confrontation, though their bilateral relationship was not a détente relationship at the time. Rather it was a Cold War relationship. What made it inevitable for the superpowers to avoid nuclear confrontation was not the type of bilateral relationship in terms of détente and/or Cold War. It was always the strategic nuclear balance between them which produced the prudent rule of nuclear-crisis-avoidance.

Mention should be made here that the U.S.-Soviet crisis of October 24-25, 1973, and the way it reached its end, paved the way for the United States to be the sole mediator between Egypt and Israel in the negotiations leading to the disengagement agreements. The Soviet Union was excluded from the whole process. Consequently, its relations with Egypt deteriorated. In compensation, the Soviets pursued daring policies elsewhere in the Third World and especially in Africa (Angola, Ethiopia, etc.) and in Central America. That was the beginning of the end for the fragile and ambivalent U.S.-Soviet détente of the 1970s.

The Aftermath of 1973:
The Lebanese Crisis, 1982-1984

The October 1973 war was the last war between Egypt and Israel. As a part of the peace process between the two countries, Egypt and Israel pursued a preventive diplomacy towards each other, which aimed at avoiding crises and particularly at preventing wars and all kinds of armed conflicts. The United States played a major role in building Egyptian-Israeli peace. In the meantime, the Soviet Union lost its influence in the Middle East as a result of the deterioration of its relations with Egypt. Therefore, after 1973, Moscow focused on its relations with Syria, which became the most important ally for the Soviets in the region. Considerable arms deliveries constituted an important means for consolidating Soviet influence in Syria.

By the mid 1970s, the Lebanese complexities and contradictions erupted in a civil war which has lasted for fifteen years. A large Palestinian presence in Lebanon was an important element of the Lebanese crisis. Coupled with the explicit intervention of Syria from 1976 and of other players afterwards (Israel and Iran) and with the escalation of Lebanese-based Palestinian guerilla operations against Israel, the Lebanese civil war turned into a regional crisis. The Israeli invasion of Lebanon in June 1982 constituted a turning point in the course of that crisis.

Before that date, both superpowers pursued a low-profile policy toward the Lebanese civil war. With the Israeli invasion things changed, particularly from the viewpoint of the United States. Within the context of the "new Cold War," which began with the Soviet invasion of Afghanistan in December 1979 and gained emphasis thanks to Reagan's policies, the Reagan administration viewed "the Soviet threat and U.S. efforts to combat it as the number one priority in the Middle East."[33] Syrian intervention and the Palestinian presence in Lebanon were regarded as extensions of Soviet power in the region. Israel, the strategic ally of the United States in the region, could play an important role in undermining Soviet influence. Therefore, the United States did nothing to prevent the Israeli invasion of Lebanon; and when the invasion occurred, the United States confined itself to calling for a cessation of hostilities.[34] But when the Israeli army laid siege to West Beirut, it became necessary to provide some sort of multinational peace-keeping force to permit the evacuation of Palestinian combatant forces. The United States contributed to that force with a military contingent. The deployment of U.S. forces in Lebanon renewed the U.S.-Soviet rivalry. The Soviet Union replied by resupplying Syria with arms. Before the exodus of the PLO from Beirut in August 1982, the Soviet Union confined itself to ineffectual verbal warnings.[35] However, the U.S. presence in Beirut in support of the Lebanese government was a very costly move: the U.S. Marine headquarters destroyed on October 23, 1983, by a truck bomb, caused considerable harm to U.S. prestige. This blow was a determining factor behind the U.S. decision to pull the forces out of Lebanon and thereby to end its military involvement in the Lebanese crisis.

Conclusion

During the past four decades, the U.S. interests in the region were the following:

1. Preventing the U.S.S.R. from exploiting the process of post-colonial change in the region.
2. Protecting the access of NATO countries and Japan to the region's oil and ensuring the interests of the U.S. business community in the region, in particular the oil industry.
3. Guaranteeing the existence, security and superiority of Israel as a Middle Eastern state.

The importance accorded to each of these interests varied from one crisis to another due to the variables mentioned earlier. For instance, the protection of oil supplies is becoming, at present, the first and foremost U.S. interest in the region as a result of the recent Gulf Crisis and the dramatic change in the general relationship between the United States and the U.S.S.R. Also, the ideological and strategic view of the Reagan administration caused it to emphasize the prevention of Soviet influence in the Middle East. Consequently, protection of Israel's security and superiority was not merely a reflection of a moral commitment or Congressional pressure. Rather, it had become a part of the strategic thinking of the Reagan administration. And since Israel was viewed as a strategic ally for the United States in its combat against the Soviet threat in the Middle East, the two interests (the ousting of Soviet influence and maintaining Israel's security) were considered closely interrelated.

The ideological orientation (the Cold War belief system) together with the U.S.-Israeli strategic alliance formed in 1981, led the Reagan administration to a policy of intervention in the Lebanese crisis from 1982 to 1984, ending a period of non-involvement (1975-82).

Due to geographic proximity, the region has always been of vital interest to the Soviet Union. As a result of the decolonization process in the Middle East, the superpowers found themselves face to face in a clash of interests. In the 1950s the United States wanted to form a defense system in the region to encircle the Soviet Union which, thanks to policies of nationalistic Arab regimes, infiltrated the Middle East in order to counter the U.S. encirclement plan. Consequently, the Soviet Union pursued a policy of defending the survival of its regional allies and friends, especially if such survival was seriously threatened during a particular crisis.

However, both superpowers practiced mutual self-restraint to prevent Arab-Israeli crises from driving them into direct confrontation. This has been the basic rule of prudence in U.S.-Soviet management of Middle Eastern crises. The Soviets were aware that the strategic balance in the Middle East favored the United States. Moreover, while U.S. relations with Israel were always, in a sense, an issue of domestic politics, the Soviets' relations with the Arab world were always merely a foreign policy issue subject to substantial ideological, social and political differences. This explains Soviet inaction and/or cautious action during some crises in the Middle East. When Kissinger succeeded in excluding the U.S.S.R. from the conflict settlement process after 1973, Moscow tended to adopt an offensive approach in conflict management everywhere (Angola, Ogaden, Central America) except in the Middle

East. Interestingly, the U.S.-Soviet conflict over Angola, Ethiopia and Afghanistan limited the possibility of their collaboration in the Middle East.

Outside the Arab-Israeli area, the U.S.S.R. seems to understand the intensity of American interest the Middle East, particularly its concern with Persian Gulf Oil. This explains the Soviet cooperation or collaboration with the United States endeavors to utilize UN Security Council resolutions and a worldwide consensus and coalition in managing the Gulf crisis.

Cautious Soviet action in treating the region's crises since 1985 (the U.S.-Libyan crisis in 1986, frequent U.S.-PLO crises, U.S.-Iraqi crises of 1990 over Iraqi armament programs, and finally the most dangerous recent crisis-the Gulf War) should be analyzed in light of the changing international order, Gorbachev's policy of disentangling the U.S.S.R. from strategic conflicts and crises of the Third World, and his policy of moving from competitive to cooperative détente with the United States. Add to this Soviet preoccupation with internal reform.

Lessons drawn from past crisis management experiences in the Middle East can be summarized as the following:

1.   Focusing on bilateral relations led the superpowers to misunderstand local political and strategic relations and even sometimes to ignore them. In this connection, the eruption of the October 1973 war proved the failure of superpower détente, as well as the goal of crisis-avoidance, due to the regional realities at the time. Also, the United States intervened in Lebanon in 1983-84 to protect a government which represented only one party to the local conflict.

2.   The superpowers have been able to exercise mutual restraint in order to prevent Middle East crises from dragging them into direct nuclear confrontation. This experience must be extended to future crisis management.

3.   However, the two superpowers have successfully collaborated and/or cooperated with each other to limit the duration and the scope of Middle East crises and wars i.e., the 1956 Suez Crisis, the October War of 1973, the 1967

War. It is in the interest of the region that such cooperation should continue in future crisis management.

4. Finally, the historical experience of crisis and conflict management in the Middle East illustrates the ineffectiveness of a regulatory structure on the global level and the absence of such a structure on the regional level.

Theoretically, there could be three mechanisms for regulating U.S.-Soviet competition and/or cooperation in conducting the region's crises and conflicts.[36] The first is a general, comprehensive bilateral agreement to prevent future military interventions in such crises. Developments in the Gulf War indicate, however, that such a regulatory mechanism is impractical. The second option is to reach *ad hoc* agreements or understandings on a case-by-case basis, concerning the definition of the interests at stake in every case and how each case should be best treated by the superpowers. Such understanding could be reached through timely and extensive diplomatic exchanges. This course could lead to practical solutions in some cases; yet, there is nothing to ensure its success every time. The third and most durable and useful mechanism is the revitalization and activation of the seventh chapter of the UN Charter and the role of the Security Council as a means of building global consensus on the norms and values designed for the peaceful, durable and just settlement of international conflicts and crises. In the recent Gulf Crisis, the moment of promise and hope was embodied in the functioning of the seventh chapter of the UN Charter, the first time this has happened since the 1950-53 Korean War. It is imperative that the two superpowers reach an agreement always to defer to the UN Security Council, whatever crises emerge. This would be the best regulatory mechanism for crisis management in the Middle East. But the important question is, would the superpowers be as enthusiastic in utilizing the UN Security Council in treating the Arab-Israeli conflict and its crises as they were with regard to the Gulf Crisis?

Notes

1. Abba Eban, *An Autobiography* (New York: Random House, 1977), p. 88, 119-122, 126.

2. Mousa Dib, *The Arab Bloc in the United Nations* (Amsterdam: N.P., 1950) pp. 41-42; see also Mark V. Kauppi, *The Soviet Union and the Middle East in the 1980's* (London: N.P., 1983), pp. 50-52.

3. Mohammed Hassanein Heikal, *Files of Suez* (Cairo: Al-Ahram Center for Publishing and Interpretation, 1986), p. 555. (Arabic)

4. Oles M. Smolansky, *The Soviet Union and the Arab East Under Khrushchev* (New York: Bucknell University Press, 1974), p. 40. See also Joseph Nogee and Robert H. Donaldson, *Soviet Foreign Policy Since World War II* (New York: Pergamon Press, 1984) p. 21.

5. Heikal, *Files*, pp. 553-5.

6. *Ibid.*

7. Smolansky, pp. 45-7; Nogee and Donaldson, pp. 121; and Heikal, *Files*, pp. 544.

8. Mohammed Hassanein Heikal, *Years of Upheaval* (Cairo: Al-Ahram center for Publishing and Interpretation, 1988), pp. 358-62.

9. Heikal, *Years*, pp. 368-71.

10. Robert O. Mathews, Arthur G. Rubinoff and Janice Gross Stein, *International Conflict and Conflict Management: Readings in World Politics* (Scarborough, Ontario: Prentice Hall of Canada, 1984), pp. 389-390.

11. Anwar Sadat, *Soul Searching* (Cairo: Modern Egyptian Office, 1978), p. 186 (Arabic); *Abd-El Nasser Documents: Speeches, Talks and Statements, January 1967--December 1968* (Cairo: Al-Ahram Center for Political and Strategic Studies, 1973), p. 226 (Arabic); and *Al-Ahram*, May 25, 1967.

12. Amin Houwaid, *Reflections on the Reasons for the 1967 Setback and on the War of Attrition* (Beirut: Vanguard House, 1975), p. 20 (Arabic); El-Sayed Amin Shalaby, "U Thant Talks about the Beginning of the 1967 War," *Al-Siyassa Al-Dawliya* 62, October p. 192 (Arabic); *Al-Akhbar*, June 13, 1967; and Eban p. 319.

134

13. Mostafa-Elwi Saif, "Egypt's International Behavior During the May-June 1967 Crisis," (Ph.D Dissertation presented to the Department of Political Science, Cairo University, 1981), pp. 191-196.

14. Majdiya Khaddour, *The Knot of the Arab-Israeli Conflict* (Beirut: United Publishing House, 1972), p. 103. (Arabic)

15. Saif, "Egypt's International Behavior," pp. 105-119.

16. Saif, "Egypt's International Behavior," p. 198.

17. *Ibid.*

18. Winston Burdett, *Encounter with the Middle East: An Intimate Report on What Lies Behind the Arab-Israeli Conflict* (London: Andre Deutsch, 1970), p. 275; Peters Mangold, *Superpower Intervention in the Middle East* (London: Croom Helm, 1978), pp. 165-6; Eban, pp. 346-7, 357-9.

19. Gregory Treverton, ed., *Crisis Management and the Superpowers in the Middle East* (London: IISS, 1981), pp. 53-4; Brigadier General Sa'ad-El-Dun Al Shathly, *Arab Military Options* (Algiers: National Book Foundation, 1984), p. 187 (Arabic); and Mohammed Hassanein Heikal, "The Explosion," *Al-Ahram*, June 25, 27, 30, 1990. (Arabic)

20. Alexander L. George, *Managing the U.S.-Soviet Rivalry: Problems of Crisis Prevention* (Boulder, CO: Westview Press, 1983), p. 74.

21. Henry Kissinger, *White House Years* (Boston: Little, Brown and Co., 1979), p. 558.

22. Treverton, *Crisis Management*, p. 60.

23. Kissinger, *White House Years*, pp. 563-4.

24. Alexander L. George and Philip J. Farley, eds., *U.S.-Soviet Security Cooperation: Achievements, Failures, Lessons* (New York: Oxford University Press, 1988), p. 562.

25. Treverton, *Crisis Management*, p. 7.

26. Mathews, *et al.*, pp. 389-91.

27. George, *Managing the U.S.-Soviet Rivalry*, pp. 145-8.

28. Kissinger, *White House Years*.

29. Kissinger, *White House Years*, pp. 548-9.

30. Kissinger, *White House Years*, pp. 584-7; Mostafa Elwi-Saif, *The U.S.-Soviet Crisis During the October 1973 War* 10, January (Beirut: Arab Strategic Thought, 1984), pp. 45-60. (Arabic)

31. Treverton, *Crisis Management*, p. 10.

32. George, *Managing the U.S.-Soviet Rivalry*, p. 151.

33. Juliana S. Plack, *The Reagan Administration and the Palestinian Question: The First Thousand Days* (Washington: Institute for Palestine Studies, 1984), p. 115.

34. Plack, *The Reagan Administration*, p. 53.

35. Paul Marntz and Blima S. Strinburg, eds., *Superpower Involvement in the Middle East* (Boulder, CO: Westview Press, 1985), p. 95.

36. George and Farley, pp. 594-7.

7 The Crisis Experience in the Middle East: Conflict Management Triumphant

Before I address the issue of the crisis experience, I propose the following definition of the term "crisis," first published by Charles F. Hermann:

> Crisis is a situation shaking the system or part of it, a subsystem, like an alliance or an individual player. More accurately, crisis is a situation bringing about a swift or most sudden change in one of the basic variables in the system or several of them.[1]

However, I would propose the following amendment: "Crisis is the situation brought about by a swift or sudden change in one of the variables, i.e., shaking the system."

A crisis situation, from the point of view of the superpowers, threatens one or more of their core interests in the area. What are these interests?

Here a word of caution is in order. The interests which have long been associated with Soviet-American competition in the Middle East will not necessarily remain the same after the sea of changes that is taking place in U.S.-Soviet relations. Today this relationship is best exemplified by the following joint U.S.-Soviet statement:

> . . . the United States and the Soviet Union believe that now it is essential that the Security Council resolutions be fully and immediately implemented. By its action Iraq has

shown its contempt for the most fundamental principles of the United Nations charter and international laws.[2]

But crisis experience dates back to a time period during which the U.S.-Soviet relationship was one of global confrontation. Then, in any area in which the spheres of influence were not clearly marked, it was an accepted custom for a superpower to "grab" whatever, whenever it could.

The superpower interests were strategic (that is, politico-military), economic and domestic. The Middle East, as a link among Europe, Asia and Africa, and as a nexus of communications, was important to both superpowers. The proximity of the Soviet Union from its southern borders to the Middle East, and therefore its interest in the area, made it mandatory for the United States to act in the region in order to contain the Soviet Union. The presence of U.S. missile-carrying submarines and of the Sixth Fleet as part of its global strategic effort in the Mediterranean compelled the Soviet Union to maintain a naval force and air elements permanently in and around these waters, and to secure naval facilities in Egypt and afterwards in Syria for the maintenance of their forces.

As to economic interests, oil was and still is of first and foremost importance to the United States as evidenced during the 1973 and 1979 oil shocks. At present more than 50% of the oil imported to the United States comes from the Middle East. In 1988, oil from the Middle East constituted 54% of all oil imported to the United States that year.[3] The dependence of Western Europe and Japan on imported oil is even greater. The Soviet Union's interest in Middle Eastern oil was indirect.

It presents a potential opportunity to interfere or to gain control over energy supplies. . . . Self-sufficiency in energy is a prime Soviet interest and, unless prices fall sharply, the Soviet Union will hesitate to depend on outside sources.[4]

Although the main instrument of the superpowers' policy in the Middle East was arms supply, until recently the Soviet Union had the upper hand in this market. Between 1977 and 1987 the Soviets supplied arms to the Middle East to the tune of 55.8 billion dollars. During the same period the United States supplied arms to the tune of 34 billion dollars.[5]

As to the domestic interests, Soviet concerns are growing about the possibility that Islamic fundamentalism will have nefarious across-the-border influence on the considerable Muslim communities in the Central Asian republics. On the American side, there is the politically influential Jewish community with its lobby, as well as an emerging Arab-American lobby. The domestic interests, though not core interests, will remain important to both sides in the foreseeable future.

The superpowers' interests clashed in every aspect of the global nuclear confrontation, particularly on the high seas. It is in the interest of the United States to have free access to the seas for its ships and submarines, which carry nuclear warheads in the Mediterranean, Red Sea and Indian Ocean. In contrast, it was in the Soviet interest to be in a position to hinder the U.S. Navy's freedom of action in case of emergency in those waters.

The protection of each side's interests demanded winning over as many of the client states in the area as possible. This meant a clash of interests, but not necessarily crisis or confrontation, because the client's posture dictated by self-interest as perceived by that nation's leadership limited the superpowers' freedom of action.

Were all the interests equal in their weight of importance? How are they going to be affected by the change in the Soviet-American relationship? We must not forget that the overall strategic interest on both sides was to avoid a nuclear confrontation. This might still remain an "umbrella interest" in the future, at least for the period during which the new global strategic structure crystallizes. In the past, the interests linked to global confrontation were the dominant ones and hence, led to the necessity to avoid confrontation.

During the coming decade or so, strategic interests linked to the nuclear aspects of naval power in the area will play a dominant role for both sides, as long as an understanding on this issue has not been reached. For the Soviet Union, the problem of its "southern borders' proximity" to the region was and remains a core interest.

Similarly, free access to Middle Eastern oil was and will remain a core interest for the United States for the foreseeable future.

The arms trade was a very important foreign policy instrument to further each superpower's interests and could therefore be called a "core issue" for both sides. Due to the present tensions in the Middle East, and given the superpowers' interests, one has to assume that arms supply will continue for the foreseeable future. From the Soviet perspective, economic considerations may play a decisive role. The Middle East would constitute a ready market for at least part of the large quantities of conventional weaponry that must be removed from the Warsaw Pact regions under the CSCE Agreement signed in 1990. This region is attractive for arms sales because states in the area are able to pay with hard currency, of which the Soviet Union has great need.

Reading the above, one might exclaim, "*Plus ca change, plus c'est la meme chose,*" were it not for the growing U.S.-Soviet understanding and cooperation as evinced by the above mentioned joint statement regarding Iraq. Real understanding and whole-hearted cooperation can go a long way in helping to solve regional problems and preventing regional crises. Crises can still erupt, about which neither of the superpowers has any foreknowledge, and either one can be presented with a *fait accompli*. Then, what is left is crisis management and resolution, which should be easier now than in the past, from the point of view of superpower cooperation.

As to the problem of regional conflict resolution, it might be some time before that degree of *entente cordiale* between the Soviet Union and the United States will be reached, when the superpowers achieve the state that will permit the collective tackling of the problems that is needed to achieve conflict resolution.

There are numerous variables that can affect a situation and bring about a crisis. As evidenced by Saddam's Iraq in 1990, the character of a state's leader can be a variable. The change in regime of a client state, bringing with it a change in the patron, as in 1958 Iraq, or a change in the patron due to a change in the client state's leadership--as with Sadat in Egypt--are additional examples of such crisis-inducing situations.

Crises have also been precipitated by a change in the other side's posture, as when one side takes an initiative to bring about a change in the situation affecting its rival's client/clients, e.g., the Soviet Union in 1967. The introduction of a new weapons systems by one patron affecting a client state of the opposing patron and the regional balance of power, e.g., surface-to-surface missiles (China to Saudi Arabia) is an example of an arms-related crisis situation.

As a client state, 1958 Lebanon, plagued by internal unrest, fanned from outside and threatening the state's regime created a crisis situation. The concentrating of military forces on a neighbor's border, e.g., Sinai 1967; the attack by one patron's client state on the other patron's client state is a clear example of a crisis situation, e.g., Syria--Jordan in September 1970, and Egypt and Syria--Israel in October 1973; or the initiating of a war by a client state with or without foreknowledge of the patron, e.g., Lebanon 1982, each exemplify a different type of crisis-inducing situation.

Each of these variables has brought about a crisis in which one or the other superpower's interest was threatened. It was not the variable that affected the superpower's perception of core and secondary interests in the region but their perception of basic interests in the region, such as oil for the United States, and their concept of the global strategic relationship. Thus, avoiding a confrontation was quickly perceived as a core interest already in 1956 and has been upheld ever since.

Looking at the various crises the Middle East has endured during the last 45 years, and the conflicts that have beset and continue to beset the region, one must conclude that the superpowers have been successful in crisis management and resolution. Not one of the various crises--Suez, 1956; Lebanon, 1958; The Six-Day War in 1967; the War of Attrition between Egypt and Israel, 1968-1970; Jordan-Syria, September 1970; The Yom Kippur War, 1973; Lebanon, 1982--brought about a superpower confrontation. Most were resolved fairly quickly, except the War of Attrition, which was a limited, stationary war, and the Lebanon 1982 War which was actually a war within a war, with superpower (U.S. only in this case) involvement being limited in volume and time.

As the crisis involves above all the superpowers' clients, the superpowers' task has been to restrain those clients. Given the nature of superpower competition in the area, this is not a black and white issue; and it does take time for each superpower to reach a point at which there is, on the one hand, fruitful cooperation with the other superpower and, on the other hand, enough inducement to the client to make it worthwhile for him to be restrained by his patron. During this time the client does his best, with superpower blessings, to improve his position militarily for the negotiating period which is to follow, while the patron shies away from confrontation.

Sometimes, as happened in 1973, the superpowers must undergo a "confrontational game" to bolster their negotiating positions, or to make it clear to the other side where each one really stands.

Only once did one of the superpowers "ignite the fuse," i.e., take steps that eventually led to war. It was in 1967, at the height of global confrontation, that it seems the Soviets were ready to take certain risks while the United States was already heavily involved in Vietnam.

My own firsthand knowledge and recent contacts with Soviet academics lead me to believe that the Soviets had two objectives in mind: one--to safeguard the strongly pro-Soviet Syrian Ba'athist regime; and two--to cut down Israel to 1947 partition borders size. The instrument for this exercise was to be Nasserist Egypt--armed, equipped, and prepared by its Soviet patron. This enabled the client to shield the patron from superpower confrontation. But the Soviets lost control of Nasser, and the rest is history. The lessons were well absorbed, and conclusions duly applied.

After the Six Day War in 1967, the Soviet Union broke off diplomatic relations with Israel as a punishment, and rebuilt and retrained the Egyptian and Syrian armies. From 1968, it trained the Egyptian army thoroughly and methodically for the crossing of the Suez Canal. It did this in order to strengthen the patron-client relationship and to ensure their clients' improved battle worthiness. At the same time the Soviets coached the Egyptian army in waging the War of Attrition in order to harass and weaken Israel, the United States' client and Egypt's enemy.

The Soviets exerted themselves to walk the narrow path between restraining their Egyptian client by trying not to satisfy his demands for additional armaments fully while at the same time trying to convince him not to risk war. No doubt the fact that this was the period of détente and the first U.S.-Soviet summit meetings had something more to do with the matter. There is enough evidence to show that Syria and Egypt postponed their plans for war against Israel from April-May 1973 to October 1973, at the request of the Soviets, since they were afraid that the war might upset the summit meeting that was scheduled to take place in Washington in June 1973. The Soviets promised the two Arab states to bring up the situation in the Middle East for "serious discussion" at the summit meeting, a promise which they did not keep. The Soviet dilly-dallying between the two courses--retaining its client Egypt by arming it, and at the same time trying to keep it from going to war--resulted in the Soviet experts' expulsion from Egypt, and in Egypt and Syria going to war against Israel on October 6, 1973. This act not only showed Soviet duplicity, but also the difficulty involved in maintaining a profitable patron-client relationship, while at the same time maintaining a détente relationship with the other person.

In settling the 1968-1970 War of Attrition between Egypt and Israel, the United States laid the groundwork for the peace effort that came after another war. During the War of Attrition, the crisis was managed more by what was going on the ground, than by superpower cooperation, so the role of confrontation avoidance was scrupulously observed. Each patron supported its client to the best of its ability. The Soviets proposed the concept of a War of Attrition, explained it, and trained the Egyptians to carry it out. The United States helped the Israelis defeat Egyptian artillery by using air power, and also supplied them with the necessary amount of aerial bombs. In the end, the Soviets were becoming dangerously involved in Egypt's air defense and both clients were suffering from battle fatigue. The downing of four Soviet planes by the Israelis made the danger palpable. The arrival of a wave of SAM batteries from the Soviet Union after the ceasefire was already in force was viewed as a Soviet breach of faith by the United States. Israel was awarded a $600 million dollar arms deal, the first of that volume. Although this was the time détente between the superpowers came into force, and relations between the two nations improved, President Nixon strongly supported Israel in its status quo position, as long as on the Arab side there was no agreement to Kissinger's "step-by-step" peace policy.

The experience gained by the Soviets in 1967 was applied during the war in 1973, when the need to avoid confrontation with the

United States was uppermost in their minds, according to the testimony of a Soviet senior official.[6] Despite their acrimonious exchanges and their military posturing exercises, in which each suspected that the other was bluffing, both patrons tried hard to resolve the crisis and to manage it so as to avoid a confrontation. Nixon viewed the crisis as the most serious international one since the Cuban Missile Crisis. But according to Kissinger, détente played an important role in settling the crisis quickly and in restoring relations between the superpowers.

As a result of the 1973 war, the United States saw a chance for moving toward peace. It felt that it should move forward on its own, i.e., as much as possible without the Soviet Union. Eventually an Israeli-Egyptian peace treaty was signed in March 1979 in Washington D.C. through the good offices and strenuous efforts of President Jimmy Carter. The only case so far in the Middle East in which successful crisis management and resolution ultimately led to conflict resolution. This process took six years--from 1973-1979.

All in all, crisis management and resolution by the superpowers has been successful. It seems the main reason for this success is derived from the will common to both patrons to avoid confrontation over the issue at hand. "Pre-resolution maneuvering/posturing," whether directly or indirectly through the client, was acceptable to both; but they always stopped short of confrontation.

In other words, when the tension between the requirements for prudent crisis management and for effective coercive diplomacy was resolved by giving priority to the requirements of crisis management, a "window of opportunity" was opened toward terminating the crisis. With the collaborative aspects of the bargaining process becoming dominant, the stage was set for a compromise settlement. This denotes a basic duality--a continued shift in emphasis and dominance between the combatants, and a concurrent wish unilaterally to "defect" by aiding their respective clients.

The picture was very different with regard to conflict resolution. Aside from the Egypt-Israel conflict, the superpowers have so far not succeeded in resolving any conflict, be it an Arab-Israeli conflict (with the Palestinians, Syrians, Lebanese and other Arab countries), or the Iraq-Iran conflict. The Iran-Iraq crisis was resolved by both superpowers and the Western European states by supporting Iraq or "tilting" toward it and thus endowing it with a military superiority, which has came back to haunt them in the Gulf crisis.

What is the reason for superpower failure in conflict resolution in the Middle East? The answer can be found in the patron-client relationship. In conflict management and resolution the clients can show much more independence while the patrons, because of domestic and superpower interests, are loath to exert the kind of pressure necessary to get the clients to be flexible enough to bring about a resolution.

Only if one superpower has enough influence over both clients can conflict resolution be reached, as occurred in the Egypt-Israel case. If this is not the case, then only sincere and full cooperation between the superpowers can achieve the same result.

Has this stage been reached? Have *perestroika* and *glasnost* also taken over the Soviet policy in the Middle East? It seems that these reforms have only partially affected Soviet policy, not enough to allow that degree of cooperation with the United States that can bring about the conditions necessary for further conflict resolution. Soviet concern for their clients and dependence on them is too strong a constraint to permit them to exact the necessary pressure to make their clients more flexible. In addition, the Soviets have only limited contact with Israel, whereas the United States has full contact with both sides.

Conflict resolution can also fail if not all the main actors participate, as was the case in Lebanon in 1983. The agreement reached between Israel and Lebanon could not hold water because Syria was not a party to it. The same might happen to a future Israeli-Palestinian agreement and for the same reason, if Syria is left out of the negotiating process, for example.

What lessons can be drawn from the crisis experience? To my mind, the main lesson is that crisis prevention and conflict resolution are much more important than crisis management and crisis resolution. With the uninterrupted and ever-escalating arms race, crises have become more and more dangerous to the people living in the Middle East. Since the Middle East will remain the most important source for all oil in the near future, if not the foreseeable one, these crises will still be a source of concern to the big powers (the United States, the Soviet Union, Western Europe and Japan).

The best way for achieving crisis prevention is not dramatic last-minute cliffhanging heroics, but early, as early as humanly possible, conflict resolution efforts. The time has arrived in which such efforts are feasible, as we talk about a post-Cold War world. In undertaking such efforts, each superpower will know relatively quickly whether or not the other patron has really changed and put Cold War psychology, behavior and tactics behind him, and thus be able to evaluate also what the chances are for conflict resolution. It is difficult to imagine the clients withstanding the combined weight of both superpowers. With U.S. success in the Gulf War the stage has been set for serious Middle East conflict resolution with good chances for success. However, dangers continue to lurk. This means that close cooperation (including intelligence) between the Soviet Union and the United States will be necessary in order to detect these dangers early on and then take the steps necessary to quell them quickly and effectively. This presupposes a U.S.-Soviet relationship free of the shackles of Cold War heritage. Isn't this what one hopes for?

Finally, there is the question of the format of superpower cooperation. Will it be on a bilateral basis, but with a fully cooperative spirit, or will it be within a UN framework which, as recent events have shown, appears to be a format preferred by the Soviets? Whichever it will be, cooperation between the United States and the Soviet Union can and must do away with crises in the Middle East and bring peace to the much tormented region. Inevitably, one cannot be oblivious to what is happening inside the Soviet Union. Internal events might neutralize the Soviet role in world affairs for at least some time. The burden will then fall on U.S. shoulders which, hopefully, will be strong enough to carry it.

Notes

1. Eytan Gilboa, ed., *International Relations--Readers*, University Library (Tel Aviv: *Am Oved*, 1979).

2. Official Text, USIA, August 6, 1990.

3. Israel Petroleum Institute Information Bulletin, April 4, 1989, p. 71. (Hebrew)

4. Gur Ofer and Joseph Pelzman, "Soviet Economic Interests in the Middle East," in Steven L. Spiegel, Mark A. Heller and Jacob Goldberg, eds., *The Soviet-American Competition in the Middle East* (Lexington, MA: D.C. Heath and Co., 1988), p.223.

5. ACDA report, U.S. State Department, 1988, p. 118.

6. Interview with a senior official from the Soviet Foreign Ministry in August 1990.

Steven L. Spiegel

8   Arab-Israeli Crises, 1945–1990:
The Soviet-American Dimension

This chapter examines the nature of Soviet-American crises in the Arab-Israeli context. I begin by exploring the nature of the bipolar system between 1945 and 1990 and the role played by the global conflict between the two superpowers in Arab-Israeli crises during this period, then turn to an examination of the emerging new international system and explore the role that crises are likely to play in that context, and conclude with an analysis of the consequences of the new order for Soviet-American relations and the potential for Soviet-American cooperation in this new era.

Bipolarity and the Middle East, 1945-1990

As the bipolar system evolved in the post-1945 period, Soviet-American competition gradually became more diffuse. The initial areas of competition were Europe and the Far East. Early post-war crises also included the Middle Eastern northern tier, Iran and Turkey. The Arab-Israeli scene was not yet part of the superpower confrontation. Thus, in the first Arab-Israeli war in 1948, both the Soviets and Americans supported Israel (with the Soviets even supplying critical arms through Czechoslovakia). Only in 1955, with the Kremlin's sale of arms to Egypt and Syria, did the Soviet-American competition break through to the Arab arena, necessarily engaging Israel in the process.

The author wishes to thank David J. Pervin, Greg Zipes, and Anissa Karney for their assistance with the preparation of this chapter.

Although shocking to Western statesmen at the time, this development was not surprising because the essence of bipolarity was the extension of the competition between the two superpowers to the entire globe. Any political-military problem worldwide could thereby potentially become a source of tension in Soviet-American relations. The engagement of one superpower in regional conflicts would necessarily raise the suspicion of its adversary. Victory or defeat for local clients could potentially affect the credibility, interests, and fortunes of both the United States and the U.S.S.R., especially since both saw the conflict as zero-sum. The net impact of this extension of the Soviet-American competition, therefore, was to make local crises, and even wars, both more likely and more dangerous. These conditions were especially perilous in the volatile Middle East, where violence, factionalism, and bitter disputes have dominated regional politics.

During the bipolar period in this area, at times one or both superpowers worked to ameliorate local crises. In other cases, however, the impact of the United States and/or the U.S.S.R. was to contribute to the outbreak of hostilities. Once war broke out, the fear of a client's loss, and therefore of the sacrifice of vital interests, meant there was a risk of escalation to the superpower level as well. But the escalatory process was delicate. Crises and conflicts were over vital interests to clients--even over survival. To the superpowers, regional interests were often peripheral, or at least of a lower order of magnitude. Both sought to avoid any possibility of nuclear war. The bipolar competition demanded that statesmen decide how to win without risking too much and determine when it was better to lose than to challenge their adversary further.

The net impact of this process was that not every crisis led to war. In all situations both local parties and superpower statesmen had to make decisions about how to react to ongoing events. It is the central thesis of this chapter that superpower actions contributed to the likelihood that war would break out. In all cases where a crisis deteriorated into open warfare, one or both superpowers in some manner encouraged bellicose behavior and one or both provided confused signals which broke down restraints and deterrence among the regional clients. As the weaker party and the challenger, Moscow played the role of instigator more often.

On the other hand, every crisis did not result in war. I therefore compare war-producing crises to crises resolved short of open hostilities. What was different about the cases where battles did not result? This study suggests that war was less likely when neither superpower encouraged conflict or when the signals against war were so clear on the part of at least one superpower that deterrence was reinforced and open hostilities were averted. With the end of the Cold War, one can predict that Arab-Israeli wars should be less frequent. Therefore, past crises which did not result in combat provide better lessons for the future of conflict management than the better-known crises that deteriorated into full-scale warfare.

I explore this process by comparing five wars: the Suez Crisis of 1956, the Six Day War of 1967, the War of Attrition 1969-1970, the October War of 1973, and the Israeli invasion of Lebanon in 1982. In each of these crises, the superpowers played a role in the origins, the shape of the war as it evolved, and in the termination of the conflict.

Five Wars

The sale of arms to Egypt by the Soviet Union in September 1955--exacerbating deteriorating Egyptian-Israeli relations and alarming both Israel and the United States, for different reasons-- can be seen as the origin of the Suez Crisis. The subsequent sale of arms in June 1956 added further fuel to the fire. The Soviet Union did not play a major role thereafter until near the conclusion of the war, although it continued to make statements and to take diplomatic positions sympathetic to the Egyptian case. It both intensified arms shipments prior to the war and sent larger numbers of diplomats and technicians to Egypt as a show of support.[1]

American policy before the crisis was clumsy and inconsistent, but clear and forthright once it began. In late 1955 Washington attempted to lure the Egyptians back to the Western camp by offering to help construct the Aswan Dam. The Eisenhower administration's decision to renege on the deal helped to precipitate the immediate crisis when Nasser retaliated by nationalizing the Suez Canal Company. By this time the United States had little leverage over either Egypt (which had been alienated by Washington's negative decisions towards its interests) or Israel (which the Eisenhower administration carefully kept at arms length). The American role during the summer and fall of 1956 was to restrain its allies (Britain and France) in the unsuccessful attempt to prevent the outbreak of hostilities. During the war, American pressure on Britain and France contributed to the conflict's resolution. Meanwhile, Israel's attack in the Sinai was facilitated by substantial prior Franco-British military and political support; indeed, coordination.

The Soviet Union, preoccupied with Hungary and limited in military instruments, made specific and dramatic threats against Britain, France, and Israel on November 5, late in the war, after the outcome of hostilities had been decided. The threats were used to gain favor with the Arab states; they did not represent a serious military alternative. Khrushchev's offer to act jointly with the United States was summarily rejected by the Eisenhower administration, which, according to the President's memoirs, did not take Moscow's threats seriously. However, his administration appears to have used Soviet statements as a subtle form of further pressure on London, Paris, and Jerusalem.[2]

The contour of the crisis in 1967 was very different. The Soviet Union, apparently concerned by the growing virulence of the competition among its Arab clients, played a central role in the origin of the tensions by spreading false rumors about an imminent Israeli attack on Syria. At least initially, Nasser appears to have believed the reports. At any rate, he thought he could transform his declining fortunes by ousting the UN peacekeeping force from the Sinai and rallying the feuding Arab states around his leadership. Because he was already receiving Soviet support, he anticipated the strong backing of the Kremlin in this particular situation as well. In the lead-up to war and during the hostilities, the Soviets assumed a staunchly pro-Arab stance at the United Nations. As the crisis escalated in May, their private messages to Cairo mixed strong backing with cautionary notes, but in the euphoria of Egypt's early political victories, the words of encouragement drowned out any comments from Moscow suggesting restraint by Nasser.[3]

During the war, the Soviets exchanged hot line communications with the White House, thereby expressing a mutual interest in limiting superpower involvement. Only after it was clear that their clients had been soundly defeated did they support American efforts at the UN to promote a cease-fire. The last day of the war, when Israel's intentions against Syria were unclear, Moscow threatened to "intervene militarily" if the Israelis did not cease hostilities immediately. The United States took this warning more seriously than it had in 1956, and, as in the previous crisis, the United States used the Soviet threat to convince Israel to end its military activity.[4] In the Six Day War, however, it was likely that Israel would have soon ended its operations even without pressure.

The strategy the Johnson administration employed was distinct from the earlier period. Eisenhower was committed to distancing American policy from Israel and to organizing the Arab states against the perceived communist threat. On the other hand, Lyndon Johnson was prepared to "tilt" toward the Israelis. Unlike Eisenhower, Johnson did not see the Middle East as a high priority, in part because he was mired in the war in Vietnam. Thus, the American response at the outset of the crisis in May was mercurial. Sympathy and support for Israel was combined with a simultaneous attempt to avoid war and to rely on multinational efforts to restore freedom of navigation, the disruption of which served as the *casus belli*. When the Israelis decided to preempt, the American reaction was that the Israeli move was justified, but unfortunate. Relief that Israeli victories would negate the need to intervene to "save" the Jewish state was mixed with fury at Arab accusations that the United States had aided Israel, worries over possible confrontation with the U.S.S.R., and concern about deteriorating relations with the Arabs. Although Washington sought an early end to the conflict, it tolerated Israel's move against Syria on the fourth day.

The War of Attrition in 1969-1970 represented a new period of superpower engagement. The Soviet Union, having been badly bruised by the defeat of its Arab allies, was involved in a massive resupply effort. Its shipment of sophisticated arms after 1967 enabled Egypt to launch the War of Attrition in early 1969, and the sale of SAM anti-aircraft missiles enabled the Egyptians to continue the war. On the Israeli side, the United States was now emerging as the country's major arms supplier for the first time. The Nixon administration attempted to keep a tight lid on new commitments to Jerusalem, lest the Israelis be emboldened to take precipitous actions against the Egyptians. Washington was troubled that the Israelis might endanger prospects for possible progress in Arab-Israeli negotiations which Secretary of State William Rogers was attempting to organize. Nevertheless, Israel's "deep penetration" raids in early 1970 led to a step-up in the transfer of Soviet supplies and arms, leading eventually to a dramatic increase in the number of military advisors and personnel Moscow was prepared to send. When a cease-fire was about to be reached in July 1970, Israeli jets shot down five Egyptian fighters operated by Soviet pilots over the Sinai.

Neither the United States nor the Soviet Union appeared interested in further escalation. Available evidence suggests that Moscow had persistent doubts about the wisdom of the effort from the outset.[5] Therefore, it is not surprising that both superpowers played a role in the termination of the conflict. The United States initiated a secret effort in late May, 1970 designed to gain Egyptian acquiescence in a cease-fire. Nasser indicated his support for the idea in mid-July, presumably without Soviet opposition, and perhaps with Soviet encouragement.[6] Despite Israeli reluctance, the administration then utilized a combination of carrots and sticks to gain the Meir government's acceptance of American terms. Pressure to agree was combined with guarantees and offers of additional military assistance. Although a cease-fire was reached, no verification procedures were arranged, and the Israelis immediately accused the Egyptians--with Soviet assistance--of violating the cease-fire. The United States subsequently confirmed these violations and compensated Israel with additional arms supplies. The degree to which the Soviets were party to the violations was never confirmed. However the violations were crucial factors in facilitating the Egyptian attack in October 1973.[7]

The progression of the three Arab-Israeli wars from 1956 to 1970 suggests that the United States and the Soviet Union were becoming more intimately involved in Middle East developments. It was thereby increasingly difficult to separate global from regional conflicts. This inter-connection was demonstrated dramatically in the

October 1973 war. The expulsion of the majority of Soviet advisors by Anwar Sadat in the summer of 1972 forced the Soviet Union to fear the loss of its major client in the Middle East. It therefore escalated arms shipments to Cairo, including a range of offensive weaponry never before shipped, even to some of its allies in Eastern Europe. These arms clearly made the Egyptians' conception of a limited war with Israel possible.[8] On the other hand, the diminished number of Soviet advisors meant that war was less risky from the Kremlin's perspective. Without the Soviet presence, there was less likelihood of immediate escalation to the global level.

While the Soviets were extending new forms of assistance to Egypt and Syria,[9] Washington was embroiled in negotiations for a Vietnam settlement and the beginnings of Watergate. In order to keep the Middle East quiet, the Nixon administration increased arms shipments to Israel in the spring of 1973. In a parallel move, the Soviets secretly extended aid to Egypt. Neither the United States nor the Soviet Union was interested in a regional conflict which might threaten their expanding détente. Yet the United States was not prepared to pressure Israel for concessions unless the Egyptians fundamentally altered their relationship with Moscow. The Soviets would not risk a collapse of their relationship with Cairo. Therefore, the Egyptians were able to prepare for war. To the United States, the Soviet failure to warn of the impending hostilities was a violation of agreements reached at the 1972-1973 summits. Brezhnev's warnings to Nixon at their June 1973 summit and the withdrawal of Soviet dependents from Cairo on the eve of the war may have been signals to Washington which were not received.

If Soviet arms shipments made the Egyptian attack possible, laggard American diplomacy after the failure of Rogers' plan in 1971 increased Sadat's incentive to "get the superpowers' attention" by initiating hostilities. Indeed, American policy may well have constituted the worst of both worlds. By continually pressuring Israel not to preempt in case of a threat of war, the United States may have contributed to diminished Israeli deterrence. By not pursuing an activist diplomacy for peaceful negotiations, Washington increased Egypt's frustration.

Part of the difference in behavior between the United States and the U.S.S.R. prior to the October 1973 War can be explained by their contrasting conceptions of how the next Arab-Israeli battle would occur. Washington assumed it would result from an Israeli preemption in the wake of a perceived threat. The Soviet Union, by contrast, accurately anticipated that war would occur as a consequence of an Arab attack caused by frustration at these countries' inability to regain lost territory through diplomacy. The Soviets were therefore prepared with a coherent set of methods for action. They immediately initiated a concerted effort to aid their clients, which included resupplies and calls for additional Arab states to join those already engaged in battle.

The Nixon administration was more surprised by the outbreak of war than the Kremlin and therefore its initial reaction was more confused. At the time of the Arab attack, Nixon and Kissinger anticipated an early and rapid Israeli victory. Therefore, the United States called for a   United Nations resolution demanding a return to the positions that existed at the outset of the war. This move appeared to be taking a step that was sympathetic to Israel. Given the anticipation of imminent Israeli victory, the maneuver was designed to help save the Arabs from a total defeat.

Despite the inconsistencies of American policy, there were several advantages to the Nixon/Kissinger strategy. They sought to achieve a stalemate of the war in order to create the basis for a peace process that the United States would lead. Although more coherent, in the end the Soviet strategy backfired. The Soviets could only back their clients, and then what?   They had no clear program for achieving Arab aims at an acceptable cost to both the United States and Israel.

Nixon and Kissinger were slow to aid the Israelis at the outset of the 1973 War. They anticipated that the Israelis would "win big" soon, and their main aim was to prevent the lopsided Israeli victory of 1967 which resulted in Arab humiliation and alienation from the United States. Once the two American leaders realized that Israel would not repeat its earlier military exploits quickly, and that the Soviets were providing their allies with arms, they initiated a massive airlift of additional weapons and supplies to the Israelis, which helped to turn the tide.[10]

Sadat had a chance to accept a cease-fire at the end of the first week, which would have provided him a clear victory. The Soviets should have encouraged him to accept, but their fears of losing influence with Cairo inhibited pressure on the Egyptian leader. In the end, Premier Kosygin was forced to travel to Egypt personally to show Sadat satellite photographs demonstrating that his forces were losing.[11] Soviets and Americans then cooperated in arranging a cease-fire of the war, but for differing reasons. The Soviets sought to save their Egyptian clients from total defeat. The United States was attempting to manipulate a stalemate to facilitate post-war negotiations.

When the Israelis used minor Egyptian violations as an excuse to break the cease-fire, the Soviets again sent a note threatening to intervene, as in 1967. In this situation, however, key American officials took the threats very seriously because of increased Soviet capabilities and reports from the Soviet Union that preparations were being made for such an intervention. There have since been analyses which question the accuracy of these reports. However, the group which gathered in the White House basement on the night of October 24 and ordered an immediate nuclear alert believed there was a strong possibility that Soviet intervention was imminent.[12] American decision-makers were also influenced by perceptions that the growing Watergate scandal might lead the Soviet Union to anticipate American weakness and by other reports (never completely confirmed) that Soviet ships in the Mediterranean during the war had carried nuclear materiel. After ordering the alert, U.S. officials placed enormous pressure on the Israelis to cease and desist from completing their encirclement of the Egyptian Third Army trapped in the Sinai. At one point, administration representatives even threatened to resupply the Egyptians themselves.

Thus, the United States and the Soviet Union both contributed to preventing Israel from inflicting a lethal and final blow on the Egyptians forces. More than any other Arab-Israeli conflict, the October 1973 War was integrally related to global politics. It came the closest to a superpower confrontation and it had the most devastating impact on overall Soviet-American relations. In this war, the United States and the Soviet Union were also most integrally related to the manner in which hostilities ended.

The last crisis which resulted in a conflict is the 1982 Israeli invasion of Lebanon. This is the only war which did not involve

Egypt, but it also engaged an American client, Israel, opposed to Soviet clients, Syria and the PLO. The origins of the crisis can by found in the April 1981 Syrian missile crisis, in which the Assad government placed missiles across the Syrian border into Lebanon.[13] The Reagan administration responded with efforts extended over several months to restrain the Israelis from retaliating. In the process, Special Mediator Philip Habib arranged a cease-fire between Israel and the PLO along Israel's northern border with Lebanon. His aim was to enhance stability on the Israeli-Lebanese frontier, and thereby prevent war. Except for its supplies of both Syria and the PLO, the Soviet Union was relatively uninvolved, but the United States was inconsistent and laggard in its efforts to restrain the Israelis in 1982. The administration was divided between one group which viewed the Palestinian issue as critical to American success in the area and another which was more concerned about the regional situation as a whole, encompassing the Iran-Iraq War and the deteriorating situation in Lebanon. The first coalition was led by Secretary of Defense Caspar Weinberger and the second by Secretary of State Alexander Haig.[14] Even though Haig and his associates in principle opposed a limited invasion of Lebanon, they did not focus upon signals of Israel's preparations for military action because they were trying to organize the area to withstand several potential problems, including a perceived Soviet threat to the region. The Israelis, led by Defense Minister Ariel Sharon, absorbed these confused signals and concluded they could act without interference.

Once the invasion occurred, however, the Weinberger group emerged victorious. Haig was fired, and the United States set about attempting to stop the Israeli assault. The devastatingly rapid and overwhelming destruction of Syrian missile sites by the Israelis did not result in an immediate Soviet response. However once the United States proposed to intervene as part of a multilateral force in early July[15] the Soviets began their resupply effort to Syria. Thus, Moscow's major response to the Israeli invasion, to the defeat of the Syrians, and to the American intervention, was the resupply of the Syrian forces, which over the next several months reached massive and unprecedented proportions. Meanwhile, during the summer of 1982, the United States was finally able to broker a deal which led to the withdrawal of the PLO guerilla force under Yasser Arafat and a cease-fire.

The 1982 crisis was essentially different from the previous wars since 1956, as there was no hint of a possible Soviet-American confrontation. In large part the muted competition between the two superpowers occurred because important Soviet interests were not being challenged. Syrian involvement was temporary and peripheral, although damaging for Damascus and embarrassing for Moscow, while the defeat of the PLO, a non-state actor, was not as compromising of Soviet interests as had been the case with previous Israeli challenges to Egypt and Syria. In addition, the Soviet Union was mired in Afghanistan.

The superpowers were integral to the initiation, progress and termination of all five wars. In 1956, the Soviet arms sale to Nasser helped to fuel the crisis by alarming Israel and emboldening Egypt. Confused American diplomacy reduced Washington's leverage over Israel and alienated Egypt, but American maneuvering was the critical factor in the termination of the war. Kremlin threats were designed to improve relations with emerging Arab clients, but the United States used Soviet statements as further leverage against London, Paris, and Jerusalem.

In 1967, the Soviet Union was primarily responsible for initiating a crisis that it hoped would unify its clients, but not escalate to war with Israel. The United States played a passive role, unwilling either to give Israel the green light for a preemptive attack or to restrain Jerusalem when the dispute could not be resolved quickly and diplomatically. The Johnson administration failed to place any pressure on Israel until the last hours of the war. Hot-line messages between the superpowers prevented miscalculations, especially in the hours following the Israeli attack on the *USS Liberty*.

In 1969-70, Soviet arms shipments and advisors enabled Nasser to continue the War of Attrition despite repeated Israeli successes in countering Egyptian moves. The United States attempted to restrain Israel by limiting new commitments for arms shipments. An American proposal for a cease-fire followed by talks led to the end of the War of Attrition, but failure to provide for verification procedures undermined planned talks and led to an improvement of Egyptian positions.

In 1973 Soviet arms shipments made the Egyptian-Syrian attack possible. The American airlift facilitated the Israeli counter-attack against Egypt. Although their objectives differed, Soviet-American cooperation and subsequent confrontation led to the end of the war.

The Israeli invasion in 1982 occurred in the wake of PLO and Syrian actions during the previous year which had been made possible by Soviet support. Yet Moscow was less relevant to the initiation of the war than it had been in the previous three. Instead, Washington was unable to prevent an Israeli preemptive strike, as it had in 1973. For the first time, the United States intervened with its own troops as part of a Western multi-national force. An Israeli-Lebanese accord ending hostilities the following year was torpedoed by the Syrians with apparent Soviet acquiescence.

None of these crises which led to war between 1956 and 1982 would have been the same without the superpowers. Their arms made it possible for the parties to pursue hostilities at a high level of combat (although the Israelis were primarily armed by the French in 1956 and 1967, and several Arab States were receiving substantial assistance from the British in the early 1950s). Either the United States or the Soviet Union or both played a role in the initiation, the continuation, and the termination of conflict. The United States was frequently unable (and in rare occasions unwilling) to restrain the Israelis. It was more successful in using its leverage on Jerusalem to terminate hostilities than in preventing the initiation of war. The Nixon administration was responsible, however, for keeping the Israelis from preempting in 1973.

The Soviet Union, always fearful of losing client support, was a greater factor in the initiation than in the termination of Arab-Israeli wars. The Kremlin was only prepared to accept conflict management when its clients had been massively defeated or were about to be devastated. It never demonstrated a willingness to risk alienating local clients by taking actions of which they disapproved. The only exceptions were its sporadic refusal to provide Arab clients with the most sophisticated technology and its reluctance to intervene directly during Middle East wars. Nonetheless, Arab confidence that the Soviets would prevent their complete defeat by the Israelis facilitated decisions to initiate hostilities and strengthened the Arab diplomatic and military position. Without the Soviet role between 1955 and 1985, the Arab war option would have surely been more limited. Even the ability to inflict terrorist attacks on Israel and on western facilities and personnel would have been more constrained without Soviet training, equipment, and supplies.

Indeed it can be argued that none of these conflicts would have occurred--at least as they did--without superpower involvement. Thus, Soviet arms shipments and American diplomacy were integral to the origins of the Suez crisis. Without the United States, Nasser would have been defeated. Without Soviet interference, the Six Day War would never have begun as it did. If the Soviets had not resupplied the Egyptians, they could not have conducted the War of Attrition or initiated the October War. In that conflict, the American airlift made Israel's ultimate military victory possible, but U.S. diplomacy ensured a stalemate. In 1982, Soviet assistance permitted the build-up of PLO and Syrian forces, while American diplomacy first permitted and then restricted Israeli military actions.

The Soviets were also more susceptible to tacit threats from local clients that they might defect to the other superpower. The Kremlin suffered the greatest single loss in the transfer of Egypt's allegiance in the mid-1970s from Moscow to Washington. Clearly, Soviet actions were in part rooted in insecurity, especially between 1967 and 1973. The Soviets were worried, justifiably as it turned out, that their enormous economic, political and military stake in the Middle East, particularly in Egypt, would come to naught. It inhibited their ability to pressure Arab clients to act in a more restrained fashion.

Particularly on the American side, specific leaders made a difference in the way that the United States conducted itself. Thus Johnson or Reagan would have been more sympathetic to the Israelis in 1956 and less able or willing to manipulate the results of the war in 1973; Eisenhower or Carter would have been more likely to try to prevent Israeli preemption in 1967. Carter has made it clear he would have worked assiduously to prevent the invasion of Lebanon in 1982 had he still been in office.[16] He might well have succeeded as he did in 1978 in persuading the Israelis to withdraw immediately from the area south of the Litani River when they moved there in a retaliatory operation. Soviet leaders also make a difference. Gorbachev would obviously have operated differently than his predecessors between 1955 and 1985. The subtle policy of providing arms to non-Communists initiated by Khrushchev was a major departure from Stalin's *modus operandi*. Comprehensible superpower alternative strategies which would have led to different regional outcomes demonstrate clearly that both the United States and the Soviet Union made critical contributions to the manner in which local conflicts were converted into hostilities.

Four Crises Which Did Not Lead to War[17]

The role of the superpowers as integral parts of Middle East conflicts during the Cold War can be seen by comparing those crises which resulted in war with several crises which did not actually lead to Arab-Israeli hostilities. We selected four cases: the Sinai crisis of February 1960; the Syrian intervention in Jordan of September 1970; the Syrian intervention in Lebanon in 1976; the deteriorating Syrian-Israeli relationship in March-April 1986.

In February 1960, recurring violence between Syria and Israel over water rights and farming in the demilitarized zone between them led to significant clashes, particularly at a point called Tawafiq. In response, Egypt ordered troops into the Sinai for the first time since 1956. Approximately 50,000 troops and 500 tanks advanced as close as the El Arish area before being detected by Israel. Israel then partially mobilized and sent secret warning messages to Egypt, which subsequently withdrew its troops.

As Avner Yaniv has noted, there was an "uncanny resemblance" between this crisis and the origins of the Six Day War.[18] Unlike 1967, Syria at this time was part of Egypt. Israel was being led by the more experienced David Ben Gurion rather than by the politically weaker Levi Eshkol. The Syrian government by 1967 was also more radical and more of a challenge to Egypt. Unlike 1960, in 1967 Egypt was bogged down in an unsuccessful war in Yemen. These are countervailing differences. On the one hand, Egyptian prestige might have been more at stake because it controlled Syria in 1960. On the other hand, the radical Syrian government was more of a thorn in Nasser's side in 1967. Similarly, in 1967 the Yemen War was clearly an impediment to Nasser. This conflict made initiation of hostilities with Israel more difficult, but also provided an incentive to offset his losses.

In both crises, the United States was relatively passive. The key difference between 1960 and 1967 was the Soviet role. In 1960 the Soviets did little to encourage Egyptian activity. The Israelis claimed at the time that Nasser moved troops into the Sinai because of a false Soviet warning that Israel was mobilizing for war.[19] There is no other evidence of Soviet incendiary involvement. Even if the report is true, in both public and private statements, the Soviets attempted to quiet the situation and did not offer the Arabs support. They did, however, try to assure Cairo that they had brought the situation under control. This behavior is in sharp contrast to 1967, when the Soviets warned Nasser of threats to Syria, but both the Egyptians and Syrians assumed that the Soviet Union would come to their aid in some manner if difficulties arose.

Two incidents in 1960 and 1967 dramatically illustrate the differences in Soviet behavior between the two crises. In 1960, the Soviet ambassador met with Foreign Minister Meir and did not even mention the crisis.[20] In 1967, by contrast, the Soviet ambassador delivered a stark message to Prime Minister Levi Eshkol about the supposed Israeli mobilization against Syria. When Eshkol offered to take him to see the front to prove no troops were there, he refused.[21] It is possible that the Soviets gained a false sense of confidence that they could manipulate Arab-Israeli crises from their experiences in 1960, but certainly--even assuming the most negative interpretation of the Soviet part in the 1960 crisis--their behavior was dramatically different than their inflammatory role in 1967. Thus these two cases help to confirm the hypothesis that Soviet-American Mideast competition exacerbated local tensions. The muted Soviet role helped avert war in 1960; Moscow directly contributed to the outbreak of hostilities in 1967.

The next case of a crisis that did not result in Arab-Israeli war is the Syrian intervention in Jordan in September, 1970. Whether or not the Soviets urged the Syrians to intervene or pressured them to withdraw, the United States played an unusually active role in coordinating with Israel and encouraging it to mobilize as a deterrent to further Syrian action. Possible Israeli military operations against Syria were discussed with Nixon and Kissinger.

American guarantees were provided that should these operations lead to Soviet or Arab threats to Israel, the United States would come to the assistance of the Meir government. Israel might have acted even without the United States, but it would have been concerned about possible American objections. Instead, the Nixon administration played the unusual role of emboldening an Israeli government. In the end, Arab-Israeli war did not result because the Syrians withdrew. If the Syrians departed Jordan because they understood that continued engagement would lead to a war with Israel, then American actions--by enhancing the Israeli deterrent--served to prevent a war which would have involved at least Israel and Syria. Certainly, Jordanian military success against the Syrians prior to the latter's withdrawal meant that in order to have any chance of success against Jordan, the Syrians would have to escalate to a point where Israeli engagement was almost certain.

In 1976, Syria again intervened, but this time in Lebanon rather than Jordan. Both the American and Soviet positions were very different in this case by comparison with 1970. The Soviets greeted the first Syrian intervention in January 1976 enthusiastically, even reinforcing their naval presence off the Lebanese coast in the spring--presumably as a sign of support. This positive backing diminished noticeably with the second, and more serious Syrian intervention in June. Moscow was visibly concerned about the Syrian vacillation and the lingering bloodshed. The Soviets grew increasingly critical of the Syrian intervention as it continued and Assad's battles with the PLO intensified. They apparently sought an end to the fighting and even a withdrawal.[22] Their behavior was generally ambivalent: They had lost their major client in the area, Egypt, and therefore Syria's role as a local proxy had grown in importance. Yet in this case two of their clients--Syria and the PLO--were engaged in direct combat with each other. They could only lose from continued conflict.

The United States understandably did not see the crisis as a direct Soviet challenge to its interests. Rather, it was anxious to mediate between the Jerusalem and Damascus governments in order to prevent war. Since Egypt had "switched sides" in the superpower competition and the United States had emerged as the central player in the peace process, Kissinger's perspective was very different from what it had been in 1970. Through his auspices "red lines" were drawn between Israel and Syria. Assad understood he could not cross them without engaging in conflict with Israel. The Israelis agreed not to employ the military option as long as the "red lines" were not crossed.

In the spring of 1986, a "war of words" ensued between Israel and Syria. Overt hostilities were threatened in the light of the Syrian build-up following 1982. However, the new Soviet government under Mikhail Gorbachev clearly was not interested in a Syrian-Israeli military confrontation. Although there is no evidence whatsoever of coordination, both superpowers were interested in the restraint of their respective clients. Syria may have been further deterred by the April, 1986 attack by the United States on Libya. Since the Syrians were similarly involved in the sponsorship of terrorism, they had no interest in challenging Washington.[23]

These four cases all have several common traits. In no example was either superpower engaged in an attempt to promote conflict. In 1960 the superpowers were relatively uninvolved. In 1976 the United States was able to mediate relatively unfettered by Soviet interference. It was clear in 1986 that neither superpower sought war. The most complicated of these cases is the 1970 Syrian intervention in Jordan. Whether or not the Soviets encouraged Syrian intervention in the first place, they were clearly uninterested in a Syrian-Israeli conflict which could have developed into a direct Soviet-American confrontation. The United States, for its part, pursued an unusual strategy. It worked explicitly to employ the Israelis as an active deterrent. Whether or not the Syrians would have withdrawn in any case once the Jordanians succeeded against them militarily, Nixon and Kissinger later concluded that the Israeli deterrent had been effective. If the analysis was accurate, and it appears to have been, in this case conflict avoidance by a "show of strength" worked. These four crises which did not lead to Arab-Israeli combat reinforce the conclusion that superpower arms shipments, political instigation, or botched diplomacy contributed to the warfare in the Middle East between 1955 and 1985. War did not occur in crises where the superpowers either did not involve themselves or they attempted to restrict conflict. (In the latter situation, either both sought to prevent hostilities or one was passive and the other actively engaged in conflict management). We can conclude that during the Cold War the actions of the United States and the Soviet Union (either in a positive or a negative direction) measurably affected the question of whether or not overt hostilities occurred between Arabs and Israelis.

The Middle East in the New Era

The issue which confronts us today is what impact the United States and the Soviet Union will have in the changed international system. In this emerging network of relationships, power is diffused in a way which would have been considered unthinkable during the bipolar era. The United States and the Soviet Union are no longer engaged in global confrontation. Their competition does not dominate world politics. They are not threatened if the other party is involved in particular local situations. Instead, they are more often likely to find themselves on the same side in local crises. The new system is dominated by localized politics in which regional activity is paramount. Even the role of great powers has altered as particular players assume dominating roles--most prominently Germany in East Europe and Japan in East Asia. There are still only two nuclear superpowers and the United States is still the only country capable of acting as a great power globally. With these exceptions, Germany, Japan, Britain, France, and China emerge as freer to act independently than even in the era of looser bipolarity in the 1970s and 1980s.

The net impact of the new conditions is that there will be more outside parties active in the Middle East, but the danger of escalation--especially to superpower confrontation, including the potential threat to use nuclear weapons--will be reduced. The possibilities of regional instability, however, will certainly be enhanced. Thus in this new era, the Middle East emerges as a post-Cold War region *par excellence*. It has three overlapping balances of power: Arab vs. Israel; Arab vs. Iran; Arab vs. Arab. Many regimes are beset by internal instability; there is extensive interference in the affairs of neighboring states; deep ideological and religious splits exist; conflict over land is critical; and the widespread involvement of countries outside the region continues.   I t   h a s become popular to suggest that terrorism will decline with the loss of guerilla bases in East Europe and the Mideast arms race will abate with the improved relationship between Moscow and Washington.   These arguments again ignore the impact of a multi-layered world politics.   The potential for arms sales may well increase with new competition for commercial benefits and political influence among such countries as Britain, France, Germany, China, and even Brazil, Argentina, and one day Japan.   In the short term, surplus weapons no longer usable on Europe's Central Front will likely be sold or given to Middle East states.

Even if the great powers successfully restrain their sales through implicit or explicit agreement, the potential for local states to independently carry out arms production remains. Prior to its defeat in 1991, Iraq's military production capabilities were impressive. Efforts, such as Saddam Hussein's, to develop independent production capabilities have been aided by various countries, including North Korea and Brazil, and by private Western companies. With the diffusion of military technology,   in the post-Cold War period it may therefore be easier for radical and wealthy countries such as Iraq, Iran, and Libya, and potentially Syria, to sow the seeds of instability because they will be dealing with secret and irresponsible collaborators. If this region became the impetus for the spread of chemical or nuclear weapons or long range ballistic missiles, it could affect the vital interests--and even the territories--of states elsewhere, including the great powers.

Local conflicts could also seriously impair the economies of advanced scientifically based countries. The high-tech states would be deeply harmed if Mideast hostilities resulted in the widespread destruction of oil-producing facilities or the serious disruption of the means of conveying energy supplies from the area. Underlying these perils is an emerging instability caused by a spreading Islamic fundamentalism from Africa to China. The Middle East lies in the middle of this diverse but virulent new force in world politics, which often assumes anti-Western and expansionist forms.

In this new post-Cold War era, the role of the superpowers in the Middle East has been completely altered. They are no longer adversaries with each war potentially leading to a superpower confrontation and each crisis exacerbated by superpower actions. In particular, changes in the Soviet Union and East Europe have altered the way in which the local parties view their interests and alternatives. The Soviet Union is no longer the ultimate guarantor of Arab security, which impedes the option for war against Israel among these states. Israel for its part is preoccupied with the absorption of Soviet Jews and its own domestic, economic, and political problems. There is little interest in decisive actions that would lead either to a negotiated peace with the Palestinians or to some kind of large scale war. Indeed the reduced Soviet relationship with Syria and Damascus' and Jerusalem's parallel antagonism to Iraq and Yasser Arafat may encourage the Israeli and Syrian governments to consider some kind of *modus vivendi*. The end of the Cold War thus makes superpower confrontation in the Middle East extremely unlikely and increases the possibility of limited Arab-Israeli agreements.

On the other hand, the reduced superpower role means that both powers have less leverage over local clients. The number of arms suppliers has increased, the political impact of outside powers has been diffused, and the guarantees which the superpowers are prepared to extend have been reduced, especially by the U.S.S.R. to its Arab clients. The inhibitions created by the fear of the superpowers confronting each other for their own purposes at the locals' expense has disappeared.

Although not an Arab-Israeli dispute, the Iraqi attack on Kuwait provides some hints as to the nature of post-Cold War crises. On the one hand, the superpowers were unable to prevent the initiation of conflict. They were not intimately involved in negotiations, and mediation was being carried out by Arab parties. On the other hand, once Iraq invaded, the United States and the Soviet Union acted in concert to try to precipitate Iraqi withdrawal, although Washington assumed by far the greater burden.

Had the Cold War been continuing, it is likely that the Soviet Union would have backed Iraq, claimed the attack was justified, continued to supply arms and vetoed the UN Security Council condemnation and the authorization to use force. The United States, for its part, would have assumed that the Soviet Union was behind the Iraqi attack, even if the Kremlin in reality could not control Saddam Hussein, given his present strength. Washington would have tried to push Moscow to pressure Iraq to withdraw from Kuwait and would have viewed the Iraqi move as consistent with the historic Soviet thrust to warm water ports on the Persian Gulf and a grab for the world's most important oil fields. Instead of Soviet-American collusion, the danger of escalation--even as far as the nuclear level--would have been ever-present. The United States would have had to take this peril into account in its decision to send troops to Saudi Arabia, but it could not afford to have ignored what would have been seen as a Soviet threat to the oil fields.

It is of course possible that the expectation of a staunch American reaction would have led Soviet officials to pressure Iraq not to attack. In this sense, there are special dangers in the current period. Moscow's reduced leverage and the lessened danger of superpower confrontation enhanced Saddam's flexibility. In particular, the attack on Kuwait occurred in a critical transition period when states were struggling with new rules. Inexperience with the new international situation may have encouraged Saddam Hussein to attack, believing falsely that declining superpower interest in the Third World would give him a free hand. Other factors may have inadvertently sent the wrong signal: the euphoria over the end of the Cold War, the talk in both Washington and Moscow about the reduced use of force in international affairs, and the failure to confront Hussein seriously over his past moves such as the use of chemical weapons against Iran and his own Kurdish citizens.

Nationalist leaders who expect bellicose actions to be resisted are likely to be deterred, as Saddam Hussein might well have been had he realized that his invasion would engender strong countermeasures. It is easier to envision Soviet-American cooperation in an intra-Arab crisis, such as the Iraqi-Kuwaiti conflict, than in an Arab-Israeli setting. First, Iraq was a regime that had alienated both superpowers and both were suspicious of it. Second, both had no particular attachment to the Baghdad regime despite past Soviet support and American flirtation with Saddam Hussein. Third, the conflict is ultimately between Arab haves and have-nots--those who share a profound interest in the economic health of the west and those who do not. In this case, Moscow and Washington are both on the side of the Arab haves.

Long-term commitments to such countries as Israel, Syria, Jordan, Egypt, and Saudi Arabia by each superpower might well inhibit Soviet-American collaboration in a future Arab-Israeli crisis. Cooperation might be more difficult, but confrontation will not be more likely. The danger of escalation to a Soviet-American confrontation is minimal in the post-Cold War era. Moreover, alliance and patron-client relations have become more diffused. American-Israeli tensions have increased at the same time as Israeli relations with East European states and even the Soviet Union have improved. The potential of positive developments in Syrian-American relations has been enhanced by the altered Soviet role and the Persian Gulf crisis. The United States even attempted a dialogue with the PLO, which proved unsuccessful. In a new Arab-Israeli crisis, the level of American support for Israel would depend on the degree to which an American administration believed Israeli actions to be justified. No foreseeable U.S. administration would be prepared to endanger Israeli security, no matter what it thought of the wisdom of prior Israeli moves. The Soviet Union under Gorbachev, or any similar leader interested in promoting Western ties, would be likely to respect the strength of American convictions. The reduced probability that the Soviet Union would come to the defense of Arab belligerents decreases the likelihood that an Arab-Israeli crisis would lead to war in the first place.

If war may be less likely in a post-Cold War environment, the prospects for Soviet-American coordinated peace negotiations may also be limited. Superpower cooperation to prevent or limit hostilities is not the same as superpower cooperation to promote a peace process. Unless American-Israeli tensions over the Palestinian issue increase measurably, or Soviet policies change further, the United States will be unlikely to cooperate with the Soviet Union in exercising pressure on Israel to accept a Palestinian state in the absence of major Arab concessions.

In the post-Cold War world, the Soviet-American relationship is most likely to resemble American relations with other European powers such as Britain or France. There will be differences over arms sales, incentives to cooperate to limit a crisis, the potential of collaboration on such arms control issues as chemical weapons and long-range ballistic missiles, and attempts--likely unsuccessful--to define common peace proposals. If during the Cold War the Soviet Union sought to demonstrate its equality with the United States through meddling in the Middle East, in the post-Cold War Moscow will likely increase its cooperation with Washington in an effort to maintain its status as coequal. In turn, because the U.S.S.R. is not as threatening and because the United States requires Moscow's assistance in the peace process, Washington is likely to go along with the game. The relationship is therefore likely to be normalized since the West will attempt to maintain the security of oil and thereby the quality of its economies. The Soviet Union will have an interest in Western economic stability, so that the option will remain of assistance to the hard-pressed Soviet economy. The Kremlin will therefore be more sympathetic than in the past to Western interests in the Middle East.

Post-Cold War Arab-Israeli crises, if and when they occur, will then evolve in an atmosphere which is the reverse of prior crisis experience. The emphasis will be on efforts to promote an environment in which crises do not occur, rather than on limiting the escalatory impact of crises which were once viewed as inevitable. If crises do occur, a degree of trust between the superpowers will facilitate their management. The possibilities of Arab-Israeli crises leading to war will be reduced. The examples of Arab-Israeli crises which did not result in war are therefore more useful in understanding the post-Cold War period than the better-known crises which escalated into full-scale hostilities. To the extent that clients cannot manipulate their patrons any longer, they will not receive the supplies necessary to take offensive actions nor will initiators of conflict receive assurances they will be saved if they begin losing. In the past, Soviet and American posturing has often been directed at the other superpower to convince it to rein in its client. Without Soviet-American competition, the tense signalling this process required has dissipated and the danger of escalation has declined as well.

The possibilities of containing and even preventing overt Arab-Israeli hostilities have been enhanced. Yet, even with all these positive developments on the superpower level, the sad fact remains that the Middle East continues to be an extremely dangerous region at the local level. The reduced threat of escalation for the superpowers and their enhanced potential for limited cooperation in conflict management and resolution does not translate into the end of raging instability among the regional parties themselves.

Notes

1. Walter Laqueur, *The Soviet Union and the Middle East* (New York: Praeger, 1959), pp. 211-246; Mohammed Heikal, *Sphinx and Commisar*, (London: Collins, 1978), pp. 56-75.

2. See Steven L. Spiegel, *The Other Arab-Israeli Conflict* (Chicago: University of Chicago, 1985), pp. 66-82.

3. See C. Ernest Dawn, "The Egyptian Remilitarization on the Sinai," May 1967, *Journal of Contemporary History*, 3:3 (July, 1968); Heikal, *Sphinx*, pp. 172-189; Speeches by Gamal Abdel Nasser of May 26 and May 29, 1967 in Walter Laqueur, ed., *The Israeli-Arab Reader*, 2nd ed. (New York: Bantam, 1969), pp. 175-179, 185-189.

4. Yaacov Bar-Siman-Tov, *Israel, the Superpowers, and War in the Middle East* (New York: Praeger, 1987), pp. 85-145.

5. See Daniel Dishon, ed., *The Middle East Contemporary Record*, vol. 5, 1969-1970, (Jerusalem: Israeli Universities Press, 1977), pp. 19-20.

6. *Ibid*.

7. See Yaacov Bar-Siman-Tov, *The Israeli-Egyptian War of Attrition* (New York: Columbia University Press, 1980).

8. See Heikal, *Sphinx*, pp. 242-55; Dina Rome Sphechler, "The U.S.S.R. and Third World Conflicts: Domestic Debate and Soviet Policy in the Middle East, 1967-1973," *World Politics* 38:3 (April, 1986).

9. Jon Glassman, *Arms for the Arabs: The Soviet Union and War in the Middle East* (Baltimore: John Hopkins, 1981), pp. 65-124.

10. See Nadav Safran, *Israel: The Embattled Ally* (Cambridge: Belknap/Harvard, 1981), pp. 476-505.

11. Mohammed Heikal, *The Road to Ramadan* (New York: Ballantine, 1975), p. 237.

12. Henry Kissinger, *Years of Upheaval* (Boston: Little Brown, 1982).

13. Itamar Rabinovich, *The War for Lebanon, 1970-1983* (Ithaca: Cornell, 1984), p. 118ff.

14. See Spiegel, *The Other Arab-Israeli Conflict*, p. 403ff.

15. *Ibid*, p. 416

16. Author's interview with President Jimmy Carter.

17. The following section in part draws on David J. Pervin, "Crises Without War: Some Middle Eastern Cases," mimeo, UCLA, July 1990.

18. For the Tawafiq incident, see Avner Yaniv, "Syria and Israel: The Politics of Escalation," in Moshe Maoz and Avner Yaniv, eds. *Syria Under Assad* (New York: St. Martins, 1986) p. 163; Avner Yaniv, *Deterrence Without the Bomb* (Lexington: Lexington, 1987), pp. 84-5; Yitzhak Oron, ed., *Middle East Record*, vol 1, 1960, (Tel Aviv: Israel Oriental Society), pp. 197-203.

19. See Gordan Shepard, "The Sinai Riddle," *The Reporter* May 31, 1960, pp. 30-1; Yitzhak Rabin, *The Rabin Memoirs* (Boston: Little Brown, 1979), pp. 85-6.

20. Shepard, "Sinai Riddle."

21. Bar-Siman-Tov, *Israel*, p. 92.

22. For slightly differing views of Soviet activity, see Ilana Kass, "Moscow and the Lebanese Triangle," *Middle East Journal* 38:2 (Spring, 1979); Robert O. Freedman, "The Soviet Union and the Civil War in Lebanon," *Jerusalem Journal of International Relations* 3:4 (Summer, 1978); James Collins, "The Soviet Union," in P. Edward Halley and Lewis Snyder, eds., *Lebanon in Crisis* (Syracuse: Syracuse University, 1979).

23. For the 1986 "war of words," see *Jane's Defense Weekly*, June 28, 1986 and *The Economist*, April 12, 1986.

Cases in Soviet–Middle East Behavior: Two U.S. Interpretations

9 The Dilemma of Superpower: Soviet Decision-making in the Six Day War, 1967

> *I think the Soviet Union has to bear a large share of responsibility for what happened. Given our influence with Nasser, given our ability to exert pressure on Egypt, we should have restrained the Egyptians from demonstrating their belligerence . . . I think our military men, more than our diplomats, are to blame. They should never have let the Egyptians force Israel into betting everything it had on a preventive attack.*

> --Nikita Khrushchev
> *Khrushchev Remembers:*
> *The Last Testament*

How much responsibility for the Six Day War rests with the Soviet Union? This chapter does not claim that the U.S.S.R. was primarily responsible for the outbreak of war; all parties to that conflict must share the blame. What it contends is that the Soviet Union played an unintentional but crucial role in the crisis in the Middle East in 1967 and that an examination of the effects of the conflict between Soviet regional objectives and global interests can help explain how and why the U.S.S.R. participated in the escalation of violence. As the Soviet Union's influence in world affairs increased, and especially as its role in the developing world expanded, Soviet leaders were frequently required to balance expanding commitments to regional allies against avoidance of confrontation with the United States. Barrington Moore called the need to reconcile communist ideology with pragmatic Soviet politics the dilemma of power; the need to manage the contradictions between regional and global interests may be termed the dilemma of superpower. Soviet leaders' failure to resolve this dilemma in 1967 ultimately led to the disastrous defeat of their Arab allies.

This chapter begins with a brief outline of Soviet interests in the eastern Mediterranean in 1967, showing how the pursuit of regional objectives risked a global confrontation. Several analyses of Soviet behavior before and during the Six Day War have concluded that the U.S.S.R. followed a predetermined strategy of avoiding risks until the crisis was essentially resolved. A reexamination of Soviet communications and actions, however, indicates that a conception of Soviet decision-making as an attempt to cope with the conflicts between regional and global goals offers a better explanation for Soviet behavior. To show how this approach can provide a more thorough explanation of Soviet risk-taking, the crisis will be divided into six phases demarcated by changes in two independent variables, time pressure and autonomous risk.

Soviet statements and actions during each phase will then be examined to identify the conditions under which Soviet leaders took risks in an attempt to secure a favorable resolution of the crisis and to discover evidence of the effect of value conflicts on Politburo decisions. A comparison of Soviet behavior in each phase of the crisis shows that Soviet leaders tended to avoid risks at points where decision-makers could be expected to accept the conflict between regional and global goals, but took substantial risks at times when attempts to deny this conflict were most likely. The chapter's conclusion discusses how focusing on the contradictions between Soviet regional and global objectives helps explain Soviet risk-taking in 1967 and suggests how further research into the effects of value conflict can contribute to the study of crisis decision making and deterrence.

The U.S.S.R.'s Dilemma in the Middle East, 1967

This section does not attempt a comprehensive discussion of Soviet interests in the Middle East at the time of the Six Day War. Instead, it outlines the general objectives of Soviet policy toward its allies in the Eastern Mediterranean, the interests which were most threatened by escalation of the Arab-Israel military conflict, and the potential for regional conflicts to result in a direct Soviet-American confrontation.[1] In the most general terms, the U.S.S.R. sought to increase its political influence in the region and reduce that of the Western powers, particularly the United States. Khrushchev inaugurated the Soviet "opening to the Third World" in 1955 by arranging for Czech armaments to be sent to Nasser's Egypt; subsequently economic and military aid was extended to non-aligned nations in attempts to break up the Baghdad Pact and exploit anti-colonial sentiment to Soviet advantage.[2] The U.S.S.R. supported the creation of the state of Israel in 1947, but before the Czech Arms Deal it had avoided openly taking sides in the Arab-Israeli conflict. As would soon become apparent, that intractable dispute offered both opportunities and dangers for the Soviet Union as it strove to attain the status of a world power.

Egypt and Syria were the U.S.S.R.'s main Middle Eastern allies in 1967, but each was important to Soviet regional interests for different reasons. Egypt possessed major strategic significance because it was the most populous Arab state, it controlled the Suez Canal, and it had excellent port facilities, to which the U.S.S.R. repeatedly attempted to gain access.[3] Egypt also played a leading role in the Non-Aligned Movement, and Nasser's stature as the most charismatic leader in the Arab world lent his country added political importance.[4] Syria, on the other hand, was probably more important to Soviet interests for its weaknesses rather than strengths. While the U.S.S.R. regarded the coup which brought the left wing of the Syrian Ba'ath to power in 1966 as a major victory for socialism in the developing world, Soviet leaders were fully cognizant of the regime's vulnerability to its internal and external enemies.[5] Increased deliveries of armaments after the 1966 coup, a joint CPSU-Ba'ath communiqué, and reports of plots against the Syrian government by internal reactionaries in collusion with American and Israeli agents indicate that the U.S.S.R. was keenly aware that the sole example of left-wing Arab socialism was uncomfortably vulnerable and had to be protected.[6]

It is not possible to determine whether the Politburo considered Syria or Egypt to be the most valuable Soviet ally in the Middle East. Egypt had greater potential for military power, economic strength, and political influence, but Syria was more dependent on Soviet support for the survival of the left-wing Ba'ath regime and therefore more likely to be a more reliable partner for Soviet policy in the region. Dependency, however, frequently increases the dependent's influence over the benefactor, and by 1967 both Egypt and Syria were beginning to be able to exploit the U.S.S.R. for their own regional ambitions.

This relationship of mutual dependency soon became the central factor in the contradiction between Soviet regional and global interests. While the term *détente* had not yet gained widespread currency in discussions of U.S.-Soviet relations, avoidance of a direct confrontation with the United States, especially a military confrontation, was clearly of paramount interest to the Soviet leadership. Soviet writings recognized that conflicts in the Middle East could ignite a nuclear war which would be catastrophic for the entire world. While America's commitment to Israel was not as strong as it later became, President Johnson and Congress were in agreement that "the Arabs should not be permitted to drive the Israelis into the sea."[7] This study is not the place for debate on whether the U.S.S.R.'s regional allies were seeking to destroy the state of Israel in 1967. It suffices to say here that Soviet officials were well aware that many political leaders among their Arab allies were striving for the annihilation of Israel. Soviet leaders who were opposed or ambivalent to this objective could not have been reassured by their allies' often evasive answers to direct questions on the subject.[8] Therefore, while U.S. and Soviet vital interests were not in direct conflict in the Middle East in 1967, the vital interests of their allies were frequently diametrically opposed. When the violence of the Arab-Israeli conflict escalated, the dilemma of Soviet superpower became more acute as the objective of maintaining relations with and influence over Syria and Egypt began to clash with the need to avoid a Soviet-American confrontation.

Value Conflict and Soviet Crisis Decision-Making

A number of studies in cognitive psychology, management science, and international relations find that decision-makers sometimes find means of resolving conflict between goals or values, but often attempt to cope with value conflict by denying its existence or blaming others for contradictions between their objectives. The findings of these studies suggest that Soviet decision-making during regional crises can be usefully characterized as a process of managing value conflicts. This section presents a framework for analysis of the effect of value conflict on decision-making and outlines how it may be used to examine Soviet actions during the crisis and war of 1967.

Table 9-1 offers a graphic representation of the dilemma of superpower which Soviet leaders faced many times in the Middle East between 1964 and 1985. It is designed to show the difficulties inherent in Soviet decision-makers' attempts to simultaneously pursue mutually conflicting regional and global objectives. The figure describes a Middle East crisis where armed conflict between U.S. and Soviet allies is occurring or imminent, but no Soviet or American forces are directly engaged. The figure is intended to represent Soviet policy options in a regional conflict; a very different matrix would be needed to model Soviet decisions in a direct U.S.-Soviet confrontation such as the Berlin or Cuban crises.

In the conflict diagrammed in Table 9-1, the Politburo must choose between pursuing its global objective, avoidance of a confrontation with the United States, or compromising it, which would increase the risk of U.S.-Soviet conflict. Similarly, the regional objective of maintaining and expanding influence in the region must be either pursued or compromised. In the context of the Arab-Israeli conflict, this often forced Soviet decision-makers to choose between supporting their regional allies against Israel or withholding support and risking increased friction between the U.S.S.R. and its Arab allies. The necessity of making these two choices created a situation where four general courses of action were possible. Of course, the actual range of options available to Soviet leaders was broader and the choices between pursuing and conceding goals were not that stark, but this representation of Soviet options illustrates the need for Soviet decision-makers to arrive at a compromise between two conflicting goals.

Each of the four cells in the figure contains a description of Soviet actions and a projection of the likely outcome. The actions outlined in each cell suggest measures the U.S.S.R. could take to implement the chosen option. These general courses of action have been abstracted from actual Soviet behavior at various points in the crises considered in this study or from reconstructions of Soviet options in previous case studies. The likely outcome presents an estimate of the probable gains and losses to Soviet interests. The actual outcome of the crisis, and the resulting impact on Soviet regional and global interests, would of course be determined by a number of factors outside the Politburo's control. Soviet decision-makers would have incomplete information on factors such as American intentions, actions of other parties to the conflict, and the results of military operations, and would therefore have to rely on assessments analogous to the estimated outcomes listed in each cell.

While each cell describes the probable effects of the chosen option on Soviet regional and global objectives, it is highly unlikely that Soviet decision-makers weighed regional and global interests equally when choosing courses of action during crises in the Middle East. A major Soviet-American confrontation could produce a disaster far worse than the loss of Egypt and Syria as Soviet allies. This study contends, however, that global interests and management of U.S.-Soviet relations did not completely dominate Soviet decision-making during conflicts in the Middle East, and that Soviet regional interests were an important consideration. A perspective which considers U.S.-Soviet relations to be the main determinant of Politburo decisions during regional crises is reflected in an alternative explanation for Soviet behavior which will be outlined later.

Each cell in the figure therefore describes an option for dealing with the conflict between the Soviet regional and global objectives and the likely results of selecting that option. In two of these options, one goal is sacrificed in favor of the other. In Option Two, in the upper right cell, Soviet decision-makers sacrifice regional interests to avoid

TABLE 9.1

The Dilemma of Superpower:
Soviet Options in a Middle East Crisis

	Concede Global Goal	Pursue Global Goal
Concede Regional Goal	**OPTION ONE:** USSR champions Arab cause publically and at the UN, but extends only limited material or military support. Probably diplomatic conflict with U.S., but little chance of serious confrontation. Good prospects for cooperation with U.S. to moderate regional conflict. High chance of alienating allies.	**OPTION TWO:** USSR abandons or chastises Arab states. No chance of confrontation with U.S. Serious breach with regional allies. Major loss of influence in Middle East likely.
Pursue Regional Goal	**OPTION THREE:** USSR supports Arab nations with major military aid and possible military intervention. Confrontation with U.S. certain, possible military conflict. Alliance with Arab states secure. Soviet role in Middle East forcibly asserted.	**OPTION FOUR:** USSR sends significant military aid, signals with military forces or threats to intervence, but stresses cooperation. Suggests joint intervention to guarantee cease-fire. Diplomatic conflict with U.S. likely; may become major confrontation. Friction likely with regional allies over insufficient support.

a U.S.-Soviet confrontation, ensuring that conflict with the United States will be avoided but entailing a high risk of a complete breach with regional allies. Confrontation, however, makes this an extremely unpalatable option for the Politburo.

In Option One in the upper left cell, Soviet decision-makers attempt to minimize risks by making a compromise on both goals. The U.S.S.R. extends some aid to its regional allies and supports their cause publicly, especially in the UN, and opposes efforts by the United States to end conflict on American terms. This situation entails risks of increased friction with Soviet regional allies and of diplomatic conflict with the United States, but the chance of a major U.S.-Soviet confrontation is minimized, and the allies may be placated with replacement of losses and Soviet support for face-saving gestures. In sharp contrast to this, in Option Four in the lower right cell the Politburo refuses to compromise on either regional or global goals and attempts to pursue both. Soviet actions in this situation cannot fail to be self-contradictory; substantial military aid to Soviet allies or threats to intervene with Soviet forces risks a serious confrontation with the United States, while limitation of effort in support of its allies to avoid antagonizing to U.S. risks alienating "progressive" Arab governments. Leaders in the United States and among the Soviet regional allies are all likely to feel deceived or betrayed, and there is significant risk of damage to both regional and global interests.

Each option outlined in the figure corresponds to a means of dealing with the value conflict faced by Soviet decision-makers. In choosing either Option Two or Option Three, where one value is sacrificed in favor of the other, Soviet leaders make a clear tradeoff between opposing goals. In Alexander George's formulation, these options describe situations where Soviet decision-makers accept the conflict between their values and decide to pursue strongly the goal they determine to be more important. Conversely, in Option Three in the lower left cell, a confrontation with the United States is almost certain, but alliances with friendly regional powers are strengthened (with the allies possibly made more dependent on Soviet support), and the U.S.S.R.'s role in the Middle East greatly expanded, if only temporarily. The risks inherent in a major U.S.-Soviet confrontation, however, make this an extremely unpalatable option for the Politburo.

Option One, making moderate concessions on both goals, more closely approximates an optimal compromise. While an all-out effort is not made in pursuit of either goal, making moderate concessions on both objectives maximizes the probability of gains while minimizing the risk of losses to both regional and global interests. This option therefore represents an acceptance of the conflict between Soviet goals and affords the best chance of a creative solution which allows pursuit of both values, which George terms resolution of the value conflict.[9] In terms of Irving Janis and Leon Mann's model of decision-making, this outcome represents successful value integration and maximization of both values, which they refer to as *vigilant information processing* or simply *vigilance*.[10]

Option Four, on the other hand, represents a suboptimal compromise. Refusing to make concessions on either opposing goal reduces the likelihood of gains on both objectives and raises the risk of losses to Soviet interests and of escalation of the conflict. Additionally, efforts to pursue both goals simultaneously are likely to contradict and frustrate each other; in this option, the U.S.S.R. is working at cross-purposes with itself. This option corresponds to Alexander George's description of coping with value conflict by avoiding it and blaming it on outside forces.[11] Why would Soviet decision-makers ever choose such an option? Studies of the cognitive effects of value conflict on decision-making identify two factors which are likely to make what would normally be an optimal compromise between goals seem impossible or unpalatable. The first of these factors is time pressure. Janis and Mann find that time pressure reduces the probability of value integration. They conclude that if decision-makers feel that they do not have enough time for a thorough search for alternative courses of action, they will tend to attempt to cope with value conflict by adopting the first option which appears to offer the possibility to satisfy both goals at the same time. Janis and Mann term this reaction to time pressure *hypervigilance*.[12] George describes this type of decision as an attempt to satisfice in one major decision rather than over a sequence of smaller decisions.[13] Time pressure could therefore be expected to impel decision-makers toward a self-defeating attempt to simultaneously pursue both conflicting goals.

Autonomous risk is another factor which could lead decision-makers to a sub-optimal resolution of value conflict or to deny that a conflict exists. Concessions on either or both values may appear less acceptable when autonomous risk is high because autonomous risk increases the probability of major setbacks to both goals. Janis and Mann find that when factors beyond decision-makers' control threaten losses on both values, they are likely to feel that no satisfactory compromise between conflicting values is possible, and they are therefore not responsible for finding one. They use the term *defensive avoidance* to describe justification of one's own actions by blaming another's and claiming that events narrowed the range of available options.[14]

Ole Holsti finds that leaders in crises frequently feel that their options are narrowing and justify their actions, and their inherent risks, by saying that their adversaries gave them no choice.[15] Jack Snyder contends that decision-makers experiencing defensive avoidance are likely to hold their adversaries responsible for the conflicts between their own goals and to adopt strategies of compellence in an attempt to force concessions, blaming the increased risks of compellent strategies on the opponent.[16] The findings of both cognitive theory and empirical studies, therefore, point to the same paradoxical conclusion: increased autonomous risk is likely to lead even risk-averse decision-makers to take risks in an attempt to pursue contradictory goals.

Defensive avoidance and hypervigilance are both coping mechanisms which help decision-makers to justify their actions by denying that a value conflict exists or that they are responsible for resolving it. Although they may attempt to deny it, leaders in situations where central goals are in conflict always have the responsibility of finding an acceptable compromise between their opposing interests. Under favorable conditions, it is reasonable to expect that leaders will arrive at a satisfactory rational compromise between mutually opposing objectives which entails a minimum risk of escalating the conflict. The circumstances of conflicts in the Middle East are rarely favorable for optimally rational decision-making, however. The effects of value conflict on decision-making discussed in this section suggest the use of time pressure and autonomous risk as independent variables for the explanation of Soviet risk-taking in regional crises. This chapter tests two hypotheses on the relationship of these situational factors to Soviet crisis behavior:

Hypothesis One. In regional crises, Soviet risk-taking tends to increase when time pressure is high and decrease when time pressure is low.
Hypothesis Two. In regional crises, Soviet risk-taking tends to increase when autonomous risk is high and decrease when autonomous risk is low.

These hypotheses contradict both intuitive expectations and the findings of empirical studies of Soviet crisis decision-making. Hannes Adomeit, for example, uses an "operational code" model to examine the Berlin and Cuban crises to conclude that Soviet leaders are likely to take risks only after careful preparations and construction of fallback positions.[17] Adomeit's studies differ from this one in that they are primarily concerned with direct confrontations between the U.S.S.R. and the United States. Certainly, Soviet leaders have shown strong tendencies toward risk-aversion in most international conflicts. This study does not dispute that Soviet decision-makers generally display great reluctance to take risks. If conditions are favorable (in terms of the framework's independent variables, if time pressure and autonomous risk are low), the most likely Soviet course of action is a low-risk strategy of moderate compromise on regional and global goals. The hypotheses tested in this study thereby fulfill Snyder's requirement that in order to be analytically useful, explanations based on the effects of value conflict must identify when decision-makers are most likely to make value tradeoffs as well as when they are most likely to avoid them.[18]

Alternative Explanations and Hypothesis Testing

This study derives its hypotheses by representing Soviet decision-making in regional crises as a process of resolving the conflict between regional and global objectives. A more conventional explanation of Soviet risk-taking tendencies can be derived by considering the U.S.S.R. as one player in a game of "Chicken" with the United States. In a Chicken game, disaster for both players occurs when both players stand firm. Submitting to the opponent's demands is therefore preferable to the "collision" which results if neither player backs down. Risk-averse decision-makers will therefore tend to "swerve" and make concessions to the opponent, thus avoiding the possibility of disaster. If Soviet decision-making in regional crises were best explained by the Chicken model, both time pressure and autonomous risk would decrease the tendencies of Soviet leaders to take risks in support of their allies. As these expectations are diametrically opposite to the two hypotheses derived in this study, the Chicken model offers an alternative explanation of Soviet behavior in Middle Eastern conflicts.

Although neither Snyder and Diesing nor Francis Fukuyama employ the Chicken model in their interpretations of the 1967 crisis, their analyses of Soviet behavior are consistent with its expectations. Both explanations contend that the general pattern of Soviet behavior was somehow predetermined, either by the structure of the conflict or by the Politburo's predisposition toward risk avoidance. Snyder and Diesing argue that the crisis is best described by a Protector game matrix where the dominant Soviet strategy is to withhold strong support from its regional allies until the Arab states meet with disaster. The U.S.S.R. then steps in after the crisis has passed to protect its clients from destruction or total humiliation.[19] Fukuyama offers a similar explanation from a holist rather than a positivist perspective, concluding that Soviet actions in 1967 fit a pattern of behavior exhibited by Soviet decision-makers in six different Middle Eastern crises. In each instance, he finds that the U.S.S.R. threatened to intervene in the conflict only after the point of highest tension and uncertainty had passed and a resolution was already in sight.[20]

If Soviet decision-makers were actually playing a game of Chicken in 1967, their best strategy would have been one of avoiding risks when time pressure or the autonomous risk of escalation was high and issuing threats or bluffs when escalation of the crisis into a superpower confrontation became a remote possibility. This strategy would allow Soviet leaders to minimize the risk of conflict with the United States and to maximize the opportunity to increase the defeated allies' dependence on, and possibly obedience to, the U.S.S.R. If Soviet behavior in the crisis were best explained by a U.S.-Soviet game of Chicken, Soviet actions which entailed the highest degree of risk would be taken when the war was essentially over. Consistent with this explanation, the action which Snyder and Diesing and Fukuyama focus on as an example of Soviet risk-taking is the hot line message of 10 June, which was received in Washington after Israel had agreed to a cease-fire.[21] (The actual timing of this message with regard to the cease-fire will be discussed later.)

The hot line message, however, was not the Soviet Union's riskiest move in the crisis. The Soviet action which involved the greatest degree of risk was the encouragement of Egypt to mobilize its forces to meet an Israeli attack on Syria in mid-May when no such attack was planned at that time. This action, which will be discussed in greater detail later, came during a period of high autonomous risk of escalation and at a point when Soviet decision-makers were likely to have felt intense time pressure. The effort to encourage Egyptian mobilization was successful, and it set in motion a chain of events which led to disaster for the U.S.S.R.'s regional allies. In an effort to limit risks and deter further escalation, Soviet decision-makers tried to put out the fire with gasoline, with predictable results.

Because the riskiest Soviet actions came before the peak of the crisis rather than after its resolution, analyses which concentrate on Soviet behavior near the end of the Six Day War do not tell a complete story. In order to test the hypotheses on the effects of value conflict advanced in this chapter against the expectations of the Chicken model, the following sections will examine Soviet statements and actions which indicate willingness to accept risks, including alerts and movements of forces, communications with allies, statements by

Politburo members, and items in the Soviet press. The effects of cognitive bias, of course, can only be directly measured in controlled psychological experiments, if even then. It is fortunate that cognition cannot be directly observed, as it is difficult to imagine an experiment with potential benefits great enough to justify a violation of the privacy of an individual's thoughts. Indirect indicators of cognitive bias, however, can be found in a variety of sources, including public statements, private communications, memoirs, published and translated documents, and press sources.

Phases of the 1967 Crisis

The 1967 crisis in the Middle East may be divided into six phases, each of which is bounded by events which produced major changes in the independent variables used in this study. The phases thus constitute periods of time within which the values of the independent variables remained relatively stable, but between which the factors of time pressure and the autonomous risk varied significantly.

Fighting near Lake Tiberias on April 7 raised the violence on the Israeli-Syrian border to a new level and signalled an increased possibility of further escalation. Soviet concern about the likelihood of larger-scale clashes is reflected in the official protest sent to the Israeli embassy in Moscow on 21 April, which warned Israel against "playing with fire" in an area close to the borders of the Soviet Union.[22] These standard expressions indicate that the incident raised the perceived probability of an escalation of conflict in the region, but delay in issuing the protest betokens a lack of perceived time pressure. For the purposes of this study, therefore, April 7 will mark the start of the first phase of the 1967 crisis, which continues until May 6. This period is characterized by high autonomous risk and low time pressure.

The boundary between the first and second phases will be demarcated by an event which the Politburo may or may not have been aware of. On May 7, Israel's cabinet took a decision to launch a limited retaliation raid against Syria if public warnings did not appear to result in a decrease in the incidence of terrorism and sabotage.[23] Nadav Safran speculates that Soviet intelligence agencies subsequently learned of an Israeli contingency plan for attack on Syria, but does not offer any evidence on when or how this might have occurred.[24] Kosygin, in his June 19 speech to the United Nations, stated that the U.S.S.R. had learned that Israel was planning to attack Syria on May 9.[25] Regardless of the provenance or accuracy of any reports Moscow may have received on the possibility of Israeli military action, it can be said with confidence that the Politburo became very concerned in early May that an attack on Syria might be imminent. The adoption of the Israeli contingency plan will serve as the start of the second phase of the crisis, May 7 to May 14. Kosygin's speech indicates that the Politburo perceived a high level of autonomous risk and very urgent time pressure during this period.

The third phase begins with the activation of the Egyptian-Syrian mutual defense treaty on May 14 and the subsequent mobilization of the Egyptian armed forces.[26] While the Egyptian mobilization heightened the risk of war, it served at first to relieve Syria of any immediate threat of an Israeli attack. Several Soviet commentators soon emphasized that even though Syria was still menaced by Israeli aggression, the UAR was a reliable ally which would aid Damascus in the Ba'ath's hour of need.[27] The third phase of the crisis, during which time pressure was moderately low while autonomous risk remained high, thus began with the Egyptian mobilization order on May 14 and lasted until May 20, when UAR forces began preparation for the blockade of the Straits of Tiran.

An Egyptian paratroop battalion dropped at Sharm el-Sheikh on May 20, and the UNEF contingent occupying the area completed its evacuation the following day.[28] By the time Nasser's speech announcing the blockade of the straits was broadcast in the early morning of May 23, it was apparent to the U.S.S.R. that Egypt's action and Israel's mobilization in response to it had created a situation where war could break out at any moment. The Soviet press carried commentaries warning that tensions in the Middle East had reached a dangerous level and that there was an urgent threat of an Israeli or American attack, probably against Syria.[29] The period from May 20 until June 5, from the Soviet viewpoint, can therefore be said to have been characterized by high time pressure as well as high autonomous risk.

The events of June 5 proved that Soviet expectations of an Israeli attack were well-founded, but the Politburo was probably surprised, and relieved, to find that Egypt and Jordan, rather than Syria, were the target of the initial ground offensives. The U.S.S.R.'s stronger ally had been attacked first, relieving the pressure on Syria at least for the moment. Soviet official statements issued during the first four days of the war sharply condemn the Israeli attack and emphasize that the U.S.S.R. and its fraternal socialist allies "reserve the right to take all necessary steps" to halt aggression in the region, they do not mention the need for immediate action.[30] By the morning of June 9, Egypt, Jordan, and Syria had accepted the cease-fire called in two UN resolutions (a third would pass that afternoon) and land combat had virtually stopped.[31] Until the Israeli offensive against Syria began in earnest, the U.S.S.R. might well have entertained hopes that the war could be ended without a renewed threat to the Ba'ath. Because a serious threat to Syria did not manifest itself until nightfall on June 9, when Israeli troops reached the edge of the Golan Heights, the phase of the Middle East crisis from the morning of June 5 until the evening of June 9 should be regarded as a period where autonomous risk was very great, but pressure for rapid Soviet action was temporarily reduced because Syria was not immediately threatened.

The success of the Golan Heights offensive posed a serious threat to the U.S.S.R.'s most vulnerable interests in the Middle East. Soviet decision-makers could not be certain that Israeli forces would stop at the edge of the heights until Israel accepted a cease-fire in the afternoon of June 10. The fall of Damascus would have had disastrous consequences for the Ba'ath and for Soviet influence in the region, and any actions intended to forestall an attack on the Syrian capital would have to be taken with all possible speed. The possibility of a continued Israeli offensive indicates that autonomous risk was high during this phase. This is supported by the language of the Soviet note announcing the breach in diplomatic relations between the U.S.S.R. and Israel, delivered on June 10, which states that "information was just received to the effect that Israeli troops . . . are proceeding in the direction of Damascus."[32] TASS reported in dispatches datelined 10 June that Israeli tanks had captured Qunaytira and would continue on to Damascus.[33]

The hot line message which Kosygin sent to Johnson on the same day, before the cease-fire became effective, warns that a "very crucial moment" was at hand and that the U.S.S.R. would act unless military operations ceased within the next few hours.[34] Even if the threat of Soviet action was a bluff, the message conveys the perception of very high time pressure. The final phase of the crisis, from the evening of June 9 until cease-fire in the afternoon of June 10, was therefore a period of both great time pressure and very high autonomous risk from a Soviet perspective.

Table 9-2 summarizes the values of the independent variables which this study expects to have influenced Soviet decision-making during the six phases of the 1967 crisis. During the first and fifth phases, time pressure was relatively low while the level of autonomous risk was relatively high. The third phase was a period of moderate to low time pressure and high autonomous risk, while phase four is characterized by high values for both independent variables. During phases two and six, high levels of time pressure were combined with very high autonomous risk and serious perceived threat to the Soviet Union's vulnerable Syrian allies. Because a pronounced element of autonomous risk runs throughout the 1967 crisis, the case of the Six Day War and the events leading up to it can serve to test the effect of variations in time pressure on Soviet risk-taking in a situation involving a high degree of autonomous risk.

With the independent variables valued as listed in the table, this study's analytical framework would expect that Soviet leaders would be least likely to take risks in phases one and five. Risk-taking would be more likely in phase three and still more likely in phase four. Phases two and six, according to this study's expectations, are the periods when the Politburo would be most likely to take risks in an attempt to simultaneously pursue the U.S.S.R.'s conflicting regional and global objectives. An explanation of Soviet behavior which structures the crisis as a game of Chicken, on the other hand, would expect that the U.S.S.R. would be least likely to take risks in phase two, more likely in phases three and four, yet more likely in phases one and five, and most likely in phase six, following Israel's acceptance of a cease-fire. The next section looks at actual Soviet behavior during the crisis in order to determine when the Politburo adopted more cautious courses of action and when it accepted greater risks. The next section will also search for evidence which suggests how Soviet decision-makers resolved, accepted, or attempted to deny the contradictions between their regional and global goals.

TABLE 9.2
Time Pressure and Autonomous Risk
in the 1967 Crisis

Phase: Dates	Time Pressure	Autonomous Risk	Likelihood of Risk-Taking
1: 7 April-6 May	Low	High	Moderately Low
2: 7 May-14 May	High	Very High	Very High
3: 14 May-20 May	Moderate	High	Moderately High
4: 20 May-4 June	High	High	High
5: 5 June-9 June	Low	High	Moderately Low
6: 9 June-10 June	High	Very High	Very High

Soviet Communications and Actions
in the 1967 Crisis

The most important point about the official Soviet response to the Lake Tiberias clash which begins the crisis' initial phase, may be that it was not issued until 14 days after the event. This indicates that the Politburo had ample time to discuss the situation before deciding to deliver an official protest, which warned that "Israeli aggression" would have "serious consequences" and suggested that Israel consider its actions carefully, but did not threaten any Soviet action.[35] This protest was read out to Israeli Ambassador Katz on May 21 by Deputy Foreign Minister Malik in Moscow, who refused to tender a written copy at the time, and the note was not published until 26 April.[36] This may indicate an unwillingness to publicly commit the U.S.S.R. to any course of action at this stage of the conflict. A subsequent message to Katz cautioned Israel to "not allow external forces to play with the fate of its people and State." but did not say that Soviet action would be part of the consequences of military operations against Syria.[37]

Commentators in the Soviet press during this period charged that the United States and other "imperialist" powers were conspiring with Israel to destabilize Egypt and Syria and stressed that Syrian-Egyptian solidarity or unity of progressive forces in the Arab world would oppose such plots.[38] No hint of Soviet involvement in the conflict is in evidence other than affirmation that "the people of the U.S.S.R. are with Syria" in its struggle with "imperialism."[39] Because the situation did not demand immediate Soviet action, and because suggestions that the U.S.S.R. might become more closely involved could have adversely affected both regional and global interests, it is not surprising that no effort was made to advertise the possibility of Soviet intervention in the conflict. In general, communications from Moscow during this phase suggest that the Politburo was concerned, but would try to keep its options open.

In the second phase, the U.S.S.R. played a crucial role in the escalation of the conflict. Sometime before May 11, Soviet officials began sending the UAR warnings of an imminent Israeli attack on

Syria. David Kimche and Dan Bawly report that an "urgent Soviet message" of an impending attack was delivered to Cairo and Damascus before Israeli Prime Minister Eshkol's speech on May 11.[40] It is easy to understand why the Politburo might have been concerned by the implications of Eshkol's speech, in which the prime minister said that Israel would choose the time, place, and means to respond to Syrian actions.[41] Subsequent Soviet communications, however, became more specific about the timing of the upcoming Israeli strike. A second message through diplomatic channels, according to Kimche and Bawly, warned that the attack would commence at 0400 on May 17.[42] The authors do not give details on the provenance of this message, but several other sources report Soviet efforts to pass warnings of an imminent Israeli attack. Anwar Sadat's memoirs include a first-hand account of one such communication; he reports that on May 13, Soviet Deputy Foreign Minister Semyonov met him in Moscow airport and told him that ten Israeli brigades had been concentrated near the Syrian border in preparation for an offensive.[43] This "confirmed" a message from Syrian Defense Minister Assad to Egyptian Marshal Amer, sent the same day, that Israel was missing its forces.[44] In fact, however, Israeli forces were making no such preparations at the time, and one account claims that the Egyptian General Fawzi reported as much to Nasser.[45]

The source of the information which led Soviet leaders to expect an Israeli attack is uncertain. Kosygin later claimed that the Knesset had authorized an attack against Syria on 9 May.[46] This "authorization" may refer to the Israeli cabinet decision, taken on May 7, to develop a contingency plan for a strike against Syria.[47] As noted above, Safran suggests that Soviet intelligence may have received information on this plan.[48] In any event, Soviet warnings appear to have had a major impact on Nasser's decision to mobilize. Heikal contends that these warnings were the primary reason for the Egyptian mobilization:

> Not a great deal of credence had been attached to the Syrian reports, but now that they were confirmed by the Russians Sadat naturally felt they must be taken extremely seriously...It

was on the basis of their warnings that on May 16 [*sic*] Nasser proclaimed a state of emergency and decided to send troops into Sinai.[49]

Because one of the objectives of his version of the events leading up to the Six Day War is to blame the U.S.S.R. for the UAR's defeat, it is likely that Heikal exaggerates the impact of the Soviet reports. It is clear that Soviet reports of preparations for an attack on Syria were not the only factor which prompted the Egyptian mobilization. It is not clear whether the overestimation of Israeli belligerence reflected in the reports was deliberate or unintentional. Nevertheless, the Soviet warnings strongly contributed to a dangerous escalation of the conflict.

Very little about the situation in the Middle East appeared in the Soviet press during the second phase of the crisis, although *Izveztiia* reported that the United States and Israel were planning a coup against the Ba'ath which was to be signalled by an Israeli attack.[50] Accounts of troop concentrations on the Israeli-Syrian border did not appear until May 16.[51] When Katz called upon Schiborin at the Foreign Ministry in Moscow on May 22 to protest the portrayal of Israeli actions toward Syria in the Soviet press, Schiborin responded, "We cannot be responsible for what is happening in the atmosphere which was poisoned by your leader's statements."[52]

Reportage in the third phase centered on the UAR's mobilization in response to the threat of an Israeli attack. Israel was again admonished against "playing with fire" and a fresh round of accusations of a plot against Syria appeared.[53] Most reports stressed, however, that the UAR and other Arab countries would come to Syria's aid if Israel were to launch an attack.[54] While the press was full of nebulous references to "imperialist plots," *Pravda* and *Izveztiia* did not emphasize the possibility of direct American military intervention into the conflict, while *Krasnaia Zvezda* and *Trud* specifically mentioned that the Sixth Fleet, a "gendarme" force, could be preparing to actively participate in Israeli machinations against Syria.[55] This could indicate that some differences of opinion on the likelihood of American action existed within the Politburo during this period, but the evidence for this is inconclusive. In general, communications from Moscow convey the message that "Arab solidarity" would be sufficient to meet the Israeli threat. This formula may have been a signal that the Politburo was not prepared at that point to commit the U.S.S.R. to intervention into the conflict.

The start of the fourth phase is marked by the UAR's preparations to blockade the Straits of Tiran. It appears likely that Soviet decision-makers were surprised by this development.[56] When reports of the blockade began to appear in the Soviet press, commentators focused on the possibility of American naval action to break it. This possibility existed, but Soviet reports of preparations for intervention appeared before the United States began to assemble its naval forces. Although Johnson discussed the formation of an Anglo-American joint task force as early as May 24, the multinational force intended to be sent to the Red Sea was still in the planning stages on June 4.[57] *Krasnaia Zvezda* reported that the United States was threatening to use naval forces to break the blockade on May 26.[58] Other papers ran items the next day which said that the "interventionist" Sixth Fleet, "the harbinger of previous invasions," was menacing Egypt and Syria.[59] These reports were premature, however, as major units of the Sixth Fleet did not actually begin concentrating in the eastern Mediterranean until May 30, and the aircraft carrier *Intrepid* passed through the Suez Canal on June 1.[60] In what may have been a belated endorsement of the Egyptian blockade, commentator Koriavin chastised the United States and Britain for sending "dreadnoughts instead of diplomats" to resolve the conflict in the region.[61]

Most Soviet diplomatic activity during this period sought to avoid war. A Soviet government note issued on May 23 warned of the danger of war and stated that the U.S.S.R. would "do everything in its power to prevent a violation of peace."[62] Kosygin mentioned this note to UAR Defense Minister Badran, who arrived in Moscow on May 24, and told Badran that Egypt must avoid giving Israel or the United States any pretext to launch an attack.[63] At 3 A.M. on May 26, Soviet Ambassador Pozhidaev asked that Nasser be awakened so that he could deliver an urgent message. He then told Nasser that the United States had informed the Soviet government of Israeli reports that Egypt was planning to attack at dawn, and he implored Nasser not to order Egyptian forces to fire the first shot.[64] Sadat recalls that "the Soviet Union consistently warned that the tempo of events was moving faster than it should."[65]

Heikal contends, however, that some Soviet back-channel communications conveyed a different message. He reports that on May 29, as Soviet Defense Minister Grechko saw Badran off on his return to Cairo, Grechko told Badran, "Stand firm. Whatever you have to face, you will find us with you. Don't let yourselves be blackmailed by the Americans or anyone else."[66] Heikal also relates that Nasser received reports from Syrian President Atassi which said that "various Soviet sources" had told Atassi during a visit to Moscow that "everything would turn out all right" without a lessening of Egyptian pressure on Israel.[67] Again, it should be noted that Heikal sought to implicate the Soviet Union in the defeat of its Arab allies. A preponderance of evidence indicates that the Politburo genuinely attempted to reduce tensions during this phase, but some conflicting signals sent by Soviet officials may have worked to undermine their efforts. Throughout the phase, the Soviet press reported that America and Israel were preparing to attack.

The reports were half right. The crisis' fifth phase began with devastating Israeli air attacks. As Egypt and Jordan bore the brunt of the initial ground offensives on June 5, Syria was not in immediate danger. The Soviet government made good use of the time made available by the fact that Damascus was not Israel's first target. Soviet diplomats repeatedly pressed for a cease-fire at the United Nations.[68] A Soviet official statement issued on the day the war started and a note to Israel sent on June 7 condemned the Israeli attack and warned that the U.S.S.R. "reserved the right to take all necessary measures" to halt aggression in the region, but neither communiqué was specific about what those measures could involve.[69] In addition to using the UN Security Council and bilateral diplomacy to attempt to secure a cease-fire, the Politburo sought to create a united socialist front in opposition to Israel's actions by convening a meeting of leaders of the Warsaw Pact countries and Yugoslavia in Moscow on June 9.[70] This effort was not completely successful; Romania refused to sign the joint communiqué, issued the day of the meeting, which reaffirmed that the

U.S.S.R. and its socialist allies would do "everything necessary" to help the Arab countries repulse the Israeli attack and to preserve peace in the region.[71]

The U.S.S.R.'s Egyptian allies were not satisfied with these diplomatic efforts and were angered when more concrete Soviet support was not forthcoming. Marshal Amer dressed down the Soviet Ambassador to Cairo on June 6, claiming that Pozhidaev's late-night call on Nasser was evidence of a Soviet-American conspiracy: "It is you who prevented us from making the first strike. You deprived us of the initiative. That is collusion!"[72] Soviet military forces scrupulously avoided provocative activity during that phase of the crisis. The Soviet Navy's Mediterranean squadron slightly increased its shadowing of Sixth Fleet vessels, and a Soviet cruiser approached to within five miles of the carrier *America* on June 8, but there is no evidence that Soviet military units attempted a show of force in the region or elsewhere during this period.[73]

The Soviet press resounded throughout this phase of the conflict with condemnations of the Israeli attack. Many commentators predicted that Israel's actions would bring disaster upon it. The United States was frequently accused of knowing of and encouraging the surprise attack. Vishnevetskiy, possibly the most vehement denouncer of U.S. policy during this period, charged America with "pouring gasoline on the flames" of the conflict.[74] Israel's methods and tactics were described as inspired by, or designed to be direct copies of, American actions in Vietnam.[75] Britain, West Germany, and Western oil companies were also accused of complicity in the Israeli attack.[76]

Despite these denunciations, the Soviet press indicated that Soviet intervention to halt the Israeli offensive was not likely. Items referred repeatedly to Soviet government statements and Soviet calls for a cease-fire in the UN Security Council as evidence of the "resolute support" of the U.S.S.R. and other socialist countries for the Arab cause.[77] One writer in *Krasnaia Zvezda* did say that "urgent steps are necessary to put an end to aggression" but did not elaborate on the measures which he felt the situation demanded.[78] For the most part, however, Soviet press reports and commentaries stressed during this phase of the crisis that although Egypt and Syria might lose the war, "Arab solidarity" would eventually defeat Israel and restore peace.[79] "V. Petrov" summed up the prospects for an ultimate Arab victory by observing that Israel could not hope to fight 100 million Arabs or the "stream of history."[80]

It soon became obvious, however, that Israel had at least secured a major short-term victory, and near the end of the crisis it may have appeared to Moscow that Israel would attempt to deal Syria a crushing blow. The sixth and final phase of the crisis began on the night of June 9, When Israeli forces began positioning themselves for an assault on Qunaytira, a strategically important city overlooking the Damascus plain. Soon after Syrian troops abandoned Qunaytira, on the morning of June 10, Soviet diplomatic activity showed signs of expectation that the worst was yet to come. After the UN Security Council had received reports that Qunaytira had been taken, but before Israel had actually occupied it, Soviet UN Ambassador Fedorenko told the Council that the Soviet government had decided to break off relations with Israel.[81] That same day, Katz was summoned to the Soviet Foreign Ministry to receive the note which announced the severance of relations. The note began by claiming that Israeli forces were advancing towards Damascus and then issued a stern warning:

The Government of the Soviet Union warns the Government of Israel that it will bear the full weight of responsibility for its treachery, for the flagrant violation of the Security Council resolution. If Israel does not immediately cease military operations, the Soviet Union, together with all peace-loving countries, will apply sanctions against Israel with all the consequences resulting therefrom.[82]

Soviet Ambassador Chuvakhin delivered an identical message to Foreign Minister Eban in Tel Aviv that afternoon.[83]

It is impossible to say whether the break in relations with Israel was intended to show support for the U.S.S.R.'s Arab allies without making definite commitments, to save face and transfer the blame for policy bungling, to prepare the way for possible military action, or all of the above. In any case, the language of the note indicates a desire on the part of Soviet decision-makers to transfer the onus of responsibility for subsequent developments from themselves onto their opponents.

The Soviet action during the crisis which most alarmed the United States was the transmission of the hot line message the same day, June 10. The communication, signed by Kosygin, said that a "very crucial moment" which threatened a "great catastrophe" had arrived, and warned that unless Israel halted all military operations within the next few hours, the U.S.S.R. would take "necessary actions, including military."[84] Johnson ordered the Sixth Fleet closer to the Syrian coast in response to this communication.[85] Fukuyama describes Kosygin's message as a bluff designed to display support for the U.S.S.R.'s allies after the real danger of an Israeli attack had passed.[86] The chronology of events on June 10 casts doubt on this interpretation. Israeli Prime Minister Eshkol and Defense Minister Dayan met with the UNTSO Chief of Staff, General Bull, at 1200 GMT and agreed to a cease-fire as of 1630.[87] Johnson received the hot line message only one hour after this meeting, at 1300 GMT.[88] It is not unlikely that a report of this meeting could have been sent to Moscow (either through the UN or Soviet intelligence), the information communicated to the Politburo and verified, and a hot line message composed and sent to Washington, all within the space of an hour. There were also indications that Israeli forces were still advancing both before and after the time Kosygin's message was received in Washington. Israeli troops had not secured Qunaytira until 1230 GMT, shortly before the hot line message was received, and additional forces were arriving at the city at 1400 GMT.[89] These troop movements could easily have raised suspicions that the announced cease-fire might not hold. The American reaction to the message increased the possibility of a U.S.-Soviet or U.S.-Syrian incident, raising the risk of a confrontation that the U.S.S.R. had sought to avoid. Kosygin's message therefore heightened the risk of escalation while the war was still hours away from its end. Both the short time between the acceptance of the cease-fire and the hot line message and the developments in the Golan Heights which probably appeared threatening from a Soviet viewpoint strongly suggest that the hot line message was not a face-saving gesture made after the crisis was over, but an action which Soviet leaders knew to involve a significant element of risk.

As the final phase of the crisis lasted less than 24 hours, the Soviet press had only a short time in which to comment on the Golan Heights fighting and the threat to Damascus. Commentaries appearing during and shortly after the last stage of the fighting, echoing the language of the June 9 joint communiqué, called for "resolute joint action" to rebuff Israel aggression.[90] Dymov in *Krasnaia Zvezda* excoriated Israel for "trying to take the opportunity to advance as far as possible" into Syria and argued that the "widest support" from socialist countries, especially the U.S.S.R., had great bearing on the situation.[91] It is difficult to determine whether this comment should be interpreted as a call for greater Soviet support of its Arab allies or an attempt to take credit for halting the Israeli offensive.

After the war, Soviet leaders claimed repeatedly that the support from the U.S.S.R. and the socialist community played a decisive role in bringing the conflict to a close. The CPSU plenum held on June 20 and 21 debated Soviet policy during the crisis and reaffirmed Soviet solidarity with the UAR, Syria, Algeria, and progressive forces within the Arab world while calling for a political solution to the Arab-Israeli conflict.[92] In his speech to graduates of Soviet military academies on 5 July, Brezhnev said that "Looking back today, we can say confidently that our actions in the critical days of the Near East crisis were correct".[93] There is, nevertheless, some evidence of recriminations following the crisis. The removals of N. Yegorichev (from the leadership of the Moscow CPSU central committee) and A.I. Shelepin (from the Ministry of Light Industry) may have been linked to their policies on the Middle East during the war, and the Ambassadors Pozhidaev and Chuvakhin were replaced without receiving new appointments.[94] These personnel changes cannot be taken as indications of post-decisional regret, however, because dismissals and demotions are normal consequences of policy failures and may not reflect upon the process by which the regretted decisions were made.

Value Conflict and Soviet Decision-Making in 1967

What do Soviet statements and actions in the 1967 crisis reveal about the effects of value conflict on Soviet decision-making? This section finds that in phases one, three, and five, Soviet communications and actions indicate that the Politburo accepted the contradictions between its global and regional objectives and acted to limit risks. Soviet behavior in phases two and six, on the other hand, provides evidence of increased risk-taking in attempts to simultaneously avoid confrontation with the United States and maintain or increase Soviet influence over regional allies. The evidence from phase four appears mixed.

In the phases of the crisis where autonomous risk was high while time pressure was at low or moderate levels, Soviet decision-makers made gestures in support of both regional and global objectives but did not take great risks in pursuit of either. Israel's actions of April 7, at the start of phase one, were answered only with an official protest on April 21.[95] The delay indicates that the Politburo used the time available to make compromises between its contradictory goals and achieve consensus on a response to the Lake Tiberias incidents. Similarly, when the initial Israeli offensives on May 5 (phase five) were directed against Egypt and Jordan rather than Syria, Soviet leaders took advantage of the brief period when the Syrian Ba'ath was not in immediate danger to convene a meeting of other socialist states in an effort to build a united front in support of its Arab allies. Although the resulting Moscow Declaration indicated some dissension in the socialist camp (from Romania), the meeting offered the opportunity for Soviet decision-makers to gauge the strength of support which the U.S.S.R.'s European allies were willing to extend before engaging in more forceful actions.[96]

While the views of the U.S.S.R.'s European allies may have had little influence in the decision adopted, the effort to show socialist solidarity offered a means to display political support for the Arab allies without making a commitment to intervene in the war. Throughout the crisis, the theme of solidarity and joint action appears in official communications and the press as a signal that strong material or military support will not be immediately forthcoming. During the third phase, commentators stressed that Arab solidarity, backed up by Soviet support, would be sufficient to deter an Israeli attack.[97] When this deterrent failed, the Politburo convened the June 9 Moscow conference in phase five to assess and rally the support of its Warsaw pact allies for "resolute joint action" to stop the fighting.[98] Press commentaries in the fifth phase likewise conveyed the message that unity among progressive forces in the Arab world, reinforced by Soviet support would eventually turn the tide and erase the gains made by the Israeli offensive.[99] While the emphasis on solidarity seems to indicate a lack of Soviet willingness to take risks in support of the Arab allies, efforts to depict the United States as an imperialist aggressor and Israel portrayed as its lackey continued during these three phases.[100] The goal of maintaining Soviet influence in the region was therefore not completely abandoned, and political conflict with the United States was heightened somewhat during the first, third, and fifth phases. This indicates that while avoidance of a Soviet-American confrontation was probably valued higher than increasing the Soviet role in the Middle East during these periods, risk-limiting compromises were made on both regional and global Soviet objectives. In addition, measures intended to insure that the U.S.S.R.'s allies were "on board" and to obtain information from a wide variety of sources and cooperation from many groups which could affect or must implement decisions are key components of vigilant information processing. These features of decision-making may be expected to accompany acceptance of a value conflict and achievement of a compromise between opposing goals.

The evidence of the effect of value conflict on Soviet risk-taking in the fourth phase is not clear. Heikal's accounts indicate that Soviet behavior in this period is characterized by contradictory signals. Three days after Pozhidaev demanded to see Nasser in the middle of the night of May 26 to plead with the Egyptian president not to attack, Grechko told the UAR defense minister to "stand firm" and to resist American pressure to de-escalate the conflict.[101] Similarly, while Badran was being told by Kosygin not to give the United States or Israel any pretext for an attack, Atassi received assurances in Moscow that continuation of the Egyptian blockade would result in a favorable resolution of the crisis.[102] These accounts, however, are not confirmed by other sources. The reports of mixed signals may reflect differences within the Soviet leadership on how to proceed, but there is insufficient evidence to determine whether this was the case. By the same token, the Soviet press exaggerated the danger of Western naval intervention during this phase.[103] However, it is impossible to determine if these statements reflect deliberate inflation of Western belligerence for propaganda purposes or a genuine concern over the possibility of American attack or U.S.-Israeli collusion. In any event, Soviet leaders generally did not exhibit an increased propensity to accept risks during phase four.

In phases two and six, on the other hand, Soviet actions indicate a significantly greater willingness to accept risks. In the second phase, the Soviet government engaged in a concerted effort to warn the UAR through multiple channels that an Israeli attack was imminent.[104] Soviet officials provided erroneous starting times for a mid-May offensive and expressed alarm at troop concentrations which did not exist.[105] These reports of Israeli preparations for an offensive had the desired effect on Nasser and the UAR's leadership in that they increased Egyptian readiness to come to the defense of Syria. However, Soviet leaders could not have been unaware of the risk that Nasser would order a further escalation of the crisis. Sadat relates how Nasser seized the opportunity for war with Israel in a meeting of the UAR Supreme Executive Council near the end of May:

> Nasser said, "Now with our concentrations in Sinai, the chances of war are fifty-fifty. But if we close the strait, war will be a one hundred percent certainty." Then, turning to Amer, he asked: "Are the armed forces ready, Abdel Hakim?" Amer pointed to his neck and said: "On my own head be it, boss! Everything's in tiptop shape."[106]

While Soviet decision-makers did not want war, they could not have been unaware that many of their allies did. Their encouragement of an Egyptian mobilization, made on the basis of false or falsified information, served only to hamper both regional and global objectives and ultimately backfired catastrophically.

The hot line message sent near the end of the crisis also involved a significant degree of risk. Kosygin's mention of the possibility of Soviet military intervention in phase six led to American actions which increased the chances of an accidental Soviet-American confrontation. Eshkol and Dayan had stated that Israel would accept a cease-fire shortly before Johnson received the message.[107] Nevertheless, the situation on the Golan front may have been very worrisome for Soviet decision-makers at the time the message was composed. The timing of the hot line message is consistent with Snyder and Diesing's characterization of it as an effort to protect defeated allies from total humiliation, and such was clearly one of the objectives of the message.[108] Another probable objective was to obtain greater American pressure on Israel to stop its offensive against Syria. It is not likely, however, that Kosygin's message was entirely a bluff, issued after the crisis was resolved, as Fukuyama argues.[109] It is more probable that this hint of the possibility of Soviet intervention, issued during a period of intense time pressure and high autonomous risk, intentionally risked some form of U.S.-Soviet conflict (if only a heightened political confrontation) in order to limit the losses to Soviet regional allies and interests.

Although the Politburo displayed greater willingness to accept risks during phases two and six, they appeared unwilling to abandon either regional or global objectives. In the second phase, they attempted to use Egyptian forces to deter an expected attack on Syria without direct Soviet involvement, which would have provoked a U.S.-Soviet confrontation. The attempt to get the UAR to mobilize succeeded, but the effort to deter war failed. In the final phase, the hot line message may have been an attempt to use American diplomatic pressure to dissuade Israel from advancing on Damascus, again avoiding direct commitment of Soviet forces. A stronger show of support for the U.S.S.R.'s regional allies was another likely goal of that communication, which in the short run served only to raise tensions unnecessarily. Essentially, Soviet actions during these phases attempted to pursue both conflicting goals by attempting to manipulate other actors into working toward Soviet objectives. The attempt to manipulate Egypt succeeded in the short run but led to a disastrous failure, while the attempt to manipulate the U.S. did nothing apart from raising the risk of accidental conflict. Soviet actions in these phases did involve lower risks than direct intervention would have entailed. In both instances, however, Soviet behavior indicates that denial of value conflict prompted efforts to pursue contradictory goals, but these efforts were worse than useless.

To summarize the preceding paragraphs, Soviet actions and statements during the 1967 crisis indicate that Soviet decision-makers took greater risks during the second and sixth phases, when time pressure was high and autonomous risk was very high, than in the other phases of the crisis. The Politburo did not exhibit an enhanced tendency toward risk-taking in phases four, when indicators of both independent variables were high. In the 1967 case, therefore, both Hypothesis One (Soviet risk-taking increases with time pressure and Hypothesis Two (Soviet risk-taking increases with autonomous risk) are supported most strongly when the two independent variables vary together and when a very high level of autonomous risk is present (phases two and six), and are supported when time pressure is low but autonomous risk is high (phases one, three, and five). Curiously, the hypotheses are not supported in one phase (four) where both are high. There is also significant evidence that Soviet decision-makers compromised both regional and global goals during periods of moderate to low time pressure and high autonomous risk, but attempted to pursue both objectives by manipulating other actors when time pressure was high and autonomous risk was very great. This evidence is also consistent with the expectations of this study's analytical framework.

With regard to alternative explanations, Soviet behavior in 1967 runs contrary to the expectations produced by conceiving of Soviet crisis decision-making as a U.S.-Soviet Chicken game, as this explanation predicts that risk-taking will be greatest in periods of low time pressure and autonomous risk and least in evidence when time pressure and autonomous risk are high. Representing Soviet crisis decision-making as a Prisoner's Dilemma game played between two conflicting objectives therefore affords a better explanation of Soviet behavior, if not a perfect one. Finally, an explanation which focuses on conflict between values can account for Soviet actions throughout the crisis, while contentions that the U.S.S.R. had a predetermined strategy of stepping in to limit damage to its allies only after the crisis was resolved cannot adequately explain the variations observable in Soviet risk-taking behavior before and during the Six Day War.

Conclusions: The Soviet Role
in the Outbreak of the Six Day War

The leadership of the U.S.S.R. played a pivotal role in the escalation from crisis to war in 1967. This study does not suggest that war would not have broken out if the U.S.S.R. had not acted as it did, as the Arab-Israeli conflict was and remains a deadly quarrel which has generated violence and war with depressing frequency. Instead, it has developed its contention that a study of the effects of value conflict on Soviet decision-making can help to explain why the U.S.S.R. contributed to the defeat of its Arab allies. There is substantial evidence that Soviet decision-makers attempted to deny the contradictions between their regional and global objectives during critical periods in the crisis which led to the Six Day War. During periods of low to moderate time pressure and high autonomous risk, the Politburo sought to control risks by extending only political support and limited material aid to its allies. At points when time pressure was high and autonomous risk was pronounced, however, the U.S.S.R. sought to maintain its influence in the region while avoiding a confrontation with the United States by attempting to manipulate other parties to the conflict into working towards Soviet objectives. These attempts met with only partial success at a high cost, especially to the U.S.S.R.'s Arab allies. The evidence from the 1967 crisis generally supports this study's hypotheses on the effects of value conflict. When Soviet leaders appeared to accept that their goals were mutually opposing, they compromised on both and succeeded in limiting risks. When a high level of autonomous risk jeopardized both Soviet regional and global objectives, however, it appears that Soviet decision-makers did not compromise one value in favor of the other, but instead took greater risks in support of both. Attempts to manipulate others into supporting one's own interests are common in international politics. Soviet decision-makers may have simply seized the opportunities for manipulation available in the 1967 crisis in order to facilitate denial of the conflict between Soviet goals. In other crises, the Politburo may have used different means to make risks more palatable. In any case, Soviet actions before and during the Six Day War show that in their efforts to maintain influence in the Middle East, Soviet leaders took substantial risks at crucial moments. Representing Soviet crisis decision-making as an attempt to deal with conflicts between goals therefore provides a better explanation of Soviet risk-taking in 1967 than either a Chicken or Protector game matrix or the contention that the Politburo followed a predetermined strategy of bluffing after the crisis was over.

Although focusing on the conflict between regional and global objectives has proven to be useful for explaining Soviet behavior in the 1967 case, some of this study's analytical framework remains untested. Autonomous risk was high or very high throughout the crisis, while the time pressure felt by Soviet decision-makers varied significantly. Further research must examine Soviet actions at points in other crises when autonomous risk was low in order to determine if this factor has an independent effect on Soviet risk-taking. Similarly, conflicts in which autonomous risk varied greatly must be studied to better understand the independent effects of time pressure. Examination of other cases is also needed to ascertain if the period in late May and early June of 1967, where Soviet risk-taking did not increase significantly when both independent variables were high, constitutes an anomaly. Subsequent findings may show that only a highly volatile situation or an immediate threat to Soviet interests can prompt Soviet decision-makers to take risks in support of regional objectives.

Political scientists have long recognized the need to incorporate cognitive factors into the analysis of decisions, but the utility of cognitive models has been limited by an inability to predict how cognitive phenomena are most likely to influence risk-taking in specific situations. The results of this chapter's inquiry into Soviet actions into 1967 indicate that study of value conflict effects may help make progress toward removing this limitation. Much attention has recently been given to the closely related question of the impact of psychological factors on deterrence. Further research on the influence of value conflict on crisis decisions may contribute to the analysis of this issue as well. The finding of this study suggests that examination of the ways in which decision-makers deal with conflicts between opposing objectives can enhance our understanding of superpower behavior in crisis confrontations.

This chapter's two hypotheses on Soviet risk-taking must be tested in other cases before any general conclusions can be drawn on the effects of value conflict on crisis decisions. With regard to the 1967 crisis, however, an examination of the events surrounding the Six Day War clearly shows that the Politburo's failure to resolve the conflict between its regional and global goals helps to explain why the U.S.S.R.'s leaders were instrumental in the outbreak of a war which they strove earnestly to prevent. As a final point, the author wishes to emphasize that the purpose of developing an analytical perspective which focuses on value conflict is not to treat decision-makers as information processing units whose actions may be predicted by psychological theory. Instead, it is hoped that this study can contribute to the understanding of the role of the human element in decisions where leaders are forced to act under the dehumanizing pressures of confrontation and crisis.

Notes

1. For detailed analysis of Soviet policy toward the Middle East before and during the war, see Walter Laqueur, *The Struggle for the Middle East* (New York: Macmillan, 1969); Arnold L. Horelick, "Soviet Policy in the Middle East, Part I: Policy from 1955 to 1969," in Paul Y. Hammond and Sidney S. Alexander, *Political Dynamics in the Middle East* (New York: American Elsevier, 1972), pp. 553-604; and Jon D. Glassman, *Arms for the Arabs* (Baltimore: Johns Hopkins, 1975).

2. Laqueur, *Struggle*, pp. 68-79; Stephen T. Hosmer and Thomas W. Wolfe, *Soviet Policy and Practice Toward Third World Conflicts* (Lexington, MA: Lexington Books, 1983), pp. 12-28.

3. Paul Jabber and Roman Kolkowicz, "The Arab-Israeli Wars of 1967 and 1973," in Stephen S. Kaplan, *The Diplomacy of Power: Soviet Armed Forces as a Political Instrument* (Washington: Brookings, 1981), p. 414; Mohammed H. Heikal, *The Road to Ramadan* (New York: Ballantine, 1975), pp. 39-40.

4. Heikal's account of Nasser's relations with Soviet leaders are very colorful, although they may be slightly colored by the author's closeness to his subject. See *The Cairo Documents* (Garden City, NY: Doubleday, 1973), pp. 1-30, 121-158; and *The Sphinx and the Commissar* (New York: Harper & Row, 1978).

5. Laqueur, *Struggle*, pp. 85-89; Horelick, "Soviet Policy," pp. 581-591.

6. Glassman, *Arms*, pp. 25-35; *Pravda*, 12 Feb. 1967, pp. 1,4 (CPSU-Ba'ath Communique); L. Koriavin, *Izveztiia*, 8 Jan. 1967, p. 4, and 10 May 1967, p. 1.

7. Lyndon Baines Johnson, *The Vantage Point* (New York: Holt, Rinehart and Winston, 1971), p. 291.

8. See for example the interchange between Nasser and Podgorny on June 23, 1967, as recorded by 'Abd-al-Majid Farid, trans. in "'Abd-al-Nasir's Secret Papers," U.S. Joint Publications Research Service Translations on Near East and North Africa #1865 (14 Nov. 1978), pp. 11-12.

9. Alexander L. George, *Presidential Decisionmaking in Foreign Policy* (Boulder, CO: Westview Press, 1980), pp. 26-28.

10. Irving L. Janis and Leon Mann, *Decision Making: A Psychological Analysis of Conflict, Choice, and Commitment* (New York: Free Press, 1977), p. 46.

11. George, *Decisionmaking*, pp. 32-34.

12. Janis and Mann, *Decision Making*, pp. 52-80.

13. George, *Decisionmaking*, p. 40.

14. Janis and Mann, *Decision Making*, pp. 86-89.

15. Ole R. Holsti, "The 1914 Case," *American Political Science Review* 59/2 (June 1965), pp. 365-378, and *Crisis, Escalation, War* (Montreal: McGill-Queen's University Press, 1972) p. 18.

16. Jack Snyder, "Rationality at the Brink: The Role of Cognitive Processes in Failures of Deterrence" (Santa Monica, CA: RAND Paper P-5740, Oct. 1976), p. 33ff.

17. Hannes Adomeit, *Soviet Risk-Taking and Crisis Behavior* (London: George Allen and Unwin, 1982), pp. 316-327; and "Soviet Crisis Prevention and Management: Why and When do the Soviet Leaders Take Risks?" (Santa Monica: RAND/UCLA Center for the Study of Soviet International Behavior Occasional Paper OPS-008, Oct.1986), pp. 17-19.

18. Jack Snyder, *The Ideology of the Offensive* (Ithaca, NY: Cornell, 1984), p. 212.

19. Glenn H. Snyder and Paul Diesing, *Conflict Among Nations* (Princeton: Princeton University Press, 1977), pp. 145-148.

20. Francis Fukuyama "Soviet Threats to Intervene in the Middle East 1956-1973" (Santa Monica, CA: RAND Note N-1577-FF, June 1980), pp. 5-25.

21. Johnson, *Vantage Point*, p. 302.

22. The text of this protest was published in *Izveztiia*, 26 April 1967, p. 1.

23. Michael Brecher with Benjamin Geist, *Decisions in Crisis: Israel, 1967 and 1973* (Berkeley, CA: University of California Press, 1980), pp. 35-36.

24. Nadav Safran, *From War to War: The Arab-Israeli Confrontation, 1948-1967* (New York: Pegasus, 1969), pp. 277-78.

25. Text of this speech published in *Pravda*, 20 June 1967, p.1.

26. *Middle East Record 1967* (hereafter *MER 1967*), pp. 185-186.

27. Koriavin, *Izveztiia*, 17 May 1967, p. 1; Yevgeniy Primakov, *Pravda*, 18 May 1967, p. 1; O. Ivanov, *Krasnaia zvezda*, 19 May 1967, p. 3; V. Rogov, *Trud*, 19 May 1967, p. 1.

28. *MER 1967*, p. 194.

29. Viktor Maevskiy, *Pravda*, 22 May 1967, p. 1; Koriavin, *Izveztiia*, 25 May 1967, p. 3; Ivanov, *Krasnaia zvezda*, 25 May 1967, p. 3; D. Volskiy, *Krasnaia zvezda*, 28 May 1967, p. 3.

30. Soviet government statement, 5 June 1967, published in *Pravda*, 6 June 1967, p. 1; Soviet government communique to Israel, 7 June 1967, pub. in *Pravda*, 8 June 1967, p. 1; Statement of the communist & workers' parties and governments of Bulgaria, Hungary, the GDR, Poland, the USSR, Czechoslovakia, and Yugoslavia, issued 9 May 1967, pub. in *Pravda*, 10 June 1967, p. 1. The last statement, often referred to as the Moscow Declaration, was prepared by a formal multilateral meeting and is highly unlikely to reflect decisions made in response to Israeli actions on the day of its issue.

31. *MER 1967*, p. 229.

32. Text of this note published in *Pravda*, 11 June 1967, p. 1.

33. *Pravda*, 11 June 1967, p. 4.

34. Quoted in Johnson, *Vantage Point*, pp. 301-302.

35. *Izveztiia*, 26 April 1967, p. 1.

36. Avigdor Dagan, *Moscow and Jerusalem* (New York: Abelard-Schuman, 1970), pp. 202-203.

37. *Ibid*, pp. 203-204.

38. Ivanov, *Krasnaia zvezda*, 12 April 1967, p. 1; Vishnevetskiy, *Izveztiia*, 16 April 1967, p. 3; Primakov, *Pravda*, 12 April 1967, p. 5, and 19 April 1967, p. 5.

39. Vishnevetskiy, *Izveztiia*, 16 April 1967, p. 5.

40. David Kimche and Dan Bawly, *The Sandstorm* (New York: Stein and Day, 1968), p. 88.

41. Charles W. Yost, "The Arab-Israeli War: How it Began," *Foreign Affairs* 46/3 (Winter 1968), p. 308.

42. Kimche and Bawly, *Sandstorm*, p. 88.

43. Anwar el-Sadat, *In Search of Identity* (New York: Harper & Row, 1977), pp. 171-172. Sadat was at that time the Vice-President of the UAR and was returning to Cairo after an official visit.

44. Laqueur, *Struggle*, p. 71.

45. O'Ballance, p. 23; Jabber and Kolkowicz, p. 425.

46. *Pravda*, 20 June 1967, p. 3.

47. Brecher, *Decisions in Crisis*, p. 36.

48. Safran, *From War to War*, p. 277.

49. Heikal, *Sphinx*, pp. 174-175. Mobilization of the UAR armed forces was actually ordered on 14 May (*MER 1967*, p. 185).

50. Koriavin, *Izveztiia*, 10 May 1967, p. 1.

51. Primakov, *Pravda*, 16 May 1967; *Izveztiia*, 16 May 1967, p. 1.

52. Quoted in Dagan, p. 213.

53. E. Tuma, *Izveztiia*, 18 May 1967, p. 2.

54. Primakov, *Pravda*, 18 May 1967, p. 1, and 20 May 1967, p. 1; Koriavin, *Izveztiia*, 17 May 1967, p. 1, 19 May 1967, p. 1, and 20 May 1967, p. 2.

55. V. Pustav, *Krasnaia zvezda*, 17 May 1967, p. 2; Ivanov, *Krasnaia zvezda*, 19 May 1967, p. 3; V. Rogov, *Trud*, 19 May 1967, p.1.

56. Dagan, p. 218; Kass, pp. 28-29; Jabber and Kolkowicz, pp. 430-431.

57. Johnson, *Vantage Point*, p. 291-296.

58. V. Vashedchenko, *Krasnaia zvezda*, 26 May 1967, p. 4.

59. *Izveztiia*, 27 May 1967, p. 4; G. Vasil'ev, *Pravda*, 27 May 1967, p.5; Primakov, *Pravda* 27 May 1967, p. 5.

60. *MER 1967*, p. 223.

61. *Izveztiia*, 4 June 1967, p. 1.

62. Text published in *Pravda*, 24 May 1967, p. 1.

63. Heikal, *Sphinx*, pp. 178-179.

64. Heikal, *Cairo Documents*, p. 244.

65. Sadat, *Search*, p. 173.

66. Quoted in Heikal, *Sphinx*, p. 179.

67. Heikal, *Sphinx*, p. 180.

68. For an account of the U.S.S.R.'s activities at the U.N., see *MER 1967*, pp. 236-241, and Eban, pp. 365-413.

69. Text of 5 June message published in *Pravda*, 6 June 1967, p. 1; note to Israel published in *Pravda*, 7 June 1967, p. 1.

70. *Pravda*, 10 June 1967, p. 1.

71. Text in *Pravda*, 10 June 1967, p. 1.

72. Quoted in Heikal, *Sphinx*, p. 182.

73. For reports of Soviet naval operations, see *The New York Times*, June 8, 1968, p. 1, and June 9, 1969, p. 1.

74. *Pravda*, 6 June 1967, p. 3. See also *Izveztiia*, 7 June 1967, p. 2, and *Pravda*, 8 June 1967, p. 3; Y. Dymov, *Krasnaia zvezda*, 8 June 1967, p. 1.

75. A. Leontiev and Y. Dymov, *Krasnaia zvezda*, 9 June 1967, p. 3.

76. Unsigned editorial, "Inspirers of Aggression," *Izveztiia*, 6 June 1967, p. 1; Polianov, *Izveztiia*, 8 June 1967, p. 5; V. Kurdriavtsev, *Izveztiia*, 9 June 1967, p. 2; Beliaev, *Pravda*, 10 June 1967, p. 3.

77. Beliaev, *Pravda*, 6 June 1967, p. 3; Vishnevetskiy, *Izveztiia*, 7 June 1967, p. 2.

78. Y. Dymov, *Krasnaia zvezda*, 8 June 1967, p. 1.

79. Report of the Soviet Committee in Solidarity with the Countries of Asia and Africa, *Pravda*, 7 June 1967, p. 5; Koriavin, *Izveztiia*, 9 June 1967, p. 1.

80. V. Petrov, *Izveztiia*, 10 June 1967, p. 1.

81. Eban, pp. 422-423; *MER 1967* p. 240.

82. Text published in *Pravda*, 11 June 1967, p. 1. Czechoslovakia, Bulgaria, Hungary, Yugoslavia, and Poland all followed suit by June 12. The GDR did not have diplomatic relations with Israel, and Romania, which had not signed the June 9 joint communique, maintained relations.

83. Eban, p. 423.

84. Text quoted in Johnson, p. 302.

85. Johnson, p. 302.

86. Fukuyama, pp. 8-9.

87. Odd Bull, *War and Peace in the Middle East* (London: Leo Cooper, 1976), p. 120.

88. Johnson, p. 302.

89. *MER 1967*, p. 230.

90. V. Matveev, *Izveztiia*, 11 June 1967, p. 3. (This commentary was quoted in a Radio TASS broadcast on 10 June, trans. in FBIS USSR 113 (12 June) 1967, p. BB23); unsigned editorial, *Pravda*, 11 June 1967, p. 1.

91. *Krasnaia zvezda*, 11 June 1967, p. 3.

92. CPSU Plenum Resolution, *Pravda*, 22 June 1967, p. 1. The resolution also warned against allowing the PRC to expand its influence in the Middle East, a concern voiced earlier by "V. Petrov" in *Izveztiia*, 13 June 1967, p. 5.

93. Text of speech in *Izveztiia*, 6 July 1967, p. 1.

94. For a discussion of these personnel changes, see Kass.

95. Dagan, pp. 202-203.

96. According to Heikal, *Sphinx*, p. 183, Yugoslavia showed more willingness to materially aid the Arab cause than the U.S.S.R. at this meeting.

97. Primakov, *Pravda*, 18 May 1967, p. 1; Koriavin, *Izveztiia*, 17 May 1967, p. 1, 19 May 1967, p. 1; TASS, Pravda, 19 May 1967, p. 1.

98. *Pravda*, 10 June 1967, p. 1.

99. Koriavin, *Izveztiia*, 9 June 1967, p. 1; "V. Petrov," *Izveztiia*, 10 June 1967, p. 1.

100. Outstanding examples of these themes are offered by Primakov, *Pravda*, 12 April 1967, p. 5; by Ivanov, *Krasnaia zvezda*, 19 May 1967, p. 2; and by Vishnevetskiy, *Pravda*, 6 June 1967, p. 3.

101. Heikal, *Cairo Documents*, p. 244, and *Sphinx*, p. 179.

102. Heikal, *Sphinx*, pp. 178-180.

103. Vashedchenko, *Krasnaia zvezda*, 16 May 1967, p. 4; Vasil'ev, *Pravda*, 27 May 1967, p. 5; Koriavin, *Izveztiia*, 4 June 1967, p. 1.

104. Sadat, *Search*, pp. 171-172; Laqueur, *Struggle*, p. 71.

105. Kimche and Bawly, p. 88; Jabber and Kolkowicz, p. 425.

106. Sadat, p. 172. Amer and Nasser both resigned on 9 June; Amer was arrested on 25 August for plotting a coup and committed suicide on 14 September. See *MER 1967*, pp. 558-561.

107. Johnson, p. 302; Bull, p. 120.

108. Snyder and Diesing, p. 147.

109. Fukuyama, pp. 8-9.

10 Competitive Politics and Soviet Policy Toward the Arab-Israeli Dispute, 1971–1972

Soviet policy toward the Arab-Israeli conflict during the early 1970s has drawn the attention of U.S. and Israeli scholars primarily because it seems so contradictory to the U.S.S.R.'s simultaneous pursuit of global détente with the United States. While eager for negotiations with the United States and its NATO allies on arms control and European security and cooperation, the Soviet Union often resisted negotiations with the United States and its Israeli ally on peace in the Middle East. While trying to resolve conflicts with the United States over Europe, the Soviet Union supplied arms to Egypt and Syria for their offensive against Israel in 1973. Arab commentators have instead tended to stress the Soviet Union's sacrifice of Egypt's and Syria's interests for the sake of preserving détente, but they too have seen the two Soviet policies as incompatible.

The most common U.S. approach to reconciling the contradiction in Soviet policy toward the Middle East has emphasized the tension within the U.S.S.R.'s motives. From this point of view, the Soviet Politburo viewed détente all along as a competitive enterprise. While trying to control risks at the level of nuclear confrontation with the United States, under the leadership of General Secretary Leonid I. Brezhnev, the Politburo simultaneously sought competitive gains against the United States in peripheral areas where conflicts were deemed unlikely to escalate to nuclear confrontation. Thus the Brezhnev Politburo willingly negotiated strategic arms control agreements with the United States and entered the Helsinki conference to relieve strains in Europe, but in a series of Third World conflicts--the Middle East, Angola, Ethiopia, and finally Afghanistan--the Politburo was ready to use force to accomplish purposes contrary to U.S. interests, on the correct assumption that the United States would limit its counter-action below levels capable of defeating Soviet purposes.[1]

This assessment of Soviet foreign policy is descriptively accurate, but in any description there is embedded a set of causal attributions. The causal attributions embedded in the assessment of Soviet policy in the Middle East visualize a Politburo characterized by homogeneous motives, concerned mainly with the geostrategic competition against the United States for global influence. When one examines Soviet leaders' statements about policy in the Middle East, however, their motives seem contradictory rather than homogeneous and their concerns appear in a different light. Among observers of Soviet Mideast policy, Dina Rome Spechler has been especially active in examining this evidence. Spechler concludes that Soviet policy in the Mideast was a victory for one Politburo faction favoring geostrategic competition with the United States over an opposing faction favoring global détente.[2]

My view of Soviet Mideast policy in 1971-1972 combines Spechler's emphasis on the heterogeneity of Politburo motives with the other account's emphasis on the compatibility between détente and competition in the Mideast. There is a paradoxical observation which seems incompatible with Spechler's conclusion: when at the end of 1972 the Politburo decided to deliver arms to Egypt for the war against Israel in October 1973, the Politburo advocates of détente (Brezhnev and Aleksei N. Kosygin, chairman of the Council of Ministers) sponsored this policy; the main advocate of geostrategic competition with the United States (Nikolai V. Podgorny, the chairman of the Presidium of the Supreme Soviet) opposed the delivery of arms.

Why would détente advocates sponsor policies of competition with the United States when advocates of competition favored restraint? Accounts that attribute to Soviet policy-makers an overriding concern with the geostrategic competition against the United States offer no ready explanation of an observation of this kind. On the other hand, the observation is unsurprising from the point of view of a theory of political competition.

According to this theory, the policy-makers of any state must concern themselves first and foremost with gaining and keeping the support of domestic constituents, for if they do not have constituency support, they will lose the ability to make policy at all. One means for a political leader to gain constituents' support is to identify with a particular global strategy the constituents find compelling and promising. Each leader must advocate a different grand strategy, since otherwise constituents will be indifferent to the choice between leaders and will offer their support to none. Because the leaders' global strategies differ, and because compromise among leaders costs all leaders' constituents less than would active intervention on behalf of their preferred leader in the event of overt conflict, leaders must choose foreign policy by bargaining in which each leader attempts to obtain the others' approval of a policy as close as possible to the leader's own grand strategy. Because each leader's leverage in the bargaining depends on the continuing persuasiveness of the leader's grand strategy in the eyes of the constituencies, developments in the world situation may produce change in foreign policy when they alter the relative persuasiveness of the various leaders.

Bargaining requires that leaders endorse policies they themselves oppose. When during 1971-1972 Brezhnev and Kosygin advocated negotiations with the United States, opponents of this policy, including Podgorny, accused them of sacrificing the Soviet Union's Third World allies for the benefit of détente. During 1971 they compromised with Podgorny by splitting the world: In return for his agreement to their pursuit of negotiation with the United States on arms control and European security, they agreed to his adamant rejection of negotiations with the United States on the issues of the Middle East and Vietnam. During 1971-1972 the negotiations with the United States on arms control and European security made progress that should have enhanced Soviet audiences' credence in the feasibility of Brezhnev and Kosygin's détente proposals, while Podgorny's policy of rejecting negotiations encountered developments in the Middle East and Vietnam that should have diminished his persuasiveness to Soviet audiences. The defeat of the Democratic Republic of Vietnam's March 1972 offensive across the Demilitarized Zone indicated that a battlefield victory was beyond the reach of the North. In the Middle East, Egyptian President Anwar Sadat viewed Podgorny's strategy as condemning Egypt to the role of a passive onlooker waiting out an indefinite and intolerable delay in recovering Sinai; Sadat's desire for action led to increasing disagreements between the Soviet Union and its Egyptian ally.

Developments in the Mideast and Vietnam that would have diminished Podgorny's persuasiveness created an opportunity for Brezhnev and Kosygin, but it was not an opportunity they could exploit by imposing their preferred strategy of negotiating a U.S.-Soviet settlement of the Arab-Israeli conflict. Under the control of Henry Kissinger, U.S. policy sought to exclude the Soviet Union from a Middle East role, and Sadat's July 1972 expulsion of Soviet military personnel and his secret contacts with Kissinger encouraged U.S. policy-makers' illusion that they were making progress toward this goal. Sadat's preferred alternative to Podgorny's policy was not a U.S.-Soviet negotiation but a war. In order to use the Mideast issue to attract domestic supporters at Podgorny's expense, Brezhnev and Kosygin needed a policy proposal that would at once defend them against the charge of sacrificing Third World allies for the sake of détente, accommodate Sadat, and not founder on U.S. unwillingness to negotiate in the Middle East. They found a policy proposal meeting all three criteria in a declaratory approval of Sadat's right to go to war. By usurping Podgorny's former control of Mideast policy, they demonstrated to domestic audiences that his grand strategy could not determine Soviet foreign policy and forced him to make a concession in the bargaining over U.S.-Soviet détente--a concession registered at the Moscow summit in May 1972 when Podgorny voiced his first approval of SALT and trade with the United States.

Political competition theory is not usually applied to Soviet foreign policy, as most students argue that Soviet leaders before Gorbachev have not depended on constituency support to maintain their hold on office. The merit of any theory, however, depends on the fit between its expectations and observations. In what follows I will show that

Soviet leaders' public discussion of Middle East policy conformed to the expectations of political competition theory that leaders will recommend different global strategies and that they will choose foreign policy by bargaining. These observations conflict with the alternative theories that Soviet foreign policy pursues goals held homogeneously among Politburo members, that these goals' content is advantage in geostrategic competition, or that global Soviet policy changes according to the domination of one faction over another. I am not arguing that under Brezhnev the constituencies whose approval the Soviet leaders sought included members of the general public; instead the leaders sought to shape opinion within the Communist Party, and perhaps only among those Party members who occupied *nomenklatura* posts. But regardless of the scope of the Soviet leaders' constituencies, observations of public differentiation of grand strategies and of choice of policy by bargaining indicate that Politburo members could no more dispense with constituent support than can the foreign policy-makers of the United States or other governments.

A brief introductory section describes the competing grand strategies advocated by Kosygin, Podgorny and Brezhnev. The second section concerns the compromise between Brezhnev and Podgorny exchanging control of European and arms control policy for control of policy toward Vietnam and the Middle East during 1971. The third section concerns Brezhnev and Kosygin's success in usurping Podgorny's control of Middle East policy in time to compel his endorsement of détente at the May 1972 Moscow summit.

In short, Soviet Middle East policy pursued geostrategic competition with the United States at the same time as Soviet global policy pursued détente because (a) compromise in favor of competition in the Mideast enabled détente advocates in the Politburo to gain assent to their policy toward Europe and the United States in 1971 and (b) advocacy of competition in the Mideast enabled the détente advocates to seize the initiative in the contest for domestic support in 1972.

Competing Grand Strategies

Political competition theory expects rivals for national leadership to promulgate distinctive grand strategies intended to guide a state's foreign policy toward all global issues. Four senior members of the Politburo fulfilled this expectation during the early 1970s: Brezhnev, Kosygin, Podgorny and Suslov. Of these four, Suslov's preferred strategy allotted little importance to the Arab-Israeli conflict. He advocated reliance on foreign communist parties to foster Soviet security by mobilizing domestic populations in opposition to U.S. plans for global war against the Soviet Union and for global aggression against the national liberation movement. Since communists were largely inactive in the Mideast, Soviet actions there could not persuasively be presented to domestic constituencies as applications of this strategy. On the other hand, with its conflicts between governments variously aligned with the Soviet Union or the United States, the Mideast was an ideal venue for convincing Soviet audiences of the urgency and effectiveness of the other three leaders' strategies.

Podgorny's grand strategy was an analog of what is known in the United States as diplomatic containment. From 1965 on, Podgorny consistently advocated competition with the United States for the loyalty of foreign governments, regardless of their domestic ideology. He said Soviet policy should attempt to assemble a global coalition of governments in opposition to U.S. policies. He envisaged the coalition including the socialist countries (except China and Albania), as many as possible of the neutrals, and even the European allies of the United States. Assembly of this coalition would be feasible, Podgorny argued, because all these governments shared a common interest in preventing the United States from carrying out its supposed plan for a new world war. The coalition members' refusal to cooperate with the United States' plans for aggression would gradually force U.S. abandonment of the plan. Until May 1972, Podgorny never endorsed bilateral negotiations between the Soviet Union and the United States.

While Podgorny sought to isolate the United States even from its allies, from 1964 on Kosygin sought to incorporate the United States into global economic and security cooperation. He consistently advocated negotiated resolution of international disputes and argued for the necessity of entry into global markets for achievement of technological and economic progress at home. Kosygin justified the practicality of this strategy by distinguishing between "forces" in the United States favoring and those opposing cooperation with the Soviet Union. He argued that the forces for cooperation were capable of gaining the upper hand in U.S. politics. At the same time Kosygin argued that cooperation must extend to the whole global community; the United States must agree to abide by an international code of conduct prohibiting military interventionism or economic penetration in the Third World.

In contrast to Podgorny and Kosygin, Brezhnev changed his grand strategy in 1970. During the first five years after he replaced Nikita S. Khrushchev, Brezhnev had been a proponent of global conflict against the United States, particularly in Third World battles exemplified by the Vietnamese communists' war for control of the South. After 1969, when he established his ascendancy over his Politburo rivals, Brezhnev tried to perpetuate his ascendancy by shifting to a centrist grand strategy between Podgorny's and Kosygin's positions. In 1970 he began to argue that U.S.-Soviet cooperation had become practical because the success of his earlier strategy of conflict had taught U.S. decision-makers that nothing could be gained from military aggression against the socialist countries or their allies in the Third World. At the same time, Brezhnev asserted that the Soviet Union should continue providing military aid to Third World movements and governments fighting the United States or its allies if Washington policy-makers failed to keep sight of this underlying reality.

Linkage Between Europe
and the Third World, May 1971

May 1971 saw a remarkable confluence of changes in Soviet policy both on the whole cluster of East-West issues and on Vietnam and the Arab-Israeli conflict. Concessions to the United States on European issues and arms control coincided with shifts to a policy more hostile to U.S. purposes in Vietnam and the Mideast. If these changes were not mutually dependent, we have no means of understanding why a shrinkage of Podgorny's role and influence in East-West issues should have accompanied an expansion of his role and influence in the Middle East and Vietnam. The confluence of policy changes in opposite directions during May 1971 was produced by a bargain between Brezhnev and Podgorny that had emerged gradually over the preceding five months.

On East-West issues, on May 20 the Soviets and the United States announced the bargain coupling an anti-ballistic missile (ABM) treaty with offensive limitations in SALT.[3] Brezhnev and Kosygin both endorsed the NATO proposal for talks on mutual reduction of conventional forces in Europe.[4] Negotiations between Gromyko and the French foreign minister produced an agreement scheduling a visit by Brezhnev to France in October.[5] A principal obstacle to a Berlin agreement was removed when East Germany's Walther Ulbricht was ousted on May 3; his successor Erich Honecker promptly acceded to tacit linkage of the Berlin agreement to the other East-West proposals.[6] Having accepted at least a tacit variant of the linkage proposed by the Western allies among SALT, Berlin, talks on mutual force reductions, and the Soviet proposal for a European security conference, Brezhnev omitted from his June 1971 speeches the denunciation of this linkage which he had repeated as late as May 27. In the German Democratic Republic on June 16, Brezhnev linked the German treaty and European conference proposals to a statement of readiness to conclude a Berlin agreement.[7] Having accepted this linkage, the Soviet leaders ceased their demands for prompt summoning of the European conference, resuming these demands only after the Quadripartite Agreement with the argument that the Berlin agreement and Soviet acceptance of talks on force reductions had removed the remaining obstacles.[8]

Brezhnev and Kosygin's endorsements of the NATO proposal for talks on reducing conventional forces should have been particularly objectionable to Podgorny. Their acceptance of these talks helped greatly to keep the United States in Europe at the very moment when the feasibility of Podgorny's strategy of expelling U.S. influence had peaked. Brezhnev and Kosygin's endorsements on May 14 and 18 occurred, respectively, five and one days before a Senate vote which might have approved the Mansfield amendment halving U.S. troop strength in Europe.[9]

Although repeating his arguments against the concession made by Brezhnev, on June 10 Podgorny acceded to Brezhnev's acceptance of a tacit linkage between the Soviet proposals and the NATO counter-proposals.[10] He agreed that "Our country considers that all European issues can be and should be decided concurrently . . ." and joined in the call for a Berlin agreement. Political competition theory would expect that Podgorny made this concession because either (a) Podgorny had lost persuasiveness or (b) Brezhnev had made some offsetting concession to Podgorny.

While no events are obvious candidates for a specific source of a deterioration of Podgorny's persuasiveness in the spring of 1971, Brezhnev did evidently make an offsetting concession. Brezhnev agreed to expand Podgorny's public role in formulating policy toward the conflicts in the Middle East and in Vietnam and to change policy toward both conflicts to accord more closely with Podgorny's aversion to U.S.-Soviet cooperation. The timing of changes in Soviet policy toward the Mideast and Vietnam, parallel reversals in the content of policy, a shift in issue linkages, and the content of Podgorny's statements all testify to an expansion of Podgorny's influence on policy toward the two regional issues at the same time as he was conceding the East-West issues.

The shift in policy toward the Mideast was marked on May 25, 1971, when Podgorny arrived in Egypt carrying a draft of a Treaty on Friendship and Cooperation for signature by both heads of state. Podgorny, who came with only two days notice,[11] told Egyptian President Anwar Sadat that the Politburo considered the treaty (which, although under consideration for some time, had languished) to be "essential right now."[12]

While the urgency of Podgorny's trip to Cairo might be attributed to Sadat's order ten days earlier for the arrest of domestic challengers who were widely regarded as Soviet proxies in Egypt, an explanation of his trip in terms of Egyptian developments alone will not explain why change in Middle East policy was accompanied by a change in policy toward Indochina that also expanded Podgorny's role. The shift in policy toward Vietnam was marked by a meeting on May 9 between Brezhnev and the Vietnamese party First Secretary Le Duan, the principal advocate in Hanoi of a strategy of conventional offensive operations in the South.[13] At this meeting Le Duan evidently obtained Brezhnev's agreement to begin talks on new arms deliveries necessary to support the conventional offensive planned for March 1972 and approved by the Hanoi Politburo during May 1971. The talks culminated in Podgorny's trip to Hanoi in October 1971 where he gave final approval to a new arms agreement.

The new policies in the Mideast and Indochina represented the abandonment of Brezhnev's previous incorporation of both regional conflicts into his overall program of East-West accommodation. In the Middle East, Soviet diplomats had displayed interest in the United States' "second Rogers plan" for an Arab-Israeli settlement in mid-1970.[14] Brezhnev had encouraged Soviet audiences to see a Mideast settlement as achievable through diplomacy in Washington.[15] Commenting on Nasser's acceptance of the second Rogers plan as the basis for negotiations, Brezhnev had said that this action had opened the prospect for a gradual settlement of the crisis.[16] Brezhnev had also recurrently encouraged the Vietnamese to pursue the then secret Kissinger-Tho contacts in Paris. In April 1970, for example, he called upon the Vietnamese to use "diplomatic" as well as "military" and "political" methods to achieve their goals. In October, after the North Vietnamese had agreed to renew the Paris sessions interrupted after the May 1970 invasion of Cambodia, Brezhnev again said that while the Vietnamese were winning military victories "worthy of admiration . . . we highly value their steps directed at a political solution."[17] Given the uncertainty during 1970 whether sustainable agreements could be reached with West Germany and the United States on any of the broad spectrum of East-West issues, it made sense for proponents of an East-West accommodation to explore privately the possibility of accords on as many issues as possible, including Vietnam and the Near East.

Since Brezhnev's overall East-West policy was controversial, the incorporation of Vietnam and the Middle East into an accommodative package became contentious as well. In accord with the expectations of political competition theory, and in contrast to theories for which bargaining is irrelevant, the contention took the form of a disagreement over issue linkage. Brezhnev tried to dissociate U.S. actions in Vietnam and the Middle East from evaluations of the chances for progress on East-West issues. Brezhnev said a person reading the newspaper about events in Vietnam and the Near East could form the impression that "in the international situation no or almost no positive changes are occurring, that the world is running in place. In fact that is not so. Positive changes are occurring, and sometimes very substantial ones."[18] By contrast, only two weeks earlier Podgorny had linked the war in Vietnam and Israeli aggression to evaluations of the international situation, citing these two conflicts as the basis for his judgment that the international situation remained "complex."[19]

Policies toward the Mideast and Vietnam became suitable for Brezhnev to use as concessions when his effort to reach accords foundered on U.S. resistance. Following Brezhnev's April 1970 endorsement of diplomatic means, United States troops invaded Cambodia; following Brezhnev's October 1970 endorsement of North Vietnamese proposals for a political settlement, U.S. aircraft resumed strikes on the D.R.V. Brezhnev reacted to these actions with concessions to Podgorny's image of the Indochina conflict, in each case expressing suspicion of diplomacy as a means for reaching a settlement and reaffirming his commitment to providing military aid.[20] Similarly, the Rogers initiative collapsed under the combination of Israeli intransigence, the Egyptian leaders' one-sided interpretation of their obligations under the cease-fire, and Kissinger's efforts to convert the issue from cooperative search for a settlement to negotiation of a preliminary withdrawal of Soviet air defense forces from Egypt.[21]

In these circumstances--progress on East-West diplomacy coupled with regress in the search for diplomatic settlements of the Arab-Israeli and Vietnam conflicts--a tacit deal between Brezhnev and Podgorny would have been beneficial to both. From a political competitor's perspective, each would have wanted to be seen conducting policy in an issue area where the course of events was increasing the persuasiveness of his global strategy. In East-West issues, Brezhnev's inclusion posture of seeking Soviet-U.S. reconciliation was working; in the Middle East and Vietnam, Podgorny's anti-U.S. posture was made to seem more appropriate by U.S. conduct.

Accordingly during 1971 Podgorny used his speeches to redefine Soviet policy toward the Middle East conflict. The redefinition began during his trip to Egypt in January and emerged with increasing clarity after his trip in May. The goal of Soviet policy in the Near East remained a "settlement by political means."[22] However, Podgorny now defined a political solution to exclude negotiations with the United States, whom he accused of using "honeyed" words about peace to lure the Arabs into a false settlement that would only enable the Israelis to dictate its terms.[23] Podgorny argued that Egypt should instead rely on the backing of the Soviet Union and on growing international support for the Arab cause.[24] The new policy urged Sadat to combine avoidance of a war, which Podgorny was convinced the Arabs could not win, with refusal of U.S.-sponsored negotiations. Instead he held out the prospect that with the passage of time growing international pressure would compel unilateral concessions from Israel. This policy was soon to draw fire from the Egyptian journalist Heikal as a policy of "no peace, no war."[25]

In Vietnam Podgorny similarly rejected talks with the United States but, in contrast to the Middle East where the military balance disfavored Egypt, encouraged the North Vietnamese plans for an offensive. The U.S. invasion of Cambodia, increasingly frequent offensive operations in the South, attacks in Laos and air raids against the North, Podgorny said, "cast light on the real essence of Nixon's 'Guam doctrine' and showed the actual worth of 'peace-making' in the U.S. manner."[26] Calling military aid "an internationalist duty" and a "principled course" and promising "modern weapons,"[27] Podgorny signed the agreements that resulted in a threefold increase of Soviet deliveries, including the tanks and artillery used in the North Vietnamese conventional offensive of March 1972.

Podgorny accepted the deal because his trips to Vietnam and to Egypt afforded opportunities to present arguments against talks with the United States, reinforcing his identification with Soviet constituencies disturbed by Brezhnev's East-West program. Podgorny did not conceal his view that his aversion to negotiation with the United States extended beyond the regional context in which he spoke. He said, "Israeli aggression poisons the atmosphere not only in the Near East but far beyond its limits," accusing "the aggressor and his transoceanic patron" of wanting to turn territorial seizures "into a norm of international relations."[28] He openly criticized the separation of Indochina and the Near East from other world issues:

Sometimes one hears arguments that the world has somehow gotten used to these conflicts, that one may even, so to say, set them to one side and occupy oneself with other unresolved problems. One cannot condone such arguments. Efforts to 'conserve' these problems speak to the desire of some circles to continue to poison the situation in the world.[29]

This last attack can hardly have been directed at anyone other than Brezhnev, who advocated exactly this argument.

Approval for a Military Solution
in the Middle East and the May 1972 Summit

While Soviet acceptance of the tacit linkage between their proposals on European issues and NATO's counter-proposals enabled negotiations with the United States to proceed during 1971, Brezhnev still had not secured the Politburo's assent to a final U.S.-Soviet accord. In order to close the deal, Brezhnev needed either to find further incentives to offer to an opponent like Podgorny or to reduce Podgorny's power to object. Policy change during the winter of 1971-1972 on the Middle East suggests how Brezhnev may have compelled Podgorny to endorse the May 1972 summit's compromise with the United States.

Brezhnev's sense of the urgency of increasing his leverage on Podgorny would have been reinforced by his expectations about North Vietnamese actions. As Brezhnev planned at the end of summer 1971 for the U.S.-Soviet summit proposed for the spring of 1972, he could anticipate that the summit might prove especially controversial. The talks with the North Vietnamese on arms deliveries could have left no doubt of their intention to stage a large-scale conventional offensive, and even if they did not inform Brezhnev of the exact date of the offensive, the proposed schedule of deliveries would have left little doubt that the offensive would shortly precede the planned summit. Brezhnev could have anticipated that a North Vietnamese offensive might evoke a violent U.S. reaction. Since Politburo opponents of talks with the United States (including formerly Brezhnev himself) had consistently reacted to escalations in Vietnam with demands for a stiffening of the Soviet negotiating position, Brezhnev could anticipate that such demands from his rivals might follow the U.S. reaction to the North Vietnamese offensive. Consequently, it was vital for Brezhnev to prepare the summit by beginning, well in advance, to position himself to reject these demands.

Therefore a political competition theory would expect that the scheduling of the May summit in fall 1971 would have motivated Brezhnev to begin building the requisite position. Sadat's resentment of Podgorny's Mideast policy would have given Brezhnev the requisite opportunity to steal the constituency that Podgorny had built over the preceding year. I will make this case first by showing that the evidence is incompatible with the customary alternative explanation of Soviet policy and then by presenting the explanation of how the goal of stealing Podgorny's constituents would have motivated Brezhnev to endorse Sadat's plans for war.

The events leading to the Yom Kippur War of October 1973 between Israel and the Arab alliance have received intense scrutiny from scholars, not in the least because the contribution of Soviet weapons to the Egyptian and Syrian attack on a U.S. ally has seemed incongruous with the contemporaneous flowering of détente. Many Western observers agree that the Soviets acted to preserve their competitive advantages against the United States in the Third World.

In this explanation, the Politburo increased weapons supplies to Egypt and Syria because Sadat's expulsion of Soviet advisers and air defense forces from Egypt in July 1972 jeopardized the Soviets' competitive advantages.

Three major observations conflict with this account of the shift in Soviet policy toward the Mideast during 1972. First, and most important, the evidence for the change in Soviet policy consists in part of a shift in Soviet rhetoric in favor of Sadat's preference for offensive war over a continuation of Podgorny's futile demands for Israeli concessions. While attributed to the July expulsion of Soviet advisers and air defense forces, in fact the shift in rhetoric began in December 1971 and was completed during Sadat's April 1972 visit--i.e., more than two months *before* the event to which the Politburo was ostensibly reacting.

Second, this account does not explain Brezhnev and Kosygin's disagreements with Podgorny. If the Politburo was pursuing a competitive advantage against the United States, presumably all the Politburo members should have endorsed it; if anyone's public commentary indicated an especially strong proclivity for competition with the United States, it was Podgorny. Yet Brezhnev and Kosygin's statements on the Mideast evolved over time from less, to equally, to more competitive than Podgorny's. They moved from advocacy of U.S.-Soviet cooperation in the Mideast in 1970, through allowing Podgorny to define policy there in 1971, to becoming the sponsors of Sadat's war aims in 1972. If their concern was to maintain a competitive advantage against the United States, why did they start by trying to cooperate? Why was the policy change in early 1972 accompanied by the exclusion from negotiations with Egypt of Podgorny, the consistent advocate of competing with the United States? Why did Podgorny continue until late 1972 to advocate the policy of seeking a political settlement without U.S. participation--the very policy which supposedly jeopardized the competitive advantage by driving a wedge between the Politburo and Sadat?

The third fact is the Soviet demand that Egypt pay cash for the promised arms. This demand caused a delay between declaratory approval for Sadat's war aims in April and the delivery of the necessary arms beginning in 1973. Both the geostrategic explanation and a political competition explanation must account for delays, of different lengths: seven months (July 1972 to February 1973) in the geostrategic case and nine months (from the end of April 1972) in the political competition explanation. In both cases, the explanation for the delay is the same: until January 1973 the Egyptians were unable to muster sufficient funds. The surmise that Soviet arms deliveries were intended to maintain a strategic advantage against the United States does not explain why the Politburo continued to alienate Sadat by demanding hard currency which the Egyptians were known to lack; political competition theory does explain why Brezhnev and Kosygin held out for cash from the Egyptians when they were willing to offer generous credit terms to other arms buyers.

Efforts to explain the Soviet switch from refusing to deliver arms for Egypt's attack on Israel rely on changes in Soviet commentary on the Arab-Israeli dispute. Scholars examining the preliminaries to the October War have routinely noted that during 1972, communiqués of Soviet-Egyptian meetings began to include statements similar to this one taken from the communiqué following the visit to Moscow by the Egyptian Premier Aziz Sidqi, whom Sadat sent there in July 1972 to explain his order a week earlier expelling Soviet troops:

> The Soviet side shares the opinion of Egypt and other Arab states that in conditions of stubborn Israeli rejection of a just political settlement of the Near East conflict . . . the Arab states have the justifications to use *all means at their disposal* for liberation of the Arab territories seized by the Israeli aggressors in 1967. . . . [Emphasis added][30]

The phrase "all means" conceded to Sadat what Podgorny had denied him: approval for either diplomatic or military action to regain the territory occupied in 1967.

Arguments attributing the change in rhetoric to the July expulsion face the difficulty that Soviet willingness to concede Egypt's right to military action against Israel *preceded* the event (the expulsion) said to have caused this concession. Sadat's renewed demands for arms during his visit at the end of April 1972[31] encountered Brezhnev and Kosygin's agreement in the communiqué that because "circles hostile to the movement for progress in the Arab East" have not stopped trying "to disrupt a political settlement. . . . Arab states . . . have every justification *to use other means* for the return of the Arab lands seized by Israel [emphasis added]."[32]

Moreover, while the April communiqué was the first to implicitly endorse military action by Egypt, Sadat's February 1972 visit had already produced a change in the Soviet position. The February communiqué was the first between the Soviets and Egyptians since at least the end of 1969 not to call for either a "peaceful settlement" or a "political settlement" of the Arab-Israeli conflict.[33] A week after Sadat's return to Egypt, furthermore, a special *Pravda* article by-lined "Observer" (generally taken to indicate a statement approved by the Politburo) introduced a further new element into the Soviet position on the Mideast: acceptance of the Egyptian position that delay in resolving the crisis favored Israel. In contrast to Podgorny's argument that the Arab-Israeli balance would change in Egypt's favor over time,[34] "Observer" now warned that Israel was seeking to consolidate its hold on the Arab territories by pretending to negotiate while "protracting the crisis without end." "Observer" therefore justified Egypt's decision "to mobilize the people and natural resources for struggle against the aggressor. . . . "[35] Finally, the communiqué of Sadat's visit promised "concrete steps" by the Soviet Union to strengthen the Egyptian armed forces.[36] While similar promises had been made in earlier communiqués, and the failure to fulfill them had intensified Egyptian distrust of the Soviets, this time the Defense Minister Marshal A.A. Grechko was sent to begin reviewing Egypt's weapons requirements.[37]

Therefore, Soviet willingness to approve Sadat's intention to wage offensive war preceded the expulsion of Soviet advisers and air defense troops by at least two months, and the first Soviet expression of approval in April culminated in a reappraisal of policy begun no later than February 1972. The shift in Soviet policy is unlikely to have been an anticipated reaction to the expulsion, which evidently took the Politburo by surprise. Various Egyptian sources record an exchange of notes between Brezhnev and Sadat expressing Soviet bewilderment at Sadat's sudden demand for the departure of the Soviet military mission. More reliable evidence for Soviet surprise is the suddenness of Sidqi's visit--unannounced and without even the customary brief biography printed in *Pravda* on the day of a ranking visitor's arrival--during which he is reported to have explained the decision taken the previous week. Finally, in August both governments recalled their ambassadors "for consultation"--a standard diplomatic response to an unexpected disagreement.[38]

Of course, one might present the shift in Soviet policy not so much as a reaction to the specific event of Sadat's expulsion order but more as a response to the general trend, observed since Nasser's death in September 1970, for the alliance with Egypt to degenerate.[39] But this account faces difficulty in explaining why the Politburo ever adopted Podgorny's proposal for Mideast policy. By January 1971, the Soviet leaders already knew that Sadat would oppose their policy of combining refusals of Egyptian arms requests with advocacy of a settlement by political means. When Podgorny traveled to Egypt in that month, he urged Egypt to focus on economic development and said that achievement of an Israeli withdrawal "by political means would be a huge success for the Arab peoples." Sadat responded that Egypt's sole aim was the recovery of the lost territories; having just declared 1971 the "Year of Decision," Sadat could not have looked favorably on Podgorny's call for restraint, flexibility, "a realistic evaluation of the situation," and "political and diplomatic" struggle while rebuilding Egyptian defenses. Since this exchange was printed in *Pravda*,[40] the Soviet leaders cannot have failed to recognize Sadat's disagreement with the policy advocated by Podgorny. Of course the Politburo may initially have misjudged Sadat's determination to recover Sinai, believing that a refusal to supply arms needed for an attack would persuade him to comply with Podgorny's policy. This surmise does not offer any explanation of two further observations: (1) the exclusion of Podgorny from a public role in negotiations with the Egyptian government from February to October 1972; and (2) the combination of Brezhnev and Kosygin's sponsorship of the new policy with Podgorny's continued advocacy of a political settlement.

Political competition theory would attribute Brezhnev and Kosygin's sponsorship of a new Mideast policy to their recognition that Egyptian recalcitrance had brought the domestic public to question the continuing persuasiveness of Podgorny's strategy in the Mideast. When Podgorny was drawing public attention to an argument that success in settling the conflict depended on Soviet-Arab cohesion, Sadat's continuing objections should have gradually eroded the persuasiveness of Podgorny's policies to his own supporters. During the October 1971 meeting with Sadat, Podgorny himself addressed the declining persuasiveness of his policy when he warned that anti-communists hoped to benefit from "a quarrel between Arab countries and their most faithful friends and allies. . .the Soviet Union and the other states of the socialist commonwealth." Podgorny then tried to reassure his constituency that the anti-communists could not successfully foment such a quarrel because experience had taught the Arabs to distinguish their enemies from their true friends.[41] Because of repeated references (clear though indirect) during the course of 1971 to the tensions between the Soviet leaders and Sadat,[42] constituencies attentive to Soviet policy in the Middle East should have been becoming increasingly available for recruitment by leaders with proposals for an alternative policy there. If Brezhnev was concerned about undermining Podgorny's appeal to constituents in late 1971 in order to secure concessions from Podgorny on U.S.-Soviet relations, Brezhnev should have exploited Podgorny's identification with a Mideast policy increasingly recognized not to be working.

Because of the diminishing persuasiveness of Podgorny's Mideast policy, if Brezhnev and Kosygin now excluded Podgorny from negotiations with Sadat, he could not anticipate obtaining enough public support to sustain an objection. Accordingly, although Podgorny had participated in all the Moscow meetings between the Politburo and Egyptian leaders during 1970-1971 and had twice led delegations to Egypt during 1971, he participated in neither meeting with Sadat in February and April 1972 nor in the talks with Sidqi in July, during which Brezhnev and Kosygin gradually redefined the Soviet position.[43]

Over the course of 1972, both Brezhnev and Kosygin publicly justified the new policy. In December 1971, when Brezhnev should have been beginning the effort to exploit Podgorny's vulnerability, Brezhnev used calculated ambiguity to float the possibility of a policy change. He described the aims of Soviet Mideast policy as "to frustrate the plans of the Israeli aggressors and their patrons and to help Arab peoples restore their legitimate rights and to aid the establishment of a just peace in the Near East." By omitting Podgorny's call for a "political settlement" (repeated by Podgorny the same day),[44] Brezhnev's statement left open the possibility of military force as a means of policy.[45] By March 1972, Brezhnev identified himself less ambiguously with the new policy. Warning of the "threat of a military explosion" in the Near East, Brezhnev contrasted the Arabs' willingness to reach a political settlement with Israeli obduracy backed by the United States. He then espoused "Observer's" definition of the situation as requiring an end to Israel's strategy of protracting the conflict: "However, this cannot continue endlessly. Sober thinking politicians can hardly count on the Arab states to tolerate the occupation of their territory." Brezhnev then noted that the military balance had shifted in the Arabs' favor. His assertion that Soviet-Arab ties had never been so "profound and all-sided" claimed credit for the policy shift's having made Soviet policy more effective.[46] At about this same time, Podgorny was describing the danger of war in the Mideast as "constant."[47] Podgorny's denial of change in the likelihood of war and his recommendation to intensify pursuit of a political settlement contrasted sharply with Brezhnev's view of increasing danger and his justification of Arab resort to war.

Like Brezhnev, shortly after the February meeting with Sadat, Kosygin said, "Some in Israel and the U.S.A., apparently, assume that in today's situation, when the Arab peoples have still not achieved the necessary unity, they will in the final analysis submit to the occupation of their lands." Kosygin warned that this perception was incorrect, noted Soviet support for "liquidation of Israeli aggression," and drew attention to the significance of the recent talks with Sadat for this shared goal. Like Brezhnev, he described the goal of Soviet policy as intended to enable the Arabs to act successfully against Israel. By October 1972, Kosygin said that:

as long as aggression is happening . . . the Arab countries have the right to struggle with all means against aggression, against encroachments on their independence and territorial integrity.[48]

Podgorny continued to defend his former policy, delegitimizing Brezhnev and Kosygin's argument for policy change. Continuing throughout 1972 to call for a "political settlement," Podgorny tried to shift the blame for tensions with Egypt. He attacked unnamed Egyptians for betraying Nasser's heritage. Thus Podgorny twice defended the pursuit of a political settlement against the specific accusation made by the Egyptian editor and unofficial spokesman Heikal:

Sometimes talk is heard of some kind of 'special' interests of the Soviet Union in the Arab East, that supposedly the preservation in this area of a situation of 'no war, no peace' is advantageous to [the Soviet Union]. Claims of such a kind are a slander on our policy and are directly calculated to do an injury to Soviet-Arab friendship. Imperialist and Zionist circles and Arab reaction of all brands and shadings direct big efforts at defaming Soviet aid to Arab states, at sowing doubts regarding the effectiveness of the Soviet Union's support for their struggle with Israeli aggression. The goals pursued in this are fully obvious: to isolate the Arab peoples from their natural allies in the anti-imperialist struggle.[49]

While Podgorny defended the old policy, Brezhnev and Kosygin defended the new one. Although, in compliance with the bargain granting Podgorny control over policy toward Egypt, Kosygin had as recently as October 1971 joined in the denial that Soviet policy was encouraging perpetuation of the Mideast conflict,[50] Kosygin now shifted to defending against a different accusation. Referring to "opponents" of Soviet-Arab alliances, Kosygin said:

> Now they have put into circulation the fiction that the Soviet
> Union has entered on some kind of 'collusion' with the
> imperialists on issues of a Near East settlement to the
> detriment of Arab countries' interests. We resolutely deny such
> conjectures.[51]

Brezhnev similarly rejected allegations that the Soviet Union had
adopted a "superpower" policy, affirming instead that the Soviet Union
"conducts a class, socialist foreign policy" in the interests of "all
peoples."[52]

While keeping the targets of their criticism anonymous, Podgorny
and the Brezhnev-Kosygin coalition in fact were challenging each
other's images and policy recommendations. Podgorny had previously
criticized Brezhnev and Kosygin's policy of a tacit agreement with the
United States to defer an Arab-Israeli settlement while proceeding on
bilateral issues; Kosygin and Brezhnev had previously criticized
Podgorny's over-emphasis on seeking a political settlement as playing
into the hands of the Israelis. Each side warned that the other's policy
would disrupt Soviet-Arab alliances. Displacing his rival's criticism
onto foreign sources, each leader tried to legitimate his own policy in
the eyes of Soviet audiences.

Brezhnev and Kosygin's verbal approval of Sadat's war aims served
to discredit Podgorny's criticism that they were betraying Third World
allies for the sake of détente. The associated arms deal with Syria
enabled them to provide a side payment to the junior Politburo
member Mazurov, a détente critic who, in his government role as
overseer of foreign aid, obtained the opportunity to lead a delegation
to Syria in February 1972. In return, in his speech in Syria for the first
time Mazurov gave Brezhnev and Kosygin (but not Podgorny) credit
for promoting European security. At the same time, Brezhnev and
Kosygin should have wanted to avoid actual delivery of the arms
promised to Egypt, as Kissinger had repeatedly warned them that this
action would severely jeopardize U.S.-Soviet cooperation. This latter
consideration explains why the Soviet leaders withheld the delivery of
arms to Egypt until 1973 despite having approved the Egyptians'
recourse to war months earlier. They finally agreed to deliver the

arms when Egypt obtained hard currency from Saudi Arabia in January 1973.[53] If their goal was to restore the competitive advantage jeopardized by Sadat's expulsion of their military personnel in July, delay in delivering the arms is extremely puzzling. A political competition account resolves this puzzle. According to this theory, Brezhnev and Kosygin's objectives in approving Sadat's war goals would have been (a) by exploiting Podgorny's vulnerability on the issue, to show their superior ability to control Soviet policy and their superior effectiveness in maintaining the Egyptian alliance, and (b) to supply a convincing counter against the accusation that they were prepared to sacrifice allies for the sake of U.S.-Soviet détente. In turn, these gains aimed at a short-run objective: to reduce the persuasiveness of potential objections by Podgorny to the May summit with Nixon at a time when Brezhnev and Kosygin anticipated that a vigorous U.S. response to the North Vietnamese offensive would place the summit at risk. At the same time, from their dealings with Kissinger, Brezhnev and Kosygin knew that an Arab attack on Israel would also jeopardize U.S. willingness to cooperate on East-West issues. Therefore they needed a policy which combined a concession to Sadat with continued restraints on his ability to act. The crux of the situation would have been their knowledge that Egypt possessed virtually no hard currency.[54] By demanding cash they could have hoped to ensure continued Egyptian restraint. The Soviet leaders may also have known that in the absence of additional weapons, Egyptian commanders were opposing Sadat's demands to prepare for an attack across Suez.[55] Consequently, the combination of declaratory approval for Sadat's war plans with the conditioning of weapons deliveries on cash payment satisfied Brezhnev and Kosygin's requirements in the domestic competition.

While the change in Soviet *declaratory policy* toward the Arab-Israeli conflict achieved Brezhnev's and Kosygin's competitive goal of undermining Podgorny's reputation for policy effectiveness in the eyes of Soviet audiences at the crucial juncture in April 1972, the Egyptians took their disingenuous offer of an arms sale--to an ally known to be unable to pay--as one more proof of the insincerity of Soviet support for the Egyptian cause. Sadat, whose image of Soviet motives in the Near East stressed the Politburo's concern with the global competition against the United States, retaliated in July 1972 by using what he thought was his only leverage to extract the promised weapons: He expelled the Soviet air defense forces and advisers.

Because his image of Soviet motives was wrong, however, Sadat's move failed to influence Brezhnev and Kosygin. "Both the speed with which the Soviet Union withdrew its military personnel from Egypt following Sadat's decision and the scope of the withdrawal indicate that Moscow was not unwilling to take this step."[56] Sadat's expulsion of the forces failed to affect Soviet policy because it played straight into Brezhnev's hand: now if a Politburo rival proposed to grant arms to Egypt, Brezhnev could blandly agree with Podgorny that Sadat was to blame for strains in the alliance. No Politburo member could very well argue for giving arms to an ally as unreliable as Sadat's expulsion of the Soviet military presence would have proved him to be, and publicly none did.

The case that Brezhnev and Kosygin's verbal approval of Sadat's war aims was aimed at Soviet domestic audiences, while their demand for cash payment was intended to restrain Sadat, depends on the assumption that Brezhnev and Kosygin misperceived the relationship between Saudi Arabia and Egypt. If Soviet leaders formed their images of the likely behavior of foreign states by evaluating the utility of these images for the competitive purpose of motivating their domestic supporters, then Brezhnev and Kosygin would not have anticipated that Saudi Arabia would give Egypt the money to buy arms. All the Soviet leaders had found it convenient to divide the Arab states into "progressives" likely to ally with the Soviet Union and "reactionaries" depicted as bound to the United States. Arguing that Israel's policy was intended to manipulate the internal political situation in the "progressive" Arab states in order to overthrow radical regimes, the Soviet leaders even depicted the interests of the Saudis, who incarnated Arab "reaction," as converging with Israeli purposes. Reference to their images of the Arab countries would have led them to discount Sadat's April claim that the wealthy Arabs would finance his arms purchases.[57]

A misperception of Saudi policy in 1972 is plausible not only because it would be merely another instance of a repeated pattern of confusing domestic appeal with international reality. There is specific contemporary evidence that the Politburo did not foresee the emergence of cooperation among the Arab governments. The Soviet leaders have frequently been accused of inciting the Arab oil boycott which followed the Yom Kippur war. It is true that during 1972 various Soviet leaders, particularly Kosygin, urged Arab governments to use oil as a weapon against the capitalist countries. But they did not recommend that the progressive states join Saudi Arabia in boycotting deliveries to allies of Israel; instead they urged the progressive regimes to nationalize the holdings of Western oil companies in their countries.[58]

There was also evidence of Brezhnev and Kosygin's sensitivity to the problem of preventing their initiative toward Sadat from interfering with the U.S.-Soviet relationship. During the talks with Kissinger to prepare for the May summit, held in April 1972 a week before Sadat's arrival, Soviet Foreign Minister A.A. Gromyko made an unexpected concession to the U.S. position on the Middle East. During the summit itself, he went even further, accepting "general working principles" which for the first time did not specifically demand a full Israeli withdrawal from all Occupied Territories. These concessions have since been taken as evidence of Soviet "willing[ness], to an unprecedented extent, to hedge their long-standing promise to their Arab allies." While Kissinger admits to "surprise" at these Soviet concessions, he also says that he opposed meaningful negotiations with the Soviets on a Mideast settlement. Describing his own participation in the Moscow exchanges as a charade, Kissinger notes, "Gromyko was experienced enough to know what I was doing; he put on no real pressure; the Soviets clearly wanted no crisis over the Middle East."[59] Despite admitting Gromyko's awareness of Kissinger's duplicity in the exchanges on the Middle East, neither Kissinger nor later analysts seem to have considered the possibility that Gromyko's concessions were equally disingenuous. By combining a public semblance of concessions to Sadat's bellicosity with a private semblance of concessions to U.S. demands for dissociation from their Arab allies,

Brezhnev and Kosygin may have hoped to manage the contradiction introduced into their own policy by the usefulness of a confrontational stance in the Mideast for the purpose of gaining domestic acquiescence to détente.

When in January 1973 Sadat unexpectedly obtained hard currency to pay for the promised arms,[60] what were Brezhnev and Kosygin to do? If they refused the arms, Podgorny and others could persuasively allege the sacrifice of allies for détente, the argument to which Kosygin had revealed his vulnerability by choosing it as the criticism meriting a public response. Moreover, if they refused the arms, the emptiness of their concession when they combined verbal approval for military action with a demand for cash payments for the necessary weapons would be publicly exposed. The Egyptians used the threat of exposure effectively in July 1973 when Brezhnev and Kosygin tried to renege on the sale of arms.[61]

The Washington summit scheduled for June 1973 remained at stake; consequently Brezhnev and Kosygin's best option would have been to continue their policy of endorsing Egypt's right to fight with Soviet arms if the Egyptians would pay.

Conclusion: Geostrategic Competition and Détente

Political competition theory explains the evidence on Soviet policy toward the Arab-Israeli dispute during 1971-1972 better than either the assumption that the Politburo homogeneously pursued geostrategic advantage or the interpretation that Sadat's expulsion of Soviet military personnel enabled a faction favoring competition to win in early 1973 over a faction favoring détente. The argument that the Soviet leaders sought to combine U.S. détente with gains in the Third World is descriptively accurate, but this argument fails to account for heterogeneity in the goals of different Politburo members and offers no explanation for the association between change in Soviet policy and change in the roles of Brezhnev, Podgorny and Kosygin. Nor does this argument explain why the Politburo sought geostrategic gains in the Middle East by a policy which first asked Sadat to delay indefinitely his goal of the return of Sinai and then made an empty offer to sell arms when the Politburo knew Sadat lacked cash. Geostrategic gains in the Mideast for the Soviet Union depended on Sadat's cooperation, yet the Soviets are viewed in this account as pursuing the gains by policies certain to alienate him. Spechler's alternative account of factional conflict does not explain why the advocates of global cooperation with the United States favored the offer of arms to Egypt, while the advocate of global competition with the United States opposed this policy.

Competitive politics theory explains all these Soviet behaviors as the product of a contest for constituency support. While this theory has not often been applied to Soviet politics, if the observable behavior of Soviet leaders conforms to the theory's predictions--as it did in the case of Mideast policy--there is no reason to reject the theory as an explanation of Soviet conduct. Brezhnev, Kosygin, Podgorny and Suslov did advocate different grand strategies. The Middle East offered opportunities to demonstrate to domestic constituencies the feasibility and urgency of the various grand strategies advocated by Brezhnev, Kosygin and Podgorny, but not Suslov's; consequently those three leaders but not Suslov made proposals for policy toward the Arab-Israeli dispute. They reconciled the resulting policy disagreements by a series of compromises. When Podgorny conceded to Brezhnev and Kosygin the control of policy toward European issues in June 1971, he received control of Mideast policy in exchange. But when Sadat's rejection of Podgorny's proposal to seek a political settlement through the exertion of mounting international pressure would have diminished the persuasiveness of Podgorny's strategy in the eyes of Soviet constituencies, Brezhnev and Kosygin seized the opportunity to take control of Mideast policy. They demonstratively excluded Podgorny from the meetings with Sadat as a means of showing domestic audiences that Podgorny's influence was declining. Thinking they could control Sadat by their demand for hard currency from an Egypt known to be bankrupt, Brezhnev and Kosygin found themselves in a quandary when wealthy Arab states agreed to underwrite Egypt's arms package. Refusal to deliver the arms would have surrendered control of policy back to Podgorny, but that would have sacrificed their competitive gains. Consequently they chose to combine delivery of the offensive arms with diplomacy during 1973 to persuade the United States to pressure Israel for a settlement and to persuade Egypt to refrain from war. When diplomacy failed, Egypt attacked, much to the detriment of the prospects for Brezhnev and Kosygin's policy of détente.

The theory of political competition offers us a general explanation why the foreign policies of many states--certainly not only the Soviet Union under Brezhnev--so often combine incompatible foreign policy goals like pursuing détente with the other superpower while arming one's own allies for an attack on the other superpower's allies. During the last three decades, both superpowers pursued self-contradictory policies, in the Middle East and elsewhere. Self-contradictory policies become understandable if we recognize that concepts like "geostrategic gains" and "détente" are, for national leaders, not goals in themselves but rather means to the more fundamental end of office-holding. Office-holding is a fundamental end not because I am making any assumption about the motivations of national leaders; regardless of whether they seek office from a selfless desire to serve the public interest or for the sake of selfish ambition or material gain or prestige, their ability to accomplish any goals depends on the allegiance of constituents. From the point of view of competitive politics theory, concepts like "geostrategic gain in a global contest" or "relaxation of tension" are linguistic devices used by the leader to provide simple, easily believable explanations to constituents why the leader merits support. By identifying themselves with alternative foreign policies, leaders pose before constituencies in a manner that communicates their political identities and secures the constituents' identification with the leader. When rival leaders use different conceptions of foreign policy to motivate constituency support, they must choose a policy by a compromise. The process of compromise combines rival global strategies in a manner likely to produce a self-frustrating policy marked by cumulative self-contradiction. The incompatibility between Soviet policy toward the Middle East and the larger program of global détente during 1971-1972 provides a dramatic example of the internal inconsistency that can afflict a state's foreign policy goals when they are chosen through a competitive political process.

Notes

1. Harry Gelman, *The Brezhnev Politburo and the Decline of Detente* (Ithaca: Cornell University Press, 1984), p. 155; Robert O. Freedman, *Soviet Policy toward the Middle East since 1970* (New York: Praeger, 1978), pp. 88, 132-134; Jon D. Glassman, *Arms for the Arabs: The Soviet Union and War in the Middle East* (Baltimore: The Johns Hopkins University Press, 1975), pp. 103-104; Paul Jabber and Roman Kolkowicz, "The Arab-Israeli Wars of 1967 and 1973," in Stephen S. Kaplan, ed., *Diplomacy of Power: Soviet Armed Forces as a Political Instrument* (Washington: The Brookings Institution, 1981), pp. 185, 441; Bruce Porter, *The U.S.S.R. in Third World Conflicts: Soviet Arms and Diplomacy in Local Wars, 1945-1980* (Cambridge: Cambridge University Press, 1984), pp. 121-122, 221-222.

2. Dina Rome Spechler, "The U.S.S.R. and Third-World Conflicts: Domestic Debate and Soviet Policy in the Middle East, 1967-1973," *World Politics* 38/3 (April 1986) pp. 440-445, 448-450, 457; cf. Philip D. Stewart, Margaret G. Hermann, and Charles F. Hermann, "Modeling the 1973 Soviet Decision to Support Egypt," *American Political Science Review* 43 (1989), pp. 35-59.

3. Raymond L. Garthoff, *Detente and Confrontation: American-Soviet Relations from Nixon to Reagan* (Washington: The Brookings Institution, 1985), p. 147.

4. *Pravda*, May 15, 19, 1971. In later footnotes, when only a date is given, it refers to the corresponding issue of *Pravda*.

5. May 8, 1971.

6. A. James McAdams, *East Germany and Detente: Building Authority After the Wall* (Cambridge: Cambridge University Press, 1985), pp. 114-115; N. Edwina Moreton, *East Germany and the Warsaw Alliance: The Politics of Detente* (Boulder, CO: Westview Press, 1978), p. 181.

7. Compare May 27 with June 12, 17, 1971.

8. September 24, October 26, 30, December 9, 1971.

9. Garthoff, p. 115.

10. June 11, 1971.

11. Lawrence L. Whetten, "The Arab-Israeli Dispute: Great Power Behavior," in Gregory F. Treverton, ed., *Crisis Management and the Superpowers in the Middle East*, Adelphi Library no. 5 (Westmead, Hampshire, England: Gower Publishing and Montclair, N.J.: Allanheld Osmun, 1981), p. 65; the announcement of Podgorny's trip was published only on May 24, 1971.

12. Anwar Sadat, *In Search of Identity* (New York: Harper and Row, 1977), pp. 221-230; Mohammed Heikal, *The Sphinx and the Commissar: The Rise and Fall of Soviet Influence in the Middle East* (New York: Harper and Row, 1978), pp. 227-228.

13. May 10, 1971; Thai Quang Trung, *Collective Leadership and Factionalism* (Singapore: Institute of Southeast Asian Studies, 1985), pp. 55-64; Victor C. Funnell, "Vietnam and the Sino-Soviet Conflict, 1965-1976," *Studies in Comparative Communism* xi, 1-2 (Spring/Summer 1978), pp. 157-158.

14. George W. Breslauer, "Soviet Policy in the Middle East, 1967-1972: Unalterable Antagonism or Collaborative Competition?" in Alexander George, ed. *Managing U.S.-Soviet Rivalry: Problems of Crisis Prevention* (Boulder, CO: Westview Press, 1983), pp. 84-86, citing a range of memoirs by American and Arab participants.

15. April 15, 1970.

16. August 29, 1970.

17. April 15, October 3, 1970.

18. April 15, 1970.

19. March 27, 28, 30, 1970; cf. June 12, July 1, 1970.

20. May 8, June 13, November 30, 1970.

21. Whetten, "The Arab-Israeli Dispute", 61-62; Henry Kissinger, *White House Years* (Boston: Little Brown, 1979), pp. 575-593.

22. *Vneshnaia Politika Sovietskogo Soiuza i Mezhdunarodnye Otnosheniia: Sbornik Dokumentov, 1971* (Moscow: *Izdatel'stvo Mezhdunarodnye Otnosheniia*, annual), document 18, p. 47 (the joint communique of Podgorny's May visit).

23. May 28, 1971; cf. May 29, June 11, 1971.

24. October 13, 1971.

25. Mohammed Heikal, *The Road to Ramadan* (New York: Quadrangle, 1975), pp. 163-164.

26. October 5, 1971

27. October 4, 8, 1971.

28. May 28, 1971. Cf. October 5, 1971.

29. September 15, 1971.

30. *Vneshnaia Politika Sovietskogo Soiuza, 1971*, document 57, p. 120. Cf. Galia Golan, *Yom Kippur and After: The Soviet Union and the Middle East Crisis* (Cambridge: Cambridge University Press, 1977), p. 23; Spechler, pp. 454-456; Porter, p. 122.

31. Yaacov Roi, *From Encroachment to Involvement: A Documentary Study of Soviet Policy in the Middle East* (New York: John Wiley and Jerusalem: Israeli Universities Press, 1974), pp. 570-571.

32. April 30, 1972. Cf. Glassman, p. 94; Porter, p. 122, fn. 19.

33. *Vneshnaia Politika Sovietskogo Soiuza, 1972*, document 7, pp. 17-18. Cf. *ibid.*, 1970, documents 59, 101; *ibid.*, 1971, documents 3, 12, 18, 54.

34. E.g., January 16, May 28, 29, 1971.

35. "The Near East--A Just Settlement," February 12, 1972.

36. February 5, 1972.

37. Grechko's trip was announced on February 15; his presence in Egypt was noted on February 21.

38. Heikal, *Sphinx and Commissar*, pp. 244-250; Golan, *Yom Kippur and After*, p. 26.

248

39. Karen Dawisha, "The Soviet Union in the Middle East: Great Power in Search of a Leading Role," in E.J. Feuchtwanger and Peter Nailor, *The Soviet Union and the Third World* (London: The MacMillan Press, 1981); Golan, *Soviet Policies in the Middle East from World War Two to Gorbachev* (Cambridge: Cambridge University Press, 1990), pp. 82-85; Glassman; Freedman.

40. January 20, 1971.

41. October 13, 1971.

42. E.g., Kosygin, February 2, October 7, 11, 1971; Podgorny, May 29, June 11, 29, 1971.

43. Cf. the texts of the communiques published in *Vneshnaia Politika* and cited previously, as well as the previously cited *Pravda* reports of the 1972 meetings.

44. December 9, 1971; cf. December 8, 1971.

45. December 9, 1971.

46. March 19, 1972. Cf. June 6, June 28, October 14, 1972.

47. April 11, 1972.

48. February 12, July 4, October 17, 1972.

49. September 15, 1972; cf. July 7, 1972.

50. October 11, 1971.

51. October 17, 1972; cf. July 7, 1972.

52. June 28, 1972.

53. February 23, 24, 1972.

54. February 23, 24, 1972.

55. Alvin Z. Rubenstein, *Red Star on the Nile: The Soviet-Egyptian Influence Relationship Since the June War* (Princeton: Princeton University Press, 1977), p. 242.

56. Sadat, pp. 213-215. Central Asian Research Centre, *U.S.S.R. and the Third World* Vol. II (1972), 208; Vol. III (1973), pp. 93, 246. Podgorny's speeches in January and May 1971 reveal Soviet awareness of Egypt's economic difficulties.

57. Janice Gross Stein, "The View from Cairo," in Robert Jervis, Stein and Richard Ned Lebow, eds., *Psychology and Deterrence* (Baltimore: Johns Hopkins University Press, 1985), p. 46.

58. Ro'i, *From Encroachment to Involvement*, pp. 570-571.

59. Kosygin, October 2, 1971; February 12, April 8, 1972. Cf. Boris Ponomarev, June 10, 1972; Podgorny, June 14, July 7, September 14, 1972; A. Vasiliev, "Oil and Politics," September 1, 1972.

60. Breslauer, "Soviet Policy in the Middle East...," p. 95.

61. George, "The Arab-Israeli War of October 1973: Origins and Impact," in George, ed., p. 143.

The Palestinian Question

11 Changes in the Arab-Israeli Conflict

Changes in the Arab Positions

In recent years there have been important developments in Arab positions toward the Arab-Israeli conflict. After 1948, many Arabs believed that the establishment of Israel had been an act of scandalous injustice that could be rectified only by the Jewish state's elimination. They argued that Israel's demise was possible because it constituted an aberrational state that had not been built on genuine nationalism, since the Jews are only a religious group. However, in the face of Israeli achievements and vitality, represented by Israel's military feats and especially its resounding victory in 1967, the belief that Israel would disappear could not be sustained. Thus Arab leaders came slowly to the conclusion that they had to resign themselves to Israel's existence, if only as a policy of "cutting losses," for only then could the Arab countries hope to retrieve the territories they had lost in the 1967 war, and the Palestinians gain a state of their own in the territories occupied in this war. In Arab discourse the change was justified with the pragmatic argument that "international legalism" (*Shar'iyya Dauliyya*) proscribed "politicide," i.e., calling for the liquidation of a state. The change in the Palestinian attitude toward recognizing Israel's right to exist and accepting the idea of partition, or the "two-state solution," was much more difficult and was slower to materialize. For the Palestinians, accepting Israel's existence meant relinquishing the hope of ingathering the diaspora population, since a smaller Palestinian state, truncated by the partition, would not be sufficient to absorb such a population. While such a plan has been only theoretical, for

Palestinians faced with the difficult circumstances of the diaspora it was comforting to entertain such a hope.

At the 19th meeting of the Palestine National Council (PNC), the parliament of the Palestinian Liberation Organization, which convened in Algiers in November 1988, the Palestinians promulgated most solemnly a fundamental change in their position. The new position was the result of long and bitter debates among the different factions. The "Declaration of Independence" that embodies the new position was endorsed unanimously, even by the PLO's hard-liners. This declaration implied a call for a two-state solution. Furthermore, repeating the all-Arab position adopted in the 1982 Fez Summit Resolution, the 19th PNC demanded that Israel withdraw from the territories occupied in 1967. Thus the PLO officially dropped its claim to 100% of Palestinian territory, decreasing its claim to a Palestinian state in about 25% of it. It is hardly thinkable that they will agree to much less.

Significantly, it calls for the "liberation of Palestine" or the "liberation of Palestine in its entirety," so frequently reiterated in the Palestinian National Covenant and in the resolutions of previous PNCs, are absent from the "Declaration of Independence" and from the text of the resolutions of the 19th PNC. Also absent is the term "armed struggle." Despite the changes in the Palestinian position, from time to time radical expressions are aired by some PLO leaders; however, an authoritative pronouncement by the PNC, and especially an august document such as a "Declaration of Independence," outweigh them.

True, the "Right of Return" is repeatedly brandished in this document. This fact is used by Israelis, including some Israeli orientalists, to contend that the PLO's change of position is only rhetorical and therefore that negotiations should not start with the PLO. This claim is based on a misunderstanding of the present function of the right of return for the Palestinians. Previously, the claim to this right had a programmatic meaning, as its fulfillment would have led to Israel's demise and replacement, through flooding it with Palestinian returnees, with a Palestinian state. Currently, its meaning is more sentimental, as a statement of the link that binds all Palestinians wherever they live.

The diaspora Palestinians continue to identify themselves as Palestinians, despite the fact that they live elsewhere. While diaspora Jews identify themselves according to the nationality of the country in which they live, for instance as "American Jews," for the time being most Palestinians have not yet adopted a similar self-identification, and a Palestinian living in Egypt does not call himself an "Egyptian Palestinian." Being Jewish is an ethnic identification, whereas a Palestinian is defined by geographic origin; the identification is thus territorial in nature. Thus the "Right of Return" does not imply a practical design, but rather symbolizes an assertion of a collective personality, the hallmark of which is an attachment to Arab Palestine.

Many Palestinians understand that once there is a political settlement, Israel cannot be forced to accept a mass influx of Palestinians without jeopardizing its being a Jewish state. At most, diaspora Palestinians originating from the territory Israel proper can demand compensation for property, but they cannot hope to reclaim it. Nevertheless, the Palestinian leaders should elucidate what they mean by the "Right of Return," stating clearly that it does not harbor a hidden agenda of destroying the state of Israel.

It should be remembered that parallel to the Palestinian claim to all of historic Palestine is the Jewish claim of a "historical right" to the whole *Eretz Yisrael* in its Biblical, though undefined, borders. To many Israelis, relinquishing this right is impossible, because it is the very basis of Zionism. However, it, too, evolved from possessing a programmatic meaning to presently having only a sentimental meaning for most Jews and Israelis. Still, from time to time verbal and written expressions of expansive ambitions and designs for a "greater" Israel appear, evoking Jewish historical rights as their justification. Israeli leaders should declare that once there is a peace settlement they will relinquish all ideas of expansion.

As long as there is no settlement of the conflict, both the Palestinian and Jewish claims can be presented in an extreme and menacing manner. A peace agreement will define the meaning of these rights in concrete legal terms. Thus the Israeli "Law of Return" will be confined to the state of Israel, and a similar Palestinian "Law of Return," superseding the "Right of Return," will be limited in its application to the confines of the state of Palestine.

Both sides may continue to hold sentimental allegiance to greater *Eretz Yisrael* or to Palestine in its entirety as their wider homeland (*moledet* or *watan*); whereas only in their smaller states (*medina* or *daula*) will they exercise their political rights of sovereignty.

The official Palestinian readiness for a two-state solution may prove time-bound. The hard-liners in the PLO coupled their acceptance of the two-state solution in the "Declaration of Independence" with the prediction that the concessions the PLO offered in changing its position would not yield any positive gains for the Palestinian cause, as Israel would cling to the territories occupied in 1967. Thus, their acceptance of the "Declaration of Independence" was meant as a tactical step to prove, in the face of expected Israeli rejection, how wrong the Palestinian moderates were in hoping that Palestinian moderation would be met with a positive change in Israeli policy. Then the PLO, including its moderate factions, would have no other option but to revert to its previous position calling for politicide, and adopt the hard-liners' strategy.

The basic view of the Palestinian hard-liners is that the conflict is essentially a *competition in attrition* in which the Arabs will eventually prevail, because of their numerical preponderance and the weaknesses in Israel's national fabric. They consider any settlement of the conflict as a danger to the Palestinian cause because the superpowers will bolster it with international safeguards and guarantees, making it robust enough to withstand any attempts to undermine it. Thus, paradoxically, the Palestinian radicals tend to reject the "stages" tactics.

An Arab moderate position in the Arab-Israeli conflict is dependent on positive responses from Israel. For instance, Sadat came to Jerusalem only because he was led to believe that he would be rewarded by the return of the Sinai peninsula. The messages that the Palestinians receive from the current Israeli Prime Minister are that they will not get one square inch of territory in return for peace. Thus, if this is the definitive position of Israel, the Palestinians actually have no reason to moderate their position. Yet, what has sustained the moderates among them has been a belief that eventually the international community will goad Israel into changing its position.

Denying the Palestinians the prospect of having a state is playing into the hands of the hard-liners and will perpetuate the Arab-Israeli conflict. The Palestinians will not resign themselves to the idea that only the Israelis deserve to have a state of their own. The Palestinians will not accept an inferior status entitling them at most to an autonomy under Israeli domination. In this they will have the support of all the Arab states, the big powers, and world public opinion. Even if the Hashemite regime collapses one day and the Palestinians turn Jordan into a Palestinian state, the almost two million Palestinians living under Israeli occupation will not accede to the suggestion that their home land is Jordan, and that they live in Israel as if in a diaspora.

The Israeli Position

The present official Israeli policy represents the position of the hard-line Likud and its allies and it advocates a one-state formula: on the west side of the Jordan river the only state will be Israel, and the Palestinians will at most be granted autonomy under Israeli suzerainty. Although the official position is that after a peace agreement and three years of autonomy, negotiations will be held on the final status of the Occupied Territories, Israel's current leaders emphatically declare that there will never be "foreign" [non-Israeli] sovereignty west of the Jordan river. Autonomy is, therefore, not a transitional arrangement, as was the intention in the Camp David Accords, but the end result. Passing from autonomy to anything beyond it will need Israeli consent, and by casting a veto Israel can *ad infinitum* freeze the status quo of autonomy. The settlements implanted in the Occupied Territories are a concrete means of anchoring Israel in the territories; they are not meant to fall under Arab authority nor do they constitute bargaining chips. Through deeds and numerous verbal commitments, Israel's current leaders have bound themselves to the position of keeping the Occupied Territories, and retreating from this position would be a catastrophe of gigantic dimensions for their political future. They ceaselessly repeat their view that any withdrawal will incur a "mortal danger" to the state and to its population, in the hope that by describing such

256

a step as suicidal they will be able to gain Israeli, Jewish, and also international support to prevent it.

Israeli leaders announce repeatedly that they are searching for non-PLO Palestinian moderates with whom to negotiate. Their efforts have been in vain not because the PLO foists its authority on the Palestinians by violence, but because for the Palestinians the PLO has come to symbolize the idea that the Palestinians constitute a collectivity deserving political recognition in the form of statehood. This position is supported by all Palestinians. Thus there are no Palestinians who agree to less than the PLO demand for a Palestinian state. It would have been a revealing exercise for Israel's leaders to define what they consider should be the position of a Palestinian moderate. For Israeli hard-liners, apparently, a moderate Palestinian is one who agrees that there will never be a Palestinian state and that Israel will dominate the Occupied Territories forever. Such a person exists only as a fantasy. Such an exercise may reveal to them that the Palestinians' demand for statehood and their refusal to remain subjugated to Israel are not an aberrational eccentricity. If the Israeli hard-liners were Palestinian, their position would not be far from the PLO's demands.

Another claim of the Israeli leadership is that negotiations should be conducted with the Arab states and not with the Palestinians. Given that the Arab states have reiterated most authoritatively that they cannot speak for the Palestinians, the Israeli hope of substituting the Arab states for the Palestinians is unrealistic. At recent summit meetings, the leaders of the Arab states have repeatedly stated that the Palestinian problem is the nub or essence (*jauhar*) of the Arab-Israeli conflict and that there cannot be any advance in relations between Israel and the Arab states in the absence of a prior settlement between Israel and the Palestinians.

Israel's hard-liners are of course aware that their position entails potential dangers, including the intensification of the *intifada*, increased terrorism against Israeli and Western targets, the possibility of war with the Arab states, and negative reaction to their policies by the world's people and governments, including those of the superpowers. They rely on the hope that Palestinian terrorism, which they allege the Palestinians cannot abstain from for long, will neutralize opposition in the international community to Israeli policies. Palestinian behavior, the Israeli hard-line leaders believe, will justify Israel's refusal to respond to Palestinian claims.

The refusal of Israel's hard-liners to negotiate with the PLO is justified by Palestinian terrorism, which they see as representing the ontologically eternal depravement of the Palestinians. In the view of the Israeli right, a Palestinian state, in which the PLO will be at the helm, will serve as a hotbed of terrorism and a springboard for greater demands against Israel. They thus see a Palestinian state as designed to bring about Israel's liquidation. Israel's insistence on keeping the Occupied Territories is therefore not presented as an expression of autonomous territorial ambitions, but as a derivative and defensive reaction to the depravity of the Palestinians. It should be noted that Arab spokesmen have previously employed the same stratagem, describing the need to destroy Israel as derivative of Israel's inherent expansionist disposition.

Hence a vicious circle is born: For Palestinians and Arabs, Israel's refusal to accept that the Palestinians deserve a state demonstrates an inability to understand that the Palestinians are fully human, which proves the basic depravity of Israelis. Thus, the use of all means in combatting Israel are justified. Furthermore, Israel's repressive measures against the Palestinians bolster this negative image. In turn, Arab and Palestinian acts of violence and terrorism support the Israeli position of keeping the Occupied Territories. A malignant mechanism comes into operation by which the hard-liners on both sides reinforce each other and both paradoxically serve as their opposite's best ally.

The strength of the Israel hard-liners' position lies in the support it received from historical Arab denouncements of Israel's right to exist. Israel's hard-liners argue that their position is the only true and straight-forward response to the radicalizing trends in the Arab world, the absence of democratic regimes, and the irresponsible behavior of some Arab states, all of which vindicate the position that compromising with the Arabs is not possible. Recently the Israeli hard-liners received a great boost from the behavior and warlike declarations of Saddam Hussein and the support that he obtained from the PLO's leaders and the Palestinian public. But if aggression is an immutable trait in Arab nature and its actuality is a permanent feature of the region, the question one must pose is how is a peace with them at all possible at any time?

The Israeli hard-liners' response to this query lies in their strategic perspective which, ironically, is the inverse of the Arab hard-liners' vision. The Israeli hard-liners also consider the conflict as a *competition in attrition*. Yet while the Palestinian hard-liners believe that Israel will eventually collapse, their Israeli counter-parts believe that it is the Palestinians who will eventually become exhausted. The Palestinians outside Israel will lose heart and those in the Occupied Territories will leave, precisely because of their reluctance to be subjugated to Israel, migrating to the Arab states and elsewhere. This emigration of the Palestinians, their "transfer," will not be by violence but by a gradual "voluntary" elegant process, which is less likely to generate international condemnation. The idea of the "transfer" of the Palestinians is also the Israeli hard-liners' solution to the demographic danger of the Palestinians becoming the majority in historic *Eretz Yisrael*. With the removal of the Palestinian problem, peace with the Arabs will become possible. Only such a vision can explain the Israeli hard-liners' position and behavior.

Furthermore, peace with the Arab states, the hard-liners claim, will become possible only when those states become democracies, which also requires a long period of gestation. Thus what is needed is time to allow the processes of Palestinian exhaustion and Arab mutation to take place. A lengthy stalemate, procrastination, and procedural delays that stall the "peace process" without excessively damaging Israel diplomatically, are thus seen as commendable.

Excluding external intervention to impel the parties to negotiations and a peace settlement, it is quite plausible that the desires of the hard-liners on both sides to prevent a compromise settlement will come to fruition. Their prophecies that such an agreement is not possible will then become self-fulfilling. It is likely that they will unwittingly collaborate in making this so: there will be acts of terrorism by the Palestinian hard-liners and the Arabs in general will regress to their old positions calling for the destruction of Israel and the rejection of the compromise of partition. On the Israeli side, there will be an increase in the repressive measures against Palestinians under Israeli control. The conflict will then be transformed into a deadly quarrel over absolute values and a war to the bitter end (*guerre a outrance*). The Israeli hard-liners may then argue that the deterioration of relations between Jews and Arabs was inexorable and that the rejectionist position of the Arabs and Palestinians reveals their true nature. The Israeli hard-liners' ideology will win to the detriment of Israel.

What the hard-liners will ignore, or forget, is that there was a possibility that things could have been antithetically different had Israel agreed to start negotiating with the Palestinians after they showed their readiness to compromise in the 19th PNC.

The visions of both sides' hard-liners are false. Neither the Israelis nor the Palestinians will become exhausted and disappear, bequeathing the land to their opponents. The continuation of the conflict will only take a heavy toll on both and wreak great calamities and havoc. A settlement of the conflict is indeed an existential necessity for both the Israelis and the Palestinians, though not for the Arab states.

World Public Opinion
and the Settlement of Conflict

So long as the Arabs adhered to their original position that Israel should be liquidated, there was no possibility for Israel to meet them half-way with a conciliatory policy aimed at compromise. An Israeli dovish position was then impossible without incurring the accusation of dishonesty in overlooking the harshness of the Arab position. Thus Israel's external policy was reduced to a strategic policy of strengthening itself to withstand Arab threats.

Originally, it was the Zionist or the Israeli side that upheld the two-state formula by agreeing since 1937 to partition proposals. Thus the Zionists and Israelis assumed a conciliatory position, for which they gained the acclaim of international public opinion and the support of many governments. Without this support, Israel could not have come into being or thrived. At that time, the Arabs called for a one-state solution, an Arab one, and argued that a Jewish state should not be allowed to emerge; after the establishment of the Israeli state, they called for its destruction.

After the PLO announced its acceptance of a two-state formula the roles have been reversed, as it is now Israel that insists on a one-state formula, a Jewish state. The historic international significance of these reversals may prove decisive in tilting the balance of international support from Israel toward the Palestinians, and eventually in influencing the modality of the settlement of the conflict. World public opinion will recognize that although the Israeli leadership proclaims that it is looking for peace, what is meant is a peace in which the Arabs and Palestinians acquiesce in Israel's retaining the territories occupied in 1967, except the Sinai. Such a peace will not be acceptable to either the Arabs or the world community.

The only possible solution to the Arab-Israeli conflict is *partition into two states*. It is a bad solution; all others are worse. Both Israelis and Palestinians deserve bigger countries, to have the whole territory of Palestine for themselves, but only a partition and smaller countries is a feasible option. Even if the Palestinian state were to be confederated with Jordan, the Palestinians would insist that the confederation be between two sovereign states, on equal footing, and not in the form of subordination of their state to the Hashemite crown.

The partition solution is derived from another exigency. A settlement of the conflict can not be a "hegemonic" settlement in which one side dictates its conditions to the other, such as the autonomy formula. There must be a negotiated settlement whereby both the Israelis and Palestinians will enjoy a similarity of status, by virtue of both having a state, even if unequal in size. Any other settlement will eventually be rejected by one side or the other.

The Recent Global Changes

Recent changes in international relations may too affect the conflict. As the relationship between the two superpowers improves, they will be less inclined to compete for clients in the less developed countries. The superpowers are doing their best to extract themselves from regional conflicts. So long as such conflicts can be localized, minimizing their global repercussions, the international community, led by the superpowers, may allow them to fester. It is doubtful whether the Arab-Israeli conflict can be localized, both because of its central geographic location and of the accumulating arsenals of unconventional weaponry in the Middle East.

The need of the Soviet Union to concentrate on internal reforms diminishes its interest in the Middle East in general and in its Arab friends in particular. The Soviet Union is now much more hesitant and reserved in supporting the Arab radical states. Soviet authorities officially warned Syria against warlike initiatives against Israel. The Soviet threat to Western interests in Middle East has declined. Thus the claim that Israel is a "strategic asset" for the United States may lose what little validity it once had.

The fiercest opposition to Israel outside the Arab countries has come from the Third World countries. However, American friendship has more than overbalanced this enmity. The declining importance of Third World countries in the international arena has in recent years led to fewer initiatives against Israel in the UN. Furthermore, Israel's position in the Third World has considerably improved.

In the short term, the changes in Eastern Europe and in the international political climate seem to favor Israel. Eastern European countries as well as some Third World countries are restoring diplomatic relations with Israel, and Israeli relations with the Soviet Union have improved. However, in the long run, the global changes will turn against Israel, and increase the pressures for a partition settlement. The end of the cold war and recent trends toward settling many conflicts in the world make the Arab-Israeli conflict look anachronistic.

The changes in Europe that came as a result of popular uprisings--*intifada*s--have produced a political climate receptive to claims for freedom as expressed in the Palestinian *intifada*. The Israeli policy of remaining in areas inhabited by Arabs, with the purpose of maintaining Israeli rule over them, seems a relic from an ugly past. The Soviet Union will have to quit Lithuania and the other Baltic republics; similar pressure by the international community may be exerted against Israel.

Post-1992 Europeans will have a greater say in international deliberations than they have now, and the position they take supports the Palestinian claim for independence. Europe has important means for exerting economic pressure on Israel. Israel had a foretaste of such pressure when it refused to comply with the European demand that agricultural products from the Occupied Territories would not be exported under the label of "Israel." Europe reacted by stopping the import of Israeli agricultural products. Israel capitulated, as it could not allow itself to be deprived of the European market. Europe may serve as a whip on behalf of the Americans against Israel. Europe, which is not constrained by a Jewish lobby, may exert pressure on the United States to take a more active, and "balanced," role in the conflict.

The United States will probably lose its position as the sole arbiter of the conflict. If it rejects American mediation, Israel will have to face the pressures of an international conference, which may take a more active role by imposing conditions. Israel will likely obtain better results by negotiating on its own volition, rather than by submitting to negotiations under duress. Any settlement will be painful for Israel, and it will be in great need of international sympathy. If the settlement is achieved in spite, and not because, of Israeli policy, such sympathy will likely not be forthcoming.

In many parts of the world the boundaries between states are considered permanent. International wars, the main purpose of which was to change borders, will become rarer. Thus future competition among states will be based less on territory and military power, increasingly veering toward commerce, economy, and technology. The developed countries will play an increasing role in international trade; the small and less developed countries may lose much of their importance in the international system, and, in many cases, may be relegated to irrelevance. In the long run this trend may negatively affect the international standing of both Israel and the Arab states, especially if they continues to waste their resources and efforts in fighting each other instead of exerting themselves to modernize their states and improve their economies.

263

The Role of the United States

The PLO's change of position had important effects on American policy. Based on the resolution of the 19th PNC, Yasser Arafat's announcement in Geneva on December 14, 1988, that the PLO had recognized Israel's existence, accepted UN Security Council Resolutions 242 and 338, and renounced terrorism convinced President Reagan, the most friendly American President to Israel ever, that American conditions for a dialogue with the PLO, dating from 1975, had been met. He thus immediately instructed Secretary of State George Shultz to engage in a "constructive dialogue" with the PLO. Until then Israel's opposition to the PLO could have been interpreted as conditional, similar to the American opposition; Israel's refusal to talk with the PLO after it had met the American, and implicitly Israeli, conditions revealed that Israel's rejection of the PLO was, and is, categorical.

The United States has traditionally registered its opposition to the Israeli policy of settlements and creeping annexation. The United States has frequently stated that new settlements are not "helpful" to peace or are an "obstacle" to peace. It can be assumed that the United States holds that Israel will eventually have to withdraw from most of the Occupied Territories, as called for by United Nations' Security Council Resolution 242, which the United States upholds as the only basis for any settlement of the conflict. The United States has called for Israel's withdrawal without specifying what will be in these areas after the withdrawal. The United States government seems to recoil from thinking about how it expects potential negotiations to conclude. Perhaps the United States government believed for some time that the West Bank would return to Jordan, but this appears unlikely in the wake of King Hussein's July, 1988 rejection of responsibility for the West Bank; nor does such a conception address the future of the Gaza Strip.

From time to time American leaders announced policy "positions" in regard to the Middle East. Examples include the Reagan "Plan" of September 1982 and Secretary of State James Baker's speech to AIPAC on May 22, 1989, in which he called on Israel "to lay aside once and for all, the vision of Greater Israel" and "forswear annexation." He added that the Palestinians should have their "full political rights." The bluntness of Baker's statement was a novelty and its implications were very serious. It meant that these territories are not areas that Israel can dispose of as it wishes, that the Occupied Territories are not and will not be part of Israel. Yet, such statements were non-consequential and could pass unheeded with impunity.

It can be assumed that American decision-makers have been reluctant to induce Israel to negotiations, much less to withdraw from the Occupied Territories, despite their conviction that peace is important for Israel. This reluctance is probably due to their awareness of the grave consequences of withdrawal for the Zionist vision and for Israeli investments in the Occupied Territories in the form of settlements. An American insistence on withdrawal may incur responsibility for its outcomes, a responsibility American policy makers apparently prefer to shun.

The traditional American declarations should be contrasted with the straightforward *demand*, in mid-1990, that Russian immigrants not be settled in the Occupied Territories. The Likud government accepted this demand without demur. Had the United States presented such a demand regarding the settlements years ago, it could have been spared many troubles for Israel. Any rejection of the vision of a Greater Israel would have been much easier before many settlements were implanted in the West Bank. The United States could have been very effective in influencing the political mood in Israel had it long ago explained to its leaders, and especially to its public, the nature of the political circumstances in which Israel was enmeshed: that the hope to annex the Occupied Territories was a will-o'-the-wisp; that American opposition to annexation was not motivated simply by American whims, but by its concern for the welfare of Israel; and that Israeli interests required it to refrain from investments in areas destined to be abandoned.

There are Americans in official circles who believe that the United States has already done its share in trying to bring about a settlement to the conflict. They argue that any additional exertion to bring about a settlement of the conflict by any Administration is politically deleterious, giving rise to domestic opposition from Congress and the American Jewish community. This argument of expediency was supported with theoretical reasoning that a solid settlement of any conflict should come from within, as an organic growth in the positions of the local parties. It has been argued that a settlement, if it is to last, cannot be artificially implanted from the outside and that the Arab-Israeli conflict is not yet "ripe for resolution." Therefore, there is a need for a lot more suffering to mellow the parties' positions, in particular Israel. Only catastrophes can bring people to their senses. Furthermore, as time goes by, Israel's internal crises will make it more amenable to reasoning and attentive to American advice. These officials may advocate the containment of the conflict as an interim measure, insulating it from spreading harmfully and allowing it to go on smoldering.

The problem with such an approach is that a delay will not improve the situation. Rather, it will cause its deterioration. The longer the wait, the more Jewish settlements will be implanted, Islamic fundamentalism will grow stronger, and the danger that the PLO moderates will be swept aside by their hard-liners will increase. Once these developments occur, the prospect for a negotiated peace will disappear completely. It can be assumed that the Gulf Crisis also showed the weakness of this approach and that movement toward the settlement of the Arab-Israeli conflict cannot be delayed for long.

After the Israeli rejection of Secretary of State Baker's proposals for negotiations with the Palestinians, a wide rift developed in relations between the Israeli Prime Minister and the American President and Secretary of State. American leaders seem to blame Prime Minister Shamir for double-crossing them, as they followed his gradual back-track from his May 1989 proposals for initiating elections in the Occupied Territories in order to compose a Palestinian delegation with whom negotiations can start. As Mr. Avraham Shweizer, a member of the editorial board of the Israeli newspaper *Ha'aretz*, correctly remarked in an editorial, it was very strange that the American leaders did not understand that given Shamir's ideological goal of achieving a Greater Israel, they could not expect him to embark on negotiations that might endanger his chief political doctrine: "[Bush and Baker] should have known that Shamir would not fulfill what his initiative promised."[1] Apparently, the American leaders have learned a lesson from their unpleasant experience and perhaps now they better understand the situation. In the United States, there are thus some indications of a process of increased disenchantment with Israel and some uneasiness with Israel's repressive policy in the Occupied Territories. The traditionally widespread American support for Israel now is combined with a desire to disengage from it.

The United States faces considerable difficulties in eventual mediating any future negotiations between Israel and the Palestinians. If the main purpose of the negotiations is to induce Israel to agree to an independent Palestinian state, the United States is not best placed to bring this about, since traditionally the United States has rejected the idea of a Palestinian state. Perhaps American decision-makers hope that an Israeli acceptance of the two-state solution will spare them the embarrassment of a volte-face in their position.

In order to direct the negotiations, the mediator needs to have some inkling of where it wants to take the adversaries. At some stage the mediator may have to propose to the parties themselves its thoughts on a solution. The United States can exert pressure, but that is not the problem. The problem is for what purpose? Because of the difficulties it faces in internal politics, the United States may prefer that others, such as the European Community or the Soviet Union, share mediating responsibilities.

The negotiations will necessarily be based on Resolution 242, but since its wording is not clear there will be need of an authoritative interpretation of its meaning. It might also be useful to ask both Israel and the Arabs to define what they consider the "legitimate rights and just requirements" of the other side. In the Camp David Accords Mr. Begin recognized that the Palestinian people should enjoy such rights, but Israel has never been asked to spell out what it meant. Such a recognition should be made symmetrical, and both parties should be enjoined to define precisely what they mean by such a phrase. Rights are not the product of negotiations, nor can they be defined by them. Rather, they are basic principles that precede negotiations.

In any future negotiations the Palestinians will have to be reminded that their case is not as impeccable as some Palestinians try to present it. For a very long period they were the main obstacle to peace. Their readiness for a compromise solution and reconciliation is only recent. While the current willingness to compromise is a development that took years to come to fruition, moderation cannot be projected backward in the pretense that the Palestinian position has been always peaceful. Palestinian support for Saddam Hussein also serves as a reminder that they need to prove the seriousness of their peaceful intentions and that they have to be ready to meet some of Israel's territorial and security demands, which the Gulf Crisis has only reinforced.

The Iraqi Crisis and Its Possible Aftermath

The foundation of this analysis was made long before the Gulf War, which does not change its basic thrust, although it does add some new elements that have to be addressed. Saddam Hussein's decision to invade Kuwait had nothing to do with the Arab-Israeli conflict. However, what can be stated for certain is that the Arab-Israeli conflict played a contributing role in the broad support for Saddam Hussein's action among the populations of many Arab states. Arabs may dislike the Palestinians, but they are passionately concerned with the Palestinian problem, which for them signifies widely felt grievances against the West for mistreating the Arabs in general.

Israeli and Jewish moderates rightly criticized the pro-Iraqi position adopted by the PLO. However, some well-known Israeli and American doves went further and sought to ostracize the PLO, presenting the PLO's support of Iraq as proof that its recognition of Israel's right to exist and its acceptance of the two-state solution were deceptive all along. By taking this stand, these doves unwittingly supported the Israeli government's position calling for the postponement of any initiative aimed at a settlement of the Arab-Israeli conflict.

The change in attitudes towards the PLO blatantly exposes some major weaknesses in the positions of Israeli and Jewish doves. They are not motivated by a serious analysis of the Middle Eastern situation, in which a sustained exploration of the changes in Arab and Palestinian positions would have convinced them that for the first time peace has become a possibility. Theirs is a cavalier, frivolous kind of moderation. For some of them, peace is a social affair, as if peace will emerge from parlor meetings and academic conferences. They do not rise to see the conflict at this stage as two-sided, in which the positions of the adversaries are interactive and mutually interdependent. They do not want to understand that once the mainstream Palestinians made a historic change in their position, parrying the scorching criticism of their hardliners, they expected that their act would be taken seriously and not be lightly spurned. Virtually unnoticed is that despite the PLO's expression of support for Saddam Hussein, it has not rescinded its acceptance of the two-state formula.

Thus, the doves do not give enough attention to the possibility that Israel's rejection of the PLO's moderation contributed to this regression in the Palestinian position. The main question to be asked has been: What incentive did Israel offer to the Palestinians to moderate their position? Why do not Israeli doves ask this question?

Once the Gulf Crisis is settled, Egypt, Syria and Saudi Arabia, now enraged with the PLO, will probably reconcile themselves to that organization. There may be personnel changes in the PLO's leadership. Thus far the Palestinians consider the PLO their leadership, and there are no signs that this attitude will change. That is what counts. Negotiating with the Palestinians inescapably means negotiating with the PLO. By ostracizing the PLO these alleged Israeli moderates have only supported the hard-liners' position that there is no possibility of peace with the Palestinians, and thus that the conflict will be ongoing.

Until now the Arab-Israeli conflict has not had a high priority on the superpowers' agenda. However, settling the Gulf Crisis may give it some urgency, as part of other arrangements in the Middle East in general. The world community may come to the conclusion that it should cooperate in bringing about some settlement of the conflict and initiate negotiations, probably under the auspices of an international conference. Egypt, Saudi Arabia, and Syria, the United States' new allies, will exert pressure on the United States to start settling the Arab-Israeli conflict. Otherwise, Arab public opinion will criticize Arab leaders for only contriving to bring about Iraq's withdrawal from Kuwait, while turning a blind eye to Israel's retention of the Occupied Territories. And while the Iraqi and Israeli cases are not analogous, this does not mean that Israel has the right to keep the Occupied Territories.

Conclusion

The internal Israeli political difficulties, the accumulation of disappointments with the national achievements and the growing bitter public discontent with all Israeli leadership, may lower the self-image of Israelis and make it easier for them to resign themselves to the need to contract to a smaller state. Yet the realization that by force of the verdict of history Israel cannot transcend, by even a small area, its narrow confines, will adversely affect the Zionist dream. It will spell dreary finality.

Once the Israeli public realizes that the hopes of annexing the Occupied Territories are a delusion, it will go through the excruciating experience of resigning itself to a smaller Israel. The pain of accepting the necessity of withdrawing will be great even if many people have had forebodings that it is inevitable and many of them have stopped frequenting the Occupied Territories. With great anxiety Israelis will ask themselves how they were blind to believe that Israel would be able to retain the Occupied Territories. They will calculate the many billions of dollars invested in the territories that, in the wake of their return, will have been irretrievably wasted. Such a huge sum of money could have solved all the formidable social and economic problems of Israel, including the absorption of the Soviet Jewish immigration. Israelis may blame their leaders for misleading them.

The crisis will spread to American Jews. American Jews will then realize that while their lobbying on Capitol Hill has been very valuable for Israel tactically, it was harmful strategically in that it allowed Israel to sink into the quagmire of erroneous policies. They will then understand that what they used to call "supporting Israel" was really supporting the wrong policy of a political party in Israel. The fact that the Likud was chosen democratically to rule is not a warrant that their policy is correct. Some of them will reproach themselves for not warning the Israeli public against the policy that was destined to court disaster.

Israel's failure does not lie in specific policies, but at the meta-level of basic modes of reasoning underlying the policies. In this domain Israeli intellectuals should have been their people's mentors on how to think rationally. The blame for the national bankruptcy should be placed on these intellectuals, as well as on the political leaders. Israeli intellectuals will now be called to make an important contribution in rethinking Zionist ideology in the aftermath of a peace settlement. The present ideology of "Zionism of Acreage," or Zionist success measured in the number of acres that are controlled, will have to be superseded by an ideology of "Zionism of Quality," in which the urge for excellence, to become a model state, will be paramount. The new ideology will have to deal with the relationship of a smaller Israel with the Jewish diaspora and the Arab world, and accommodate and explain faithfully both the past conflict and its settlement. The historical narrative will have to be revised and so will its accompanying collective memory.

The role of the Jewish religion in the conflict and in the politics of the state will have to be examined and conclusions drawn. The phenomenon of religious groups spearheading annexationism will have to be examined. They erred not only politically, but ideologically by making God collateral to their policies. Israelis and Jews will have to reflect on the role of a smaller Israel in the historical perspective of Jewish destiny. Self criticism will be a great blessing. Narrow parochialism will have to be overcome in order to view Israeli problems and policies against what is permitted and what is forbidden in the emerging new world order. Israel, like the rest of the world, will have to think internationally before thinking nationally.

Notes

1. *Ha'Aretz*, November 5, 1990.

12 Historical Cases of U.S.-Soviet Conflict Management in the Middle East: The Palestinian Question

This chapter examines the Palestine question as a historical case of Soviet-U.S. cooperation in conflict management in the Middle East, with a focus on four issues: (1) the way the two superpowers have perceived their interest in the Palestinian issue and the factors that have affected their perceptions; (2) the nature of each superpower's relationship with the parties to the Palestine conflict, in particular Israel and the Palestine Liberation Organization (PLO); (3) the areas of agreement and disagreement between the superpowers regarding the Palestine question; and, (4) the factors that are likely to influence the future policy of the two superpowers towards the Palestine question, the possibility of cooperation between them, and the impact of this cooperation on the prospects for the resolution of the Palestine problem.

Clearly there are methodological and practical difficulties in any attempt to draw a demarcation line between the Palestine conflict and the Arab-Israeli conflict. This chapter tries to avoid any serious overlap among themes that are clearly intricate. Reference to other related issues, which are outside the direct scope of this essay, is made only in the context of the Palestine question.

The United States and the Soviet Union have perceived their interests in the Palestinian issue as an integral part of the Arab-Israeli conflict, of their interests in the Middle East, and of their global interests.

During the last four decades or so, the interests of the two superpowers in the Middle East were defined in the context of the Cold War: The United States had sought to contain the Soviet expansion of communist influence which it perceived as a threat to its strategic and economic interests in the region, whereas the Soviet Union attempted to prevent Western--particularly U.S.--domination of the region, in order to protect Soviet economic and strategic interests there.

The protection and promotion of U.S. interests in the Middle East required the support and protection of pro-Western governments vis-à-vis anti-Western governments, and revolutionary and radical movements. In this context, Israel has been perceived as an asset and strategic ally, since Israel's interests and those of the United States have coincided significantly. U.S. support to Israel has emanated from moral as well as political commitments. Since its creation, Israel has been perceived and therefore valued by the United States as a democratic state. The presence of a powerful Zionist lobby in the United States has been an important factor in extending American support to Israel. In this context for many years the question of Palestine did not figure as an issue of any significance to American foreign policy. The United States dealt with the Palestine question as a refugee problem.

The Soviet Union's perceived interests in the Palestine question were embedded in its broader regional and global interests, which encompassed ideological, strategic, geopolitical, military and political considerations. Although the Soviets during the period of their active and widespread involvement in the region did not derive any real economic gains, economic interests could have been one of their underlying long-term objectives.

Soviet objectives and policies in the Middle East, and towards the Arab-Israeli conflict and the Palestine question in particular, have contradicted those of the United States. The relationship between the two superpowers, in this respect, has been characterized by competition. Each superpower tried to extend its influence and deprive the other of access to regional interests and clients. The Soviets tried to achieve this objective by extending political, military, and other forms of material support to anti-Western governments. In accordance with its perceived interests, the Soviet Union, especially after the 1967 war, has allied itself with the Arab world. It treated Israel as the aggressor in the Six Day War. In a show of support to the Arabs, the Soviet Union severed diplomatic relations with the Jewish state during the final phase of the conflict.

The nature of their adversarial relationship resulted in accusations from each of the superpowers that the other was deliberately creating or perpetuating instability in the region, as a means of gaining access. With regard to the Palestine problem, for example, the Soviet Union accused the United States of supporting Israeli aggression against the Arabs, while the United States accused the Soviet Union of lending support to Arab radicals and Palestinian "terrorism."

Over the years, however, the Soviet Union has conceded the strategic significance of the Middle East to the United States' vital interests. Instead of trying to push the United States out of the region, the Soviet Union has sought to secure itself a place and a role in resolving the region's conflicts, the most important of which is the Arab-Israeli dispute.

The Soviet Union's perception of its interests in the Middle East and in the Arab-Israeli conflict has been undergoing significant change under Gorbachev and his new policies. It seems that the old Soviet objectives and policies in the area are giving way to the requirements of the new Soviet internal and external orientations.

In an age of détente, which has culminated in an end to the Cold War, both the United States and the Soviet Union recognize, though in different terms and ways, and perhaps to varying degrees, the significance of resolving the Palestinian problem as a key to resolving the broader Arab-Israeli conflict. Both superpowers perceive their interests, regional and global, as better served through a peaceful resolution to this conflict. But this realization has not necessarily entailed a concerted effort by the superpowers to resolve the conflict.

The American Approach

U.S. attitudes toward the Palestine question have differed from those of the Soviet Union in terms of defining the issue and proposing a solution to it. Initially, the United States viewed the Palestine problem as one of refugees and therefore viewed potential solutions in this light. Hence the United States sponsored or supported refugee resettlement plans of the 1950s.

After 1967, the United States refused to recognize the Palestinian resistance movement as a movement engaged in a struggle for national liberation. The Palestinian guerrilla groups were predominantly viewed as terrorist organizations. During the 1970 civil war in Jordan, the Nixon administration sympathized with the crushing and expulsion of the Palestinian resistance movement from Jordan.

It took the United States a number of years to acknowledge that there was a political component to the Palestinian problem and the Palestinian people. This acknowledgement was not, however, a clear cut one. Rather it was hesitant, ambiguous, and inconsistent. The evolution of the United States perception of the Palestinian question and the Palestinian people was reflected in the kind of plans the United States sponsored or supported over the years to solve the problem.

The first American initiative after the 1967 war, the Rogers Plan of December 1969, aimed at achieving a unilateral solution to the Egyptian-Israeli conflict. The plan addressed the Palestine question as one of refugees, as evidenced by the plan's language: "There can be no lasting peace without a just settlement of the problem of those Palestinians whom the wars of 1945 and 1967 have made homeless."[1]

The United States-orchestrated disengagement agreements between Israel and Egypt, and Israel and Syria in 1974 made no reference to the Palestinian problem, or the Palestinian people. Nor did the second disengagement agreement between Egypt and Israel in September 1975. Yet in an address by Secretary of State Henry Kissinger on September 16, 1975, Kissinger stated, "And we are fully aware that there will be no permanent peace unless it includes arrangements that take into account the legitimate interests of the Palestinian people."[2]

The United States was opposed to the proclamation by the Rabat Arab Summit Conference of October 29, 1974, of the PLO as the sole legitimate representative of the Palestinian people. After this proclamation, Kissinger reconfirmed the United States' position towards the PLO:

It is impossible for the United States to recommend negotiations with the PLO until the PLO accepts the existence of Israel as a legitimate state. As long as the PLO proposals envisage, in one form or another, the destruction of Israel we don't see much hope for negotiations with the PLO.[3]

On another occasion, Kissinger commented on the decision of the Rabat Summit saying it "made negotiations over the West Bank impossible,"[4] the reference being to a perceived disengagement agreement concluded between Israel and Jordan, similar to those disengagement agreements concluded between Israel and Egypt, and Israel and Syria. It was clear that the United States perceived the PLO and the Palestinian resistance movement as an obstacle to the resolution of the Arab-Israeli conflict.

In 1976, a reference was made to the political dimension of the Palestinian issue. In a hearing of the U.S. House of Representatives, then-Deputy Assistant to the Secretary of State for Near Eastern and South Asian Affairs Harold Saunders, talked about the aspirations of the Palestinian Arabs and their legitimate interests. He also referred to the Palestinians as a political factor that should be dealt with if peace is to prevail between Israel and its neighbors.[5]

The U.S. sponsored Camp David Accords of 1978 dealt with the Palestinians neither as refugees, nor as full-fledged people entitled to equal political rights. The Accords advocated that the Palestinians in the West Bank and Gaza be granted "full autonomy," and within a transitional period of five years, negotiations among Egypt, Israel, Jordan, and the elected representatives of the inhabitants of the West Bank and Gaza take place.

If the intention of the Camp David Accords and the autonomy plan was ultimately to recognize the legitimate rights of the Palestinians (self-determination and statehood), the Accords and the plan would have referred to that option or implied it. Instead, the plan made vague references to these rights. It states that the negotiations, among the four parties mentioned above, "shall be based on all the provisions and principles of UN Security Council Resolution 242."[6] The plan also stated that the Palestinians will participate in the determination of their own future, through a variety of measures, none of which alone, or put together, amounts to an actual exercise of the right of self-determination. The Camp David Accords meant practically that the West Bank and Gaza would remain for a period of five years under Israeli sovereignty, and that after the status of these two areas was determined, they would be linked either to Israel or Jordan, or both.

President Reagan's plan of September 1, 1982, articulated a continuation in the same vein. While the President talked about "legitimate rights of the Palestinians" and their "political aspirations," and acknowledged that the Palestinian cause is more than a question of refugees, he stressed the necessity of dealing with the Palestinian people in conjunction with another sovereign state (Jordan). The Reagan Plan, as it became known, emphasized the autonomy plan included in the Camp David Accords. It differed from the Accords in being very explicit in ruling out the options of establishing a Palestinian state by determining ahead of time the future status of the West Bank and Gaza:

> Beyond the transition period, as we look to the future of the West Bank and Gaza it is clear to me that peace cannot be achieved by the formation of an independent Palestinian state in those territories. Nor is it achievable on the basis of Israeli sovereignty of permanent control over the West Bank and Gaza. So the United States will not support the establishment of an independent Palestinian state in the West Bank or Gaza, and will not support annexation or permanent control by Israel.[7]

It is worth mentioning that the Palestinians saw a positive side to the Reagan Plan, which was rejected by Israel, and that the conclusion of the Jordanian-Palestinian Accord of 1985 should be viewed in that context. It is also worth mentioning that the United States welcomed this Accord since its principles coincided with the Reagan Plan to a large extent. The Accord does not make any reference to an independent Palestinian state, and talks about Palestinian self-determination within the framework of a Jordanian-Palestinian confederation.

The Reagan Plan further stated:

> The final status of these lands must, of course, be reached through the give-and-take of negotiations. But it is the firm view of the United States that self-government by the Palestinians of the West Bank and Gaza in association with Jordan offers the best chance for a durable, just and lasting peace. We base our approach squarely on the principle that the Arab-Israeli conflict should be resolved through negotiations involving an exchange of territory for peace. This exchange is enshrined in UN Security Council Resolution 242 which is, in turn, incorporated in all its parts in the Camp David agreements. UN Resolution 242 remains wholly valid as the foundation stone of America's Middle East Peace effort. It is the United States position that--in return for peace--the withdrawal provision of resolution 242 applies to all fronts, including the West Bank and Gaza.[8]

It is often suggested by U.S. apologists for the Reagan Plan that while the U.S. government will not support the establishment of an independent Palestinian state in the West Bank and Gaza, it will not oppose the idea in principle if the various parties to the conflict, mainly Israel, agree to such an option.

The Reagan Plan did not fail to reiterate the United States' strong commitment to Israel's security: "And make no mistake, the United States will oppose any proposal--from any party and at any point in the negotiating process--that threatens the security of Israel. America's commitment to the security of Israel is ironclad."[9]

The U.S. decision in December 1988 to open a dialogue with the PLO, after the latter had met U.S. conditions, was considered a turning point, despite the fact that the opening of the dialogue was less than what the PLO was once promised if it recognized the legitimate existence of Israel as a state. It was Henry Kissinger who said that the United States would negotiate with the PLO, and not only open a "substantial dialogue" with it, if it recognized Israel.

While opening the dialogue in itself did not amount to a *de jure* recognition of the PLO as the sole legitimate representative of the Palestinian people, and did not mean in any way that the United

States recognized the Palestinian people's right to self-determination, or their right to statehood, it was construed as a *de facto* recognition of each. But from the opening of the dialogue to its suspension on June 20, 1990, the United States did little to indicate a change of policy in the direction of the suggested prospects.

The Baker proposals of 1989 tried indirectly to involve the PLO in the peace process by giving it some leverage in the selection of the Palestinian negotiating team to the Cairo talks to discuss the Shamir election plan for Palestinian self-rule in the West Bank and Gaza. Nonetheless, the thrust of the proposals towards these two areas and their inhabitants remained vague. Unlike the Reagan Plan, the Baker proposals do not clearly state that the West Bank and Gaza should be associated with Jordan. In this respect, the spirit of the Baker proposals, in essence, is more consonant with the Camp David autonomy plan. It leaves the future status of the West Bank and Gaza open. Like all other American proposed plans designed to resolve the conflict, the Baker proposals make no reference to Palestinian self-determination, Palestinian statehood, or PLO representation.

In its attempts to resolve the conflict, partially or comprehensively, the United States has tried a variety of mechanisms. It employed or attempted bilateral arrangements (the Rogers Plan, and the Camp David Accords), interim arrangements (the Israeli-Egyptian, Israeli-Syrian disengagement agreements, and the Baker proposals), and comprehensive arrangements (the Geneva Conference of 1973).

U.S. sponsored plans to resolve the Palestine question have been characterized by two fixed attitudes. First, they have been consistent in their rejection of what the Palestinian people and the PLO have been insisting upon as an acceptable basis to resolve the conflict, illustrated in self-determination, statehood, and PLO representation. The United States has not even considered plans that carry within them the prospect for achieving such goals at some point in the future.

The glimmer of an exception to this position was President Carter's vague references to a Palestinian homeland. On March 16, 1977, Carter spoke of the need for a Palestinian homeland: "There has to be a homeland provided for the Palestinian refugees who have suffered for many, many years".[10] But on July 12, 1977, Carter indicated that his personal preference was "that the Palestinian entity . . . should be tied in with Jordan and not be independent."[11]

Reference to "the legitimate rights of the Palestinian people" was made again in October 1, 1977, in a joint communiqué issued by the governments of the United States and the U.S.S.R.[12] This communiqué, which was later played down by the Carter administration due to Israeli and Jewish lobbying in the United States, was issued in the context of discussions aiming at the resumption of the Geneva Conference.

It is suggested that the "definitive statement"[13] of the Carter administration on self-determination was made by the President at Aswan, Egypt, on January 4, 1978, where he talked about:

a resolution of the Palestinian problem in all its aspects. The problem [sic] must recognize the legitimate rights of the Palestinian people and enable the Palestinians to participate in the determination of their own future.[14]

Secondly, U.S. sponsored plans have been consistent in excluding the Soviet Union from efforts to resolve the conflict. The only significant case for joint U.S.-Soviet cooperation was the Geneva Conference of 1973, which the Soviet Union and the United States co-chaired. It should be mentioned, however, that the conference was not a U.S. sponsored plan. Attempts to reconvene this conference never succeeded, stumbling over the question of PLO representation. While the United States objected to PLO participation in the conference, the joint Soviet-American communiqué of October 1, 1977, called for the participation in the work of the conference "of the representatives of all the parties involved in the conflict including those of the Palestinian people."[15] It was clear, however, that the reference was not made to the PLO, but to Palestinian participation through a joint Jordanian-Palestinian delegation or a unified Arab delegation.

The Soviet Approach

Although the U.S.S.R. emerged as a superpower at about the same time the Arab-Israeli conflict became a world concern, the Soviet Union's visible role in the Arab region dates only from 1955.

Soviet support for the 1947 UN Partition Plan for Palestine and subsequent recognition of the state of Israel in 1948, as well as the later switch in the Soviet position in favor of the Arabs and the Palestinians, is explained in ideological as well as strategic terms.

The Soviet Union supported the 1947 partition plan and recognized the state of Israel immediately after its foundation out of a hope that the establishment of Israel would lead to the exit of colonial Britain from the Middle East. The Soviets were also counting on the evolution of a new socialist state in the Middle East, since many Jewish immigrants to Palestine brought with them socialist ideas. Furthermore, the socio-economic organization of the new Jewish state had many socialist attributes. In addition, the Soviets had very little sympathy for the pro-colonial backward regimes in existence at the time in many Arab countries, especially those surrounding Israel.

It is, however, sometimes argued that the Soviet decision to recognize Israel was an example of the imperatives of the state taking precedence over ideological imperatives. The Soviets did not pay much attention to the questions of rights and justice, and they overlooked the fact that Israel was a Zionist state and that the Soviet communist ideology was hostile to Zionism. Such Soviet conduct repeated itself on more than one occasion, as it has with current Soviet Jewish immigration to Israel, an act which is believed to be dictated by state interest.

The Soviet position towards Israel changed when it became clear that Israel was becoming a strong pro-Western, primarily American, ally in the region, and a guardian of Western interest.

The Soviet Union's shift in support of the Arabs and the Palestinians can also be explained in ideological and strategic terms. When certain Arab countries (Nasser's Egypt, Qassim's Iraq, and Ba'athist Syria) began to adopt socialist or anti-Western stands, the Soviets decided that these countries had become worthy of Soviet support. Needless to say, the Soviet interest in these countries was not purely ideological. The strategic drive, challenging and competing with Western interests in the region, was a primary consideration. To Soviet thinking, however, even that strategic drive can be explained ideologically, since communism's ultimate purpose is to stand up to world capitalism.

In this context, too, the Soviet Union extended its support to the Palestinian national movement. It was President Nasser of Egypt who, in 1968, introduced the leaders of the Palestinian resistance movement to the Soviet leadership. Only then did the Soviet Union begin to deal with the Palestinians as a national liberation movement, having viewed their guerrilla actions, for a time, with suspicion. Political as well as material support was extended to the movement, and over the years, the level of this support gradually increased. The Soviets coordinated their stance regarding the Palestine question with the PLO. Furthermore, they provided the Palestinian movement with weapons and military training. Political as well as ideological guidance was extended to those Palestinian groups which had ideological affinity with the Soviets. Palestinian students were admitted in large numbers to Soviet universities and institutions.

The Palestinian national movement was to the Soviets an active anti-imperialist, anti-Zionist force, as well as an agent of revolutionary change in the Arab world. The Soviets felt they could rely on the movement as a regional ally. This movement has been significant not only because it has provided the Soviets with an avenue of access to the region, but also because it has moral, political and material presence in most Arab countries.

Initially, the Soviets and the Palestinians differed in their views towards Israel. While the PLO called in its original program for the liberation of the whole area of Palestine, the Soviet Union, which recognizes Israel and its right to exist in secure borders, did not share that view. Over the years, however, the views of the Soviet Union and those of the PLO regarding Israel and the Palestine question evolved in a way to coincide. Both parties agree now on the Palestinian people's right to self-determination, their right to have a state of their own, and on the PLO as the sole legitimate representative of the Palestinian people. Furthermore, both parties agree on Israel's right to exist as a state within secure borders. This standard Soviet position toward the Palestine question determined Soviet attitudes towards the U.S. plans which were advanced to resolve this question and the Arab-Israeli conflict.

Before 1967, the Soviet Union was officially committed to the UN Partition Plan of 1947. However, the Soviets took little or no action on this official stance. The practical Soviet position was more inclined to view the Palestine question as one of refugees. This attitude was reflected in the Soviet acceptance of UN Resolution 242.

After 1967, the Soviet Union opposed U.S. proposed solutions to the problem which excluded the Palestinians and their legitimate rights as the Soviets understood them. While none of the U.S. sponsored plans to resolve the Palestine conflict explicitly, or even implicitly, recognized Palestinian national rights as they were defined by the Palestinians themselves, the Soviet attitude in this respect was in total opposition to that of the United States.

The Soviet view of how the conflict should be resolved has also been different from that of the United States. While the United States has often embraced plans that would exclude a Soviet role in an attempt to bypass the Soviet Union in the region--for example the Camp David Accords--the Soviet Union has instead, and almost from the very start, advocated a resolution to the Palestine question in the broader context of resolving the Arab-Israeli conflict. The formula which has been consistently advocated by the Soviets is an international peace conference which is to be attended by all the parties concerned, including the PLO. From the Soviet point of view an international peace conference is bound to produce a comprehensive, just and permanent settlement to the conflict.

Implications of the End of the Cold War

Today, the Soviet Union seems to be more amenable than ever to U.S. sponsored initiatives to resolve the Palestinian conflict. This Soviet amenability was manifest during the United States' attempts to hold a meeting in Cairo between Israel and Palestinian representatives from the Occupied Territories, as ascribed by the

Baker proposals. The PLO's acquiescence to hold the meeting underscores the new Soviet attitude.

With the demise of the Cold War, foreign policy objectives of both the United States and the U.S.S.R. are bound to change. The two superpowers have to perceive and define their interests in a different light, now in a context of détente and cooperation instead of Cold War and conflict. Hostile competition is likely to fade away. Regional conflicts should be reduced to their actual size, and not drag the two superpowers into confrontation. These regional conflicts are not likely to be used as an avenue of access for hostile or aggressive rivalry. The rivalry may continue, but in a context of mutual coexistence and recognition of legitimate interests of both superpowers. The U.S-U.S.S.R competition in the Middle East is likely to evolve into something similar to that which exists between the United States and its Western European allies, or the United States and Japan. The U.S.S.R. has clearly conceded the region to the United States. It cannot pursue its interests as it used to.

It is not certain after the ascendence of Gorbachev, and after the initiation of his policies of *perestroika* and *glasnost*, that the Soviet Union will adhere to its classical attitude towards the Palestine question and its resolution. If Soviet global and regional objectives have become subject to change, the change is bound to include Soviet stands on the Arab-Israeli conflict as well as the Palestine question. Preoccupation with Soviet internal affairs, and the future of the Soviet Union itself will, by necessity, entail a reassessment by the Soviets of their objectives in the Middle East and their attitudes and policies towards the Arab-Israeli conflict and the Palestine question.

The reconstruction of Soviet society will require the highest degree of understanding and cooperation with the United States. A relationship of understanding and cooperation requires the removal of tension between the two superpowers, or at least the reduction of its level to a minimum. The Soviet Union will find itself, if not by inclination, then by necessity, forced to cooperate with the United States in American attempts to resolve regional conflicts peacefully. The Soviet Union cannot afford, for some time to come, to be involved in regional conflicts, nor can it afford to alienate the United States.

Such considerations underlie a new Soviet orientation towards Israel and the Palestinian issue. The new and more favorable Soviet attitude toward Soviet Jews and toward Israel is an outcome of this new orientation. This attitude is consonant with the process of change and gradual democratization taking place in the Soviet Union, but is also a reflection of the improvement of U.S.-Soviet relations. The Soviet Union is also aware of the great influence the Jewish lobby can exercise over the U.S. Congress.

Change in Soviet positions toward the Palestinian question has been evident in the Soviet attitude towards Jewish immigration from the Soviet Union to Israel and in the restoration of consular relations between Moscow and Tel Aviv in October 1990. Furthermore, on a few other occasions, the Soviets have indicated that the rules of the game with regard to the Arab-Israeli conflict have changed. The Soviets, who have exercised a moderating influence on their old Arab allies, have made it clear that they will no longer sympathize with, or can even tolerate, radical Arab or Palestinian stands, let alone extend support to any military adventure. Also, they no longer need to take hard-line positions vis-à-vis Israel at a time when the Palestinians themselves express a willingness to negotiate directly with Israel.

Favorable Soviet attitudes toward Israel were also reflected in the Soviet reluctance to reject Israel's credentials to UN membership in 1989, as it did in 1988. In 1989, the Soviet Union abstained. Mutual visits by Israel and Soviet officials to Moscow and Tel Aviv, after a long boycott, is another indication of improved relations between the two countries. On one occasion Alexander Zotov, the Soviet Ambassador to Damascus, stated (and it is significant that he did so in Damascus) that new facts now exist in the Soviet Union, and that these facts will affect his country's ability to meet Syria's military needs, especially with regard to supplies of sophisticated weapons. Zotov further indicated that the Soviet Union does not wish to see Syria acquiring military capabilities that would exceed its defensive needs and which would inflict unacceptable losses on Israel, if Syria tried to retaliate to an Israeli attack.[16]

Even before the Zotov statement there were indications that the Soviets might alter some of their "fixed" stands. On one occasion, Gorbachev suggested that it was up to the Palestinian people to determine the form of their representation in an international peace conference. According to Gorbachev, the Soviet Union would not mind if the Palestinians went to such a conference in a joint Palestinian-Jordanian delegation, or as part of a unified Arab delegation. This position differs from previous Soviet attitudes which insisted on the independent representation of the PLO. It is also different from the attitude the Soviets once held towards the Amman Jordanian-Palestinian Accord of 1985, which the Soviets openly opposed.

Finally, change in the Soviet attitude towards the Palestine question and its resolution has manifested itself in the Soviet reaction to the Baker proposals and the persistent U.S. efforts to hold a meeting between Israel and Palestinian representatives from the West Bank and Gaza. The Soviet attitude has been rather acquiescent. These Soviet gestures, especially if they evolve in the direction Israel and the United States desire, may improve the chances of the Soviet Union playing a role in resolving the Palestine question and the Arab-Israeli conflict.

After the change in Soviet priorities and preoccupations, it is clear that the United States will become more free-handed in dealing with the Arab-Israeli conflict and the Palestine question. While the Soviets will be more forthcoming in accommodating U.S.-sponsored plans, it is unlikely that they will share identical views. The Soviets may oppose those American policies they do not like, but they may not be able to impede them, even if they want to. The U.S.S.R.'s dependence on U.S. understanding and support to overcome its internal problems prevents the Soviet Union from challenging the United States in the Middle East or elsewhere, at least at present. Suffice to say that the Middle East, the Arab-Israeli conflict, and the Palestine question will not be of more importance to the Soviet Union than Eastern Europe. If the Soviets let Eastern Europe go, it is unlikely that they will fight the United States for the Middle East, or the Palestine question. They will, however, keep in mind that they have both current and future interests in the region, and are likely to take into account certain internal considerations when they make policies regarding the Palestine question. For the Muslims of the Soviet Union, the Palestine issue is a Muslim concern.

If the Soviet attitude towards Israel is changing, the American attitude towards the Palestinians and the PLO can change too. There is room for such an assumption, at least from a theoretical point of view. U.S. objection to granting the Palestinians the right to self-determination emanates, it is suggested, from "concern for the safety of Israel," and from some reasons "rooted more in [American] domestic politics."[17] It is also argued that concern for Israel may justify the imposition of restraints, but not the denial of self-determination altogether.[18]

American denial of Palestinian self-determination is of questionable soundness on geopolitical as well as moral grounds. Old concerns pertaining to a Palestinian state becoming a pro-Soviet radical enclave, and as such a threat to U.S. interests, are no longer valid. It is no longer convincing that this mini-state, perhaps demilitarized, emerging in phases, would pose any real threat to Israel. There has not been sufficient evidence to back the argument that this state would be a factor of instability in the region.

On the moral plane, with regard to the American denial of self-determination to the Palestinian people, the United States cannot forever exclude the Palestinian people from a universal right, which it champions in other parts of the world. The United States cannot indefinitely defend double standards.

In the aftermath of the Cold War, Israel cannot be of the same strategic importance to U.S. interests in the Middle East. Communism in the region is no longer the threat which Israel was to help contain. The remaining "radical" Arab states are eager to establish cordial and mutually beneficial relationships with the United States. The Palestinians are competing with the Israelis to win U.S. understanding, sympathy and support.

Pro-Israel advocates and apologists in the United States will continue to promote Israel's strategic significance to U.S. interests, and will continue to invoke U.S. moral responsibilities towards "the only Jewish state and the only democracy" in an unpredictable Arab region. After the demise of the communist threat, Israel and its friends will try to stress Israel's significance in fighting terrorism. Israel's name will always be raised in contrast to Islamic fundamentalism which could be detrimental to U.S. interests in the Middle East.

Nevertheless, U.S.-Israel relations are bound, as they did in the past, to go through ups and downs. The two countries' views regarding the Palestine question have not always been identical. The Israelis, for example, have rejected the Reagan Plan, as well as the United States' opening of dialogue with the PLO. By recognizing Israel's right to exist, accepting UN resolution 242, and renouncing terrorism, in November 1988, the PLO has made it difficult for the United States to support Israel blindly or tolerate its intransigence. But it is not clear, however, under what circumstances U.S. and Israeli views would diverge, if it is at all possible, to the point where the United States would recognize the PLO or the Palestinian people's right to self-determination.

As for future cooperation between the United States and the U.S.S.R., the apparent trend is that the two superpowers will cooperate, not only in defusing tension in the region, but also in opposing the eruption of war, and in helping the Arabs and the Israelis resolve their conflict. Because of the current internal Soviet preoccupation, the American role is bound to be more active and visible.

The problem which will confront the two superpowers in this regard is twofold. First, even if the two superpowers have the genuine desire to resolve the conflict, as a matter of principle, it is not certain whether the two of them can develop an identical vision to the way the conflict should be resolved. The two countries may favor a compromise and try to bridge the gap in views, and adopt a bottom line basis for the resolution of the conflict. Second, it is also not certain to what degree the two superpowers can persuade the Palestinians and the Israelis to narrow the gap between their respective stands and accept a compromise formula devised and sponsored by the two superpowers.

Because of internal and regional changes, the Israelis and the Palestinians will be, at this point, reluctant to embrace an attitude of compromise. An ultra-rightist government in Israel is not likely to make any meaningful concessions. The PLO cannot make further concessions, after those it made at the 19th Palestine National Council in Algiers, without actually endangering its legitimacy, until Israel in some way reciprocates. The PLO is further constrained by the rise of a militant Islamic movement, in the West Bank and Gaza, opposed to the PLO program.

The regional changes are symbolized in the acquisition by some Arab states of strategic and chemical weapons. This is bound to offset the military balance of power, alarm Israel, exacerbate tension, and further complicate the situation. While the Arabs argue that these weapons are for defense purposes, Israel is not likely to rest assured and seek a peaceful settlement to extricate the region from disaster. The solution of the Palestinian-Israeli conflict cannot be found in total isolation from the resolution of the Arab-Israeli conflict.

Prospects for U.S.-Soviet cooperation in resolving the Arab-Israeli conflict, or the Palestine question as a prelude to resolving the broader conflict, or as part of it, can take more than one form. In spite of the constraints, the two superpowers can try to use whatever leverage they have with their respective friends in the region to demand more flexibility and compromise. U.S.-Soviet understanding and agreement cannot be ignored, especially if it is public, and if the two superpowers' commitment to this agreement is serious.

The two superpowers can, for example, lend credibility and legitimacy to any joint plan they co-sponsor in order to resolve the Palestine conflict. They are in a position to provide the mechanisms for a solution in the West Bank and Gaza, for example, as a first step. This solution can be gradual, interim, or even comprehensive. The superpowers have a variety of means to induce the Palestinians and Israelis to see the value of a resolution to the conflict. The question is whether they can give the resolution of the Palestine conflict the due attention and the priority it requires on their agendas.

Notes

1. The Rogers Plan, December 1969 in *The Quest for Peace: Principal United States Public Statements and Related Documents on the Arab-Israeli Peace Process 1967-1989* (Washington: United States Department of State, 1984), pp. 23-29.

2. "Address by Secretary of State Henry Kissinger, September 16, 1975 (Extract)" in *The Quest for Peace*, p. 65.

3. "The second Egyptian-Israeli Disengagement Agreement, September 16, 1975" in *The Quest for Peace*, p. 57.

4. "Address by Secretary of State Henry Kissinger," in *The Quest for Peace*, p. 61.

5. House of Representatives, "The Palestine Issue in the Middle East Peace Efforts," *Hearing, Committee on International Relations, 94th Congress* (Washington: 1976), p. 176.

6. "Framework For Peace in the Middle East, Agreed at Camp David, September 17, 1978," in *The Quest for Peace*, pp. 76-81.

7. "Address by President Ronald Reagan, September 1, 1982," in *The Quest for Peace*, pp. 108-114.

8. *Ibid.*, p. 113.

9. *Ibid.*, p. 114.

10. "President Jimmy Carter's Comments Regarding a Palestinian Homeland, March-July 1977," in *The Quest for Peace*, p. 66.

11. *Ibid.*

12. "Joint Communiqué by the Governments of the United States and the Union of Soviet Socialist Republics, October 1, 1977," in *The Quest for Peace*, pp. 70-71.

13. Seth P. Tillman, *The United States in the Middle East: Interests and Obstacles* (Bloomington: Indiana University Press, 1982), p. 59.

14. "Remarks by President Jimmy Carter, Aswan, Egypt, January 4, 1978," in *The Quest for Peace*, p. 73.

15. *Ibid*, p. 71.

16. *The Washington Post*, November 20, 1989.

17. Tillman, pp. 60, 62.

18. *Ibid.*, p. 60.

13 The Palestinian Question and the End of the Cold War

One dominant characteristic of Palestinian leader Yasser Arafat --both a weakness and a strength--is that he has avoided making difficult decisions, especially in choosing allies. Although this strategy may have prevented bold leaps forward, it has also assured the longevity of the Palestinian leadership. The Gulf Crisis of 1990, which split the Arab world like never before, was the type that has in the past enabled Mr. Arafat to exploit a difficult Arab situation. However, during the Gulf War, by taking sides, Mr. Arafat made an uncharacteristically bold decision--one that has cost him dearly, at least in the short run. The question is, why?

Simplistic analyses of Mr. Arafat's personal strengths and weaknesses could not do justice to the widespread Palestinian sentiment that preceded Iraq's invasion of Kuwait. Palestinian journalist and leader Hanna Siniora captured the Palestinian feeling well by explaining metaphorically that "when a drowning man sees land disappear slowly in front of him, and suddenly a man throws him a rope, he will not stop to ask who that man is."[1] Were the Palestinians "drowning" prior to Iraq's invasion of Kuwait?

An examination of both Palestinian perceptions and the objective chances for deliverance from a desperate status quo reveal that Mr. Siniora's explanation was not far off the mark. At the heart of the prevailing sentiments was a Palestinian fear that the end of the Cold War would have devastating consequences for the Palestinians. By the end of the Arab Summit Conference in May, the Palestinians were expecting the worst.

The Palestinians
and the Decline of the Soviet Union

Several assumptions drove the Palestinian view, which was also shared by many Arab leaders. Mr. Arafat himself sounded desperate about the potential implications of the changed global political climate. In his speech to his Arab colleagues at the May 1990 Summit Conference in Baghdad--which was televised across the Arab world--Mr. Arafat declared:

The threats against pan-Arab security and the security of each individual Arab country are growing and are being fueled by the temptations of the transnational period through which the world is passing before a new and different détente is formed. They are also being fueled by the dramatic changes among the Arabs' traditional friends, who are now up to their ears in domestic problems. To help solve some of these domestic problems, the United States has set conditions that blackmail Eastern European countries and weaken their role in the search for a just peace for the Middle East. It is using the emigration of Jews--the emigration of people and brains--and setting other economic, political, and diplomatic conditions for providing assistance.[2]

Indeed, Soviet Jewish immigration was the central issue of the conference. It symbolized for Arabs all that was perceived to be wrong with the end of the Cold War, and all the threats that faced the Arab nation. Across the board, Arab leaders and elites did not see the end of the Cold War as a victory of democracy over dictatorship, or as the victory of consensus politics over power politics. Instead, the end of the Cold War signaled the decline of the Soviet Union as a major superpower, ushering in an era of American hegemony, which implies Israeli regional hegemony.[3] The Arab view was summarized by Saddam Hussein in a speech that he delivered to the Arab Cooperation Council in February 1990:

Given the relative erosion of the role of the Soviet Union as the key champion of the Arabs in the context of the Arab-

Zionist conflict and globally, and given that the influence of the Zionist lobby on U.S. policies is as powerful as ever, the Arabs must take into account that there is a real possibility that Israel might embark on new stupidities within the five-year span I have mentioned. This might take place as a result of direct or tacit U.S. encouragement.[4]

While Egypt and Syria agreed with this assessment, they also understood that the United States is the only game in town. Even if the United States could not be persuaded to take the Arab side vis-à-vis Israel, good relations with the United States were perceived to be critical in preventing disaster for the Arab side.[5] However, for the Palestinians and the Jordanians, the situation looked more ominous.

First, the Palestinian and Jordanian perception was not only that the Arab-Israeli peace process and the Baker plan had completely failed, but that the United States was "in collusion with Israel." Mr. Arafat believed that the Bush administration's efforts were motivated by the desire to get ever more and more concessions from the Palestinians, to buy time, and to destroy the *Intifada*--without any serious intent to work toward Israeli compromise.[6] The Jordanians shared this assessment.

Second, a resolution by the United States Congress declaring united Jerusalem the capital of Israel aggravated deep wounds. Mr. Arafat expressed the sentiment to his Arab colleagues at the Baghdad summit, questioning how the U.S. Congress could give itself the right to issue a resolution to consider holy Jerusalem the capital of Israel. Arafat called the resolution invalid, and argued that it constituted an attack against "Arab pride, Islamic pride, and international will."

Third, a U.S. veto of a United Nations resolution regarding the situation in the West Bank and Gaza in May contributed to the view that there was "collusion by the United States." Complaining to Arab leaders, Arafat promised to "convey to you in secret session what happened to me in Geneva as a result of U.S. collusion and maneuvering."[7] In the closed meetings, Arafat tried to convince his Arab colleagues that the United States had promised not to veto the UN resolution if the PLO accepted the proposed formulation; once the PLO agreed to make the requested concession, "the U.S. voted as it had planned to all along."[8]   Arafat would not accept the possibility of miscommunication or misunderstanding, despite the fact that most of the negotiations involved intermediaries.[9]

Palestinians further chose to interpret the killing of several innocent Palestinian workers by a lone Israeli, south of Tel Aviv, as part of a general conspiracy to inflict fear in the Palestinians and drive them to leave the Occupied Territories.[10]   Subsequent bloodshed in confrontations between Palestinians and the Israeli army fueled Palestinian suspicions.

Finally, Palestinians and other Arabs alike interpreted Soviet Jewish immigration in the worst possible way: as an attempt to fulfill the dream of Greater Israel. "This immigration," concluded Arafat:

> which tops the list of priorities for Israeli policy and the world Zionist movement--with flagrant U.S. support and exposed collusion, and the closing of the doors of the United States and other countries in the face of immigrants-- constitutes a new attempt to revive the Zionist myth and dream of Greater Israel.[11]

Indeed, Arafat tried to convince Arab leaders that the threat of Soviet Jewish immigration is not just a threat to the Palestinians but a threat to the rest of the Arab world. Producing maps at the Arab summit, he argued that Israel is now implementing plans for a Greater Israel:

> The map covers all of Jordan, the entire Lebanon, all of Palestine, half of Sinai, half of Syria, two-thirds of Iraq, and one-third of Saudi Arabia up to Medina . . . this is the Greater Israel from the Nile to the Euphrates. They printed it on their currency and published it in newspapers and magazines without hesitation.[12]

This picture added up to one thing for Arafat: the end of the Cold War, the decline of the Soviet Union, and U.S. "collusion" with Israel, meaning that Israel is now in a position to implement designs for a Greater Israel, without serious opposition from the international community. Arafat was expecting that, unless Arabs take serious counter-measures, Israel would launch an attack against Jordan within months, leading to the expulsion of Palestinians from the Occupied Territories.[13] He was unconvinced by the argument that the Israeli public would not support such an incursion, especially given the lessons that the Israelis have learned from the adventure in Lebanon.[14] To his Arab colleagues, Arafat chanted: "Brother Arabs, the Israelis are beating the drum of war."[15] In short, for Arafat, disaster was imminent.

A similar sentiment was expressed by Jordanian elites and leaders about the imminent danger to the Arab nation.[16] So desperate was King Hussein at the Baghdad summit, so tragic was the tone of his televised speech that some of his most loyal citizens felt humiliated by the king's tone.[17] The king, a man with legendary talent for the game of survival, ended his speech with the following warning to Arab leaders:

> I have talked about my country with such candor and
> bitterness in the hope that the day will never come in which
> I and my people in Jordan--men, women, children and young
> men--have nothing to repeat on every lip but that painful cry
> by the Arab poet: "They have lost me, and what a brave man
> they have lost, for he would have defended their frontiers on
> the evil day." Peace be upon you.[18]

The unusually harmonious views of Arafat and King Hussein further consolidated a relationship already strengthened by the Jordanian riots of April 1989 protesting tough economic measures. Jordanian analysts argue that besides the economic factor, Jordanians were inspired by the Palestinian uprising (*Intifada*), and the perceived heroics of the people in South Lebanon.[19] The demonstrations were especially threatening to the king since they took place almost exclusively in Jordanian, not Palestinian communities. There was a sense that, had the PLO not advised its supporters in Jordan against joining the demonstrations, King Hussein would have been in serious trouble.[20] Expecting more difficult economic times ahead, complicated by the fear emanating from Soviet Jewish immigration to Israel, the king sought to diffuse the situation and spread the blame by holding elections. The PLO, on other hand, had every incentive to help the Jordanian monarch survive, lest instability in Jordan give Israel and opportunity to implement the "Jordan option" of turning Jordan into a Palestinian state.

Arab Legitimacy
and the Question of Palestine

The devastating defeat of Iraq, and the PLO's difficulties with the rich Arab states must be counted as a setback for the Palestinians in the short term. However, it would be a major mistake to conclude from this that a fundamental transformation has occurred in the general Arab perception of the question of Palestine, if only for the fact that the PLO's political position during the Gulf War was probably in line with the majority of the Arab masses outside the Gulf. It must also be recognized that, as usual, Arab governments cannot ignore the Palestinian question.

At the core of Arab politics are patterns of relations resulting from the need for all Arab governments to balance their interests as leaders of nation-states, with the political legitimacy required for their survival. Despite transnational, ideological, cultural, and religious movements linking all Arabs, governments in the Middle East, like governments around the globe, are driven first and foremost by the interests of the nation-states. However, since most political movements within each state profess broader Arab and Islamic objectives, any Arab government must present credentials on those issues; what the governments of Egypt or Syria do for their own interests must always be advocated for the good of all Arabs or Muslims.

This common Arab need creates an uncomfortable interdependence which alters the priorities of Arab governments. What happens in Arab and Islamic political movements *outside* a given Arab state affects political movements *within* that state. Arab governments thus cannot remain oblivious to political trends in other parts of the Arab world. For this reason, many Arab governments continually engage in a competition for regional political leadership;

the closer these states are in their ideology, and thus in their legitimacy, the fiercer the competition for leadership. Two examples tell much about the current configuration of Arab alliances in the Gulf War.

One pertains to Syria and Iraq, the only two Ba'athist states in the world. It is an ideology centered on a single priority: Arab unity. Yet Syria became the Arab world's only ally of non-Arab Iran during the eight years of the Iraq-Iran war. In the recent crisis, Syria, one of the Arab world's most staunchly anti-American states, joined the United States to make sure that Saddam Hussein's influence in the Arab world did not rise at its expense.

The case of Egypt and Iraq in 1961 is even more telling. The regime of Abd al-Kareem Qassem of Iraq had come to power in 1958, to the pleasure of Egypt, by overthrowing the pro-British, anti-Egyptian monarchy. Qassem was as anti-British as Egypt's Nasser, advocating similar pan-Arab ideals. But he was unwilling to subordinate himself to Nasser and quickly became Egypt's most targeted opponent. Nasser adamantly opposed Qassem's plan to control Kuwait following British withdrawal, although the plan was consistent with Nasser's pan-Arab ideals. So sharp was Egypt's opposition to Iraq's designs on Kuwait that it was willing to reconcile its differences with its ideological opponent Saudi Arabia and risk the dissolution of its union with Syria. More embarrassing, Egypt found itself unable to oppose the deployment of British troops in Kuwait to defend against potential Iraqi attacks.

While Arab governments are interdependent for their legitimacy, there are few specific issues on which the competing ideological movements agree. One stands out: the Palestinian question. Much of the recent debate about the role of the Palestinian question in Arab politics and how this question will be affected by the Gulf War misses the point.

To be sure, Arab states have abused this question for their own ends, with the Palestinians always paying a price. Nonetheless, the Palestinian issue remains at the core of every major Arab, Islamic, and anti-Western political movement, providing the lens through which the Arabs must view the world, and the cement that binds these movements together. And whenever the legitimacy of an Arab government comes into question, it will rush to wrap itself in a Palestinian flag.

Though its importance is largely symbolic, the power and persistence of the Palestinian issue should never be underestimated. Its history is closely linked to the inception of Arab nationalism, anti-imperialism, and all those defining moments of Arab relations with the rest of the world. Its value for government legitimacy will not diminish, no matter how Arabs come to perceive the PLO and its leaders. And as a result of the Gulf War, the legitimacy of every Arab government is being put to the test. This crisis of legitimacy in the region will guarantee that the Palestinian question will be high on the Arab agenda.

Even before the Gulf Crisis began, however, Arab governments were already preparing themselves for an expected regional crisis that could threaten their very survival. Arab fear was not only related to the ramifications of the end of the Cold War for the Arab-Israeli conflict, but also to a broader concern about superpower designs for the Middle East in the new global political climate.

Taken together, the shifts in the distribution of the military, economic and political power that the world has witnessed in the past few years are in some important respects on par with the end of World Wars I and II. From the point of view of most Middle Easterners with political memory, this comparison is an ominous one. Indeed, King Hussein's perception of current Western designs to "reorganize the area in a manner more dangerous to our people than the Sykes-Picot agreement"[21] of 1916, dividing the Middle East into European spheres of influence, is neither accidental nor unique to the thinking of the King. Many in the Middle East expressed fears about the regional consequences of the end of the Cold War months before Iraq's invasion of Kuwait.

Consider the sources of regional fear. The end of World War I brought a completely new political system in the region, one that fell far short of the aspirations of its people. The Ottoman Empire, which had ruled the region for centuries, finally collapsed, giving way to a European mandate, dominated by Britain and France. The end of World War II forced a substantial British and French retreat, but not before it created a new political order in the region that seemed more suited to serving British and French interests from afar than to responding to the political and economic realities in the region. States were created in regions where no unique geographic or ethnic identities had ever formed, and boundaries were drawn in places where none had existed before--King Hussein's Jordan being only one case in point. This occurred while most indigenous political movements were either pan-Islamic or pan-Arab. Even geographic political movements like the Greater-Syria and Greater-Maghreb movements were antithetical to the boundaries drawn.

While newly established governments struggled to maintain control over the new nation-states, popular movements continued to present a challenge to their legitimacy. And while states in the region have become an inescapable reality in the past four decades and have succeeded in giving life to new political allegiances, the old movements have never died away. Hiding the ever existing tension, and perhaps accounting for the survival of many Arab governments, has been the Soviet-American competition that has prevented the altering of the system. The end of bipolarity will no doubt unleash many of the hidden forces.

Making matters worse for states in the region is that, despite their partial success at building national allegiance, they have failed their people. The vast majority of Arabs live in states where the per capita GNP is less than $1,000 a year. Most Arabs are under the age of 20. Seventeen Arab states have declining per capita GNP. In short, most Arabs are young, with a pitiful economic present and a future that looks even worse. The political uncertainties unleashed by Soviet disengagement will no doubt push these popular concerns to the surface.

If Saddam Hussein understood anything, it was his Arab colleagues' fear and apprehension about the new global political order. He was the first to articulate a comprehensive interpretation of the meaning of the end of the Cold War for the Arab world, in February, 1990.[22] Going beyond the typical interpretation of the end of the Cold War as the beginning of an era of American hegemony, and therefore Israeli hegemony, Saddam Hussein offered Arabs an alternative: if Arabs act jointly and consolidate their oil and financial resources, they will have to be taken seriously by the United States.

In pursuit of his ambitious designs for Kuwait, Saddam had Arab public opinion going his way by the early summer of 1990. Following a June visit to five states in the region, I concluded that "anti-Americanism at the popular level is approaching the anti-British sentiment of the 1950s," that "Iraq is gaining influence in the region at a faster rate than anticipated," and that "the personal popularity of Saddam Hussein has increased dramatically"[23] despite his all too obvious shortcomings. Summarizing Arab despair, a former Egyptian ambassador to the United States put it this way: "Arabs are sick of their governments begging the United States to plead with Israel to please let them have peace."[24] By flaunting his military capabilities, targeting Israel, and highlighting the Palestinian question, Saddam Hussein filled the gap of Arab despair and helplessness.

Indeed, if Saddam made any miscalculation by invading Kuwait, it was about Arab, not American, reaction. He had been saying for months that he expected the United States to have fewer constraints in advancing its interests now that the Soviets were out of the picture. But he believed that the United States could not succeed without Arab cooperation. And given the regional despair and anti-Americanism, he must have calculated, not unreasonably, that Arab governments would be reluctant to accept the deployment of American troops to attack an Arab state. What he seemed to forget, however, is that the very competition that makes Arab governments concerned about the Palestinian question to begin with would prevent Syria and Egypt from allowing Saddam Hussein to claim the mantle of Arab leadership.

Short-Term Impact of the Gulf War

Although the Gulf governments' relations with the PLO are strained and some, especially in Kuwait, are resentful of Palestinians generally, their temporary ability to snub the PLO derives from the fact that both Syria and Egypt were on their side during the Gulf War. As soon as Arab relations become more competitive again-- as no doubt they will--Arab public opinion will become critical for legitimacy, and the question of Palestine will be up there. Moreover, both Syria and Egypt have Arab-leadership ambitions--

and both understand the value of the Palestinian question in this regard. In the 1950s and 1960s, Egypt could claim Arab leadership only by projecting military leverage on behalf of the Palestinians; as soon as it concluded a peace treaty, it was expelled from the Arab League. In the late 1980s, in the absence of any serious Arab military option, Egypt regained a leadership role by projecting political leverage to bring about a dialogue between the PLO and the United States; as soon as it became clear that the peace process was getting nowhere by the spring of 1990, Egyptian leverage diminished and, symbolically, Arafat was beginning to spend more time in Baghdad, which moved to project a military option. A high level Syrian official explained the apparent decline of Syrian influence in the Arab world in the summer of 1990 by claiming that Syria had forgotten a key axiom of Arab politics: he who leads the Arab world must champion the Palestinian cause.[25] In short, both Syria and Egypt will have incentives to win the Palestinians over, which will translate into some Palestinian leverage.

Still, there are costs to the Palestinians in the short-term. First, PLO relations with the United States are seriously strained at a time when U.S. influence is supreme. Second, it will probably take some time before a new alignment emerges between the PLO and Egypt or Syria. Third, and perhaps more importantly, both the PLO and its Palestinian constituencies will suffer serious economic difficulties as a consequence of the war; the PLO has lost an estimated $480 million in annual contributions from the Gulf Arab states, for an overall annual Palestinian loss of over $1.3 billion. This does not include the billions in lost assets and depreciation of properties.[26] The per capita income of the average Palestinian in the West Bank and Gaza may eventually decline by 15-20 per cent.[27]

And in the long term, the evolution of Arab identity, and therefore the means of legitimacy, may not be so favorable to the Palestinians; if the Gulf War accelerates the decline of Arabism in favor of stateism, will the value of the Palestinian issue diminish in Arab politics?

Dialectic Weakness in
the Palestinian Position

At the heart of the dilemma for the PLO is a dialectic between pan-Arabism on the one hand and Palestinian nationalism on the other (*qawmiyya* vs. *wataniyya*). Since its early stages, the Palestinian national movement has symbolized pan-Arabism and provided the rallying point for the pan-Arabist forces. Since the Camp David Accords, however, it has become clear to the Palestinians that, despite the rhetoric, Arab governments behave primarily in accordance with their own national interests. This view was reinforced when the PLO found itself fighting Israeli forces in Lebanon almost alone. Syria interfered only when its forces became endangered. The Palestinians have had a difficult time dealing with a dilemma. On the one hand, they cannot subordinate themselves to selfish Arab regimes in the name of pan-Arabism. Independence is sought even at the cost of leaving the Arab world; after the Israeli invasion of Lebanon, Palestinian publications moved their headquarters to Cyprus. In the early days of the PLO's presence in Tunis there were reports that it was unhappy with the freedom of operation available to it and was considering opting for non-Arab Greece.

On the other hand, total abandonment of the pan-Arab cause is not likely. This is the case not simply because of the ideological attachment to this cause by a great many Palestinians who have come to be politicized and mobilized in an era of rising Nasserism. There are other practical reasons. The Palestinians need the Arab states for financial and political backing, and cannot afford a major break in relations.

To be sure, the Arab states also need to appease the Palestinians. In spite of the reality of state nationalism at the governmental level, the Palestinian issue remains a major issue in the minds of Arabs at large. Many Arab governments feel that they need to pay at least lip service to the Palestinian cause to establish their legitimacy in the minds of their people. Unhappy Palestinians are also in a position to cause unrest in many Arab states, especially in the Gulf region. The predicament of the PLO, however, is that a role totally independent of the Arab states would not only result in isolation from Arab governments, but also could result in the erosion of support among Arab masses. If Palestine is strictly a Palestinian issue, then how can other Arabs be expected to make it their major concern? This dilemma for Arabs at large can be seen in a letter to the editor of *Falastine Al-thawra*, the central organ of the PLO, by a Saudi student, requesting an explanation for the choice of Cyprus as the center for Palestinian publications, following the Israeli invasion of Lebanon. "Why," asked a student, "did you not choose an Arab state as your center, as we all would have expected? . . . I had not expected that the PLO would be so ungrateful to all the aid provided to it by the Arabs . . . especially since the liberation of Palestine is primarily an Arab concern."[28] The editor's reply was also telling. "The PLO is not ungrateful," the editor replied:

> The deposits of one Arab state in the United States provide a sufficient budget for the liberation of Palestine in a year. Payment in blood cannot be compared with monetary payments. This revolution is indeed Arab, but Palestinian decisions shall remain independent regardless of the cost.[29]

Yet the same *Falastine Al-thawra*, in considering the debate on *qawmiyya* vs. *wataniyya* concluded that the Palestinian considers himself "first Arab, second Arab and third Palestinian."[30] This dilemma for Palestinian nationalism will become more difficult as a consequence of the Gulf War.

But the weakening of pan-Arabism will not necessarily lead to the end of trans-nationalism in the Middle East or to the weakening of the power of the Palestine question in mobilizing masses in the region. The alternative is likely to be a string of trans-national Islamic political movements, for which the symbols of Palestine and Jerusalem are even stronger that they have been for the Arab nationalist movement.

Indeed, it would be a tragic mistake to conclude from the immediate regional quiet following Iraq's defeat that the worst is over, that the source of regional despair has disappeared, or that Arabs are pleased that an ambitious and ruthless Saddam Hussein has been defeated. Most Arabs, like King Hussein, believe that the

Gulf War was "a war against all Arabs and all Muslims and not against Iraq alone,"[31] that the defeat of a strong Arab state, even one led by Saddam Hussein, is not good for the Arabs, and that their leaders have betrayed the Arab cause in order to score points with Washington. While these sentiments will not necessarily translate into major political changes in the Arab world, the survival of governments will be assured only by more oppression. Since oppression means the absence of legal means of opposition. the populace will likely turn to available structures for mass political opposition, in this case the mosques. And the issue of Palestine will again be an instrument of political mobilization.

Conclusion: Palestinian Nationalism and Transnationalism

Fouad Ajami saw the rise of Palestinian nationalism in the mid-1970s as an indication of the death of Pan-Arabism. Although there is little doubt that Arabism declined in the 1970s, announcing its death may have been premature. Still, Ajami's metaphorical point holds: there is a direct link between the question of Palestine, the pan-Arab movement, and other transnational political movements in the Middle East--whether Arab or Islamic. Palestine remains the fuel that drives transnationalism in the region, and prevents the "normalization" of the state system in the Middle East. Although resolving the Palestinian issue would not remove many of the serious economic and political problems in the region, it would go a long way in weakening transnationalism, and removing the interdependence of regional problems that has made it difficult to deal with them constructively. No global power configuration can transform this regionality.

Notes

1. Personal interview, Jerusalem, December 1990.

2. Foreign Broadcast Information Service (henceforth, FBIS) NES-90-103, May 29, 1990, p. 12.

3. This view was consistent among Arab elites and leaders in Egypt, Syria, Iraq, Jordan, and the West Bank in May-June 1990. This assessment is based on dozens of interviews that I conducted in the region during that period in preparing a report for Representative Lee H. Hamilton, Chairman of the House Subcommittee on Europe and the Middle East.

4. FBIS-NES-90-039, February 27, 1990.

5. Interviews in Egypt and Syria, June 1990.

6. Personal interview with Yasser Arafat, Baghdad, Iraq, June 5, 1990.

7. FBIS-NES-90-103, May 29, 1990, p. 16.

8. Personal interview with Yasser Arafat, Baghdad, Iraq, June 5, 1990.

9. *Ibid.*

10. *Ibid.*

11. FBIS-NES-90-103, May 29, 1990, p. 15.

12. *Ibid.*

13. Personal interview, June, 1990.

14. *Ibid.*

15. FBIS-NEW-90-103, May 29, 1990, p. 13.

16. Interviews in Amman, Jordan, June, 1990.

17. *Ibid.*

18. FBIS-NES-90-104, May 30, 1990, p. 9.

19. Interview with a Jordanian political scientist, Amman, Jordan, June, 1990.

306

20. This view was expressed by Jordanian analysts as well as by PLO Chairman Yasser Arafat, during my meeting with him on June 5, 1990.

21. *The New York Times*, February 7, 1991.

22. See his speech to the Arab Cooperation Council in FBIS-NES-90-039, February 27, 1990.

23. Report to Representative Lee H. Hamilton, June, 1990.

24. Personal interview with Ashraf Ghurbal, Cairo, June, 1990.

25. Personal interview, Damascus, Syria, June, 1990.

26. See Bishara A. Bahbah, "The Economic Consequences on the Palestinians," in *The Palestinians and the War in the Gulf* (Center for Policy Analysis on Palestine, February, 1991).

27. *Ibid.*

28. *Falastine Al-thawra*, January 22, 1983.

29. *Ibid.*

30. *Ibid.*, January 15, 1983.

31. *The New York Times*, February 7, 1991.

Lebanon, Syria, and Israel

14 Triangle of Tension

Before looking specifically at Soviet policy toward the "triangle of tension," let us first briefly examine the Soviet approach to the Third World in general, and the Middle East in particular, in the pre-Gorbachev era.

Soviet policy before Gorbachev represented a strange mixture of ideological and geopolitical concepts, and both dimensions possessed peculiar traits that mirrored the ambiguity of Moscow's stance in the international arena. It is probably not easy for a foreigner to assess the true nature of the ideological dimension of Soviet foreign policy, which was less a genuine belief in the ultimate global victory of communism over capitalism or in the inherent superiority of the socialist system, than a dogmatic adherence to an established set of rules postulating--in an axiomatic manner--irreconcilable contradictions between the two systems. Nobody would have dared oppose or openly doubt the official wisdom that predicted the inevitable collapse of capitalism and, in relation to the Third World, its utter incapacity to solve the enormous and painful problems of the developing countries. However, the downfall of the totally evil and rotten capitalist system had to be accelerated--in the ultimate interests of mankind--by means of the active struggle of all anti-imperialist forces, the main element of which being an unshakable alliance of the socialist world community and the national-liberation movement in the Third World.

Can this kind of thinking be called ideology? Obviously only to a limited extent. Rather, it was a peculiar sort of pseudo-ideology, a set of concepts dictating unthinking obedience to rules of conduct that did not necessarily reflect genuine ideological convictions and spiritual values of either political leaders or executive officials. The acceptance of this given "reality," namely the division of the world into two opposing blocs, inevitably led to a zero-sum game being played in the sphere of foreign policy. All the rest was just routine work aimed at promoting and improving Soviet positions in the Third World and--logically--undermining the influence of an adversary that, at the same time, was a bitter enemy of newly-liberated nations, threatening their independence through its subversive neo-colonialist activities.

The geopolitical dimension may be divided into two broad categories: great power politics and superpower politics. Russia has always been a great power and--even had the October Revolution not occurred--would have had certain legitimate interests in many areas of the world, interests that at times quite naturally would be opposed to and clash with those of other great powers, which is perfectly normal in the "game of nations." As to superpower politics, this dimension was closely linked to the pseudo-ideological factor and reflected Moscow's self-perceived position in the world as champion of the "just cause," defender of the oppressed, and vanguard of progress. It is doubtful that the very notion of "superpower" could have emerged in the modern world without an ideological connotation. For instance, if neither the Bolshevik Revolution in Russia nor the Nazi revolution in Germany (both countries subsequently claiming virtual superpower status precisely as a result of those revolutions) had occurred, it would have been difficult to imagine any nation asserting itself as a superpower. In this writer's view, it would be erroneous to link superpower status to possession of nuclear weapons and inter-continental missiles coupled with huge territory and population. After all, China has all of these attributes but has never been considered a superpower. To be a superpower, a nation also has to be one of the main global centers of power, a dominant figure in a network of world alliances and an ideological leader of at least a significant part of mankind. From this definition it follows that the Soviet Union has recently been losing--or has already lost--its claim to superpower status.

Superpower pretension based on a quasi-ideology, constantly bolstered and fed by the situation of confrontation and the Cold War mentality, played an important role in drawing blueprints for Soviet foreign policy. Now in the Gorbachev era, this combined "ideological" and "superpower" dimension has been reduced in a fundamental way and in some situations may be considered a negligible element in Soviet foreign policy. What remains is "normal" great power realpolitik based on legitimate and understandable geopolitical interests.

Turning to practical politics in the Middle East, it would be correct to assume that of the three main factors that have determined the importance of the region to each superpower, namely its strategic value, oil, and the ideological competition, only the first can be said to have been almost equally vital to the United States and the U.S.S.R. The second factor, oil, was immeasurably more important to the Americans than to the Soviets, while the ideological dimension was vital to a Soviet leadership anxious to constantly claim new successes for the socialist cause. Let us not forget that there was a period when the Middle East was the area of the highest concentration of regimes of socialist orientation.

Now, of course, the strategic dimension has lost its former importance to both superpowers. It would be surprising to find the highest military echelons in Moscow and Washington still thinking in terms of a Soviet-American war being played out in the deserts and oases of the Arab East. However, a powerful inertia remains and it may be assumed that quite a few young diplomats entering the Foreign Service in both capitals still tend to believe that the Middle East is so vital that any withdrawal from this area is unthinkable. Formerly, these people would have said: "We must drive the other side the hell out of the Middle East." Now they are more moderate and more prepared to compromise.

From these general reflections, let us come now to the "triangle of tension."

Superpower Interests: The United States

The two main preoccupations of every American administration since World War II have appeared to be: a) security of Israel and b) the maintenance of dominant American influence in the Arab East in general and in the triangle in particular.

The reasons for the American preoccupation with Israel's security have been amply described and analyzed. They stem not only from the Jewish state's value as the main American ally in the Middle East--a value that might be called virtually unique in the era of Soviet-American confrontation--and not only from the considerable influence of the Jewish lobby within the United States, but also from humanitarian feelings and the Christian tradition. As people of the Old Testament, Jews occupy a special place in American thinking and the guarantee of security of the new-born Jewish state has always been given high priority by Washington. The United States seems to have been anxious to prevent a repetition of the situations of 1967 and 1973, when Israel had to wage war at least on two fronts, with Syria, along with Egypt, being a menace to the very existence of the Jewish state. After Camp David, Syria's possibilities and its capacity to take on Israel were drastically reduced since it was obvious that in any bilateral confrontation its chances of victory were practically nil. Syria, however, has always had a great potential for trouble in American eyes, since it could become a spark setting off a huge fire, the Golan Heights being a constant irritant. Preventing a new flare-up in the Syrian-Israeli confrontation has been one of the primary tasks of American diplomacy, but unless the Israeli government had agreed to a solution acceptable to the Syrians on the issues of the Golan Heights and the West Bank--and there has never been a chance that it would--the situation was doomed to remain explosive.

Nobody knew how long the Syrian regime could tolerate the stalemate over the Golan Heights without a fatal loss of face among its own population, resulting in an internal explosion. A risk always existed that Syrian President Hafez el-Assad would choose to provoke a new round of hostilities, reckoning on support in the Arab world. It could have been argued, however, that the very nature of Syria's relations with Egypt and Iraq--the only Arab nations of real military value in these circumstances--precluded any genuine alliance with either of them. Still, the possibility of a new conflagration between Syria and Israel has always remained high, and the only feasible course of action for the United States, given Israel's adamant stand, has been to procrastinate, to voice from time to time new initiatives, hardly more promising than previous ones, for a Middle Eastern settlement.

As to Lebanon, it seems that this country--at least until the Israeli invasion of 1982--did not have a special, independent place of its own in American thinking. President Reagan's disastrous attempt to ensure American predominance in the settlement of the Lebanese conflict and to thwart Syria's hegemonic ambitions was probably the high point of the U.S. involvement in Lebanese affairs, the last occasion of direct American intervention.

As regards the upkeep of U.S. influence and prestige in the triangle, as part of the larger Middle Eastern area, it must be noted that this region has been unique in the sense that here, and nowhere else, principal clients (or allies) of both superpowers have been directly facing each other with virtually no significant middle-of-the-road states in between. Between Camp David and the start of the Gulf War, Israel's only real adversary was Syria, which at the same time was Moscow's chief ally in the area. Thus, keeping Syria isolated in the Arab world with no hope of any other state in the area coming to its aid in the event of an attack on Israel has appeared to be the bottom line of the American regional policy. At the same time it has been necessary not to drive Syria to desperation nor humiliate Hafez el-Assad. Thus, Washington sought not to deprive him of the hope for possible flexibility in American policy, and to convince him that his interests would be best served by patient diplomacy, allowing him to reject confrontation with America in favor of a search for common ground and accommodation. In short, the basic character of American policy has been to weaken and isolate the Syrian leader but not to corner him, to make him realize that eventually it is Washington, not Moscow, that can help him out of his predicament.

Superpower Interests: The Soviet Union

Before the Gorbachev-Reagan breakthrough the key to Soviet policy in the Middle East had been the deep-rooted conviction, never openly challenged, that the area was absolutely "vital to our interests," that it was imperative to maintain and promote Soviet influence and "progressive social trends" in the region and prevent U.S.-led imperialist forces from establishing control or dominance. It was taken for granted that the Middle East was one of the principal battlefields in the superpower confrontation.

It is in light of this overall approach that Soviet policy in the triangle must be considered. The clear-cut confrontation between Syria and Israel greatly pre-determined the Soviet attitude there, as Israel was the main American client directly confronting the main Soviet ally in the area. Lines were drawn rather sharply. However, this was only a part of the picture: major differences between Syria and Iraq--another Soviet ally--as well as fundamental contradictions between Hafez el-Assad and PLO Chairman Yasser Arafat and, lastly, Syria's role in the Lebanese civil war tended to make Moscow's policy toward Syria rather complex. Of course, this policy must also be viewed against the background of Soviet-American relations. It was realized in Moscow that the Middle East was equally, if not more, vital for the other superpower, and it was felt that the local confrontation between Syria and Israel must never be allowed to escalate into a large scale armed conflict liable to lead to a Soviet-American clash.

These basic and unavoidable contradictions in and restrictions on Soviet policy tended to complicate considerably the Soviet Union's initially simplistic and clear-cut "black and white" approach to the Syrian-Israeli situation. Soviet aims in the triangle were contradictory: to promote Soviet influence and socialist trends in the Middle East, but in such a way as to not provoke a serious conflict with the United States; to protect Syria's interests and, if possible, to ensure the Israeli withdrawal from the Golan Heights, but without a new Syrian-Israeli war that could escalate into a Soviet-American confrontation; to behave in such a manner as to guarantee Syrian loyalty to Moscow, leaving Damascus in no doubt as to the ability of the Soviet Union to help Syria achieve its legitimate objective of restoring its lost territory, but at the same time not to jeopardize Soviet-Iraqi relations by appearing to support Syria's hegemonic ambitions in the region; to recognize Syria's interests in Lebanon but not at the expense of either the PLO or the Lebanese left-wing forces. Taken as a whole, Soviet diplomacy can be said to have coped quite successfully with this delicate situation.

One wonders just what has changed in this respect since the introduction of Gorbachev's new political thinking and his historic accord with Reagan marking the substitution of the global confrontation of the Cold War with a new concept of cooperation. Here we must return to the idea of differentiating between the Soviet Union's former superpower interests, closely linked to and partly derived from the ideological--or quasi-ideological--dimension of its foreign policy, and normal, legitimate great power interest. While the former seem to have gradually disappeared, the latter evidently remain as strong as ever.

Hardly anybody in Moscow would now think in terms of the Middle East as a battleground in the confrontation between the United States and the U.S.S.R.; the very notion of combating imperialism all over the globe and thus accelerating the ultimate and inevitable victory of socialism has become obsolete. One neither fears an American attack on the Soviet Union from many directions, including the Middle East, nor pins any hopes on Hafez el-Assad building a happy socialist society in Syria. As to the Soviet attitude towards Israel, for 20 years Moscow has said that the renewal of diplomatic relations depended on Israel's withdrawal from the West Bank and Gaza. Now, the Soviet Union has only asked that the Israeli government state its commitment to peaceful negotiations, including with the Palestinians in some form, by joining an international conference--in short, to make a meaningful gesture that would enable Moscow to explain to the Soviet people, the Arabs, and the whole world why it has changed its position.

At the same time it must be categorically stated that, as a great power (if probably not a superpower any more) the Soviet Union is not willing to be pushed out of the picture in the Middle East and firmly intends to play a role commensurate with its status in any peaceful settlement in the area. Therefore, Syria remains and will remain an ally since one has to rely on somebody in any given area, even if this somebody does not ideally suit one's idea of a staunch friend and efficient, useful ally.

The Superpower Experience: The United States

The long American relationship with Israel has demonstrated at least two things. First, it has confirmed Israel's unparalleled value as an ally, one more reliable than any other state in the area if only because the Jewish state, unlike any Arab country, is not likely to fall victim to revolutions, coups, and changes of regime. Stability and loyalty being, along with efficiency, the main qualities needed in an ally, America may be quite satisfied to be able to lean on Israel in such an important and at the same time volatile area as the Middle East.

Second, Israel's obstinacy, its intransigent and adamant stand on the Palestinian issue must have been a source of deep irritation, bordering on sheer despair, to many an American official. What has been clearly demonstrated in the course of 43 years is that Israel is a unique and peculiar kind of client (if such a term is appropriate), a very tough customer indeed, stubborn and self-willed, not in the least eager to meekly obey its protector's wishes. More than once the Israeli government succeeded in spoiling the American game in the Middle East, refusing to subordinate what it saw as the Jewish state's national interests to the broader designs of the State Department's policy.

It is widely believed that even acute American displeasure with Israel's policy would not result in the imposition of some kind of economic or military sanctions or in a meaningful reduction of U.S. aid to that nation. Israel has good reason to believe that it is more or less free to act as it wishes as long as it does not create a situation that may result in the United States being drawn into a dangerous confrontation with the Soviet Union or in a sharp increase of anti-American feeling throughout the Arab world.

However, now that the danger of a superpower collision in the Middle East has virtually disappeared, it may be argued that Israel's value to the United States as a strategic ally is steadily declining. Perhaps in the future Israel will not be able to afford to thwart American efforts at proving to the Arabs that they can trust the United States to bring pressure to bear on the Zionist state in order to gain concessions.

In relations with Syria, the Americans have had the opportunity to reassure themselves of that nation's moderate and even relatively sensible position on most relevant issues. Of course there is a limit to Damascus' moderation and reasonableness. One should not forget that "the first goal of a leader is to survive," and that Hafez el-Assad could not survive if he appeared less than totally bent on restoring Syrian authority over the Golan Heights and on ensuring Palestinian rights in the West Bank and Gaza. Still, it may be argued that Assad has proved to be much less of a vicious adventurist than he has been accused of being. In fact, Lebanon aside, and genuine Syrian interests in that country cannot be denied, Hafez el-Assad has not been guilty of taking steps that actually threatened regional stability. It seems that his reputation as an evil genius has been vastly exaggerated and that it is not impossible for the Americans to try and reach some kind of accommodation with this leader.

American experience with Lebanon may be summarized very briefly: a hopeless business. The only possible course of action must be preventive, preventing either Syria or Israel from establishing total and unilateral control over Lebanon because such a development would seriously affect the fragile balance of forces in the area. He who grabs Lebanon instantly gains advantage over the opposing side and so provokes that side to take counter-measures, the likely result being the rapid escalation of the existing conflict.

The Superpower Experience: The Soviet Union

In regard to Syria experience has shown a clear limitation of Syria's possibilities. That country's potential for either good or evil has proved to be less than had been anticipated. As a socialist-oriented country, Syria has been an obvious failure, although not a downright disaster as has been the case with most other countries of this category. In any case, this angle has lost its former importance in the perception of Soviet policy-makers due to the demise of the ideological dimension of Soviet policy. Syria's capacity to influence the course of events in the Middle East is rather limited. If anyone in Moscow believed at one time or another that

Syria could play a major part in a settlement of the Arab-Israeli conflict beneficial for Soviet--as well as Arab--interests, such beliefs by now have been definitely dashed.

Socialist orientation aside, Syria could have been useful to Soviet policy in two ways: first, as a strategic bulwark in a possible confrontation with the United States (naval facilities and all that), and second, as a spearhead of an Arab alliance, armed and inspired by Moscow and aiming at restoring Arab authority over the Israeli-occupied Palestinian territories.

The strategic dimension of Moscow's interest in the Middle East having all but disappeared by now in the light of the new relationship with the West and the improbability of a major power war, what can be said about the second factor? It has always been tempting to contemplate the following scenario. Under pressure from the Arabs, the UN, and the world community, Israel sooner or later gives way and agrees to pull back from the Occupied Territories; post-Camp David Egypt placed on the sidelines and American counter-efforts thwarted, credit for this remarkable and historic achievement goes to Syria, the PLO, and of course--last but not least--to the Soviet Union. An American defeat, a Soviet victory; Moscow's position in the Arab world is stronger than ever, virtually unshakable from now on.

Since the PLO contribution to the realization of this scheme in a practical, not propagandist, sense could only be secondary, Syria would have been the principal architect of victory, but the whole world would have been aware that all this was possible only thanks to Soviet aid, Soviet weaponry, Soviet political and moral support.

Now it is clear that Syria is incapable of playing the part of the spearhead. Even if eventually Israel has to come to some kind of new arrangement involving relinquishing its hold on the Occupied Territories, it is doubtful that credit for this would have been given primarily to Syria and the U.S.S.R., although it is equally clear that without those two countries any Middle East settlement is improbable.

Syria still has a useful role to play as Moscow reappraises its priorities in the Middle East. Obviously, Syria is the only remaining Soviet ally in the area. Great power (if no more superpower) politics necessarily envisage existence of allies or partners in any important region.

With regard to Israel, most Soviet analysts would concede today that the rupture of diplomatic relations in 1967 was a mistake, a meaningless gesture, although quite natural and organic for the Brezhnev regime. Now, as has already been mentioned, Moscow's conditions for restoring relations with Israel have been fundamentally changed. In Soviet eyes Israel is not such a horrible villain any more. With the Soviet confrontationist approach abandoned and the anti-imperialist crusade forgotten, there is no more need for bitter struggle against "the American stooge in the Middle East," especially since Israel has demonstrated that, notwithstanding all its intransigence and obstinacy over the Palestinian issue, it is not eager to start a major regional war that would put the Soviet Union in an embarrassing situation.

Superpower Influence: The United States

Within the framework of the new Soviet-American relationship, with geostrategic factors having ceased to play a crucial role, Israel's value to Washington as a strategic ally ought to dwindle but, on the other hand, the Iraqi aggression against Kuwait may have led American policy planners to some new thinking. By this I mean the following. The Arab world is still far from being stable and, as such, reliable from the American point of view. The dust has not yet settled. Saddam Hussein's brutal action against Kuwait has amply demonstrated both the inability to predict the conduct of Arab leaders and the fragility of Arab alliances. All in all, Israel remains the only reliable partner for a Washington anxious to ensure permanent access to Middle East oil since, in the worst case scenario, Israel's ability and willingness to provide military support for any American action aimed at safeguarding this access is indispensable.

Furthermore, the Arab world has a long way to travel yet before it becomes a truly civil society. Popular Arab reaction to Iraq's aggression has showed the extent of an anti-American "crusading" feeling in the region, and the growth of Muslim fundamentalism, demonstrated in quite an ominous way during the recent Algerian elections, has proven that any American complacency in regard to social and political trends in the Arab world would be premature.

Having said this, one should not rush to the conclusion that the United States can afford to relegate the Arab countries to a secondary position in its hierarchy of Middle Eastern priorities, cultivating exclusively its friendship with Israel. On the contrary, efforts to come to terms with the Arabs have to be redoubled in the interests of regional and global security since it is impossible to bet only on Israel. But any accommodation with the Arabs must naturally include settlement of their conflict with Israel. It is precisely from this conflict that the anti-American sentiment manifested today on the streets of Arab cities has been derived for years and decades.

In order to achieve this goal, a tougher policy vis-à-vis Yitzhak Shamir and the Israeli government seems to be called for, if the deadlock is to be broken at last. One of the lessons of the Gulf Crisis appears to be this: Until and unless America succeeds in guiding Israel to a compromise solution acceptable to mainstream Arab opinion, it cannot be sure of safeguarding its, and the Western community's interests in the Middle East. Only after the main source of nationalist frustration, the Palestinian humiliation, is removed from the Arab mentality, will it become possible to hope for a gradual transition of the Arab world from authoritarian to democratic systems.

Superpower Influence: The Soviet Union

Soviet influence on Syria has been exaggerated in the West. Moscow does not have enough leverage to dictate to Syria, and even if it did, what sort of *diktat* would be realistic to expect in the present economic and political situation of the Soviet Union? What should our aims be? Nobody in Moscow would think of pushing Syria to a more extremist position; as to a moderating influence, Syria has been relatively moderate as it is, without Soviet advice.

Several years ago, when Hafez el-Assad was after Yasser Arafat and tried to dominate the PLO as well as lord over Lebanon, the limits of Soviet influence were quite obvious. The Syrian leader has failed on both fronts--Palestinian and Lebanese--because he physically could not make it, not because he heeded Soviet moderating counsel.

As the question of clients' influence on patrons, I believe that, as regards U.S.-Israeli relations, Washington has been gravely and permanently handicapped in its Arab policy by its inability--or unwillingness--to bring pressure to bear on Israel over the issue of the West Bank and Gaza. Apart from this factor of major importance it is difficult to discern any concrete signs of Israeli influence on the United States.

In the sphere of Soviet-Syrian relations it would be hard to separate specific Syrian influence from that of the Arab world in general, and this has been demonstrated more than once in two ways: Soviet reservations with respect to restoring diplomatic relations with Israel and Moscow's reluctance to side with the West in the Gulf Crisis. However, it can be argued that in both cases Soviet internal political factors have weighed at least as heavily in determining Moscow's stand as foreign policy considerations.

The Implications of the Gulf War

If this chapter had been written before August 1990, it would have been possible to say that the prospects for Soviet-American cooperation in helping to resolve the Arab-Israeli conflict were quite favorable. Events since then have dramatically changed the situation. The impact of the Persian Gulf crisis on the Arab-Israeli dispute has been considerable. One of the most important and negative trends relates to the situation concerning a major party to the conflict, i.e., the PLO.

The fact that Arafat swung his allegiances to the Iraqi side is certain to have grave and lasting implications for the destiny of the PLO, without which it is impossible to arrive at a peaceful settlement of the conflict over Palestine. Arafat's fortunes are likely to decline. While the sympathies of the broad Arab masses may continue to be both with Saddam Hussein and with Arafat, Egypt, Saudi Arabia and the smaller Gulf states will never forgive Arafat and will probably refrain from continuing to provide him with financial aid and political support. Even more important, Arafat and the PLO in general are sure to lose all credibility in the eyes of the Western world, primarily the United States, and any American-Palestinian dialogue will be highly unlikely in the foreseeable future, Israeli and American hawks being certain to strengthen their influence.

As Saddam sinks, Arafat sinks too. A leader backing the wrong horse at a crucial moment can hardly expect to maintain his hold over his following. Arafat's many enemies from within his own ranks may try to use this opportunity to deal him a mortal blow. Even though Arafat, this unrivalled survivor, has managed yet again to avoid terminal disaster, he is paying a great deal for his stand during the crisis, and it is hard to imagine him successfully climbing up from the depth of the well into which he himself chose to descend.

After Saddam's collapse new people will in all likelihood take charge of the PLO, but, since in the eyes of Arab, and particularly Palestinian, public opinion the name of the fallen Iraqi leader will be surrounded by a martyr's halo, it will not be easy for the new team to dissociate itself from Arafat's fatal pro-Iraqi policies of 1990. This will mean that the PLO will in any event find it hard to reassert itself in the world community outraged by the Iraqi dictator. A serious split in the PLO is more than probable. What this all means is a prospect of sharp disequilibrium, a dangerously asymmetrical situation in the Arab-Israeli conflict in which the organized forces opposing the Israeli occupation are seriously weakened and forces of unrestrained desperation, spontaneous revolt, and terrorism are unleashed.

As to the actual Soviet-American cooperation in the area, it is likely to be seriously hindered as a result of the Soviet Union's inevitable dissociation from the American tough and militant stand in the Gulf. This unfortunate situation will not, in my view, jeopardize or undermine the new Soviet-American détente on the global scale, factors and trends determining it being too powerful and deep-rooted. But it may postpone for an indefinite period a Middle Eastern settlement based on the mutual will of the participants themselves to find a compromise solution and on Soviet-American cooperation.

PART FOUR

Policy Implications:
Potential for Soviet-American
Cooperation in the Middle East

15 Bilateral Soviet-American Relations, Including Control of Arms Supplies and Regional Economic Development

Clearly the Iraqi invasion of Kuwait had direct implications for international relations, for relations between the superpowers and for relations between them and their regional allies and clients. This situation bears heavily on prospects for international and regional security. It raises a host of complicated practical questions about the rationale for great power understanding and cooperation in regional conflict management, possible Soviet and American roles in curbing the regional arms race, preventing the proliferation of mass destruction weapons and the means of their delivery, etc.

Though one could only wish the recent tragic situation had never arisen, it presents a perfect illustration of the complexities of U.S.-Soviet involvement in the Middle East, the danger of arms proliferation in the region, and the necessity of superpower cooperation in conflict management. I therefore use the Gulf War as the main case study for presenting my views thereon.

Big Power Responsibilities for Regional Instability

It must be stated quite bluntly that whether they want to admit it or not, the U.S.S.R. and the United States bear heavy responsibility for much of what has transpired in the Middle East, in the negative sense, during most of the post-war period. They played out their rivalries in the region, with very little regard for the interests of local peoples and societies; they used the region as a trial ground for their own models of socio-political organization, in the process disrupting indigenous ways of life and existence, traditions and human values, and destroying traditional forms of social organization without providing viable alternative forms that would be consonant with local requirements and capabilities; they exploited existing regional contradictions in order to promote their own vested interests and policies, again much to the detriment of the interest and policies of indigenous populations; they exacerbated local conflicts, imbuing them with additional bitterness; they provided participants therein with material means (financial, military, etc.) to wage modern warfare, leading to the destruction of innumerable human lives and property accumulated by many generations; and they facilitated the militarization of local societies, including the wide dissemination of militant philosophies and the advent to power of regimes based on military force rather than democratic self-rule.

Eventually each side may admit that these were indeed the effects of their regional policies; yet, at present, they attribute responsibility for these disastrous consequences to the opposite side and shun any responsibility of their own. Yet if the bitter superpower rivalry may to a large extent be in the past, then the sense of responsibility for the present state of affairs has so far failed to imbue American and Soviet policies.

Saddam Hussein's regime epitomizes many of the adverse consequences of the great power presence in the region. During the Iran-Iraq war it was aided and abetted by both superpowers, directly and indirectly, in building an impressive military machine, clearly beyond any reasonable national security requirements. Apparently such a machine, once created, begins to live--or run--on its own, and it needs more than additional inputs of military hardware to remain functional. It also must find an enemy target to be directed against and overrun to prove its virility and justify its existence. Iraq may have pursued certain political and economic ends in lashing out against its militarily weak, but financially prosperous neighbor. However, it was equally important for Baghdad to demonstrate its strategic superiority to anyone around and to expand for the sake of expansion.

And yet, Iraq is not an exception. Other regional powers with the willpower for expansion have acquired similar potentials, mostly through the "good offices" of the U.S.S.R. and the United States, not to exclude France, Great Britain, China, as well as Brazil, Argentina, etc., all of whom for various reasons supplied arms, military technology, and know-how to countries of the region.

Deficiency in Security Arrangements

The intense nature of local conflicts may be explained not only by an unruly arms race, outside intervention and internal instability, but also by lacunae and voids in multilateral security arrangements (as opposed to bilateral ones that, on the contrary, proliferated).

A comparison between the Middle East and Europe is quite in order in this connection. Europe's division into two opposing military blocs may have been counterproductive in more ways than one: in particular it exerted tremendous pressure on European societies on both sides of the dividing line in terms of military allocations and the loss in revenue for the civilian sector. However, this division was also a "blessing in disguise," as it effectively led to the emergence of an extremely well-cemented bipolar power structure that reduced uncertainty and prevented any secondary disruptions, such as local conflicts, from occurring in Europe throughout the post-war period. In contrast, the virtual absence of such mutually exclusive, albeit hostile, structures in the Middle East paved the way for the emergence and reemergence of numerous conflicts--some of them of overbearing magnitude--that would erupt in any part of the region.

Indeed, one may claim that one of the reasons Turkey avoided all the trouble that constantly occurred south and east of its borders was its membership in NATO. By the same token one may ponder what would have happened had the Baghdad Pact survived in the Middle East, and, even more, if it had been complemented by an opposing pro-Soviet alliance. Both alliances could have disciplined their members in different ways, much like the model of Europe.

Does this mean that a European type NATO-Warsaw Pact rivalry-in-power should be introduced into the Middle East? Hardly so, if only because such a structure in Europe is already on its way to extinction and there seems to be no authentically viable indigenous *raison d'etre* for its emergence in the Middle East. However, the historical absence of such alliances in the Middle East may be lamented. Its absence again may be "blamed" on the superpowers, who could have tried it, but did not, notwithstanding its advantages for preserving regional stability, even if at a fairly high cost. In the conclusion of this chapter we will propose an alternative mutual security arrangement, one that may take care of some of the existing regional tensions and even eliminate the foundation for chaotic regional policies. Unavoidably the U.S.S.R. and the United States will have to play leading roles in its introduction.

Yet at this stage we would venture to observe that a system of mutual superpower guarantees to consenting states of the region (especially small and virtually defenseless ones--such as Kuwait) will have to be devised to become one of the centerpieces of this security arrangement.

Commonality and Mutuality in Big Power Activities

Similar ways of thinking--and acting--characterized the superpowers during the decades of playing out their rivalries in the Middle East. It was expressed in the "zero sum" equation of their regional policies: fighting over clients; subdividing them into "ours" and "theirs"; considering any gain for one side as a loss for the other, etc.

Could this element of traditional, albeit contentious, interdependence be transformed and used for constructive, rather than destructive purposes?

The realization of the importance of coordination, parallelism, and mutuality of actions in the region, chiefly in conflict avoidance, prevention, management and resolution, comes through experiences gained by the superpowers in other contexts of their relationship, primarily in bilateral attempts at strategic and conventional disarmament and multilateral efforts at restructuring European policies.

Dangerous regional realities push in the same direction. Already in the Afghan and Iran-Iraq wars, at their late stages, there emerged signs of such an understanding between the superpowers. Attempts at the practical implementation of such understanding include the Geneva agreements on an Afghan settlement, including the withdrawal of Soviet forces, which were made possible only through a modicum of Soviet-American cooperation. The same goes for UN Security Council Resolution 598, the termination of Iran-Iraq hostilities, and actions in providing for freedom of navigation in the Gulf.

A real breakthrough in the direction of cooperation took the form of the joint Soviet-American declaration of August 3, 1990, condemning the Iraqi aggression against Kuwait. Although it remains to be seen what will be realized in practice, the joint statement may already be assessed as marking a qualitatively new stage in regional cooperation, thinking, and acting in the wake of concurring interests in the face of common dangers. What a difference from the similar, but ill-fated attempt of October 1977! Clearly the superpowers, and the world, have come a long way in assessing such dangers and finding the willpower to address them jointly.

Unavoidable Steps to be Taken

There is a Russian saying that "even an unloaded gun shoots by itself once a year." Massive arms accumulated in the Middle East present the acute danger of undermining regional and world peace as the result of "just being there." In conditions of thorough regional instability, the easy availability of arms is a source of danger in itself. In addition, the qualitative improvements in the Middle Eastern arms race may lead to a situation in which many regimes and even groups fighting for power acquire lethal weapons having capabilities of mass destruction: primarily chemical agents and substances but also, in the case of some regimes, nuclear weapons.

The general tendency in the region is toward increased sophistication and the proliferation of both conventional and unconventional arms and the means of their delivery. As far as the delivery means are concerned, their improvement and proliferation pose additional difficulties for powers outside the region since their territories become reachable by those who possess them.

The two main sources for the local militarization and arms race are easily identifiable: outside transfers and indigenous production. In most cases both sources are at work in providing particular regimes with more and better arms. As is known and documented, Iraq in particular tried to acquire or acquired its conventional, chemical, missile and nuclear capabilities from without. This was done through cooperation with outside powers, illegal operations in foreign countries, purchases in international markets and domestic production activities. When coupled with military-political doctrines that prescribe virtually unlimited use of any weapons at the regime's disposal, the situation really is potentially disastrous.

It must be admitted that a great deal of time has already been lost for curbing the Middle Eastern arms race and preventing what are potentially the most expansionist and destabilizing regimes from acquiring capabilities to withstand outside pressures. However, this does not mean that strategies and steps appropriate to changing the situation, at least in the long run, should not be envisioned and introduced to the region. All parties could clearly be working for the following goals: 1) an announcement by the great powers, and others, placing an immediate ban on the further supply of arms to Iraq; 2) the freezing of Iraqi assets outside the country that could be used for starting a resupply of arms; and 3) national and international arrangements to check any attempts at this resupply.

Further practical steps, in particular on the side of those who have cooperative agreements with Iraq, including the U.S.S.R., France, Brazil, and various Arab states, could include the withdrawal of military and civilian personnel involved in projects of cooperation; the cessation of political, trade and economic agreements with the regime; and an economic embargo against Iraq.

However the problem is not Iraq alone. Other "unloaded guns" may start shooting in the Middle East on the slightest provocation, or even without it. Hence it is imperative to start the immediate elaboration and implementation of comprehensive programs of arms limitation, nonproliferation and disarmament in the Middle East, using, as the most obvious rationale, the consequences of the militarization of Iraq. An additional and convincing argument in favor of these programs could be the growing threat of the unauthorized use of various weapons, including those of mass destruction, by terrorists and other violence-prone groups, inside and outside the region.

The following program might serve as an outline for normalizing and limiting arms transfers, the proliferation of non-conventional weapons, and the local production of weapons in the Middle East:

1. the adoption of the principle of reasonable sufficiency by local parties and their patrons, already widely accepted in the European context, as a guiding force in establishing permissible levels of arms transfers to specific countries of the region;

2. the abandonment of the "dual standard" approach whereby major suppliers of arms (the U.S.S.R. and the United States) involve themselves in bilateral arms reduction and disarmament efforts, but proceed to pump arms into Third World regions, primarily the Middle East;

3. the strengthening of international controls over the peaceful uses of atomic energy;

4. the introduction of similar international controls for the production and use of chemical and biological agents and substances;

5. the expansion of arrangements against nuclear proliferation, including the NPT (Non-Proliferation Treaty), should be emphasized and increased in effectiveness;

6. the strengthening of the role of the IAEA (International Atomic Energy Agency) and elaboration of similar organizational arrangements on chemical, biological and other technologies of mass destruction;

7. the conclusion of agreements among suppliers of arms, concerning limitations, both qualitative and quantitative, on the types of arms, materials, technologies, etc. they may export;

8. the elaboration of appropriate agreements on similar issues and between suppliers and buyers of arms;

9. the introduction of international monitoring and control mechanisms on the transfer of specific categories of arms and production activities in various regions and/or countries, preferably within the system of existing international and regional organizations, but also on an independent basis.

Bilateral as well as multilateral efforts leading to the goal of arms limitation play a complementary role. Clearly the U.S.S.R. and the United States. must play a leadership role in these efforts, as envisioned by the UN Charter and as befits their status as the most powerful military powers. This has become particularly relevant since they have finally started on the road of practical disarmament and elimination of dangers of mutual self-destruction, debilitating confrontation and futile competition over issues unrelated to their true national interests.

Methods of Implementation:
Concordance, Persuasion, Pressure, Use of Force

Various situations demand a specific choice of ways and means to help limit threatening forces and increase elements of stability. Under any circumstances it is eminently preferable that agreements on reducing and eliminating various dangers, including those involved in arms proliferation, should come through mutual understanding, coincidence of views, and conscious efforts at improving the situation. We have had several salient examples of these forces at work, as in the bilateral and multilateral negotiations leading to treaties on the non-proliferation of nuclear and chemical weapons, limiting nuclear testing, as well as strategic, medium and shorter range nuclear weapons, etc.

However, more often than not, consensus, as a force leading to the achievement of positive results, is nonexistent or even unattainable. Persuasion and pressure may then be tried in various combinations, especially in situations where there are dependency relations among the parties involved.

It is common knowledge that the U.S.S.R. and the United States used arms transfers in order to attain levers of influence and control over their clients. Though this mechanism did not always work to perfection, it was fairly effective compared even to the instrument of foreign economic aid. Yet, if we have now arrived at a situation in which the superpowers are prepared to work together in eliminating the danger of war, then it is logical that their influence should be put to productive use in regional situations. In practice this means that each superpower should undertake to convince its partners, allies and clients, and, if need be, use pressure tactics against them, in order to alter their policies and positions in such a way as to make an appropriate agreement possible.

Before long this will be called "big power condominium," and almost everyone, especially those who may become targets of these tactics, will complain loudly and even try to counteract them. Indeed, it is not impossible that certain Soviet and American clients that are otherwise at odds will join forces in order to oppose the perceived Soviet-American condominium. Yet, while passions may rise, the question remains: what is the lesser of two evils, especially if a particular trend, as in nuclear and chemical proliferation, for example, may lead to everyone's demise?

Another stage in "escalating" superpower efforts at obtaining concessions, especially in military matters, is the threat and use of force. Clearly this is the worst of options but, as a final resort, it may not be dismissed.

It appears that the world is rapidly moving to a situation in which civilization may be confronted with a threat to its well-being, and even survival, coming from a particular source. Imagine a regime bent on violence, aggression, and expansion that, knowing no limits to its ambitions, will be prepared to start a nuclear war that may destroy millions. Do we not already see a specter of such a totally unacceptable possibility in the behavior of Saddam Hussein's regime? May there be any room for complacency under such circumstances?

Unpalatable as it may be in a political, moral, and human way, the use of counterforce should be considered in case the entire fabric of orderly international life is threatened with rupture. It seems that Hitler, Pol Pot and now Saddam Hussein have sent strong enough signals to the entire human race to start at least contingency planning for a situation that borders on genocide, holocaust, even apocalypse.

At least two major elements should characterize any use of military power in such situations when only superior force can counter evil: a broad international consensus in favor of such action and, even more important, the participation of both superpowers in any forceful actions and operations.

The experience of the unilateral use of force, especially in a preemptive way to counter threats to national and sometimes international security, demonstrates that even if the desired aim is achieved there is little, if any, improvement in the overall regional or international situation. A well known example is represented by the Israeli action against the Iraqi nuclear facility near Baghdad. Even if from the vantage point of our contemporary understanding of the Iraqi regime it may be assumed that this action prevented a fairly dangerous development in the region in the short term, it is evident that in the long run it did not prevent Iraq from sliding down the road of aggressive behavior, expansion and militarization. As a matter of fact, it might have produced an opposite effect that cumulatively led to contemporary problems.

International peace keeping operations, predominantly dating back to the Cold War and the period of divisiveness in superpower positions, may be used as a better model--however, one that needs considerable refinement. The UN Charter may provide the legal basis and authority for expanded operation of peace keeping with participation of the U.S.S.R., the United States and other great powers, however, again some of its provisions will have to be amended or even changed. The sooner international consultations on these matters begin the better. As such they may sound a warning call for those who might choose to play the role of international outlaws.

Internal Change in the U.S.S.R.
and Prospects for Soviet Involvement
in Regional Situations

The deep transformation of Soviet society is far from being completed. Liberalization of public life, in particular as expressed in the policy of *glasnost*, helped reveal the magnitude and intensity of problems confronting the country internally and externally.

Soviet foreign policy, especially towards developing countries, is not immune from criticism. Debates over the Soviet role in the Afghan war, as well as Soviet economic and military assistance to various Third World regions and client-states, are becoming more and more involved. They touch upon basic questions related to the process of policymaking: establishing responsibility for practical foreign policy decisions, ascertaining the "cost-effectiveness" of relations maintained with various allies and partners, etc.

It is impossible to predict the outcome of change in the U.S.S.R., and also of the debates of foreign policy issues. However, some of the new variables are already taking shape and should be considered in trying to evaluate the future Soviet role in managing regional situations. These variables include the de-ideologization of Soviet politics which is gradually depriving formerly predominant power structures, such as the CPSU (Communist Party of the Soviet Union) Central Committee, of their role in foreign policymaking; new and influential structures, more consistent with ideas of openness and democratic process, such as Commissions on Foreign Policy and National Security in the Soviet and Republican Supreme Soviets, which have emerged; the different republics' growing demand for a greater role in reviewing and making foreign policy decisions that affect their interests, a notable example being the Russian Federation's decision to stop transferring locally-produced arms to Afghanistan; and the role of public opinion, as expressed by various "informal organizations" and many mass media sources, which is growing in importance in demanding accountability in foreign policy matters and in actually shaping this policy.

Will these processes, coupled with a deteriorating economic situation that limits resources available for the projection of Soviet power abroad, lead to Soviet self-isolation in foreign policy? The answer is again uncertain; but Soviet obligations abroad will be shrinking further under the influence of both subjective and objective factors, including new Soviet perceptions of itself and the outside world as well as a lack of moral resolve and physical capability to involve itself, especially in situations that are clearly unrelated to important Soviet interests.

Various factors may accelerate or slow down this process. The military industrial complex, for example, loathes any decrease in expenditures of foreign military aid and is constantly speaking in favor of maintaining their high level, using traditional arguments to the effect that "the U.S.S.R. cannot abandon it reliable allies abroad" or that "selling arms earns the country the hard currency without which it will become totally bankrupt."

However, these arguments become fairly unconvincing when data about the debts of Soviet clients receiving Soviet arms becomes known. The Soviet consumer is appalled to learn that India or Syria, which sell some basic consumer goods in the Soviet market at high prices, owe the U.S.S.R. huge sums of money for arms. The rhetoric of some Soviet allies, such as Cuba and certain Arab states, directed against Soviet internal and external policies, also works against supporters of an activist Soviet foreign policy, especially oriented towards these very clients.

The mood of public opinion in favor of self-restraint in Soviet foreign policy may change, however, if any real or perceived outside threats to the U.S.S.R. emerge. One such threat may come from the Middle East in the form of Muslim fundamentalism or regional proliferation of weapons of mass destruction and missiles.

An issue that grows in importance in debates over Soviet foreign policy is that of "morality." On several occasions it was discussed in the Supreme Soviet, at least once in connection with Soviet arms transfers to Iran. it seems that Soviet eagerness in supporting the cause of Kuwait in its conflict with Iraq also depends in large measure on the sense of fairness and righteousness in foreign policy.

Future Soviet involvement, in particular Third World situations, will depend to a growing extent on the position of the United States and other Western countries. If during the Cold War the U.S.S.R. more often than not acted in opposition to what the West was doing, calling this "the line of principle," then supporting Western initiatives now may give greater credence to changed Soviet intentions internationally and help bring the U.S.S.R. closer to the rest of the "civilized world." There is evidently considerable potential for the Soviet Union to participate with the United States in activities aimed at preservation of world peace, and international as well as regional security. The joint Soviet-American declaration of August 3, 1990, was a clear demonstration to this effect, as was the general Soviet support for Western attempts to deprive Iraq of the fruits of its aggression against Kuwait.

Nevertheless, certain Soviet and American clients still preserve a capability to "throw a bone of contention" into superpower relations. This is particularly the case in the Arab-Israeli conflict. Evidently more time devoted to building mutual Soviet-American confidence has to pass before they can withstand the contradictory influences of clients that have mastered "the art" of manipulating their patrons and using divisions between them to their own advantage.

Regional Economic Development and Cooperation

Attempts to influence the internal economic and political development of regional clients was part and parcel of superpower policies in the Middle East, as elsewhere in the Third World, during the Cold War. Regardless of whether they were called "capitalist modernization" or "the socialist way of development" these policies were fairly imperialistic in nature. They largely ignored local traditions and peculiarities, as well as the needs and requirements of indigenous populations. Both superpowers failed in pursuing these policies, sometimes miserably (the U.S.S.R. in Afghanistan, as in Egypt before it; the United States most notably in Iran). And while lessons were learned on both sides, a recurrence of attempts at influencing the course of regional socio-economic development may not be excluded.

One of the best recommendations to both the U.S.S.R. and the United States could be to let local traditions, mode of production, and types of social organization have their natural way, in the background of their involvement in the international division of labor. Most countries of the region hardly need any substantial outside help for their development. However they are all interested to a larger or smaller extent in cooperation with close and not so close neighbors.

In the area of aid, the U.S.S.R. is unable to play the role of a major contributor to solving economic problems of the lesser developed Middle Eastern countries. Soviet economic difficulties that, according to some estimates, are leading the country towards the abyss disqualify the U.S.S.R. for this role. Certain adjustments in this respect could, however, be brought about by reductions in Soviet military aid to traditional Soviet clients in the Middle East. Moreover, the Soviet role may not be insignificant if the U.S.S.R. chooses to channel whatever it can spare through international relief and aid organizations. A worthwhile example could be set by arranging for a cooperative relief effort, similar to the Marshall Plan, in favor of war-ravaged Afghanistan. Apparently the U.S.S.R. would by an eager participant, not only because it admits its responsibility for the destruction of the Afghan economy but also because, due to internal political reasons, it would be more palatable to direct Soviet aid to that country through international channels, hoping also that this would precipitate an overall settlement in that country.

If there is a further shift by the United States in accepting the U.S.S.R. as a *bona fide* partner in economic cooperation in the Middle East, rather than perceiving it as a military-political "trouble maker," then there can be mutual benefits both for the Soviet Union and for those regional countries who might choose to participate in this cooperation. Some regional countries, in particular the unfortunate Kuwait, have recently started evaluating the risks and advantages of doing business with the U.S.S.R. A $300 million loan extended by Kuwait to the Soviet Union in early 1990 could have brought a promising new beginning in dealings between the two countries, had it not been brutally disrupted by the Iraqi aggression against Kuwait.

Undoubtedly any economic and trading ties are conducive to better political understanding. Both the U.S.S.R. and Israel learned this, in a small way, since some kind of rapprochement began between the two in the last few years. Trade and economic exchange could play their role in similar circumstances where there is a need to open up a political relationship. Hopefully in the future there will also be an opportunity for the U.S.S.R. to enter into relations with regional economic groupings, especially centering on combustible raw materials.

Toward a System of Regional Security

Let us return once again to the predicament of Kuwait and of some other states in the region that may be drawn into situations beyond their control. Mindful of the dangers of the regional arms race, proliferation of mass destruction weapons, etc., a case may be made for a speedy elaboration of a reliable system of regional security that would address these and other complicated political, military and even economic problems of the Middle East. The process leading to the emergence of such a system could be based on the successful example of the Conference on Security and Cooperation in Europe as well as negotiations on various military-political issues that arise in the European context.

A central role in establishing the system of mutual security obligations between the states of the region could be played by great power guarantees to all those who might want them and would be able to accept them. In general terms the U.S.S.R. and the United States should play a leadership role in promoting regional security and initiating appropriate security arrangements. As was mentioned before, since the problem of Soviet-American "condominium" may be raised at any stage, both superpowers should strive to portray their cooperation as beneficial, and not detrimental, to the interests of Middle Eastern states.

It happens that the superpowers may have an improved chance to set such a positive example in the zone of the Arab-Israeli conflict. Both Israelis and Palestinians seem to be thoroughly tired of the stalemate in the conflict between them; yet expectations that by themselves they would be able to break the remaining ground before entering into direct negotiations, with everyone else waiting idly for that to happen, have not materialized. Could the U.S.S.R. and the United States try to accelerate the process by, for example, launching a joint peacemaking initiative? Such an initiative could take the shape of still another joint declaration (1) inviting involved parties to come to the negotiating table; (2) specifying the venue of negotiations; and even (3) setting the broad guidelines for them. One of the procedural approaches could be to resume the process of the Geneva Conference on the Middle East, where the U.S.S.R. and the United States play the roles of co-chairs. Could this start something that for years was identified as the international conference on Middle Eastern settlement?

Regardless of what turn the events will take, it is obvious that the two superpowers should increase the level and expand, maybe even make permanent, their bilateral consultations on problems of the region. These consultations should be concerned not only with local conflicts, if and when they flare up, but also with the entire range of economic, political, military, and social affairs of the Middle East. Evidently they should draw heavily on academic expertise available in both countries and in the countries of the region.

16 Arms Races and Arms Control in the Middle East

This chapter discusses arms races and the prospects for arms control in the Middle East. In particular, it treats the Middle East situation before the Gulf crisis that erupted on August 2, 1990, with the Iraqi invasion of Kuwait. While that crisis, the ensuing war, and its aftermath have made significant changes in the region, the broader and underlying issues presented here are still relevant, as seen, for example, by the resumption of arms buildups in and arms transfers to the region following the war.

Our approach is to identify the major and minor actors of the region (Section 1); to review their past arms interactions (Section 2); to consider past examples of arms control in the region (Section 3); to determine the most important arms race/arms control relationships among the major actors of the region (Section 4); to note the inappropriateness of applying Soviet-U.S. arms race and arms control concepts to the Middle East (Section 5); to introduce alternative future scenarios for arms races and arms control in the region (Section 6); and, based on these scenarios, to analyze the prospects for arms control in the region.

Our main conclusions are the following: (1) There is evidence for both arms races and arms control in the region; (2) the application of Soviet-U.S. arms race and arms control concepts to the region is inappropriate and even dangerous; (3) a more appropriate way of

We would like to acknowledge the extremely perceptive observations and useful suggestions of Shlomo Aronson, Simin Amini-Sereshki, Bennett Ramberg, and Etel Solingen and the research assistance of Daniel Lefler, an intern at the UCLA Center for International and Strategic Affairs. We also received helpful suggestions from W. Seth Carus, Steven Rosen, and Steven L. Spiegel.

analyzing arms races and arms control in the region is with a multilateral and multidimensional approach which may, in fact, be more and more relevant in the global context as well; (4) there are possibilities for further arms control initiatives of various types-- unilateral, bilateral, and multilateral--in the region that could represent useful steps toward an overall arms equilibrium, but, for the foreseeable future, such an equilibrium will continue to be at relatively high levels of armaments; and (5) probably the most reasonable and desirable future arms control scenario would include Israeli determination of a specific plan for the future of the West Bank and Gaza Strip, and U.S. economic assistance and political involvement to foster greater economic cooperation and political dynamism in the region.

Major and Minor Actors in the Middle East Region

By the *Middle East* we shall mean the region involving the interactions of 14 actors, which we divide into nine major actors and five minor actors.

The nine major actors are the major confrontation states of *Israel, Egypt, Syria, Iraq, Jordan*, and *Saudi Arabia*; the *Palestinians* which, while not having their own state, nevertheless play a major role in the region; and the global powers of the *United States* and the *Soviet Union*, which, while not in the region, have significant influences in the Middle East. These actors are the principal ones determining the future of the Middle East region.

The five minor actors, being relatively less important, are excluded from consideration for now, recognizing that they may have played major roles in the past and/or that they could play major roles in the future. These include another state in the region, *Lebanon*; states in the broader region, namely *Iran* and *Libya*; and the major power states of the *United Kingdom* and *France*. We exclude Lebanon in view of its virtual collapse as a meaningful nation as well as a meaningful actor on the international scene. We also exclude Iran and Libya because of their preoccupation with other matters, and their distance, although we recognize that Libya does play a role in terms of providing financing for arms acquisitions by Arab states in the region and Iran has played an important indirect role in the past and could play such a role in the future. Finally, we exclude the United Kingdom and France due to their relatively less significant role in the region than that of the global powers, recognizing that both have played major roles in the region in the past. Thus, while in times past or in the future another definition of the region might be required, for the present and near future, the Middle East will be treated here as the region defined by the interaction of the nine major actors.

Arms Races in the Middle East

An *arms race* consists of the interactive and dynamic process of weapons acquisition among two or more states.[1] Such arms acquisitions are typically based on perceived security interests, particularly in terms of retaining a balance or equilibrium with rival powers. As each state seeks such a balance, the result is an interactive and dynamic arms race. There are, however, other reasons for arms acquisitions, including the role of the army, prestige, and the desire for regional hegemony.

In the Middle East region there are, in fact, multiple and multi-faceted arms races. There is an arms race between Israel and the Arab confrontation states, stemming, in part, from underlying enmity, but further stimulated by each side seeing its security interests threatened by arms acquisitions on the other side. As each side attempts to correct the perceived imbalance, the result is the acquiring of yet additional weapons, with arms acquisitions by Israel stimulating responses from the Arab states and with the acquisitions of arms by the Arab confrontation states stimulating responses on the part of Israel.[2] The wars that have been fought in the region and the long state of conflict in the region have further aggravated this arms race. In fact, there are recurring cycles of military buildup, followed by the outbreak of war, particularly in the case of Syria and Israel. It should, however, not be concluded that arms races inevitably lead to the outbreak of war in the region.[3] Of the major Arab-Israeli wars that have been fought since 1948, perhaps only the 1956 war was related directly to arms acquisitions, as it was due, in part, to Israeli concern that the growing supply of Soviet weapons to Egypt would disturb the status quo and lead to an eventual Egyptian strike against Israel.[4]

Another arms race in the Middle East is that among the Arab states. These states are concerned about their own security vis-à-vis one another, but they are also competing for power and influence in the region. The desire of Egypt, Syria and Iraq each to be the dominant military power in the region further aggravates the Middle East arms race, as do the major arms acquisitions by Saudi Arabia. There are, in fact, multiple links among the arms races in the Middle East.

A major influence on both arms races is the role of the army in the Arab states of Egypt, Syria, Iraq and Jordan, which are, in effect, praetorian guard states with large standing armies. The role of the armies in these states is decisive, and they form the backbone of these regimes. The armies play a significant political, social, and economic as well as military role in these states. While Israel relies on reserves, its army also plays a significant role, going well beyond military considerations and leading to a type of civilian-military-industrial complex. All of these armies will continue to demand major resources, both human and financial, in their procurement policies, almost regardless of any conceivable circumstance. These resources must be specifically taken into account when considering any future scenario for the region. Ironically, any arms control measures must explicitly allow for resources to be channelled to the armies of each of the confrontation states.

Another major influence on both types of arms races in the Middle East is the presence of significant arms supplies from outside the region, particularly past arms transfers from the global powers of the United States and the Soviet Union (and also other powers, including France, China, and North Korea). To some extent, the global powers have used their arms transfers to compete for influence in the region, and these arms transfers, in part, have driven the arms race in the region. In particular, arms transfers by one global power have in the past tended to stimulate both additional transfers by the other global power and responses from the competing nations in the region. The United States has played a major role in the supply of arms to Israel (a total of $20 billion in military aid by 1988), while the Soviet Union has played a similar role in supplying arms to Syria and Iraq. The global powers have been willing to provide vast quantities of weapons to the region, including certain modern weapons systems, such as high performance aircraft and missiles. From 1980 to 1983 arms transfers to the Middle East represented 59 percent of U.S. transfers and 40 percent of total Soviet transfers, while in subsequent years the percentage reversed in favor of the Soviets. Syria and Iraq have been the two largest Middle Eastern recipients of Soviet arms in recent years. Iraq has continuously received arms from both the West, especially France, and the Soviet Union. Arms supply to the Middle East is, however, by no means limited to the global powers. By 1988, for example, Saudi Arabia purchased long-range Chinese surface-to-surface missiles and signed a $30 billion order with the British for fighter aircraft and other military equipment.

Yet another major influence on arms races in the Middle East is the presence of government economic assistance programs and private remittances to the states in the region. The global powers, in addition to providing arms to the region, also provide economic assistance to states in the region, including budgetary and foreign exchange support. Such economic assistance programs give states in the region resources not only for consumption, investment, etc., but also, directly or indirectly, for arms acquisition and maintenance, given the underlying fungibility of economic resources. As to the United States, Israel and Egypt are, in fact, the two largest recipients of U.S. foreign assistance programs: in fiscal year 1985, for example, the United States provided Israel $3.35 billion in economic and military aid and provided Egypt $2.5 billion, the two largest aid levels from a total aid figure for all countries of $13.7 billion. The Soviet Union has provided substantial economic support to Syria. Other states and private groups also provide economic assistance to the region, some of which is translated, directly or indirectly, into arms acquisitions. In particular, the oil-producing Arab states provide economic assistance to the confrontation states. Private groups also provide economic assistance, such as the contributions of Jews worldwide to Israel and the remittances of Egyptians and Palestinians working abroad, especially in the oil-producing Arab states.

Arms Control in the Middle East

Arms control consists of initiatives undertaken to achieve or to increase strategic stability among the states involved in a potential conflict. With this broad definition, arms control includes any measures that decrease the danger of war.[5] Secondary goals, as in the discussion of arms control in the context of the global powers, would include the limitation of damage in case of war and reduction in the cost of armaments.[6] While arms control can include limitations or reductions in the numbers of weapons, it is not restricted to this approach alone.[7]

Arms control can involve *unilateral, bilateral, or multilateral initiatives*. In fact, all three types of initiatives can be illustrated in the Middle East region, and these illustrations serve to emphasize an important point, namely that arms control, broadly construed as initiatives that reduce the chance of war, *does* apply to this region.[8] In fact, arms control has played an important role in reducing, but not eliminating instabilities in the region.[9]

Unilateral arms control measures have included initiatives undertaken by parties both within and outside the region. Israel has exercised restraint in terms of not overtly introducing nuclear weapons to the region. In fact, its policy of nuclear ambiguity not only shows self-restraint, but also has the effect of limiting nuclear weapons developments by other Middle East states or transfers of nuclear weapons from the nuclear powers through the threat of their overt introduction by Israel. This policy of nuclear ambiguity has, in fact, been a model which has been used in other regional conflict situations, e.g., India-Pakistan, where, as in the Middle East, it induces caution and restraint by both the confrontation states and the nuclear powers. The possibility of Israeli possession of nuclear weapons has some restraining influence on other states, but overt nuclear weapons would entail destabilizing repercussions and nuclear power state reactions. However, Israel's covert nuclear weapons have had the destabilizing effect of encouraging other states in the region to build chemical weapons and expanded conventional capabilities. Israel has also relied on a unilateral preemptive strike in destroying the Osirak reactor near Baghdad in 1981.

Another unilateral action is the refusal of the global powers to supply certain types of weapons systems to states in the region. While the United States and the Soviet Union are major arms suppliers to the region, both have established certain limitations in terms of which weapons they supply, the numbers of such weapons, and how these weapons can be used. In particular, they have refused to supply nuclear weapons to the region. They have also established quantitative limitations on numbers of high-performance aircraft and missiles supplied to the region. These unilateral arms control actions are reinforced by the potential threat of a disruption of weapons supply or an embargo on weapons shipments, which induces caution on the part of the Middle East parties in their use of not only the specific weapons supplied by the global powers but other weapons as well. Such caution adds to stability against the outbreak of war and thus represents a type of arms control initiative exercised unilaterally by each of the global powers for the region.

Bilateral arms control also exists in the region, specifically in the Egyptian-Israeli peace treaty. This treaty ended a state of war, which had significantly added to the arms race and instability in the region. Ending the state of war had the effect of significantly reducing regional political tensions and potential instabilities and thus can be considered an important arms control measure. Even before the Egyptian-Israeli peace treaty, however, there were elements of bilateral arms control in the region, however, in the form of demilitarized zones, buffer zones, limitations on deployments of weapons systems in certain areas, implicit agreements to avoid certain targets, and implicit agreements limiting the nature of war.

Multilateral arms control also exists in the region in the form of the Camp David agreement, involving Israel, Egypt, and the United States. A specific example of a multilateral arms control initiative is the presence of U.S. observers in the Sinai, agreed to by both Egypt and Israel, to provide early warning and protection for both sides. Another aspect of multilateral arms control is the cooperation of the global powers and other nuclear and non-nuclear powers in establishing a nonproliferation regime. By 1990 a total of 140 states had signed the Nuclear Non-Proliferation Treaty (NPT), including Egypt, Iraq, Jordan, and Saudi Arabia, but not Israel. There are also proposals for a Middle East nuclear weapons-free zone. The

United States and the Soviet Union have taken an active interest in ensuring that constraints and incentives exist for states in the region not to develop nuclear weapons. These nonproliferation measures, which can be interpreted as a type of arms control initiative, have, to some extent, been offset by nuclear developments in the region and by nuclear exports to the region but, they, together with the unilateral restraint exercised by Israel, have been largely successful in preventing the overt introduction of nuclear weapons in the Middle East. The Middle East could have been significantly more dangerous and unstable in the presence of overt nuclear weapons.

Interactions Among the Major Players

Having treated some of the major aspects of both arms races and arms control in the Middle East, we consider now the nine major actors of the region, as discussed earlier, namely Israel, Egypt, Syria, Iraq, Jordan, Saudi Arabia, the Palestinians, the United States, and the Soviet Union.   In particular, we consider the bilateral interactions between each pair of these nine major actors. Altogether there are 36 such bilateral interactions, and 26 are ranked in terms of their relative importance, from the standpoint of arms races and arms control, in Table 16.1. (These rankings are subjectively rather than objectively determined, on the basis of our judgments. They could, however, conceivably be estimated on the basis of objective interactions among each pair of states.)

The most important of these arms race/arms control bilateral relationships in terms of the future stability of the region is that of Israel and Egypt, shown as the "1" in Table 16.1. This relationship is considered the most important in terms of the Middle East arms race, for which Israeli weapons acquisitions are based, in part, on Egyptian capabilities and vice-versa, and in terms of Middle East arms control, of which the Egyptian-Israeli peace treaty is one of the most important examples. It therefore is a catalytic dyad that influences many of the other bilateral relationships. The second most important bilateral relationship is the Israel-Syria relationship, particularly in view of the substantial Soviet arms transfers to Syria, the high proportion of Syrian GNP devoted to arms acquisitions (which even exceeds that of Israel), past wars, and the current perception of Syria as Israel's principal potential enemy in view of the peace treaty with Egypt. The third and fourth ranked of the 36 bilateral relationships are the Israel-Palestinian and Israel-Jordan relationships, based on past wars, terrorism, the continuing Palestinian problem, and the question of the future of the West Bank and Gaza Strip. Sixth is the Israel-Iraq relationship, while the Israel-Saudi Arabia relationship is ranked 19th. These six important bilateral relationships are treated as a group as **Israeli-Arab interactions**. All of these bilateral relationships, derived largely from the defense and arms control objectives of Israel, involve a perceived need for military superiority in the region in order to provide some degree of security against a surprise attack. Such superiority would deny any opponent or coalition of opponents the option of resorting to force. In addition, there are other security concerns for Israel: self-sufficiency in arms, given the fear of a possible arms embargo; acquisition of high technology weapons systems, both for security and for certain economic and political goals; a settlement of the Palestinian issue; a reduced burden of military expenditure, given an extremely high ratio of military expenditure to GNP; and certain political objectives, including ones involving Israeli-U.S. and Israeli-Soviet relationships. Israel's concern for self-sufficiency is both political and economic. Politically, Israel is concerned about the possibility of an arms embargo and needs to obtain sophisticated weapons systems for security purposes. Economically, the high ratio of military expenditure to GNP creates enormous problems for the state of Israel, limiting resources needed for investment and consumption.

The next group of bilateral relationships each involve the United States, the Soviet Union, or both, and are therefore treated as **global power interactions** in the Middle East. These include the United States-Israel interaction, ranked 5, involving U.S. arms transfers and economic assistance and its involvement in the peace process; and the U.S.-Egypt interaction, ranked 7, involving economic assistance and the peace process. The U.S.-Soviet relationship is ranked 8, involving both post-global power competition in the Middle East and the application of the global power-supported nonproliferation regime in the region. The U.S.-Iraq interaction is ranked 9, while the Soviet-Syria interaction is ranked 10. Also in the group are the Soviet-Iraqi interaction (14), the Soviet-Israeli interaction (18), the U.S.-Syria interaction (23), and the Soviet-Egyptian interaction (26). As in the case of Israeli interactions, the global power interactions derive, in part, from the objectives of each of the global powers. For the United States, the principal concerns have traditionally been those of maintaining stability in the region; ensuring the survival of Israel; keeping good relations with Egypt, Jordan, and other Arab countries; maintaining Western access to oil; and retaining general influence in the region. The region is, in fact, vital to U.S. interests. The Soviet Union has traditionally been concerned with protecting its client state, Syria, and retaining and expanding its influence, both political and military, in the region.

The third and final set of bilateral relationships are the **Arab-Arab interactions**, involving Jordan-Palestinians, Syria-Iraq and Egypt-Syria, ranked 11, 12, and 13 respectively; Syria-Jordan, Iraq-Jordan, and Iraq-Palestinians, ranked 15, 16, and 17 respectively; Egypt-Iraq, Egypt-Jordan, and Egypt-Palestinians, ranked 20, 21, and 22 respectively; and Syria-Palestinians and Iraq-Saudi Arabia, ranked 24 and 25 respectively. These relationships change over time as coalitions change, involving varying patterns of conflict and cooperation, with implications for arms races and arms control in the Middle East.

These rankings represent an average over the recent period since they can and do change considerably over time and can be highly influential at certain times. As in the case of the two previous sets of bilateral interactions, the Arab-Arab interactions are based on the objectives of the Arab actors. For Egypt, the goal is security, particularly against a surprise attack, but in addition, Egypt is concerned with maintaining a military option; preserving its traditional dominant political and military role in the region; settling its economic problems; and resolving the Palestinian issue. Syria is concerned with its own defense, ensuring that it plays a major or even dominant role in the region, and regaining the Golan Heights. It also has the broader and more ambitious goals of creating a "Greater Syria," assuming control over traditional Palestine, including Jordan, Lebanon, and most of Israel. Iraq, like Syria, is concerned with its own defense and ensuring that it plays a major or even

TABLE 16-1

Rankings of Importance of 26 Bilateral Interactions Relevant to Arms Races and Arms Control in the Middle East

MAJOR ACTORS:	I	E	S	Q	J	A	P	U	R
Israel (I)	1	2	6	4	19	3	5		18
Egypt (E)			13	20	21		22	7	26
Syria (S)				12	15		24	23	10
Iraq (Q)					16	25	17	9	14
Jordan (J)							11		
Saudi Arabia (A)									
Palestinians (P)									
United States (U)									8
Soviet Union (R)									

Israeli-Arab interactions . . . 1,2,3,4,6,19

Global power interactions . . 5,7,8,9,10,14,18,23,26

Arab-Arab interactions 11,12,13,15,16,17,20,21,22,24,25

dominant role in the region. It has, like Syria, ambitious goals of creating a "Greater Iraq." Jordan is concerned with security, both in terms of an external attack and in terms of internal revolution. It is also concerned with the Palestinian issue, particularly the future of the West Bank, but its principal concern is the preservation of its independence and territorial integrity. The Palestinians are concerned with their survival and security, establishing a state of Palestine, resolving their factional differences, and ensuring their economic well-being. Saudi Arabia is concerned with preserving its independence and the traditional form of its government and society.

The remaining rankings are of lesser importance, and they are not shown explicitly in Table 16.1, although, over time, they could become more important. Also, over time, many of the rankings can change.

The Inappropriateness of Applying
Soviet-U.S. Arms Race and Arms Control
Concepts to the Middle East

In analyzing arms races and arms control in the Middle East, it is important to take into account the specifics of the region, including the nine major actors and their various interactions, the important role of the global powers, the lack of (overt) nuclear weapons, the role of the army, and related political and economic considerations. It is inappropriate to consider arms races and arms control in the Middle East in the same category as the Soviet-U.S. arms competition, given these special considerations. The application of Soviet-U.S. concepts relating to defense or arms control in the Middle East can be misleading and even dangerous. In particular, defense and arms control concepts that have been applied to Soviet-U.S. strategic interactions, such as mutual assured destruction, counterforce targeting, strategic defense, détente, and strategic arms reductions are probably not applicable to the region in view of the many actors involved, their proximity, and the types of weapons available.

Given the nature of the region, it is necessary to study it in multilateral terms, rather than in bilateral terms, and to treat explicitly the military, political, and economic interests of all parties, rather than focusing on purely bilateral military issues. In fact, if one were to treat the Middle East situation in strictly bilateral military terms, specifically in terms of Arab and Israeli military balances, one might overlook the fact that two of the potentially most important arms control initiatives for the region are political/economic, not military, and unilateral/multilateral, not bilateral. As to precedent from other regions, the most appropriate one might be conventional arms control in Europe, when the CFE--

when the CFE--Conventional Forces in Europe--agreement and the confidence-building negotiations under CSCE, the Conference on Security and Cooperation in Europe, might be appropriate models for possible multilateral arms control agreements in the Middle East.

Interestingly enough, current Soviet-U.S. strategic interactions may also be more appropriately analyzed in multilateral and multidimensional terms, particularly in view of both future weapons deployments by the British, French, and Chinese and the important interactions among military, political, and economic variables. Thus, rather than using Soviet-U.S. strategic relations as a model for studying arms races and arms control in the Middle East, it may be that precisely the *opposite* is true. That is, the Middle East military, political, and economic interactions may be a prototype of likely future global strategic interactions. A major difference between global and Middle East strategic interactions, however, is precisely the role of the global powers in the region.

Alternative Future Scenarios:
Baseline, Pessimistic and Optimistic

Alternative future scenarios can be envisaged for the Middle East in terms of the possibilities for arms races and arms control. As in quantitative forecasting, it is instructive to bracket a particular forecast with a "low" and a "high" estimate. Here a "baseline" scenario, representing the most likely future, is bracketed by "pessimistic" and "optimistic" scenarios, in terms of arms race/arms control possibilities for the region.

The **baseline scenario** is a continuation of the status quo, but coupled with anticipated political, economic, and military developments. In this scenario, Israeli-Arab interactions would involve a continued "cold peace" with Egypt (i.e. observance of the peace treaty, but continued tensions between the states and little political or economic interchange between them) and a continued "cold war" with Syria and Jordan, coupled with political activity and low-intensity conflict of skirmishes and terrorist acts by the Palestinians. In terms of global power interactions, this scenario would also involve reduced economic assistance to the region but continued arms sales on a bilateral basis. In terms of Arab-Arab interactions, this scenario would likely involve continued shifting alliances and low intensity conflict. The result would be continued arms acquisitions in the region, with no significant arms control initiatives. If some potential arms suppliers are reluctant to deliver weapons for political reasons, then other suppliers will do so for commercial reasons.

High and rising oil prices have, in the past, led directly or indirectly to increased arms acquisitions in the region by the Arab parties, through both governmental support of the oil-producing states and remittances from guest workers, especially Egyptians and Palestinians. Reductions in oil prices and expectations of relatively depressed oil prices over the short-to medium-term however, have not led to the reverse anticipations of major reductions in arms acquisitions. Because of the influential role of the army in the Arab states, these states have been unwilling to make significant cuts in arms acquisitions, particularly given the high levels and major acquisitions of arms by Israel and by some of the other Arab states. Rather, the result of reduced oil revenues would probably lead not to a significant reduction in arms purchases but rather to a reduction in investments, imports, and living standards.[10] Budgetary restrictions or limitations in the United States may require limiting its economic support for Israel and Egypt in the future. Similarly, the Soviet Union has reduced its support for Syria due to its own economic difficulties and falling domestic oil production. Such reduced support of the global powers would have some effect in terms of reduced arms purchases, but, as in the case of falling oil prices, the more significant effects would probably, again, be reduced investments, imports, and living standards.

The **pessimistic scenario** would involve, in terms of Israeli-Arab interactions, a further deterioration of Israeli political relations with Egypt as Egypt seeks to improve its position vis-à-vis other Arab states; skirmishes or even open conflict with the Syrians; the escalation of low-intensity conflict with the Palestinians; further disaffection, revolt, and uprisings in the Occupied Territories; the termination of conflict between Iraq and Syria; and especially a militarily and politically strong axis of Iraq, Syria, Jordan, and the

Palestinians. Another aspect of the pessimistic scenario would be the overt introduction of nuclear weapons by Israel.[11] While covert nuclear weapons may have stabilizing implications, overt nuclear weapons could have significant destabilizing repercussions, including a nuclear arms race in the region and adverse Soviet-U.S. reactions.

In terms of global power interactions, in this pessimistic scenario there would be added transfers of arms to offset reduced economic assistance and fewer restrictions on the numbers or the use of weapons supplied to the region as a result of competition from other suppliers.

As to Arab-Arab interactions, in this pessimistic scenario there would be greater tensions and conflicts due to reduced external support and the repatriation of Egyptian and Palestinian guest workers. A particularly pessimistic scenario would be severe economic pressures in the Arab states leading to significant reductions in living standards. The result could be economic disaster, leading to possible social and political upheaval, conceivably with the advent of revolutionary fundamentalist and apparently irrational regimes in the region. These developments would make the prospects for peace in the region even more remote as, for example, a revolutionary fundamentalist Egypt renounces the peace treaty with Israel and once again seeks the elimination of Israel. The result would be the emergence of long-term conflict in the region, with an accompanying acceleration of the arms race.

The **optimistic scenario** would involve, in terms of Israeli interactions, a significant improvement in its relationships with Jordan and the Palestinians through a decision on its future role in the West Bank and Gaza Strip. A national debate on future options in these occupied zones could lead to a national commitment to a particular plan and a timetable for its implementation. Such a plan could play a major role in settling the issue of the future of the Palestinians. Some sort of resolution of this issue, accepted by all parties to the conflict, could represent one of the most significant arms control initiatives for the region in terms of reducing the chance of war.

In this optimistic scenario, Egypt would take significant steps to foster peace in the region by promoting closer ties with Israel, including greater trade, tourism, cultural and scientific exchange, etc.

It would also assume a greater role in expanding the peace process, particularly by encouraging the involvement of Jordan.

As to global power interactions, in the optimistic scenario the global powers would take some important steps unilaterally or, even better, cooperatively to reduce the chance of war. The most important of these steps would be restraints on certain weapon systems, particularly offensive systems, such as first-strike weapons, that could undermine any arms equilibrium in the region.[12] At the same time, the global powers would ensure the continued supply of defensive systems, such as warning systems. Furthermore, the United States would, in this optimistic scenario, play an active political and economic role to promote arms control. It would promote improved Egyptian-Israeli and Jordanian-Israeli relations via political dynamism in the region, leading, for example, to Jordanian participation in the peace process. The result could be an Israel-Jordan peace treaty, based on some variant of the "peace for land" formula in the Egypt-Israeli peace treaty. Meanwhile, continuing this optimistic scenario, the Soviet Union could play a similar role in fostering a Syrian-Israeli peace treaty with provisions such as the establishment of jointly manned Syrian-Israeli-Soviet observation stations in the Golan Heights to provide early warning and protection to both sides in this sensitive area and also restrictions on deployments of potentially offensive weapons systems.

As to Arab-Arab interactions, in this optimistic scenario there would be greater economic and political cooperation among the Arab states due, in part, to the positive steps taken by Israel and the global powers.

Prospects for Arms Control

The discussion of future possible scenarios--baseline, pessimistic, and optimistic--suggests that there are some significant possibilities for arms control in the region that could build on past efforts. (Here a broad interpretation is given to "arms control," not just arms reductions.) Such arms control initiatives could help stabilize the region by reducing the chance of war. Nevertheless, for the foreseeable future, the region will probably continue to have a relatively high level of armaments.

Certain arms control initiatives could play a significant role in promoting stability in the region. For Israel the most important arms control initiative would be that of determining a reasonable future for the West Bank and Gaza Strip. It is important that Israel recognize the potential problems of continued occupation of these territories, the attitudes of the people of these territories, the interest and involvement of the other states and of the Palestinians, and the security concerns of all interested parties. This initiative would be an important and perhaps essential step toward other arms control initiatives, such as an expanded peace agreement to include Jordan.

For the United States, the most important arms control initiative would be economic and political activities to foster economic cooperation and political dynamism in the Middle East. Only the United States (ideally, with help from Europe and Japan) can provide the financing, administrative expertise, and the capability of working as a friendly third party with both Israel and the Arab states of the region. Economic cooperation in the form of expanded trade and investment, joint major capital projects, and labor and capital mobility could play a significant role in terms of facilitating arms control in the region. Unilateral U.S. initiatives, building upon its interactions with several states in the region, could foster regional economic cooperation, which, in turn, could promote political as well as economic cooperation. They could lead to results in both bilateral arms control agreements in terms of Israeli-Arab interactions and multilateral arms control agreements in terms of Arab-Arab interactions, leading to reduced arms transfers to the region. The region, particularly the Arab states, suffers from chronic economic problems, including the lack of skilled manpower, an obsolete and aging capital stock, poor economic planning, overpopulation (in Egypt), and a limited national market (in Jordan). These traditional economic problems are being compounded by newer problems, e.g., those stemming from reduced oil prices, including reduced government funding from oil-producing states, reduced remittances from Egyptian and Palestinian workers in such states, and repatriation of these workers. The resulting economic pressures, when combined with demands of the military for continued support, could lead to severe reductions in living standards with possibly disastrous political consequences, particularly in Egypt, which already faces severe economic pressures. Economic cooperation in the region, fostered by the United States as part of its economic support and political involvement in the region, could avoid this disastrous future and thus play a significant role in terms of arms control. U.S. action in writing off its $7 billion loan to Egypt is an important step in that direction.

Various people have, for some time, referred to a possible U.S. Marshall Plan for the Middle East. While this is primarily a slogan, and there are dramatic differences between post-war Europe and the Middle East today, it would, in fact, be extremely useful to have an integrated plan and overall concept for economic assistance and cooperation in the region. Other nations, particularly those of Western Europe, and international organizations, particularly the IMF and the World Bank, could also play an important role in fostering economic cooperation in the region, provided the fundamental socio-economic-political conflicts in the region could be overcome. Economic cooperation resulting in economic growth could prevent the advent of revolutionary fundamentalist regimes, could provide the resources needed to keep the armies intact, and could improve the political climate. Such economic cooperation could be an important step in a process of political, military, and social change in the region which would result in greater stability. Economic cooperation, particularly when combined with political dynamism, could, in fact, be one of the most important instruments of arms control in the region.

Both forms of arms control, the political determination by Israel of a future for the West Bank and Gaza Strip, and U.S. activities to promote economic cooperation and political dynamism in the region, involve political and economic rather than military initiatives. Each would be initiated by the unilateral actions of one of the major actors in the region, and each could lead to positive bilateral and multilateral arms control responses. Furthermore, they are mutually reinforcing, with a resolution of the status of the West Bank and Gaza Strip helping to promote economic cooperation and political dynamism in the region and vice-versa. These two initiatives,

TABLE 16-2
Past and Possible Future Arms Control Initiatives
in the Middle East
(future initiatives are in **bold**)

MILITARY/POLITICAL

UNILATERAL — No introduction of overt nuclear weapons by Israel; Refusal by the global powers to supply certain types or numbers of weapons. **Israeli determination of a future for the West Bank and Gaza Strip.**

BILATERAL — Egypt-Israel peace treaty; **Israel-Jordan peace treaty. Egypt-Israel, Israel-Jordan, and Israel-Syrian improved political relations.**

MULTILATERAL — Soviet-U.S. cooperation to prevent nuclear proliferation in the region: **Egypt-Israel-Jordan peace treaty.** Camp David agreement of Egypt, Israel, United States; **Expanded peace agreement to include Jordan. Soviet and U.S. cooperative political and diplomatic activism in the region.**

ECONOMIC

UNILATERAL — **United States actions to promote economic cooperation.**

BILATERAL — **Bilateral economic cooperation.**

MULTILATERAL — **Multilateral economic cooperation, involving states of the region and the global powers.**

particularly when taken together, represent the most reasonable and desirable prospects for arms control in the region. Even with either or both of these initiatives, however, the likelihood is that there will continue to be a relatively high level of armaments in the region for the foreseeable future, given the present level of arms, military production and transfers, the lack of an overall political solution, and the significant role of the armies in all states in the region. Nevertheless, arms control, particularly multilateral approaches, involving several parties, and multidimensional approaches, involving political and economic as well as military initiatives, could play an important role in stabilizing the region and avoiding some extremely undesirable alternatives for the Middle East.

A summary of past and possible future arms control initiatives for the region appears in Table 16-2. This table highlights some important past steps and possible future ones, particularly the unilateral/political initiatives of Israel vis-à-vis the West Bank and Gaza Strip and the unilateral/economic initiatives of the United States in fostering economic cooperation in the region. Both of these unilateral steps have important potential bilateral and multilateral consequences. They may include improved political relations between Egypt and Israel, Israel and Jordan, and Israel and Syria, bilateral economic cooperation, an expanded peace agreement to include Jordan, an Israel-Jordan (or multilateral Egypt-Israel-Jordan) peace treaty, and further bilateral and multilateral economic cooperation in the region. These initiatives could lead to greater transparency in the region, confidence-building measures, and, eventually, a possible multilateral arms limitation agreement for the region.

Notes

1. Our previous work on arms races appears in Dagobert L. Brito, "A Dynamic Model of an Armaments Race," *International Economic Review* 13, 1972, pp. 359-375; Michael D. Intriligator, "Strategic Considerations in the Richardson Model of Arms Races," *Journal of Political Economy* 83, 1975, pp. 339-353; Michael D. Intriligator and Dagobert L. Brito, "Formal Models of Arms Races," *Journal of Peace Science* 2, 1976, pp. 77-88; Michael D. Intriligator and Dagobert L.

Brito, "Can Arms Races Head to the Outbreak of War?" *Journal of Conflict Resolution* 28, 1984, pp. 63-84; and Dagobert L. Brito and Michael Intriligator, "Strategy, Arms Races and Arms Control," in J.V. Gillespie and D. A. Zinnes, eds., *Mathematical Systems in International Relations Research* (New York: Praeger, 1977). For a review of the literature on conflict theory, including arms races, see Michael D. Intriligator, "Research on Conflict Theory: Analytic Approaches and Areas of Application," *Journal of Conflict Resolution* 26, 1982, pp. 307-327.

2. For a formal model of this interactive process see Michael D. Intriligator and Dagobert L. Brito, "Heuristic Decision, Rules, the Dynamics of the Arms Race, and War Initiation," in Urs Luterbacher and Michael D. Ward, eds., *Dynamic Models of International Conflict* (Boulder, CO: Lynne Rienner, 1985).

3. For a theoretical analysis of the relationship of an arms race to the outbreak of war see Intriligator and Brito, "Can Arms Races Head...?"

4. See Yair Evron, *The Role of Arms Control in the Middle East* (London: The International Institute for Strategic Studies, Adelphi Paper No. 138, 1977). Of course, there were other and more fundamental factors that led to the 1956 Anglo-French-Israeli coalition against Egypt, including the nationalization of the Suez Canal and the potential threat of the Nasser regime to British oil interest in the Arab world.

5. Our previous work on arms control appears in Brito and Intriligator, "Strategy;" Michael D. Intriligator and Dagobert L. Brito, "Non-Armageddon Solution to the Arms Race," *Arms Control* 6, 1985, pp. 41-57; Michael D. Intriligator and Dagobert L. Brito, "Arms Races and Instability," *Journal of Strategic Studies* 9, 1986, pp. 113-131; and Michael D. Intriligator, "A Better Alternative for START," *Bulletin of Peace Proposals* 20, 1989, pp. 225-227.

6. For a discussion of the so-called "canonical" goals of arms control, as applied to the Soviet-U.S. arms conflict, see Thomas C. Schelling and Morton H. Halperin *Strategy and Arms Control* (New York: Twentieth Century Fund, 1961); and Thomas C. Schelling, *The Strategy of Conflict* (Cambridge: Harvard University Press, 1963).

7. As has been noted in the general arms control literature, in certain contexts arms *increases* can stabilize an otherwise unstable

situation and thus can be considered as arms control initiatives. See Schelling and Halperin, and Schelling. For a formal model implying that in certain situations arms *increases* can reduce the chance of war see Intriligator and Brito, "Can Arms Races Head...?" See also Intriligator and Brito, "Arms Races and Instability." for further discussions of the relationships between arms acquisitions and war initiation. Some specific examples in the Middle East were the U.S. transfers of Phantom jets to Israel in 1970 and the Soviet transfer of Scud surface-to-surface missiles to Egypt in 1973. The former strengthened Israel and thus deterred Arab attacks, while the latter forced Israel to restrict attack to military objectives, avoiding countervalue air strikes against Egyptian population and economic infrastructure in order to avoid Egyptian countervalue retaliation against Israel. For a discussion of these cases of arms transfers as arms control measures in the region see Evron, *Role of Arms*. Evron notes that while the transfer of Phantom jets secured some stability, war was not ultimately prevented. He also notes that while the Scud missiles limited the destructiveness of war by restricting targets to military objectives, they did strengthen Egypt's intention to start the 1973 war in the first place.

8. For previous analyses of arms control in the Middle East see Yair Evron, *The Middle East: Nations, Superpowers, and Wars* (New York: Praeger, 1973); Evron "Arms Races in the Middle East and Some Arms Control Measures Related to Theory," in G. Sheffer, ed., *Dynamics of a Conflict: A Reinterpretation of the Arab-Israeli Conflict* (Atlantic Highlands, NJ: Humanities Press, 1975); and Evron, *Role of Arms*. See also Colin S. Gray, "Arms Races and their Influence upon International Stability, with Special Reference to the Middle East," in G. Sheffer, ed., *Dynamics of a Conflict*; Michael Mihalka, "Understanding Arms Accumulation: the Middle East as an Example," in J. Benkak, ed., *International Conflicts: the Methodology of their Assessment*, (New York: 1973); Jeffery Milstein, "American and Soviet Influence, Balance of Power, and Arab-Israeli Violence," in B.M. Russett, ed., *Peace, War, and Numbers* (Beverly Hills, CA: Sage Publications, 1972); H. Rattinger, "From War to War: Arms Races in the Middle East," *International Studies Quarterly* 20, 1976, p. 59; Steven J. Rosen, "What the Next Arab-Israeli War Might Look Like," *International Security* 2, 1978; James A. Bill, *Politics in the Middle East* (Boston: Little, Brown and Co., 1984); Gabriel Sheffer, ed., *Dynamics of Dependence: U.S.-Israeli Relations* (Boulder, CO: Westview Press, 1987); and Anthony H. Cordesman, *The Gulf and the West: Strategic Relations and Military Realities* (Boulder, CO: Westview Press, 1988).

9. An exception may be in time of war. During the 1973 war there were reports of possible Soviet nuclear weapons on ships approaching the region.

10. In economic terms, the marginal propensity to buy arms is high when income is rising, but low when income is falling, a type of ratchet effect.

11. See Shai Feldman, *Israeli Nuclear Deterrence: A Strategy for the 1980s* (New York: Columbia University Press, 1982), and the critiques of his position in Beres, Louis Rene, ed., *Security or Armageddon: Israel's Nuclear Strategy* (Lexington: Lexington Books, 1986). See also Steven J. Rosen, "A Stable System of Mutual Nuclear Deterrence in the Arab-Israeli Conflict," *American Political Science Review* 71, 1977, 1367-1383.

12. An important precedent for supplier cooperation in limiting arms transfers to the Middle East is the Tripartite Declaration of 1950, under which the arms suppliers to the region, at the time, the United States, Britain, and France, regulated arms transfers. It was a major arms control agreement which was effective until the emergence of the Soviet Union as a major arms supplier to the region in the arms deal with Egypt in 1955.

17 Bilateral Soviet-American Cooperation in the Middle East: An Israeli View

Soviet-American cooperation in the Middle East has often struck Israeli governments as more of a potential threat than a diplomatic opportunity. It was the superpowers' *de facto* joint stand after the Suez Campaign that helped promote Israel's eventual withdrawal from the Sinai in 1957. And according to the then-Israeli Foreign Minister Moshe Dayan, actual Soviet-American cooperation in their 1978 Joint Declaration would have worked to the detriment of Israel's position at the Geneva Conference that was being planned to be the centerpiece of Middle Eastern peacemaking before the Sadat visit.[1]

Generally, Israeli trepidations about Soviet-American cooperation in the Middle East have been of three types. First, given the differences in both superpowers' interests and policies toward the Arab-Israeli conflict, Soviet-American cooperation has been seen to require concessions by Washington to Moscow in the area of policy; modifications of the U.S. position on Middle Eastern peacemaking, it must be remembered, have been of greater significance to Israel than the value of the concessions Moscow has made to Washington.

Second, Soviet-American cooperation has frequently implied to Israeli governments the prospect of some sort of imposed solution. Much of the domestic debate in Israel over the international conference idea in 1987-88 centered on the authority of the conference plenum to dictate a solution to diplomatically deadlocked parties.

Even Israeli advocates of the conference idea, like Labor Party leader Shimon Peres, focused their diplomatic energies on neutralizing the potential power of the conference sponsors through oral understandings attached to the 1987 London Agreement. According to its Israeli advocates, the main contribution of a superpower or broader five-power sponsorship of the conference idea was to provide a legitimizing framework for Israeli-Jordanian negotiations, and eventual Jordanian territorial concessions.

Thirdly, Soviet-American cooperation has often conveyed some hint of the substitution of superpower guarantees for Israeli defensive capabilities. Thus in the aftermath of the Six Day War, the Johnson administration considered delaying aircraft deliveries to Israel while a Soviet-American regional arms transfer agreement was under consideration. However, massive Soviet arms sales to Arab clients undermined the notion that Israel's need for Skyhawks could be ameliorated by a Soviet-American understanding.

Likewise, when consideration is given to Israeli territorial defensive capabilities in the territories that the Israel Defense Forces (IDF) took control of in the 1967 Six Day War, the substitution of forces stationed in the West Bank by joint Soviet-American guarantees in the past has been considered by American policymakers.[2]

The purpose of this paper is to examine whether these traditional Israeli concerns with Soviet-American cooperation in the Middle East have any relevance for the arena of regional arms control. Would increased superpower management of the flow of arms into the region bring about a fundamental alteration in U.S. policy toward Israel out of deference to Soviet perspectives in a manner similar to the concern in the 1970s with peace process issues? Does a superpower arms control process in the Middle East necessarily imply imposed security arrangements for the states of the region? Is the whole idea of guarantees worth examining in the arms control context as it has been explored in the framework of the issue of the territories?

Superpower and Israeli Arms Control:
Interests and Priorities

First, with regard to the possible effect of Soviet policies on evolving U.S. positions, it is important to stress that even without

Moscow's input, substantial discrepancies already exist between the basic interests of the superpowers. On the one hand, differences exist over issues concerning Israel as well as other smaller states in the region, while on the other hand, discrepancies exist over the priorities of any future Middle East arms control agenda.

Prior to the Persian Gulf Crisis of 1990, the clearcut stress of U.S. arms control policies toward the Middle East over the last decade has been the threat of the proliferation of non-conventional weapons and ballistic missiles. Regular Soviet-American consultations have been held since 1982 over the implementation of the 1968 Nuclear Non-Proliferation Treaty. By the mid-1980s, these consultations came to include the proliferation of chemical weapons as well.

As late as the February 7-9, 1990, ministerial meeting in Moscow, Secretary of State James Baker and Soviet Foreign Minister Eduard Shevardnadze agreed on the need to consider increasing their cooperation "in all areas of non-proliferation--chemical, missile, and nuclear." The words "conventional proliferation" were notably absent.

The prioritization of missile arms control has been even more pronounced than the non-conventional concerns stated by U.S. policy. Some of this stress on ballistic missiles has been unintended. For example, one of the side-effects of the 1987 Intermediate Nuclear Forces (INF) Treaty has been the effective prohibition of the transfer of intermediate-range missiles from the superpowers to Middle Eastern countries. By banning the very production of ballistic missiles in this category, the INF treaty eliminated the possibility of these systems being transferred to the Middle East after they were prohibited in Europe.

International U.S. activism in the missile arms control area had been evident since April 16, 1987, with the establishment of the Missile Technology Control Regime (MTCR)--a non-binding set of declaratory policy guidelines governing technology transfer of missile systems capable of carrying warheads of 500 kilograms or more at distances greater than 300 kilometers.

The Reagan administration added missile proliferation to its arms control discussions with the U.S.S.R. during its last year in office. Moreover, at the same time, the Reagan team explored the idea of confidence-building measures in the missile field when it suggested to Egypt and Israel the idea of giving prior notification of missile launches.

The missile/non-conventional focus of the U.S. arms control agenda in the Middle East is understandable considering the U.S. interest. Ballistic missiles reaching into the intermediate range allow hostile, anti-Western states in the Middle East to put American bases in the Mediterranean at risk. The attempted Libyan missile strike at Lampedusa in 1986 would have been a far more serious matter if Libya possessed non-conventionally tipped missiles capable of reaching the Italian mainland or Greece. Certainly for the U.S.S.R., the proliferation of intermediate-range ballistic missiles in the Middle East affects not just overseas bases, but the territory of the Soviet homeland itself.

The missile/non-conventional threat also places constraints on U.S. power projection capabilities in areas where the United States has no permanent bases. The ability of the United States to deal with Iraq would have been an entirely different matter if all Turkish and Saudi airbases were within striking range of a future generation of accurate Middle Eastern missiles. Disembarking American forces would be extremely vulnerable to missile attack, in a manner that would compromise U.S. capabilities to respond to regional crises in the Third World. Nations vulnerable to ballistic missile attack may be far more reluctant to host American forces, thereby diminishing U.S. access to global facilities in future scenarios. From an Israeli perspective, missiles have introduced new vulnerabilities to Israel's rear areas by giving rejectionist Arab forces assured penetrability of Israel airspace. However, missiles have not been regarded as the main threat to Israel's existence; nor have they been seen as the principle destabilizing element in Arab rejectionist force structures.

It must be remembered that at present the Arab rejectionist ballistic missile forces--given their accuracy, range, deployment and lethality--cannot deny Israel its second-strike capability by assuring the shut down of IAF airbases throughout Israel. Even the Iraqi missile strikes on Tel Aviv during the "Desert Storm" operation, while tragic for the families that were displaced from their destroyed homes, could not be described as a strategically decisive event; Kuwait's fate was decided by an Iraqi conventional ground force attack while Israel, as a whole, was barely wounded by Iraqi missile attacks.

Thus the consensus of most Israeli military analysts has been that the principle threat to Israel is based on the asymmetry in the number of active duty conventional ground formations between Israel and its Arab neighbors.[3] The majority of Arab ground divisions are active duty units, in Israel's case the majority of ground divisions are reserves. When Arab ground divisions are massed along Israel's borders, extremely unfavorable force ratios result that are only partially ameliorated by the reserve call-up within forty-eight hours.

It must be added that the conventional force pre-occupation in Israeli threat assessments is not reflected in formal Israeli arms control proposals. During the 1980s, the Israeli government put forward in the United Nations proposals for nuclear and chemical free zones in the Middle East MBFR (Mutual and Balanced Force Reductions). But the general stress of formal proposals by the Israeli government has also been in the non-conventional field, as is the case of the United States.

Nevertheless, it can be asserted that the United States and Israel may have different arms control interests and agendas that are occasionally expressed in terms of their actually-stated priorities. Certainly differences have already been expressed in the last decade over the continuing massive conventional arms sales to the Middle East by the United States, its European allies, and the Soviet Union.

While careful criteria were set by the United States regarding missile technology or dual-use chemicals, no similar criteria limiting destabilizing sales were established in the conventional arms arena. When the U.S.S.R. was denounced in 1989 for transferring the SU-24 to Libya, Syria, and Iraq, there was some basis to the Soviet argument that the West itself had placed no qualitative restrictions on similar sorts of ground-attack aircraft sales, like the Tornado, and had not ruled out the eventual sale of the F-15E.

It is possible that now that the Gulf Crisis has passed, the United States will begin to give more attention to conventional arms control than it did before, although its basic interests will still be in the non-conventional/missile field, as explained below. Asked at the World Affairs Council on October 29, 1990 whether the "Iraq situation . . . taught us anything about the sale of weapons by developed countries to the developing world," Secretary of State James Baker responded ". . . we ought to give some thought to the degree to which . . . we should look at conventional weapons proliferation."[4]

Appearing before the House Foreign Affairs Committee on December 6, 1990, Secretary Baker was asked by Representative Mel Levine (D-CA) what the administration's "long-term vision" of the Middle East looked like; Baker again made explicit reference to the conventional arms control area:

> With respect to your questions on arms control, I think that we must, in the aftermath of this crisis, spend a lot of time examining those issues. And I wouldn't limit it . . . just to arms control or proliferation of weapons of mass destruction, *I think we need to consider the question of proliferation of conventional arms in the tinder box region.*[5]

This new conventional orientation appeared formally to enter U.S. postwar policy on February 6, 1991 when Secretary Baker outlined the basic headings of American Middle East diplomacy after the liberation of Kuwait. After stating the need for security arrangements in the Gulf region as the first matter of business, Baker described "regional arms proliferation and control" as the second challenge to the United States. Baker now put unusual stress on conventional arms control:

> This includes both conventional weapons and weapons of mass destruction. The terrible fact is that even the conventional arsenals of several Middle Eastern states dwarf those of most European powers. Five Middle Eastern countries have more main battle tanks than the United Kingdom or France. The time has come to try to change the destructive pattern of military competition and proliferation in this region and to reduce arms flows into an area that is already overmilitarized.[6]

This evolution of U.S. arms control policy towards the Middle East certainly means that some of Israel's most fundamental security concerns--the size of Arab conventional forces--may at long last be addressed. But at the same time other American post-war priorities could pull American policy in another direction; the need to establish security arrangements for the Gulf region could very well lead to an acceleration of arms sales to Saudi Arabia or to Egypt.

The Carter administration faced a similar dilemma of trying to get a handle on conventional arms sales to the region while at the same time it was concerned with Gulf security; ultimately it made enormous arms sales to the region. The current dilemma will likely lead to an American policy focussing on the nonproliferation of unconventional munitions and missiles, which is in fact similar to the policy that existed prior to the Gulf Crisis. Only one month after Baker's testimony, President Bush's March 6, 1991, address to both the Senate and the House dropped the call for conventional arms control in the Middle East. American ambivalence towards conventional arms control has been reasserted.

Within the missile arms control field, important differences between U.S. and Israeli perspectives are worth noting. The MTCR governs the transfer of missile technologies in ranges which are significant for the types of U.S. interests that are noted above. Missile capabilities below the 300 kilometer level are not affected by MTCR. While a 100 kilometer range Soviet SS-21 may not be a significant weapon for U.S. or Western interests, it is actually a system of enormous concern from the Israeli perspective. What may be dismissed in the West as a battlefield weapon is viewed by Israel as a strategic weapon in the narrow geography of the Middle East.

Having adhered to MTCR guidelines in February 1990, Moscow can continue to sell SS-21 missiles to Syria without violating this missile regime. For its part, Washington could conceivably upgrade Saudi MLRS (Multiple Launch Rocket System) units with U.S. Army 120 kilometer range ATACM's (Army Tactical Missile System), and not be guilty of missile proliferation. Thus, in the case of Middle East arms control, potentially substantial differences in perspectives already exist between Israel and the United States even before Soviet policies are taken into account. In this case, the Soviet contribution would not necessarily lead to a wider policy gap between the United States and Israel, as would be the case in the peace process.

In fact, given the Soviet Union's repeated declaratory interest in considering the utility of confidence-building measures (CBM) in the Middle East, first raised by Foreign Minister Shevardnadze in February, 1989 in the form of a regional crisis prevention center, Moscow might have some understanding for Israel's conventional forces pre-occupation in any proposed arms control arrangements. Soviet visitors to Israel, like Sergei Rogov, put particular stress on the relevance of the CBM idea for the Middle East.

It would not be farfetched to surmise that the occasional American remarks about the need for Middle Eastern CBM's that were made in 1990, especially those by the State Department's Director of Policy Planning, Dennis Ross, at the Middle East Institute during October, grew out of Soviet-American discussions in this area. It is noteworthy that in the January 29, 1991 Joint Statement by Secretary of State James Baker and Foreign Minister Alexander Bessmertnykh, specific reference was made to the need for "working to reduce the risk of war and miscalculation"--reflecting perhaps the Soviet influence on American policy regarding the application of some confidence building measures to the region.

Superpower-Managed Arms Control
and Imposed Solutions

A second traditional Israeli concern with superpower-managed peacemaking has been the prospect of imposed solutions. In the arms control field, the destabilizing effects of imposed solutions overshadows a solution to the territories. A particular Israeli concern, in this regard, has been the repeated attempts of Arab diplomacy to stress Israeli refusals to sign the Nuclear Non-Proliferation Treaty. Israel's counter-offer of a nuclear-free zone in the Middle East underlines, almost paradigmatically, the difference between an externally managed arms control arrangement and one that is freely negotiated by the states of the region.

The philosophical underpinning of the nuclear-free zone concept is that arms control cannot just eliminate specific weaponry alone, but must have a wider purpose of bringing about some general political accommodation. In any arms control process, each side has its own relative advantage in specific weapons categories; only if the level of general hostility is reduced can states be expected to take risks in areas in which they might enjoy some relative advantages against their adversaries. Otherwise, states are engaging in a process that they will regard as virtual unilateral disarmament--which may actually destabilize the military balance rather than serve to advance the cause of peace.

For Israel, the externally managed NPT regime allows Arab states to assure for themselves that Israel might not have a qualitative option for countering their quantitative superiority. Were Israel to sign onto the NPT, Arab states might be relieved from the threat of an Israeli nuclear deterrent, while maintaining for themselves the right and capability of waging conventional or chemical war against Israel.

To alleviate this danger, the Israeli nuclear free zone concept requires direct Israeli-Arab talks; by reducing the degree of hostility between the parties, it might also have the effect of lowering the prospects of conventional war, as well as nuclear war. Moreover, by insisting on a regional arms control framework that could involve regional verification, the nuclear free zone concept requires a considerable relaxation of Arab-Israeli tensions. In this sense, Israel prefers that verification be conducted by Syrian officers rather than by Swedes belonging to the International Atomic Energy Agency (IAEA) in an NPT regime.

The Israeli view of the NPT versus the nuclear free zone concept is of direct relevance to any superpower-managed arms control process in the future. A superpower-managed process might focus on weaponry that is first of all important to the superpowers' interests, as noted earlier. The chances of Israel's concern with conventional force growth in the Middle East being addressed in a superpower-managed arms control process are very small. Secondly, a superpower-managed process that served to substitute externally imposed guidelines for direct Arab-Israeli talks might, like the NPT, cut back a particular capability, but would not allow Middle East arms control to move beyond into a general process of Arab-Israeli reconciliation.

The impact of the Gulf Crisis on superpower views on the appropriate mechanism for Middle East arms control--and their role in that mechanism--is complex. The United States continues to support the NPT, as in the past. But considerable doubt was expressed by Bush administration spokesmen, during the deployment of U.S. forces against Iraq, concerning the reliability of IAEA inspections. The United States was claiming that Iraq was much closer to obtaining an atomic device than what the IAEA inspections might have indicated.

Moreover, during an interview given to the Cable News Network (CNN) in early February 1991, Defense Secretary Richard Cheney came closer than any American official before him in recognizing the fact of Israel's reputed nuclear capacity; asked if Saddam Hussein was deterred from a chemical attack on Israel by the possibility that Israel would retaliate with nuclear weapons, Cheney answered:

> I assume he knows that if he were to resort to chemical weapons that would be an escalation to weapons of mass destruction and that the possibility would then exist, certainly with respect to the Israelis, for example that they might retaliate with unconventional weapons, as well.[7]

No American qualification was expressed as to whether Israel's reputed capacity in this area was within American interests or not.

For its part, the Soviet Union reiterated its support for a nuclear and chemical weapons free zone in the Middle East during the Baker-Shevardnadze ministerial meeting in Houston on December 10-11, 1990. Both superpowers, thus, may be open to alternative nuclear arms control mechanisms to the NPT, without disqualifying the NPT structure entirely.

Superpower Guarantees
and Middle East Arms Control

Since superpower guarantees have been considered in the context of a reduction of Israel's territorial capabilities, they might also be considered in the context of a reduction of weapons capabilities as well. The limits of guarantees have been examined in the past in a relatively broad spectrum of literature. Nonetheless certain general points must again be examined considering the radical international developments of 1989-90. For the entire discussion of guarantees in a Cold War context is entirely different than in a post-Cold War reality.

The most profound change in the superpowers' relationship to the Middle East in the last year has been the relative reduction of Soviet power in the region that has been a function of its internal economic preoccupations. If indeed the Soviet Union does not plan to have any Soviet troops outside the borders of the U.S.S.R. by the year 2000, as Soviet spokesmen have claimed, the same cannot be said for the United States. Looking only at the beginning of the 1990 Persian Gulf Crisis, the U.S. military presence in the Middle East could very well be greater in the post-Cold War environment than at any other time since 1945.

This disparity in U.S. and Soviet positions in the region must be factored into the relative value of Soviet versus American guarantees. If during the Cold War period, in a possible arms control scenario, the U.S.S.R. might provide guarantees of a certain sort to Syria, while parallel guarantees were provided by the United States to Israel, in the post-Cold War period the value of U.S. guarantees would be considerably different than those given by the U.S.S.R.

Should the Middle East evolve from a region dominated by superpower bipolarity to a region dominated by American supremacy, then clearly the only alternative to superpower guarantees, in an arms control context, would be a unilateral American umbrella. Here, a whole other set of difficulties would be encountered. The United States views Israel, Egypt, and Saudi Arabia as local allies, while countries like Libya, Syria (even with its participation in the coalition), Iraq, and Iran, have been regarded in varying degrees as local adversaries.

Even with some improvement in Washington's relations with its local adversaries, can the United States be "evenhanded" in future arms control guarantees between its local allies and adversaries? If the strength of its allies affects the United States' ability to project power effectively to the Middle East, then an "evenhanded" arms control posture by the United States would damage American security interests.

One option for the United States under these circumstances might be to alter the mix of responsibilities between the United States and its Middle Eastern allies in a manner that would increase the American burden in regional security. In the Persian Gulf, for example, while local Arab capabilities were built up over the last decade in order to counter local threats, U.S. power projection was regarded as necessary to deter the extra-regional Soviet threat. Since the Kuwaitis and Saudis were unable to stand alone against Iraqi armor, perhaps regional threats will have to be the responsibility of the United States. Such a conclusion would mitigate against massive arms transfers to the Gulf, and allow for some Middle Eastern arms control under American sponsorship.

However, it is extremely unlikely that Washington will assume a position of regional policeman throughout the Middle East in lieu of its regional allies. Moreover, with the exception of the oil-producing states, where clearcut American interest dictates continual American engagement, Arab states would be extremely reluctant to replace their own self-defense capabilities even with American guarantees. In the long term, without a central motivating theme of the threat of communism, the support of overseas military engagement by the American public will be taken for granted by resource-poor allies of the United States.

The deployment of U.S. Patriot missiles and their crews to defend Israeli cities from repeated Iraqi extended-range SCUD attacks, as well as the allied air coverage over launch sites in western Iraq, may mistakenly lead observers to the conclusion that Israel might be ready to accept a superpower guarantee in lieu of its own capability. For Israel, the U.S. Patriot deployment does not mark any fundamental doctrinal change according to which Israel might be ready to accept external protection in lieu of a self-defense capability. If anything, the deployment is seen as a stop-gap measure allowing the Patriots to become operational before Israeli crews could complete their training.

One notable development that did occur in the crisis was not the substitution of Israeli capability with American capability, but rather the *addition* of American capabilities in highly advanced areas where

Israel was essentially unable to defend itself. Thus former Defense Minister Yitzhak Rabin confessed that now every civilian knows "what we have known for several years . . . that Israel has no early warning against missile attack"[8] Israel's five minute warning for Iraqi missile attacks came about only as a result of the assistance of U.S. spaced-based satellites.

To the extent that advanced American technologies can add stability to the Middle East by introducing capabilities that neither side can either afford or technologically manage, a superpower presence can serve as a vital security arrangement for the region but can not necessarily act as a vehicle for regional arms control.

Conclusion

Superpower involvement in Middle East arms control poses many of the same questions that arise in the context of superpower involvement in peace process issues. It also poses unique problems for the states of the region. The superpowers have very distinct interests which dictate their own views of the Middle East arms control agenda. Nevertheless, the Gulf Crisis may have narrowed these differences as a greater emphasis is placed on the need to address conventional imbalances.

Superpower involvement in imposing arms control arrangements that might be sought by some Middle Eastern players could undermine the evolution of the arms control process into a greater process of political reconciliation. Finally, their involvement might suggest to some that their guarantees could be of value in lieu of specific military capabilities.

With these difficulties, the superpowers do have a potential contribution to Middle East arms control that ought to be considered. They themselves have made the leap from distrust to the destruction of weaponry. Superpowers can establish the general rules of the game in diplomacy for the Middle East. In this sense, they can serve as instructors to their regional clients. They can suggest frameworks that the states of the Middle East might explore. In the absence of goodwill among the states of the region to investigate arms control by themselves, the superpowers can serve as

378

a substitute for this lack of goodwill, and provide the impetus for discussions between Arabs and Israelis in the future.

Notes

1. Moshe Dayan, *Breakthrough: A Personal Account of the Egypt-Israel Peace Negotiations* (New York: Knopf, 1981), p. 65.

2. *Ibid.*

3. Mordechai Gur, "Destabilizing Elements of the Middle East Military Balance" in Dore Gold, ed., *Arms Control in the Middle East* (Jerusalem and Boulder, CO: *The Jerusalem Post*/Westview Press), pp. 9-16.

4. Address by Secretary of State James Baker, World Affairs Council, Los Angeles, California, October 29, 1990. Federal News Service.

5. Hearings, U.S. House of Representatives, Committee on Foreign Affairs, December 6, 1990. Federal News Service, Washington, D.C.

6. Hearings, U.S. House of Representatives, Committee on Foreign Affairs, February 6, 1981. Federal News Service, Washington, D.C.

7. IUT, February 4, 1991.

8. *The Jerusalem Post*, February 22, 1990.

18 Beyond the Cold War: The Superpowers and the Arab-Israeli Conflict

The striking developments of the late 1980s in the Soviet Union and Eastern Europe marked the end of the Cold War and the resolution of a myriad of regional conflicts. The reunification of the two Germanies, the downfall of the totalitarian regimes in Eastern Europe, the settlement of the conflicts over Afghanistan, Namibia, Cambodia, and Nicaragua signalled the beginning of a new world order.

Despite the definitive outcomes of the discontinuation of the Cold War in many parts of the world, the Middle East remained largely unaffected by the unfolding of these dramatic events. Notwithstanding the emerging trend toward political liberalization in Jordan, Tunisia, Algeria, and South Yemen, the democratic trend is far from being a region-wide phenomenon in the Middle East. Likewise, the peaceful resolution of the various conflicts in the Middle East has continued to be an elusive goal. The position of many of the local players remains intractable. Indeed, the proliferation of weapons of mass destruction is making conflicts in the region deadlier.

The Sources of Instability in the Middle East

The presence of a multiplicity of conflicts, the race for the acquisition of advanced weaponry, and the existence of numerous barriers to political compromises have, over the years, hindered the search for a peaceful resolution to many Middle East disputes. The

Middle East remains an arena for high intensity conflict as numerous threats continue to challenge regional security.

One of the oldest of these challenges has been the enduring popular appeal of trans-national ideologies--Arab nationalism and Islam--both of which have rendered the boundaries of the territorial state permeable. A second threat to regional stability emanates from the presence of ethnic minorities wanting a greater degree of autonomy, and in some cases, complete independence from their states of residence. The uneven nature of the process of economic and political modernization, the legitimacy problems that confront many Arab regimes, and the presence of religious and ethnic divisions account for much of the internal instability of several Middle East countries.

The intensity and the frequency of interstate competition furnishes another source of conflict in the Middle East. The struggle for power and leadership in the Arab world has been, in part, behind the interstate violence. Over the years, bitter rivalries have broken out between Egypt and Iraq, Syria and Iraq, and Iraq and Iran. These rivalries and animosities will continue to fuel the interstate violence.

Several Middle Eastern countries pursue incompatible objectives and conflicting sovereignty claims over territories under the control of another state.[1] Indeed, the quest for regional hegemony and commitment to irredentist interests has been behind the recurrent phenomenon of war in the Middle East. Countries like Israel, Iraq, Libya, Algeria, Morocco, and Syria harbor territorial ambitions toward their weaker neighbors. Their expansionist tendencies have been driven by ideological, historical, security-based territorial, or economic objectives. Still others may carry on wars to emancipate other people or help them reconstruct their territorial and national rights. For many years, the Arab states have supported the Palestinians' goal of recovering their lost territories. Finally, other countries--including Israel, Syria, Iraq, and Egypt--have differed over the configuration of a neighboring government where the discontented country has tried to install a new regime that would be more disposed to serve its interests.

The Arms Race in the Middle East

The bitter rivalry among these countries has not only resulted in the frequent recurrence of the phenomena of interstate wars and internal violence, but has also heightened the race for the acquisition of the most advanced weaponry. The proliferation of missile technology, including surface-to-surface medium-range missiles, and the attempts by several Middle Eastern states to acquire chemical and nuclear defense capabilities attest to the intense nature of the arms race in the region.

Given the deep-seated hostilities and conflicts in the Middle East, the introduction of weapons of mass destruction is destabilizing to the regional order. The availability of these long-range rockets gives local adversaries the option of mounting them with nuclear or chemical warheads. The existence of a technological gap among the various adversaries may induce certain countries to launch a preemptive attack to destroy the military facilities of their opponents. Israel's destruction of an Iraqi nuclear reactor in June 1981 is an example of such a contingency.

The volatile nature of some of the governments in the Middle East may prompt the leaders of those states to use their offensive arsenals against one another. This contingency is reinforced by the fact that many of the Middle Eastern elite accept the use of military force as a legitimate vehicle for the pursuit of political objectives.

The Impediments to a Palestinian-Israeli Peace

While not underestimating the various types of conflicts in the Middle East and the multitude of obstacles emanating from such disputes, the Palestinian-Arab-Israeli conflict is potentially the most lethal and volatile of these, and the most difficult to resolve. The incompatible territorial objectives of both Israel and the Palestinians render the attainment of peace an elusive goal. More seriously, the possession by both sides of some of the world's most sophisticated weapons makes the cost of future wars more devastating than ever before.

To reach a political compromise, both the Israelis and the Palestinians would have to retract their initial positions and demands. The two sides should acknowledge that the price of continuing the conflict is higher than the cost of reducing their demands.[2] Israel and the Palestinians are obstinate about their stands, thus making the progress toward a settlement an arduous process.

Several barriers stand in the path of an historic reconciliation between the two sides. While the Palestinians have broken away from their maximalist goal of liberating all of Palestine and have confined themselves to the construction of a West Bank-Gaza state, the present Likud government has assigned to the Occupied Territories a high ideological importance. This is a reversal in the attitudes of the early Israeli governments.

During the initial years that followed the 1967 war, the struggle over the Occupied Territories centered on Israel's need for secure and defensible borders. The Israeli Labor government was prepared, during the first decade of occupation, to give back to the Arabs a portion of the Occupied Territories in return for security and peace. Since 1977, however, the Likud government has infused the dispute with political rhetoric. The Likud regards the West Bank and Gaza Strip as liberated land and as an integral part of Greater Israel. This gives the Jews the right to settle anywhere in the Occupied Territories. The Likud politicians have described Israel's perpetual control over the West Bank and the Gaza Strip as being crucial to the moral and the spiritual well-being of the Jewish people.

Thus, the fusion of concrete territorial dispute with ideological rationalization has made the attainment of political compromise an exceedingly demanding task. The retraction from such a symbolic position is seen by a growing number of Israelis as a sacrifice of some lofty principle.

The frequent outbursts of violence are another impediment to an Arab-Israeli compromise. The cycle of violence prevents reconciliation and also broadens the distance between the two sides.

The absence of channels for open communication between the antagonists constitutes an additional barrier to political reconciliation. Until the mid-1980s, the Palestinian Liberation Organization (PLO) did not sanction a direct dialogue between the West Bank-Gaza

Palestinians and the Israelis. In the second half of the 1980s, the Israeli government passed a law making contacts with the PLO a crime for which violators would be jailed.

Compromise is also thwarted by a lack of trust among the adversaries. The relationship between Israel and the Palestinians is characterized by conditions of mutual suspicion and mistrust. The pervasiveness of such sentiments inhibits responsiveness to each other's needs and wants and precludes the emergence of cooperative forms of behavior. The feelings of mistrust also explain why peace gestures are dismissed as misleading and empty and why malicious intentions are ascribed to the enemies' peace moves and actions.

Over the years, the Israelis have argued that the PLO is not a trustworthy party and that any agreement signed with it would be futile and inconsequential. Likewise, mistrust has led some of the Palestinians and the Arab countries to conclude that they cannot negotiate with Israel except from a position of strength. They argue that, in the absence of military parity, Israel will continue to exploit the Arab and the Palestinian weaknesses.

The skillfulness and the reputation of the bargainers could also play a crucial role in the success of any diplomatic effort. Presently, both the Israelis and the Palestinians lack effective politicians who employ diplomatic skills and visions for the future. The politicians on both sides perceive each other to be inflexible and unimaginative. Moreover, the history of the Palestinian-Israeli dispute does not have too many successes to build upon.

Patience is another essential prerequisite for successful bargaining and negotiations. While the Palestinians are anxious to speed up the negotiating process and reach an agreement with Israel for the establishment of a Palestinian state, Israel's desire to do so is minimal. The Israeli government's anticipation of a final victory has been an ardent barrier to compromise. Many of the Israeli politicians expect that they will ultimately achieve their goals even if through the exercise of military force.

The diplomatic persuasion of allies and friendly states is another important factor that would affect the chances of reaching a compromise. In 1988, Egypt, Saudi Arabia, and the Soviet Union swayed the PLO to launch a diplomatic initiative. In contrast, the various American administrations were reluctant to exert sufficient pressure upon Israel to make meaningful territorial concessions. The Bush administration, for instance, has failed to bring about enough pressure to get the Israeli government to accept Secretary of State James Baker's plan to conduct democratic elections in the Occupied Territories.

The Israeli refusal to accept the Palestinians' right to choose their political representatives is also a serious obstacle in the path of any compromise. The PLO does not have sufficient support in the United States and in some Arab quarters, and is an unacceptable partner for Israel. A peace settlement is not plausible, however, without the active participation of the Palestinians.[3] The United States and Israel do not recognize the PLO's legitimacy and the Palestinians' right for self-determination.

Due to the pro-Israeli stance of the various American administrations, the Palestinians do not want to see the United States in control of the peace talks. Such an eventuality will favor Israel and, as such, preclude any outcome that would satisfy the Palestinians' national aspirations. As a consequence, the PLO relishes the convening of an international peace conference in which Western Europe and the Soviet Union will participate actively.

The asymmetry in the capabilities of both sides does not lend itself to the achievement of a diplomatic compromise. The contestants on the Palestinian-Israeli divide do not have resources of parallel sufficiency that would enable them to offer equally credible threats or rewards. In this context, the capabilities of the Palestinians are strikingly inferior to those of Israel. In particular, Israel's possession of the West Bank and the Gaza Strip together with the military supremacy of the Jewish state has convinced the Likud government that the grip on the Occupied Territories can be maintained indefinitely.

The Israeli government hopes that, over time, the Arab states and the Palestinians will simply accept the new status quo of the Occupied Territories as partially legitimate. An ensuing development of this sort would induce the Palestinians to desist from their exuberant search for the establishment of an independent state. The approbation of the new situation would also lessen Arab commitments to the formation of a West Bank-Gaza state.

Due to the aforementioned barriers and considerations, the Arab-Israeli dispute cannot be expected to become a passive conflict. On the contrary, the obstinacy of Palestinian nationalism and Israel's unyielding opposition to relinquishing the Occupied Territories are bound to lead to violence and counter-violence. This dismal prognosis necessitates a joint action on the part of the superpowers. The end of the Cold War and the diffusion of tension between the United States and the Soviet Union provide a congenial milieu for the initiation of serious mediating efforts to resolve the Arab-Israeli dispute.

The End of the Cold War:
Implications for the Middle East

As a result of the termination of the Cold War, the Third World lost its value in an era of competition with the West. Consequently, the quest for the sweep of international communism and the dissemination of socialism among the developing countries are no longer a preoccupation of Soviet foreign policy. In its efforts to expand socialism, the Soviet Union was willing to extend economic and military assistance to its Third World clients. Presently, such resources are not readily available, as they are needed for internal Soviet economic development.

The net effect of this change was a reduction in the tension between the United States and the Soviet Union, resulting in the superpowers' indifference to the outcome of regional conflicts.[4] The cessation of the Cold War has also diminished the opportunity for American-Soviet intervention on behalf of their local clients. Without the Cold War, the ideological justification for active involvement cannot be easily produced. Indeed, the retreat of Soviet global power has undermined the rationale behind the containment policy which provided the cornerstone for American foreign policy in the post-World War II era.

The New Thinking in the Soviet Union

A configuration of consideration and incentives has led the Soviet Union to adopt a new attitude toward the Middle East. The presence of weapons of mass destruction in the hands of several Middle East players can pose a direct threat to the Soviet-Asian mainland. Israel and Iraq, in particular, possess long-range missiles that can reach the Soviet Union's southern flanks in a relatively short time.

The perpetuation of the Arab-Israeli conflict may lead to the further spread of Islamic fundamentalism in an area adjacent to the volatile Soviet-Asian boundaries. Soviet republics in this region have a large Muslim population that may be susceptible to the spread of Islamic fundamentalism. The Soviet interest in avoiding such a situation would induce the leadership to find a solution to the Arab-Israeli dispute.

Considerations of bureaucratic inertia also sustain Soviet interest in the Middle East. The Cold War created an economic, political, and military interdependency between some of the Arab countries and the Soviet Union. The Soviet Union has also backed the Arab world in its confrontation with Israel. In addition, the geographic propinquity led to the development of ideological affinities between these regimes and the socialist camp.

In addition to these incentives, many of the barriers that previously stood in the path of an active Soviet participation in the peace process were removed. As early as April 1987, Gorbachev declared that Soviet-Israeli relations could not be considered normal.[5] Since that date, Israel restored full diplomatic relations with the various East European countries. Moscow and Tel Aviv exchanged consular delegations and in October 1990, the relationship between Israel and the Soviet Union was restored at the consular level. More significantly, the Soviet government removed travel restrictions from the Soviet Union, thus enabling a large number of Jews to emigrate to Israel.

The new image of the Soviet Union has been further reinforced by the dramatic changes in Eastern Europe. The collapse of the totalitarian regimes has had an adverse impact upon international terrorism. The Palestinian extremists can no longer depend upon Eastern Europe for military supplies, training, finance, and refuge.

The new Soviet thinking toward Israel has lessened the state's support to radical Arab countries. The Soviet leadership no longer believes in the efficacy of military force as a means of resolving the Arab-Israeli dispute. Unlike the past, the sale of arms to the Arab states does not aim at checking the influence of the pro-Western Arab countries or the achievement of strategic parity with Israel. The trade of weapons with Arab countries is presently made for purely commercial and economic reasons.

In addition to the constructive stand toward Israel, the new Soviet Middle East policy has incorporated diplomatic overtures toward the conservative Arab countries. The Soviet government has upheld the institution of amicable relations with Third World states which are implementing a capitalist path for development. Moscow has discontinued the search for an Arab radical bloc in favor of fostering friendly relations with conservative Arab regimes. Thus, the Soviet political pragmatism has contributed to the establishment of full diplomatic ties among the Gulf states, and the Soviet Union.

The Soviet Union's new thinking on the Middle East has undoubtedly caused a deep sense of anxiety among its Arab clients. Many of these hard-line clients--including Syria, Algeria, South Yemen, and the PLO--have modified their foreign policy after feeling betrayed by their long-time ally. Syria, a long-time Soviet friend, terminated its political radicalism and isolationism by restoring diplomatic ties with Egypt. Syria also backed the American-led economic, military, and political blockade of Iraq in the wake of the latter's occupation of Kuwait. Likewise, the PLO's political initiatives in the late 1980s, including its acceptance of United Nations Resolution 242, its recognition of Israel, and the declaration of an independent state were partly in response to the pressure of the Soviet Union.

The end of the Cold War, the retreat of Soviet global power, the shift in Soviet-Middle East policy, and the political moderation of some key Arab players have thus created new opportunities for addressing the problems of the region. The prevention of future Arab-Israeli wars, the encouragement of negotiations between the

388

Palestinians and the Israelis, the maintenance of any settlement to the conflict, and the prohibition of weapons of mass destruction are all issues that demand immediate attention from the superpowers.

The Potential for Superpower Mediating Efforts

In view of the impediments that stand in the path of a final Palestinian-Israeli compromise, the good offices and mediating efforts of the superpowers assume added urgency.[6] As mediators, both countries can perform numerous services and functions for the disputants. First, given the intractable nature of the Palestinian-Israeli conflict, the two superpowers could try to diffuse the tension between the adversaries and enable them to withdraw gracefully from their previous obdurate attitudes. By taking specific actions, the United States and the Soviet Union can help the combatants begin bilateral talks. Both countries can play an active role in breaking down false images and stereotypes, dismissing spurious information, and identifying the presence of overlapping interests between Israel and the Palestinians. They could also introduce new proposals to encourage the two sides to accede to these suggestions.

Second, the United States and the Soviet Union can provide the combatants with a channel of communication: passing messages and proposing sites for the beginning of talks between the enemies. The two superpowers can also furnish the opponents with relevant and undistorted information.

Third, the elucidation of the issues that surround the conflict is another critical service that can be offered by the two superpowers. By enunciating their understanding of the issues and by suggesting basic principles and mechanisms for formal bargaining the two superpowers can bring both the Arabs and the Israelis closer together. Rather than allowing the enemies to focus on their own demands, the United States and the Soviet Union can try to generate sufficient pressure upon the opponents to accept a compromise settlement.

Superpower Collaboration in the
Post-Settlement Phase

The provision of security and confidence-building measures is another vital area for superpower cooperation. Such arrangements are needed to ensure the long-term stability of the settlement and to allay the fears of both Israel and the Palestinians.

Due to the demilitarization of their state, the Palestinians need firm superpower security commitments and guarantees. The stationing of American and Soviet forces on the borders between Israel and the future Palestinian state would guard against the infiltration of terrorists across state boundaries.

Another area of confidence-building measures is for both superpowers to try to reduce the chances of misperceptions and misunderstandings between the Arabs and the Israelis. In this connection, the establishment of American and Soviet early warning stations on strategic West Bank mountaintops and advanced satellite capabilities would provide information for the Arabs and the Israelis alike about the movement of armies, military maneuvering, or deployment of troops. In addition, the two superpowers could help the Palestinians and the Israelis resolve any dispute that may arise between them in the future.

The imposition of a nonproliferation regime in the areas of nuclear, chemical, and biological weapons is an arena for serious superpower coordination.[7] The risk of military confrontation among the Middle East states mandates a joint endeavor in this field by the superpowers. The creation of a security regime would include an end to the sale of long-range missiles and an end to the exportation of military technical know-how that contributes to the production of unconventional weapons.

The two superpowers need to encourage the countries of the Middle East to declare the region as an unconventional weapon-free zone. In order to encourage the cooperating states, the superpowers should offer them firm security assurances, while at the same time, they should impose sanctions upon those countries which develop and maintain the unconventional weapons.

The Effectiveness of Superpower
Mediating Efforts

It will be arduous, however, for the superpowers to perform their mediating roles and services without pre-conditions.[8]   The incompatible political objectives of both the Israelis and the Palestinians require the exertion of substantial American-Soviet pressure upon the protagonists.   The impartiality of the two superpowers as go-betweens is another crucial requirement for conducting successful mediating efforts.   The objectivity and the open-mindedness of the American and Soviet intermediaries are important for the building of trust between the Israelis and the Palestinians.   Should the two superpowers continue to espouse biased opinions concerning the nature, origin, and preferred means of resolving the Arab-Israeli conflict, the local antagonists are unlikely to accept such mediating efforts.

The diplomatic competence, sway, and stature of the negotiators, as well as their willingness to offer rewards, issue threats, and impose sanctions, are additional important requirements for successful mediation. The two superpowers must arrange for payoffs for the Palestinians and the Israelis in order to sustain their continuing interest in the ongoing peace process. Both sides should realize that through cooperation rewards will be augmented.

In addition, the mediating role of the two superpowers will depend upon the attitudes of Israel and its Palestinian and Arab neighbors.   The presence of a number of overlapping interests between the Israelis and the Palestinians would provide an impetus for both sides to start negotiations. The chances for a compromise will also be enhanced if the issues under contention are explicitly delineated rather than obscure and figurative. The dissociation from violence by Israel and its Arab and Palestinian neighbors would expedite the beginning of the negotiating process.

The Crisis in the Gulf and Beyond

The Iraqi occupation of Kuwait and the crisis resulting from that certainly deflected attention from the Palestinian-Israeli dispute.

Yet, several lessons can be drawn from the imbroglio in the Gulf. In the first place, the crisis highlighted the rising importance of crisis management by the two superpowers in the post-Cold War era. Indeed, the predicament in the Gulf has confirmed the emerging partnership between the two superpowers for conflict management in the Middle East. Coordination rather than competition is the new mode of interaction between the two superpowers. Such coordination was evidenced in the convening of a summit conference for President Bush and President Gorbachev in Helsinki on September 9, 1990.

The second lesson refers to the widespread support and acceptance of the sanction of the United Nations in conflict resolution. This international organization played a leading role in the coordination of the sanctions against Iraq's invasion of Kuwait. Should the United Nations' coordinating efforts succeed in convincing Iraq to withdraw from Kuwait, this would legitimize the UN's role in the resolution of the Arab-Israeli conflict. The increasing legitimization of the United Nations would also facilitate the convening of an international peace conference and compel Israel to comply with the wishes of an emerging international consensus.

The emergence of such a consensus for the resolution of the Arab-Israeli dispute and the convening of an international conference under the supervision of the United Nations would enable the Bush administration to resist the pressure of the pro-Israeli lobby.

The insistence upon Iraq's withdrawal from Kuwait is a third pertinent lesson to be learned from the Arab-Israeli conflict. The opposition to the Iraqi invasion has implications for Israel's twenty-three years of occupation of the West Bank and the Gaza Strip. Following the end of the Gulf Crisis, the Bush administration needs to advance some proposals for the resolution of the Palestinian-Israeli conflict. The Arab states that sided with the United States in the Gulf Crisis would most likely insist upon the launching of a serious diplomatic initiative to address the Palestinian predicament. The Bush Administration's support of the Security Council resolutions criticizing Israel for the death of twenty Palestinians and the Jewish state's refusal to receive a United Nations mission to investigate the incident came in response to Arab wishes for a tougher position toward Israel. The Bush Administration also indicated that the convening of an international conference is one of the ideas that is being examined to achieve peace in the Middle East.

Finally, with the end of the Cold War, Israel's traditional opposition to the Soviet participation in the peace process is no longer tenable. The improvement in relations between Tel Aviv and Moscow and the unrestricted emigration of Soviet Jews removed many of the barriers that hampered Soviet participation in the peace process in the past.

Notes

1. For a theoretical discussion of these for the sources of internal conflict, see K.J. Holsti, *International Politics: A Framework for Analysis* 5th ed. (Englewood Cliffs, NJ: Prentice Hall, 1988), pp. 398-405.

2. For a discussion of the various barriers to a political compromise see Fred C. Ikle, *How Nations Negotiate* (New York: Harper & Row, 1964); and *ibid.*, p. 408.

3. Robert G. Neumann, "Can the Broker's Role be Resuscitated for the United States? " *The Washington Quarterly* 10 (Spring 1987), pp. 143-150.

4.   Richard Haass, "The Superpowers and Regional Conflicts in the Post-Cold War Era," *The Middle East in an Era of Changing Superpower Relations*, ed., David Segal (Washington, D.C.: The Washington Institute for Near East Policy, 1990), pp. 7-16.

5. Galia Golan, "Gorbachev's Middle East Strategy," *Foreign Affairs* 66 (Fall 1987), pp. 41-57.

6. For a theoretical discussion of the role of mediators, see Oran Young, *The Intermediaries* (Princeton: Princeton University Press, 1967), pp. 31; Thomas C. Schelling, *The Strategy of Conflict* (Cambridge: Harvard University Press, 1967), pp. 143-144; and K.J. Holsti, *International Politics: A Framework for Analysis*, pp. 412-419.

7. For additional information, see Haass, "*The Superpowers and Regional Conflicts in the Post-Cold War Era.*"

8. For a theoretical discussion of factors needed for successful mediation, see Holsti, *International Politics: A Framework for Analysis*, pp.   412-419.

19 The Soviet Union and Middle East Settlement: New Factors

The rapidly changing situation in the Middle East makes many of yesterday's notions and ideas for the settlement of the Arab-Israeli conflict hopelessly outdated. The primary reason for this lies in the fundamental changes in the socio-political, economic and strategic military factors of the region.

Only recently many scholars spoke of the Palestinian revolt in the Occupied Territories as a crucial new factor affecting the course of the Arab-Israeli conflict. More recently the mass immigration of Soviet Jews to Israel became another new factor affecting the conflict. Today, we have a whole host of new factors in the wake of the Gulf War, resulting from Iraq's invasion of Kuwait, the response of the United States and other Western nations to this invasion, and the reaction of the Arabs and other Muslim nations to the West's actions.

We are now probably faced with a new stage in the North-South strategic confrontation after the end of the Cold War. The Arab-Israeli conflict is becoming an integral part of this confrontation, with numerous unpredictable elements. First, we shall turn not to the question of relations between Palestinians and Israelis nor to the methods, ways, and forms of possible settlement, but to the new threats to peace and security which add unpredictability to the region. Let us start with mass destruction weapons.

If we take Egypt, Iraq, Iran, Israel, Libya and Syria and ask what these countries have in common, we notice that all these countries are, at the beginning of the twenty-first century, likely to have at their disposal the technology to develop nuclear weapons. Indeed, most experts assert that, by the end of the 1970s Israel had already become a nuclear state. To have done so it, along with South Africa, must have staged a nuclear explosion in the south Atlantic, and by now it must be building up its arsenal of warheads. If such is the case, there can be no guarantee that, in the event of a sharp confrontation, the Middle East conflict will not assume new proportions, from which unpredictable consequences will inevitably follow.

It is not by accident but by design that the starting-point of this essay is the prospect of the appearance and proliferation of nuclear arms in the Middle East, rather than the more obvious subject of the *intifada*, the Palestinian uprising, to which we shall later return. The nuclear factor has the greatest potential for devastation if we contemplate the terrifying prospect of its capacity not only to shatter peace and security in the area and to detonate a wider conflict, but also possibly to culminate in the self-annihilation of the embattled parties.

At present the Middle East is becoming saturated with medium-range missiles, capable of hitting targets 1,000 kilometers away. All previously-held ideas of military invulnerability and national security, based on a country's technological and military superiority over its neighbors, are rapidly becoming obsolete. But missiles are not the only evil. Iraq's possession of the "nuclear weapons of the poor," i.e. chemical weapons, is proven. The Iraq-Iran war has revealed the ugly face of this weapon of mass-destruction. Because of the thirst for vengeance and the climate of mutual hatred and distrust, this kind of weapon could well be used in any future Arab-Israeli conflict. In such circumstances the former political myth of Israel's unfailing military and technological superiority over its neighbors may boomerang if it leads other countries, that possess immeasurably lower levels of technology, but nevertheless are able to create weapons capable of overwhelming or impairing any means of defence, to adopt such weapons. Not surprisingly, at all conferences Arabs of different outlooks, from left-wing radicals to Islamic fundamentalists, have started to uphold the idea of the development of a missile and chemical potential in Arab countries as a deterrent against Israel.

However, these are not the only factors that affect the situation in the Middle East. As a consequence of the termination of the war with Iran, Iraq emerged with a dominant, experienced, and well-armed army on the Arab scene. It directed its might not against strong Israel but against weak Kuwait. Baghdad's actions aroused a wave of support in Jordan--which borders Israel--in the Occupied Territories, and in other areas. Of course, the Israeli government can achieve a *modus vivendi* with Baghdad, as it did with Damascus over the confrontation in Lebanon. One would think that the traditional rivalry between Cairo and Baghdad and the cooperation between the Egyptian leadership and the United States should ease Israel's position. However, fundamentalist pressure on Egyptian President Hosni Mubarak and growing anti-Western and anti-American sentiments in Egypt deprive this course of any guarantees of stability. Islamic fundamentalism is a phenomenon which is not new, but is increasingly influential on the Middle East scene. Nowadays we are witnessing the second wave of fundamentalism. The fundamentalists reject compromise of any kind with "Zionism" and reject out of hand the very idea of the existence of the Israeli state on any part of what was Palestinian soil. Their hand is strengthened by the growth of Jewish fundamentalism. The political weight of these extremist positions decreases the chances for an Israeli-Arab compromise.

The mounting Palestinian unrest makes the need for moves toward a comprehensive settlement increasingly pressing. This is clear to all sober political forces in Israel. The great potential of this popular movement lies in its mass base, and despite the actions of the occupying army, in a deeply democratic and up to now non-extremist nature. Before the Gulf Crisis, it was winning ever-widening international support and gaining sympathy in different strata of Western society. The position of the PLO's leadership during the crisis has changed this, but not forever. The movement has shown that the Palestinians are the key factor in a Middle East settlement, a settlement that will never be reached unless their future is decided. The Israelis' illusions that they would be able to perpetuate their colonial sway over the occupied West Bank and Gaza Strip, gradually squeezing out the Palestinians by confiscating their land, have been explosively discredited.

A brush-stroke that has brought a new and different color to the Middle Eastern canvas is King Hussein's decision to renounce his administrative authority over the West Bank, which was once integrated into the Kingdom of Jordan. This decision seems entirely logical, though it undermines the position of those who expected Jordan to represent the Palestinians of the Occupied Territories. It eliminated the Israeli government's previous peacemaking proposals that advocated Israel's continued military presence in the Occupied Territories, its retention of the expropriated lands and waters, and the continued existence of settlements in the territories. Under such conditions the return of the West Bank to Jordan would have meant Jordan would have had to perform police functions and shoulder an economic burden, while Israel would have been the only beneficiary. To suppose that such a wise and experienced politician as Hussein would ever have accepted a political settlement of this kind was a very naive assumption--an illusion. Now, after the three year long uprising in the Occupied Territories, it is clear that the Palestinians are determined to decide their own future through representatives they appoint. Behind King Hussein's action there lay the recognition of realities.

On the crest of the Palestinian revolt the PLO finally passed a series of historic resolutions. In November 1988, the extraordinary 19th session of the Palestine National Council, the PLO's supreme body, recognized UN Security Council Resolutions 242 and 338, effectively recognizing Israel's right to exist. The Council also condemned terrorism and declared the establishment of a Palestinian state. All this effectively annulled the National Charter which had proclaimed the complete liberation of Palestine by armed methods as the main goal of the PLO. In other words, the PLO leadership, too, has recognized the "land for peace" formula.

However, the hand extended by the Palestinian leadership to Israel was ignored. The Shamir government continues to reject the idea of a Palestinian state and is counting on complete annexation of the Occupied Territories. The leaders of the Labor Party do not mention the subject of a Palestinian state either. That is why neither the Mubarak nor the Baker plans have worked out, while Israeli Prime Minister Yitzhak Shamir has backed out of his own suggestion of elections in the Occupied Territories. The wave of

Jewish emigration from the U.S.S.R. is another factor which has prompted the Israeli leadership to adopt a tougher stand.

Turning to the demographic factors that need to be considered, the fact that emigrants from Israel outnumbered immigrants just a few years ago tells us more about Israel's future than the noisy blasts of tear-gas grenades and the ring of shots in the Occupied Territories. There were more Arab births in the Occupied Territories and in Israel than there were Jewish births. If this tendency persists, the Arab and Jewish population on the territory west of the Jordan River could be almost the same by the year 2000. However, the grave socio-political and economic crisis in the U.S.S.R., combined with the easing of the emigration rules, has led to a mass exodus of Soviet Jews to Israel. Some 500,000 to 700,000 of them are expected to arrive in Israel within the next few years. As a result, the demographic situation is Israel is changing in a radical way. The right-wing forces are growing stronger and the Israeli leadership is becoming more intransigent. There is ever more talk of the deportation of the Palestinians to Jordan, of the establishment of "Palestine" there, and of the complete assimilation of the Occupied Territories. All this creates a dangerous impasse.

What, then, of the future? The gamble of using armed force as a means of settling the conflict is now wholly discredited. To avoid mutual annihilation in the future the emphasis should lie on working to abate rather than aggravate current differences, to aim at an agreement for a political settlement--on resolving the conflict today for the sake of survival tomorrow--and at meeting the level of threat with a new, commensurate way of thinking. But on what terms and principles is agreement to be based? Through what mechanism is it to be devised? The first question to ask is: Does the Israeli leadership want peace? Apparently it does--but what does it mean by "peace"? Until recently it has interpreted the word as an official and legal recognition of its "exclusive" rights and privileges. "Peace" of this kind was to be imposed by military pressure and separate agreements, with the stronger dictating its will to the weaker. The fallaciousness of such thinking is self-evident. The balance of forces is unstable, and a foreign policy concession made by a government under pressure can be resisted by the mass of the population. In the final analysis the masses can play the same role in the

Arab-Israeli conflict as they played in the Iranian revolution. In such an event the technological superiority of a small country with a tiny population will be no substitute for the possession of a corresponding force. Finally, the very principle of driving one's enemy into a corner flies in the face of political wisdom and common sense. The essential ingredient of any long-term political settlement must use compromise rather than *diktat* if the national rights of others are to be respected and not treated in a way that breeds a sense of humiliation in a people, thus sowing the seeds of future conflicts.

The Israeli-Egyptian agreement has formally established "peace" on Israeli terms, but, leaving aside its impact on the region as a whole and the fate of the Arab people of Palestine, there is still a long way to go before genuine peace is established between the two countries; Israel is boycotted by Egyptian society at large, and the situation is aggravated by the growing mood of Islamic fundamentalism. In this connection, it is worth recalling that Lebanon has rejected the separate agreement once imposed on it at gun-point. The Arabs have legitimate interests and legitimate demands, which include the withdrawal of Israel from the Occupied Territories and the capacity of the Arab people of Palestine to exercise their legitimate right to self-determination. If rightly understood, the proposal to accord the necessary rights also takes into consideration Israel's interests and it's need to guarantee national security, including the security of its borders. In this connection it is important to note that the safety of borders is not determined today by geographical factors such as their location in mountains, or along rivers, or their remoteness from the economic centers of a state, i.e. "strategic depth." Such safety is determined by the readiness of neighbors to live in peace and by the existence of appropriate international guarantees. Therefore, when speaking of the security of borders, it should be emphasized that those Arabs who live close to Israel are as, if not more, interested in their security as Israel is interested in its security.

Escalation of the conflict, then, or any attempt to impose peace "Israeli-style" though separate agreements, runs counter to the interests--rightly interpreted--of all sides, Israel included. It may, of course, be argued that the majority of the Israeli people support the government and, accordingly, its policy. Indeed, in the atmosphere of the "garrison state" generated by the mass media with emphasis on religious fanaticism and nationalism, chauvinistic attitudes have exerted an influence on most Israelis. Still, Israeli society is not all that uniform, and the possibility of its evolution is quite conceivable. In this specific situation the vital interests of the people and the country are perceived, not by the majority, but by the minority pressing for a political settlement. There are historical precedents for this kind of phenomenon. Let us take, by way of example, the support given by the majority of the French to France's colonial war in Algeria; the victory was in fact won by the critically-minded minority, which convinced the nation, in the long run, of the rightness of its thinking. There is, then, a need for a political solution--for a political dialogue directed towards compromise. Here the formula of compromise is well known: "territory for peace."

To end any conflict a well-defined mechanism needs to be worked out. But before dealing with the question of a mechanism, we must make a necessary digression and examine the nature of regional conflicts, so that we can identify the place for a Middle Eastern settlement within the system of Soviet foreign policy priorities.

Regional conflicts are born and develop on local breeding-grounds, but they take shape under the influence of various factors. External factors may play an important role here. Be that as it may, to ignore internal regional reasons for conflicts and focus exclusively on the "the hand of Moscow" or "Washington's encroachments" would be absurd. When it comes to the settlement of conflicts, peaceful settlement aims at two things: the removal of the threat to international security, the abatement or elimination of regional tensions and the threat of mutual annihilation, on the one hand, and, on the other, the removal of the inclination to view regional conflicts in terms of confrontation, as in the traditional questions of "Whose side are you on?", "Where do you stand in the confrontation of the great powers?", and "Which great power will benefit by the victory of one side or the other in a regional conflict?" The zero-sum logic behind such questions spawned the concept of "the scoring of points" in global confrontation as well as the view that damage suffered by the other side was a "gain" for one's own side. Yet the prompting of reason leaves us in no doubt as to the truth of the matter; in inflicting damage on the other side, one's own side cannot avoid losses, however small, or great, as the case may be. But one can, and should, adopt another stance based on the thesis that, if a balance of interests is maintained, another side's gain does not necessarily entail losses for one's own side--and vice versa.

The export of arms is viewed by some students of politics and by some political leaders as an extension of political influence. To some extent, this view was logical in conditions of confrontation. But experience in real life has shown that a recipient of arms does not necessarily become the client of the supplier. Moreover, even if the recipient purchases weapons from only one source, that fact alone does not preclude political re-orientation on the part of the client. The "180-degree shifts" of such Soviet arms-buyers as Egypt, the Sudan, and Somalia or such recipients of U.S. weapons as Iran speak for themselves. Turkey and Greece, both armed with U.S. hardware, came to the brink of war over Cyprus. And everyone knows whose armaments Uganda and Tanzania used to wage their brief war.

The role of the United Nations is a subject in itself. Its potentially most effective instrument--the Security Council, designed to preserve international peace and security--has hitherto not been sufficiently active because of the conflicting groupings into which the world has been split. But if all permanent members of the Security Council should be in agreement in principle on a question of a regional conflict, why should that body not resort to force for the sole purpose of attaining a cease-fire and joining in the search for political solutions--or for curbing the aggressor? Is it not perhaps possible for the international community, as represented by the United Nations and its Security Council, not only to recommend but also to impose civilized behavior on offending countries? Maybe. But, for such a policy to succeed, the members of the Security Council themselves need to set an example of good behavior; they should never bomb another country if its leader is uncongenial to them, nor should they occupy a small island state after every coup d'etat or send a "limited contingent" of its troops to a neighbor country to defend an unpopular regime. The great powers themselves should set the example of unswerving obedience to the norms and principles of international law. The UN General Assembly has adopted Resolution 41/43D, confirming the need for an early convocation of an international peace conference on a comprehensive Middle Eastern settlement acceptable to all concerned parties. The first practical step has already been taken; by 123 votes, the UN General Assembly has approved an appeal to establish a working party involving all the permanent members of the UN Security Council. It was a Soviet proposal. It is time to ponder the most constructive methods for its success. In its proposals, the Soviet leadership regulated neither the future conference nor arrangements for it; it did not impose its viewpoint. The Middle Eastern conference must be a product of multilateral efforts, which, without compromise and diplomatic methods of agreement, are meaningless.

The Soviet Union favors an international conference under the aegis of the United Nations, which the UN General Assembly has urged for several years. Critics dub the Soviet proposals as "propaganda" or "pro-Arab." But at best, they read the proposals casually. The Soviet stand is not "in favor of the Arabs"; it is in favor of a consistent approach to the Middle Eastern conflict, to the inadmissibility of aggression, and the forcible seizure of other people's territories; it is in favor of a peaceful solution, the observance of the legitimate rights of both the Arabs and the Israelis on the basis of international law, and the establishment of peace and security in this region. A careful analysis of the Soviet principles of settlement shows that they in no way infringe upon the rights and security of Israel.

Until recently the Soviet leadership believed that conditions were highly favorable for resolving the Middle Eastern crisis. The more deeply new thinking sinks into world public opinion and penetrates political life, the quicker a new political situation conducive to the settlement of disputes and regional conflicts could take shape. Such optimism was emanating from Moscow.

The Soviet approach to a Middle Eastern settlement was spelled out by Mikhail Gorbachev at his meeting with Yasser Arafat on April 9, 1988. For the balance of force he substituted the balance of mutual interest. Only on the basis of consistently adhering to the principles of equality and equal security for both sides is it possible to realize the cherished aim of peace, he insisted. Experience gained in the world peace drive teaches the benefit of firmness and patience as well as the need for flexibility, realism, and readiness to recognize and consider the legitimate rights of an opponent. "The Palestinian people enjoy wide international support," said Mikhail Gorbachev:

which is a guarantee that the most vital question for the Palestinians--on self-determination--will be solved. But the recognition of the state of Israel and the consideration of its security interests are also an indispensable element of the establishment of peace and good-neighborliness in the region on the principles of international law.

It should be stressed that this statement reflects the Soviet approach: a balance between Israeli and Palestinian interests. "The Soviet Union," continued Mikhail Gorbachev:

is working persistently in favor of a just and comprehensive settlement taking account of the interests of all the Arabs, including the Palestinians, and the Jews. This country is ready to contribute constructively to the efforts of all the participants in the peace process. . . . The Palestinian people have the same right to self-determination as Israel. The ways the Palestinians will make use of this right is their own business.

The countries concerned would not attend the conference to raise questions which are no longer disputable, namely Israel's obligation to observe the Security Council's Resolutions 242 and 338 and to withdraw from Arab territories occupied in 1967. There would be no discussion of the Palestinian people's right to self-determination, which the world community recognizes. Also indisputable is the very fact of the existence of the state of Israel. The Security Council's Resolutions 242 and 338, as well as the recognition of the legitimate rights of the Palestinian people, including the right to self-determination, must constitute the legal basis for the conference, which ought to be attended by all the parties involved in the conflict, including the Arab people of Palestine, as well as the members of the Security Council. And what progress could be achieved without some PLO participation? At the same time, the interests of Syria, Jordan and Egypt should also be taken into consideration. Bilateral meetings, give-and-take, and even the most unexpected solutions are quite possible within the framework of the proposed conference.

Naturally, it is the direct participants in the talks, above all others, that would need to reach agreement; several long decades have not brought them to a comprehensive settlement which is so favored by the international community. Therefore, the participation in the conference by the authoritative Security Council members--above all, the U.S.S.R. and U.S.--could be expected to promote success. Quite apart from all else, both the U.S.S.R. and the United States have legitimate interests in the Middle East. By "legitimate interests" we mean economic and other relations established in the region by the Soviet Union and the United States. We do not mean anything tantamount to domination or subjugation nor do we suggest the establishment of military alliances or military bases.

The Soviet Union is not against any intermediate measures or stages on the way to comprehensive settlement. But it would need to be discussed and implemented within the framework of the conference and in connection with the conference's ultimate goals. The success of this undertaking would largely depend on the great powers, above all, the U.S.S.R. and the United States.

The more concrete details of the Soviet settlement proposals were outlined by the Soviet Foreign Minister Eduard Shevardnadze, during his Middle East tour in February 1989. He notably said:

We believe that it is precisely such a conference that offers a chance of a historic compromise between the Arabs and the Israelis. We would like the government of Israel to know that its choice in favor of a conference and the consent to begin dialogue with the Palestine Liberation Organization would enable our two countries to make another step forward along the road to restore full diplomatic relations.

While the breakoff of diplomatic relations between the U.S.S.R. and Israel may not have achieved anything, even though it was prompted by actions qualified in Moscow as "aggressive," the only obstacle to the restoration of relations now is the Israeli refusal to accept the Soviet leadership's involvement in the peace conference plans. All other relations with Israel, political, economic, cultural, and scientific alike, are successfully developing. The most important thing from the Israeli viewpoint which eclipses all others, is the permission for the mass emigration of Soviet Jews. Accordingly, the existence or non-existence of diplomatic relations between the U.S.S.R. and Israel in these conditions is a matter of secondary importance.

Various forms of Israeli-Palestinian compromise can be contemplated. The following ideas are hardly new, but they have been ignored in recent decades.

Why should the Palestinians and Israeli Jews not create a joint state on a federative, confederative, or any other chosen basis, so that the territory west of the Jordan can be their common home? There, they could create a one-chamber parliament or a parliament of the Supreme Soviet type with a "Chamber of the Union" based on proportional representation of the population and a "Chamber of Nationalities" with quotas for every ethnic group and each chamber having the right to veto the decisions of the other. That joint state would be called "Palestine" in Arabic and "Israel" in Hebrew. Other countries would have the right to refer to this state by either name. At this juncture the Soviet position formulated before the 1947 decision on the division of Palestine was taken should be recalled. The U.S.S.R. urged the establishment of a united democratic Palestine with equal rights for both communities. Thus, this proposal simply echoes the old Soviet idea at a new point in historical development.

What prerequisites are required for the unlikely development of a joint state? First, both Israel and the Palestinians have found themselves in a stalemate, an impasse of hatred and discord. So, they need a non-orthodox way out of the deadlock. Second, at present the Palestinians are the best educated and most dynamic of the Arab peoples and have wide-ranging connections. To become part of the Middle East, Israel needs support. Provided there is partnership, it could be buttressed by the Palestinians, who, incidentally, bear grudges not only against the Israelis but also against some Arab states. For the truth is that the number of Palestinians killed by Arabs is many times greater than the number of Palestinians killed by Israeli Jews. We will not dwell here on the matter of who incited the Arabs in question. The massacres in Sabra and Shatila were provoked by certain Israelis, but not carried out by them. Backed by international guarantees, sharing the common capital of Jerusalem, having approximately the same level of population and an equal cultural and educational level, both communities could become a vehicle for progress, and diminish potential for conflict in the Middle East.

To reach this sort of solution, both sides would have to abandon many stereotypes. But is confrontation preferable? Israeli leaders have repeated time and again that the territory to the west of the Jordan has insufficient space to accommodate two states. But there are similar states already in existence--Luxembourg and Singapore, for example--and their future excites no apprehension. The crux of the matter lies not in room for the states, but in the Israelis' concern over their security.

Nowadays, when the phrases "Palestinian self-determination" or "Palestinian political rights" arise more often, the possibility for creating statehood or federative or confederative links with Jordan is taken as implied. But, in this context, why should one not envisage a free choice, by the Palestinians, of federative, confederative, or other links with Israel? And what of special ties such a Palestinian-Israeli state would have with Jordan?

It is clear, of course, that the convening of a peace conference on the Middle East is a difficult task, with much preliminary give-and-take attached to it. But the main thing is goodwill, a real desire to create, in the Middle East, a change for the better, that would contribute to an improved international climate. A durable peace in the Middle East is inconceivable without the removal of all the basic ingredients of the conflict, all of which are too well known.

Other methods have been tried, too, but not the conference. None of them has worked out. So why not the conference? When can it be held? I do not believe this can happen soon. The passions are running too high throughout the region and too many hopes again are being pegged on a forceful settlement of the problem.

So what can the world count on? Certain mutual understanding and cooperation between the U.S.S.R. and the United States. Let us be frank. Until very recently the U.S. refused to consider even the very idea of cooperation with Moscow on a Middle East settlement. The logic of confrontation was "to keep the Soviet Union out of the region," "to oust" it from the positions which it had already gained, and "to ward off the communist threat" from the region where the West has vital interests. But if one is to admit that a new era has set in and that the U.S.S.R. is gaining credit of confidence in the West and has not yet lost it with the Arabs, then constructive cooperation with the U.S.S.R. in the name of peace and security in the region is simply a must.

The war in the Gulf has left a mixed heritage. On the one hand, it has produced more hatred and distrust between the Palestinians and the Israelis. On the other hand, Soviet-American cooperation during the crisis proved once more that the Cold War and global East-West confrontation is over. But this also implies the loss of interest of both Moscow and Washington in the Israeli-Arab conflict as a regional projection of the global confrontation. The basis of the superpowers' cooperation in finding ways and means for a resolution of the Arab-Israeli conflict has thus broadened.

20 Soviet-American Cooperation and the Future of the Arab-Israeli Conflict

Any attempt at Soviet-American cooperation with regard to the future of the Arab-Israeli conflict must ultimately be based upon at least a minimal degree of mutuality of interests and approach to the conflict. While such a mutuality existed in the past on specific aspects of the conflict and in certain situations, the advent of *perestroika* and "new thinking" in Soviet foreign policy has created an entirely new set of circumstances and therefore possibilities in this respect. In its broadest terms, "new thinking" adheres to the idea of global interdependence, generated by the existence of a world economy and the universal nature of such problems as nuclear conflict, the environment, and international terrorism. The interdependence created by the modern era dictates a "deideologization" of foreign policy and the search for a balance of interests between states rather than the pursuit of zero-sum game competition.

The primary interest shared by both superpowers is the prevention of the outbreak of war in the region; beyond this they have a mutual interest in the achievement and preservation of stability in the region. Such interests include the avoidance of rising tensions which might upset the delicate balance and cooperation created by the new order or jeopardize the developing Soviet-U.S. relationship in political and economic spheres. In this respect both powers have an interest in restraining and moderating their respective clients.

The interest in restraint would apply as well to the realm of arms production and development, as concern deepens in both countries regarding the spread of the potential for nuclear, chemical and biological warfare. Missile development in the region threatens the agreements reached by the superpowers, and alterations or exploitation of material provided by the powers (such as the Iraqi alteration of Soviet surface-to-surface missiles or the Israeli development of the Jericho missile or Arrow ABM project) raise questions at least for the Soviets, given their proximity to the area. Moreover, too strong a regional power, disturbing the internal balance of power within the region, could not only restrict the process of disarmament at the superpower level, but it could also limit the superpowers' inclination or ability for intervention, including military intervention, in the region.

If proximity renders regional stability of particular interest to the Soviet Union, the flow of oil to the West is the primary strategic American interest in stability. A strong regional power could and did (in the Persian Gulf Crisis) create a threat to the supply of oil from the Middle East to the West and Japan, and to oil prices. Crises in the region threaten the flow of oil and therefore the security of clients within and beyond the region. Although the Soviet Union profits from higher energy prices, it is also interested in the basic stability of energy markets, for the Soviet Union increasingly relies on a growing and prosperous world economy for the success of its own economic reforms.

Both superpowers would appear to have an interest in the containment of Islamic fundamentalism, which tends to be nurtured by the unresolved conflicts and uncertainty within the region. The fundamentalist movement also has the potential for creating crises inside the region, endangering not only the stability and security of clients, but also the security and integrity of the Soviet Union and other regions, such as central Asia. While the United States may be the more direct target of fundamentalist hostility, the connection between the Islamic renaissance and Soviet ethnic problems, particularly in the southern border areas of the Soviet Union, constitutes a major concern for Moscow.

The violent, messianic nature of Islamic fundamentalism also raises the issue of international terrorism, which has been declared a major concern of the Soviet as well as American leadership. The Soviets themselves have increasingly become victims of domestic if not international terrorism, while their desire to improve the international climate and their own image in the world have led them to what is probably a genuine interest in eliminating international terrorism.

Domestic considerations of an economic and particularly political nature could generate similar interests on the part of both superpowers in disengaging from the conflict or at least reducing involvement in the area. Waning public support for Israel in the United States could lead Washington to reduce its involvement. This breakdown has been primarily the result of what is increasingly perceived as unjustified intransigence on the part of the Israeli government. Israel's failure to live up to American perceptions and expectations regarding a Western-style democracy in its response to the *intifada* is part of this disillusionment. Further, the absence of a Cold War-related rationale for continued American involvement has contributed to the change in public attitude and to the gradual erosion of support for Israel. Indeed Israel's importance as America's strategic ally in the region has been placed in question by what may be perceived as the country's "irrelevance" with regard to the American response to Iraq's invasion of Kuwait. With Egypt and Syria having played a significant role in legitimizing the American moves in the Gulf, loyalty to these two newer "allies" may further the deterioration in public American commitment to Israel. Coincidental with these factors, American, particularly Congressional reassessment of foreign aid priorities in view of the revolutions in Eastern Europe could lead to a reappraisal of Washington's commitment to Israel on economic grounds.

Domestic factors may be leading the Soviet Union in the same direction of an interest in reducing involvement in the area of the conflict. At the very least domestic factors are beginning to complicate the determination of Soviet policies toward Israel and the conflict.

Possibly one of the few, if not the only, foreign policy issues to be so domestically relevant, the Middle East issue has become tied up with domestic Soviet anti-Semitism, particularly on the part of Russian nationalists. Opposition by many to the rapprochement with Israel is fortified by resentment over the "privilege" accorded the Jews to emigrate from the Soviet Union. Professional "Arabists" within the Soviet foreign policy establishment add their criticism of what is perceived as a decline in Soviet support for the Arab world to the benefit of Israel. And on the other side of the argument, domestic critics of Gorbachev from the pro-democracy forces, such as Boris Yeltsin, have urged a hands-off approach to the Arab-Israeli conflict (at the expense of support for the Arabs) together with strong condemnation of anti-Semitism.

In a sense, support for Israel has become something of a test of support for *perestroika*, change in the policy toward the Arab-Israeli conflict being associated with over-all change in Soviet policies-- domestic and foreign. Thus Moscow now faces what has long been a familiar phenomenon for Washington, that is, the advent of the Arab-Israeli conflict as a major political football on the domestic scene. For this reason too, both superpowers may find they have a mutual interest linked to domestic politics, in detaching themselves or at least reducing their own involvement in the conflict.

Some of the above interests, such as a mutual Soviet-American interest in avoiding the outbreak of war in the region, are not entirely new. Most important, however, is the altered interest in the Arab-Israeli conflict itself. If indeed the Cold War is over, and the zero-sum game approach and ideological competition to be eschewed, continuation of the conflict serves neither superpower. The conflict was always an irritant in U.S.-Arab relations; it is now becoming an irritant in Soviet-Arab relations. While one might argue that with the end of superpower competition, each power would have less interest in wooing the Arabs, both nonetheless have at least some interests, such as economic interests, which would lead them to prefer the absence of such irritants in their relationships with the Arabs. Nonetheless, it may be argued that neither superpower, particularly the Soviet Union, has nearly the same interest as they once did in pleasing the Arabs, given the end of Cold War competition. This in turn might facilitate the achievement of a settlement of the conflict, for the absence of the Cold War competition eliminates or greatly reduces the leverage of clients (or of rejectionist forces among the clients) over the superpowers. Clients may no longer be able to resist pressures for moderation by playing off the superpowers in the Cold War game, nor remain intransigent with the confidence that the wherewithal to continue the conflict would still be forthcoming. Moreover, joint pressures on both or either client would presumably be more likely to succeed than pressures of one patron on its own client.

The United States might share the Soviet interests in this cooperative role at least in a general way. There is a shared interest on the part of both in asserting their status in the new order created by the post-Cold War environment, and they share an interest in proving that this new order can work better than the old international system. Specifically, they may share an interest in proving that cooperation in conflict management and resolution can create a more stable global environment, and that this can be done with less direct intervention by the superpowers. Thus Soviet-American cooperation in defusing conflicts elsewhere--in Southern Africa, Southeast Asia, Central America, and Afghanistan--is viewed as a model which can be imitated in the region, both with regard to the Persian Gulf and the Arab-Israeli conflict.

Moscow may be motivated to demonstrate its continued great power status as much as possible in the framework of cooperative efforts (with the United States alone or through international bodies). In this way, the Soviet Union could maintain its apparently equal status with the United States, even without equal economic or political power or the will to project military power. Aside from simple great power nationalism on the part of the leadership, public opinion in the Soviet Union also dictates an attempt to maintain superpower status. Recent Soviet opinion polls have demonstrated that Soviet foreign policy elites favor the withdrawal of the Soviet Union from involvement and expansion in the Third World but nevertheless are desirous of maintaining the U.S.S.R.'s power status. This became particularly apparent with the growing influence of conservative military and Communist Party elements during the Gulf Crisis. Thus, given its weakened position, its continued interest in remaining a great power, and its greater stake in proving the efficacy of the new order which the Soviet Union has largely been responsible for creating, the Soviets have a strong interest in cooperative efforts. However, it is not clear that the United States is fully committed to the cooperative approach in every situation, specifically with regard to the Arab-Israeli conflict.

Changes in the Superpowers
Necessary for Cooperation

In order for Moscow to play the role it seeks in this conflict, it might have to proceed along some or all of the following lines: 1) development of relations with all the parties to the conflict, meaning Israel as well as the Arabs. For this it would have to meet more of Israel's demands in the bilateral sphere, such as diplomatic and commercial relations, and the speedy emigration of Soviet Jews; 2) reduction of Moscow's advocacy position vis-à-vis its clients by shifting to a more neutral or flexible position regarding the nature of a settlement; 3) pressure on clients as well as on the Israelis to compromise in the interests of a resolution; 4) reduction or introduction of new restrictions to the supply of arms to clients; and 5) withdrawal of support of any kind for terrorist activities and cooperation in the prevention of terrorism.

For its part, the United States might make it easier for Moscow to cooperate openly were it to imitate conditions two through four, that is, reduce its own advocacy position vis-à-vis Israel, bring pressure upon the Israeli Government, and reduce U.S. aid to Israel. Improvement of U.S. relationships with the Palestinians could also serve to alleviate Arab pressures on Moscow with regard to Soviet-Israeli relations. In view, however, of the advantage the United States already enjoys as mediator, none of these conditions is actually required in order to gain Soviet agreement to cooperation. As the party with little to no leverage for bringing about a settlement alone, Moscow is not in a position to dictate conditions to the United States.

In what appears to be the beginning of an American belief in the genuineness of the changes in Soviet foreign policy, Washington has been more willing than in the past to permit the Soviets into the peace process. While it is not clear that the United States will agree to more than symbolic Soviet participation at this stage, Gorbachev has hinted that this would be sufficient. In talks with President Bush, the Soviet leader cited the consultation which occurred with the Soviet Union over the Shultz proposals as the type of participation which would satisfy Moscow. Washington does not appear, however, to be interested in anything beyond this in the way of a genuinely cooperative approach to Middle Eastern diplomacy. Its references to an international conference have been more a threat (to pressure Shamir into talks) than an option. The Americans have claimed that Soviet participation would only complicate the already difficult negotiation attempts. The United States may believe that precisely because of the weakened Soviet position, that country is no longer necessary as a player in the resolution of the conflict--either because of reduced Soviet interest, capability or influence in the region.

There may, however, be a tendency in Washington to exaggerate the weakness of the Soviet Union (not unlike the previous tendency to overestimate its capabilities). Even if less than equal to the United States, the Soviet Union still has some influence on a number of players in the region. And even if the value of its services were less than half of the total, these services may nonetheless be essential to bring the parties to negotiations and a settlement.

The United States might change its position if the Soviets were to undertake certain concrete steps to demonstrate not only their interest in cooperation but also their abandonment of the pursuit of strategic or political gain. One such step might be drastic limitations on arms supplies to Syria (well beyond the cutbacks that have already taken place) or the withdrawal of all military advisers and military facilities, that is, steps similar to those being taken by the Soviet Union in Europe. This may prove difficult, as aside from Moscow's continued hope for repayment of the debts owed for past supplies, two of the internal dilemmas of "new thinking" are the contradiction between the idea of withdrawal from overseas involvement and the desire to remain a superpower, and the clash between the goal of the political resolution of regional conflicts and the Soviet economic need for the hard currency revenues brought in by arms sales to Third World countries involved in these conflicts. However, some debate within the Soviet Union as to the actual value of these sales inasmuch as almost half of the foreign debt owed the Soviets today grew out of the failure to pay for arms supplies, including the supplies to the Middle East.

If, in the meantime, the main obstacle to Soviet-American cooperation is American reticence based on mistrust of Soviet

If, in the meantime, the main obstacle to Soviet-American cooperation is American reticence based on mistrust of Soviet motives, there are few additional obstacles to cooperation with regard to the actual components of an Arab-Israeli settlement. Both superpowers agree that Israel must relinquish the Occupied Territories, with possibly minor differences over just how much territory should be evacuated. They are probably not too far apart regarding the creation of a Palestinian entity in these territories: an idea accepted as a distasteful inevitability by the United States, which would prefer to see a greater role for Jordan, while the Soviets, for their part, have no objection to Jordanian participation in a confederation and, more importantly, have tried to open options by espousing the less exact formula of Palestinian self-determination. Both agree to security precautions and at least compensation to Arab refugees, any return of the refugees being primarily limited to the territories accorded the Palestinians. Neither has ever accepted even West Jerusalem as the capital of Israel, much less Israeli annexation of East Jerusalem, and neither views the Israeli settlements in the occupied territories as desirable or permanent (or legal).

Major differences do exist, however, as to the means of reaching a settlement and its implementation. For example, the pace and form of Israeli withdrawal is viewed differently: the Soviets prefer a comprehensive agreement with uniform, minimally staged Israeli withdrawal, while the United States advocates very gradual moves, involving interim agreements such as autonomy and confidence building measures among the parties. The superpowers also disagree on the role or status of the Palestinians in such agreements: the Soviet Union calls for the direct participation of the PLO while the United States generally accepts Israel's preference to deal with Palestinians residing in the occupied territories as distinct from those outside and directly associated with the PLO. None of this is of paramount importance, at least for the Soviets.

More important, Moscow's approach still favors the opening of talks, i.e., movement of almost any kind, with less concern over prior agreement on the issues or any certainty over the outcome of such talks. The United States continues to be more concerned over content, with the desire to have the main issues more or less worked out prior to the convening of an international forum. Whether Washington's position stems from a genuine wish to avoid a failure of the talks or is simply meant to maintain American exclusivity is difficult to determine. In any case, the stated U.S. position calls for prior understanding, and a conductive environment--meaning confidence building measures and, probably, also interim agreements--prior to formal, multilateral negotiations. This places the United States position closer to that of its client Israel, which rejects multilateral negotiations altogether.

Areas of Potential Cooperation

There may be steps the superpowers could take cooperatively to press the peace process forward. Since the Six Day War in 1967, there has been speculation about the possibility of an imposed solution, a peace agreement forced upon the parties in the region. In Israel, at least, the idea has held some attraction, for it would have the effect of relieving the respective leaders from the responsibilities and onus attached to the concessions necessary for a peace accord. It is unlikely, however, that either superpower would be willing or even able to impose a solution given their limited control and the deteriorating relationships of each with their clients.

Both superpowers can still bring pressures upon their clients, however, and one of the pressures could be the threat of, if not actual, cooperation between the superpowers. An example of this from the past is the October 1977 joint Soviet-American communique which signalled to the parties in the Middle East superpower willingness to collaborate on the peace process. The communique, with its apparent restoration of a Soviet role, led to Sadat's dramatic trip to Jerusalem and the beginning of bilateral talks resulting in the Israeli-Egyptian peace accord.

In a sense, it was a threat of joint action which did the trick. Similar threats, even on the part only of the United States, might have a similar effect on Israel, which is the party that opposes internationalization of the peace process. The Arabs concerned, and particularly the Palestinians, still demand and find support in the superpowers toward convening an appropriate international forum, might influence the actors' behavior--even if only to the point of spurring them into bilateral talks (such as those proposed by the Mubarak-Baker proposals) in order to avoid the broader forum.

A Soviet-American proposal to host preliminary talks, if not a full-fledged conference, might be more likely not only to break-up the log-jam but possibly even to receive some consideration from the parties involved. Israeli Prime Minister Shamir is on record, as recently as the beginning of 1989, as favoring, or at least not rejecting, the idea of such a forum. Interestingly, it is the Arabs--Palestinians and Jordanians in particular--who oppose the idea. There are numerous signs that they fear a Soviet-American "deal" at their expense: both Jordan and the Palestinians believe they have more loyal backers in Europe (Britain for Jordan, the EEC countries for the Palestinians). It seems likely, however, that this opposition could be overcome if there were a genuine prospect for bringing Israel to such a meeting, particularly since both Jordan and the PLO have been seriously weakened as a result of their support for Saddam Hussein.

Confidence-building measures on the part of each superpower might include the following: renewal of full Soviet diplomatic relations with Israel; Soviet renunciation of the "Zionism is racism" resolution in the UN; the re-opening of stable U.S.-Palestinian communications; and the granting of American permission for leading Palestinians to enter the United States. Joint measures on the part of the superpower might include security proposals such as those suggested by Shevardnadze during his 1989 Middle East tour. For example, Soviet-American discussions for the establishment of a crisis control center in the region (or what the Soviets called a military risk reduction center) and joint peace-keeping mechanisms such as early-warning systems might alleviate some of Israel's security concerns.

More immediate and perhaps more important, joint limitations of arms transfer (dependent upon commitments from alternative sources such as France and China) and control of the introduction and/or development of new technologies, particularly in the area of non-conventional weapons, might also alleviate local concern. These could include on-site inspections as well as other measures, such as prior notification of exercises or troop reductions along certain lines, mutual and international verifications, and steps against terrorism. There might also be talks for eventual disarmament of the region along the lines proposed by Mubarak for a region free of weapons of mass destruction. Regional steps could not substitute for a settlement, but they might bolster the security elements of a settlement and thus facilitate Israeli agreement. At the very least, the superpowers might offer their experience in the area of arms control and security as contributions to original thinking on this matter to the parties involved in the conflict. To work jointly and cooperatively in the realm of arms control and security measures would appear to be logical and necessary, and it need not cost either power in its relations with its clients or each other.

In view of the Soviet-American cooperation in the Gulf Crisis, including Moscow's at least passively cooperative posture during the war, sufficient trust may have been created between the two powers to encourage them to seek out other joint steps in the region. The crisis itself may have driven home the unpredictable dangers of ongoing conflict in the region, which might cause both powers to accord greater priority to the remaining crisis there, namely the Arab-Israeli conflict. Despite the brief, apparent Soviet deviation from American plans in the closing phase of the Gulf War, the role and appeal of Soviet-American cooperation was enhanced. The Gulf Crisis led to the beginning of a sensitizing process among the nations of the region, as well as those outside, with regard to the type of superpower cooperation that can be expected in the post-Cold War era. It was not necessarily the cooperation of equals or totally symmetrical, nor was it sufficient to break down domestic resistance to cooperation within the two countries, but it may have legitimized consideration of the uses of this precedent for the future of superpower behavior in the region. It did highlight the need the Soviets apparently feel for placing superpower cooperation in a broader international framework, if possible. On the one hand, Moscow runs the risk of being totally eclipsed by the Americans now that the Soviet Union is unwilling or unable to use or threaten to use power projection. An international framework would minimize the asymmetry and provide the possibility for some token Soviet role even of a military type, if necessary. On the other hand, the costs of Soviet cooperation with the United States in any act perceived by its Arab clients as counter to Arab interests would also be diluted if the actions were taken in a broader international framework.

Economic Cooperation for
the Promotion of Peace

Beyond the area of security and arms, Soviet-American cooperation in the economic arena might also play a role in the achievement of an agreement by offering incentives and, possibly, the economic wherewithal for the solution of anticipated problems. The economic burden imposed on the parties to the conflict is very heavy, even when outside aid is taken into account. Most countries in the region spend between fifteen and twenty-five per cent of their GNP on defense, and there are additional heavy costs that are not accounted for in the respective defense budgets. The present state of the Soviet economy (and to some extent the American) is testimony to the consequences of a long-lasting heavy defense burden, and there is no question that the economic price paid by the parties to the conflict is very high. It is even higher when one considers the economic potential of the region under conditions of peace, particularly with the increased global emphasis on economic performance under conditions of openness and the directing of major technological efforts toward new civilian uses. With the opening up of Eastern Europe, large sums of capital will be moved across borders, but high risk regions will be avoided. It may well be that countries that do not join this trend in the near future will simply be left behind. The alternative costs of missing this double opportunity are, therefore, much larger than even the present high direct costs.

Thus on the face of it, and in the longer run, movement toward a settlement of the conflict would create economic benefits for all the parties involved. Yet it seems that the economic factor has so far played only a marginal role in pushing the parties toward a settlement. Until recently, economic motivation was lacking because of the large oil revenues on the Arab side, because of American and, to a lesser extent, Soviet willingness to foot some of the bill in the form of both military and economic aid to the parties. This situation has also undergone change and, despite the aid, the main regional states to the conflict, as well as the Palestinians in the West Bank and Gaza Strip, are experiencing a serious economic crisis. This crisis is the result of the *intifada*, the new wave of immigration to Israel, and the decline in outside aid (to the Arab side), as well as the accumulated long-term outcome of the military burden.

While there may be a growing realization among the parties of the increasing costs and of the missed economic opportunities, one should not overestimate the likely impact of economic difficulties on the willingness of the parties to reach a settlement. Unfortunately, economic considerations become important only when they directly affect the military capabilities of the parties to defend themselves. This does not mean that economic considerations have no effect, and, indeed, the "moment of truth" with respect to the military implications of the economic crisis is approaching. One could, therefore, envisage the superpowers' use of an economic "stick," presumably in an even-handed fashion, to encourage the regional parties to progress in the peace process. There might be, for example, an effort to restrict or condition additional economic assistance.

On the other hand, and given the skepticism regarding the potentially persuasive power of economic factors, there is also ample room and a need for economic "carrots" to counter-balance the "stick." Despite the long term definite benefits from a peace settlement to all sides, there are economic needs in the shorter term that the parties themselves may not be able to provide for in full. Some of these needed investment resources may be repaid in the future from the resulting economic benefits and the peace dividend. The major needs and projects include security, water, immigration, and the economic requirements of a Palestinian entity.

The transitional, as well as longer term security needs may be higher rather than lower. This would be the case particularly if the settlement were to advance in stages, with the Palestinian question first, for example. There would be a need to compensate with equipment and installations for some of the security risks imposed on the parties by territorial concessions, or in order to secure against outside opposition to a partial settlement. In addition there would be the costs of minimizing the security risks during the transition period, including the deployment of international superpower forces.

In terms of water, the acutely short supply of this natural resource is the cause of much mutual distrust, and a potentially immoveable obstacle in any settlement. Economically it is much more significant than land, which has been positioned as the eye of the dispute. While its economic significance may not be very high in the overall picture of future developments, it may have more than symbolic importance in the initial stages of a settlement, first of all in the West Bank and Gaza, but also as part of the peace treaties with Jordan and Syria. A regional-international research effort to increase the availability of water to the Israeli-Palestinian basin, be it through innovative transportation means, desalinization, or radically new preservation and efficiency-of-use enhancing methods, could provide an important incentive to move forward with the peace process, and it might also alleviate somewhat part of the territorial problem. Even if the results of such efforts were able to provide more water only at a considerably higher cost than ordinary sources, the difference might be off-set by the costs saved by the avoidance of conflict, i.e., the peace dividend. An economic solution to the water shortage may come in the longer run; it must be preceded by a commitment to multi-party agreement as part of any settlement. However, the early launching of an effort, immediately if possible, and a superpower commitment to its solution could ease one of the most serious sources of present and future conflict.

In addition, a major source of mutual suspicion and tension is the fear of instability created by prospective immigration of people on both sides, to Israel and to the Palestinian entity, and by long-standing "temporary" refugee status of large numbers of Palestinians inside and outside the West Bank and Gaza. The Arabs' fear of expansionary tendencies of Israel has been manifested recently in connection with the large influx of Soviet Jewish immigrants under the Law of Return. Likewise, Israel, worried by the external refugee problem, rejects the Palestinian insistence on the Right of Return. There may be an opportunity to deal with the mutual fear of population movements in a symmetric way within a political settlement. A political agreement on this issue would not, however, remove the fears unless it were backed by a feasible economic plan that would alleviate the initial absorption problems with minimal hardships and replace the physical infrastructure of the refugees with permanent and normal communities. Social turmoil similar to that created in Israel in connection with the massive Soviet Jewish immigration could be repeated on the Palestinian side. Indeed it might develop into a much more extreme situation unless a proper absorption plan were prepared and the required economic means pre-committed and put aside. Here too, the long term economic impact of both immigrations has the potential to contribute to more rapid economic growth and development. It is the investment needed up front that should be provided in order to prevent mutual tension from developing. It would certainly be preferable for the political negotiations to have sufficiently progressed so as to embark immediately on an international plan for resettlement on both sides of an agreed upon border. Short of this, however, an announcement of intentions and the formation of some big power sponsored planning body could serve as a potential incentive for agreement. Any execution would, nonetheless, have to be conditioned upon progress in the negotiating process.

Finally, there is the question of the immediate economic requirements of a Palestinian entity directly following its establishment. The literature is full of discussions concerning the economic viability of a Palestinian state. We do not share any doubts regarding this question, including the case of a full-fledged Palestinian state without special economic relations with any body or state. Modern economic growth at the present time depends less and less on natural resources, including agriculture, but to a growing extent on new products and services designed and produced by sophisticated equipment and human capital, which the Palestinian people possess in abundance. True, there are clear disadvantages to small size, and a common market or an economic union of a group of countries would be advantageous, but full participation in the world market combined with liberal policies of an open economy could compensate for small size. In the long run, the Palestinian entity would be able to take part in and take advantage of whatever long term regional development plans that might evolve.

The economic hardships of the transition period, however, would be of much more concern. There are mainly two sources of worry.

The first is that the establishment of the state might be accompanied by political problems causing internal instability and tensions, some of which might overflow across the new borders.   Second, the settlement might bring about a temporary or permanent disconnection from economic relations with Israel, connections that are providing at present more than a third of the combined GNP of the West Bank and Gaza.   A severing of these connections, especially those of Arab workers in Israel, would create an extreme rise in unemployment and decline of income, proven sources for social and political instability.   If such an event were to coincide with an influx of Palestinians from other countries, the situation could get out of control.   For the sake of the initial steps of the new entity, and in order to partly pacify Israeli nightmares of a resulting terrorism across the border, a ready plan, and the needed resources, should be prepared in advance.   Such a plan should minimize the use of the regulation or restriction of the movement of people; it may also have to consider perhaps temporary continuation of economic relations with Israel.

Finally, in the long run, all of the above mentioned programs could be integrated into a larger program of regional cooperation. And a regional program might well be incorporated into or at least considered in conjunction with broader international plans.

As already noted, while many of the positive economic programs and needs discussed above would have to come only at a later stage in the negotiating process, indeed following a significant break-through on questions of basic principles, it is nonetheless important to begin discussions and planning, as well as a commitment of resources.   Such early preparations might serve as incentives to the parties and the flip side of the coin of economic pressures.

Given an agenda for international and superpower cooperation in the economic aspects of the peace process in the Middle East, there is also the question of the forms such cooperation might take and the role of the individual parties.   Indeed, the capability of the United States and of the West to take part in such a cooperative effort is straight forward, although the demand for resources would definitely impose a significant burden on them.   The real problem lies in the limited ability of the Soviet Union to play a role that would be proportionate to its status as one of the two big powers.

Under the present circumstances of extreme domestic difficulties in the Soviet Union (political, economic, even psychological), the Soviet ability to commit resources to cooperative efforts is very limited. But even if committed, Soviet aid resources would be received with less trust, and therefore might be less effective, in view of the growing revelations about the inefficiency of the Soviet economic system, the low quality of its products, and its radically decreasing economic credibility as a role model for a successful strategy of economic development for Third World countries. Indeed the Soviet Union will turn for the foreseeable future into a major recipient of economic aid, and a major importer of technology and manufactured goods not only from Western powers but also from many of the newly industrializing countries, Israel included.

Turning to the cooperative efforts listed above, the Soviets would be able and willing to participate in any peace-keeping force that a future settlement might require. They probably would also be ready to provide some of the parties with the arms and military infrastructure required as part of compensatory security measures in such an agreement. This might ease the Soviet dilemma regarding the continuation of arms sales. They would clearly wish to participate in the planning and managing of the various economic projects, but at the same time, they would try to minimize their share in the overall financial package needed, be it grants or long term loans. The Soviet Union would, however, be able to become directly involved in the implementation and provide real inputs to some of the investment projects discussed above, for example in the spheres of water projects, the development of energy resources and power generation, physical infrastructure, or housing projects. Under most favorable conditions, one could envisage multilateral economic cooperation, mutually beneficial cooperation that might include various development projects in the Middle East as well as in Eastern Europe and the Soviet Union, in which every party contributed according to its resources and comparative advantage. However, under such a scheme, the Soviet Union would remain a net long term debtor to the rest of the world.

Conclusion

In view of the limitations outlined above, the United States would have to weigh the political benefit of Soviet participation in the economic aspects of a settlement. As in some of the political aspects of the peace process, so too in the economic, there is not a symmetry between the two superpowers. Yet, as in the case of differing views and differing degrees of influence and capabilities, the overall benefit of cooperation--in terms of world stability and the potential for bringing about the resolution of the Arab-Israeli conflict--may well outweigh the relative costs from the American point of view. The advent of the new order, the end of the Cold War, makes this cooperation possible; the dangers to the stability and future of this new order may make it essential. This was in fact one of the lessons of the Gulf War. Superpower cooperation was both possible and necessary for the multinational effort to reverse Iraqi aggression. Yet the outbreak of war severely tested this cooperation, contributing to the strength of the forces within each superpower, in particular the Soviet Union, opposed to such cooperation. Thus the fragility of the new order was highlighted, leading perhaps to the conclusion that regional conflicts pose an even greater threat to the new order than previously considered. Even if efforts at the resolution of regional conflicts (especially in the Middle East) have been spurred, the degree of superpower cooperation will be greatly affected by the problem of asymmetry. Most notably, domestic Soviet forces will have to be convinced that cooperation, which is part of "new thinking," will not merely enhance the asymmetry, that is, America's strength relative to that of the Soviet Union, while the United States will have to be convinced that the benefits of cooperation outweigh the benefits of maximizing this strength.

About the Contributors

Ziad Abu-Amr is Assistant Professor at Bir Zeit University. In 1991 he was a visiting researcher at Georgetown University. He has recently published on the Islamic movement in the West Bank and Gaza Strip.

Richard D. Anderson, Jr. is Assistant Professor of Political Science at the University of California, Los Angeles.

Abraham Ben-Zvi is Associate Professor of Political Science at Tel Aviv University and a senior researcher at the University's Jaffee Center for Strategic Studies. His recent books are: *The Illusion of Deterrence: The Roosevelt Presidency and the Origins of the Pacific War* (Westview Press, 1987), and *Between Lausanne and Geneva: International Conferences and the Arab-Israel Conflict* (Westview Press, 1989).

Dagobert L. Brito is Peterkin Professor of Political Economy at Rice University.

Graham E. Fuller is a Senior Political Scientist at the RAND corporation. He has published in *Foreign Policy*, *Current History*, and *Middle East Insight*.

Galia Golan is Darwin Professor of Soviet and East European Studies and Director of the Mayrock Center for Soviet and East European Studies at the Hebrew University of Jerusalem. Her most recent book is *Soviet Policies in the Middle East From World War II to Gorbachev* (Cambridge University Press).

Dore Gold is the Director of the U.S. Foreign and Defense Policy Project, at the Jaffee Center for Strategic Studies. He is the author of *America, the Gulf and Israel* (Westview Press, 1988).

Janice Gross Stein is Professor of Political Science at the University of Toronto and a fellow of the Royal Society of Canada. She is co-author (with Raymond Tanter) of *Rational Decision Making: Israel's Security Choices* and (with Robert Jervis and Richard Ned Lebow) of *Psychology and Deterrence*.

Yehoshafat Harkabi is Hexter Emeritus Professor of International Relations and Middle Eastern Studies at the Hebrew University of Jerusalem. During 1991 he served as a visiting Professor at Princeton University.

Mark A. Heller is a Senior Research Associate at the Jaffee Center for Strategic Studies at Tel Aviv University. He was co-editor of *The Soviet-American Competition in the Middle East*. His recent works include *Between Old Thinking and New: the Changing Dynamics of Soviet Policy in the Middle East*.

Michael D. Intriligator is Professor of Economics and Professor of Political Science at UCLA, where he is also Director of the Center for International and Strategic Affairs and Director of the Jacob Marschak Interdisciplinary Colloquium on Mathematics in the Behavioral Sciences.

Richard Ned Lebow is Professor of Government and Director of the Peace Studies Program at Cornell University. He is the author of numerous books and articles, including the forthcoming *We All Lost the Cold War: Can We Win the Peace?*, co-authored with Janice Gross Stein.

Benjamin Miller is Lecturer in the department of International Relations at the Hebrew University of Jerusalem. He is now completing a book on great power cooperation in conflict management, tentatively entitled, *When Opponents Cooperate: Great Power Collaboration in World Politics*.

Georgi Mirski is a member of the staff of the Moscow Institute of International Relations.

Gur Ofer is Professor of Economics at the Hebrew University of Jerusalem.

Emile Sahliyeh is Associate Professor of International Relations and Middle East Politics at the University of North Texas. He is the author of *The PLO After the Lebanon War, In Search of Leadership: West Bank Politics Since 1967*, and *Religious Resurgence and Politics in the Contemporary World*.

Mostafa-Elwi Saif is Associate Professor of International Relations at Cairo University.

Andrei Shoumikhin is a member of the staff at the USA and Canada Studies Institute in Moscow.

Steven L. Spiegel is Professor of Political Science at the University of California, Los Angeles. He is the author of *The Other Arab-Israeli Conflict: Making America's Middle East Policy, from Truman to Reagan*.

Shibley Telhami is Associate Professor of Government at Cornell University and served as the Council on Foreign Relations Fellow, advising the United States Mission at the United Nations during the Gulf Crisis. He is the author of *Power and Leadership in International Bargaining: the Path to the Camp David Accords* (Columbia Press, 1990).

Alexei Vassiliev is a member of the staff at the Institute of African Studies in Moscow.

Fred Wehling is a consultant with the RAND/UCLA Center for Soviet Studies.

Aharon Yariv is Director of the Jaffee Center for Strategic Studies. He is also a retired general in the Israel Defense Forces, and a former member of the Israeli Knesset.

About the Book and Editor

This book explores efforts being made to create Russian-American cooperation in managing recurrent conflict in the Middle East. Theoretical, historical, and policy sections provide the framework for chapters that represent the most current, multinational thinking on issues of war prevention, crisis avoidance, and conflict resolution.

The contributors—including scholars from the United States, Russia, Israel, and Arab states—examine the specific aspects of such crisis experiences as the 1967 Six Day War and the 1973 October War. The history of the Palestinian question is reviewed, and then the Lebanese-Syrian-Israeli triangle of tension is evaluated, with a focus on the impact of the recent crisis in the Gulf. Finally, the authors turn to policy implications and prospects for Russian-American cooperation in the Middle East in the future. They discuss the practical steps that must be taken to achieve lasting peace in the region, particularly in the area of arms control, and look at the effects that changing international superpower policies will have on stability in the Middle East.

Steven L. Spiegel is professor of political science at the University of California–Los Angeles.

Index

436

renounces authority over West Bank, 398
speech at Baghdad summit, 295
Hussein, Saddam
appeal to Palestinian-Israeli confict, 17
argument of "Arab machismo" and, 10
collapse of, 320
on deterred chemical attack by, 374
efforts toward military production by, 55
on Israel as alien imperialist power, 20
Israeli hard-liners on, 257
miscalculations by, 6-9, 299-300
misperception of a "power vacuum," 100-101
motivated by opportunity and need, 48-49
new international order impact on, 169
Palestinian support of, 267
on power of Arab unity, 299-300
response of superpowers to, 4
statements to Glaspie, 7
on threat of Greater Israel, 294-295
U.S.-Soviet cooperation against, 99
on U.S. Zionist lobby, 292-293
Hypervigilance, 183

IAEA. See International Atomic Energy Agency (IAEA)
Ideological rivalry, 92
IDF. See Israel Defense Forces (IDF)
IMF, role in economic cooperation, 358
Immediate deterrence, 35
See also Deterrence
Immediate reassurance, 36-37
See also Reassurance
Imposed solutions, 372-374
Informal regimes, 37
INF. See Intermediate Nuclear Forces (INF)
Intermediate Nuclear Forces (INF) of 1987, 98, 367
International Atomic Energy Agency (IAEA), 331-332, 373
International conference, legal basis of Soviet proposed, 404-405
International outlaws, 331-332
International system
changes in, 379
impact of Persian Gulf crisis on, 325
impact of recent changes in, 72, 260-262
nuclear confrontation reduced in new, 166
Soviet action in changing, 131
superpowers' impact in changed, 166-172
terrorism in new, 167

Intervention
crisis management and conflict resolution as, 56
defining rules of graduated, 58-59
threats used in bargaining, 87
Intifada
inspiration of, 295
Palestinian uprising, 397-398
U.S. attacks on, 293
Intriligator, Michael D., 341
Iran, 342, 375
Iran-Contra scandal, 5
Iranian revolution, 400
Iran-Iraq war
aided by superpowers, 326-327
impact on Gulf crisis of, 144-145
superpowers' cooperation in, 329
use of chemical weapons, 396
Iraq
aided by superpowers in Iran war, 326-327
arms race and, 344-348
as Ba'athist state, 297
Israeli action against nuclear facility, 334
lack of support for, 11
motivated by opportunity and need, 48-49
revolution of 1958, 115-116
as threat, 396-397
U.N. sanctions against, 391
as U.S. adversary, 375
use of chemical weapons ignored by U.S., 4
Irrevocable commitments, use of, 37-38
Islamic fundamentalism
as growing influence, 317-318, 386, 400
military threat of, 336
opposed to PLO program, 288
support of missile and chemical potential, 396
terrorism and, 410-411
Islamic nationalism, 380
Israel
action against Iraqi nuclear facility, 334
as active deterrent, 163-164
arms race and, 343-349
on autonomy, 255
behavior during Syrian missile crisis, 158
bilateral relationship with Egypt, 347-348
bilateral relationship with Syria, 348-349
casus belli and, 32-33
changes in the external legitimacy constraint, 64
concerns with Soviet-U.S. cooperation, 365-368
framework for Jordanian negotiations, 366

438